HISTORY OF WOMEN IN THE UNITED STATES

HISTORY OF WOMEN IN THE UNITED STATES
Historical Articles on Women's Lives and Activities

Edited by Nancy F. Cott

Series ISBN 3-598-41454-4

1. Theory and Method in Women's History
   ISBN 3-598-41455-2 Part 1
   ISBN 3-598-41477-3 Part 2

2. Household Constitution and Family Relationships
   ISBN 3-598-41456-0

3. Domestic Relations and Law
   ISBN 3-598-41457-9

4. Domestic Ideology and Domestic Work
   ISBN 3-598-41458-7 Part 1
   ISBN 3-598-41475-7 Part 2

5. The Intersection of Work and Family Life
   ISBN 3-598-41459-5 Part 1
   ISBN 3-598-41476-5 Part 2

6. Working on the Land
   ISBN 3-598-41460-9

7. Industrial Wage Work
   ISBN 3-598-41461-7 Part 1
   ISBN 3-598-41693-8 Part 2

8. Professional and White-Collar Employments
   ISBN 3-598-41462-5 Part 1
   ISBN 3-598-41694-6 Part 2

9. Prostitution
   ISBN 3-598-41463-3

10. Sexuality and Sexual Behavior
    ISBN 3-598-41464-1

11. Women's Bodies: Health and Childbirth
    ISBN 3-598-41465-X

12. Education
    ISBN 3-598-41466-8

13. Religion
    ISBN 3-598-41467-6

14. Intercultural and Interracial Relations
    ISBN 3-598-41468-4

15. Women and War
    ISBN 3-598-41469-2

16. Women Together: Organizational Life
    ISBN 3-598-41470-6

17. Social and Moral Reform
    ISBN 3-598-41471-4 Part 1
    ISBN 3-598-41695-4 Part 2

18. Women and Politics
    ISBN 3-598-41472-2 Part 1
    ISBN 3-598-41697-0 Part 2

19. Woman Suffrage
    ISBN 3-598-41473-0 Part 1
    ISBN 3-598-41696-2 Part 2

20. Feminist Struggles for Sex Equality
    ISBN 3-598-41474-9

HISTORY OF WOMEN IN THE UNITED STATES

Historical Articles on Women's Lives and Activities

8. Professional and White-Collar Employments

PART 1

Edited with an Introduction by

Nancy F. Cott
Yale University

K · G · Saur
Munich · New Providence · London · Paris · 1993

Publisher's Note

The articles and chapters which comprise this collection originally appeared in a wide variety of publications and are reproduced here in facsimile from the highest quality offprints and photocopies available. The reader will notice some occasional marginal shading and text-cur common to photocopying from tightly bound volumes. Every attempt has been made to either correct or minimize this effect.

Copyright information for articles reproduced in this collection appears at the end of this volume.

Library of Congress Cataloging-in-Publication Data

History of women in the United States : historical articles on women's lives and activities / edited with an introduction by Nancy F. Cott.

p. cm.

Includes bibliographical references and indexes.

Contents: 1. Theory and method in women's history -- 2. Household constitution and family relationships -- 3. Domestic relations and law -- 4. Domestic ideology and domestic work -- 5. The intersection of work and family life -- 6. Working on the land -- 7. Industrial wage work -- 8. Professional and white-collar employments -- 9. Prostitution -- 10. Sexuality and sexual behavior -- 11. Women's bodies -- 12. Education -- 13. Religion -- 14. Intercultural and interracial relations -- 15. Women and war -- 16. Women together -- 17. Social and moral reform -- 18. Women and politics -- 19. Woman suffrage -- 20. Feminist struggles for sex equality.

ISBN 3-598-41454-4 (set)

1. Women--United States--History. 2. Women--United States--Social conditions. I. Cott, Nancy F.

HQ1410.H57 1992

305.4'0973--dc20 92-16765

CIP

Die Deutsche Bibliothek - CIP - Einheitsaufnahme

History of Women in the United States: historical articles on women's lives and activities / ed. with an introd. by Nancy F. Cott.

- Munich ; London ; New York ; Paris : Saur.

ISBN 3-598-41454-4

NE: Cott, Nancy F. (Hrsg.)

Vol. 8. professional and white-collar employments

Pt. 1. - (1993)

ISBN 3-598-41462-5

Printed on acid-free paper/Gedruckt auf säurefreiem Papier

A Reed Reference Publishing Company

Printed in the United States of America

Printed/Bound by Edwards Brothers Incorporated, Ann Arbor

ISBN 3-598-41462-5 (vol. 8/part 1)

Contents

CONTENTS

Part 2

CONTENTS

Series Preface

In the space of one generation, women's history has become the fastest-growing area of scholarship in U.S. history. Since the resurgence of feminism in the late 1960s and 1970s, insistent questions about the historical meanings of "woman's place" have sowed and reaped a garden of scholarship. Where scholarly works used to be bare of mention of women, academic enterprise has now produced a vigorous growth of books and articles, bringing to light diverse women of every region, race, class and age. This research is marked by a renovating intent that refuses to accept as "human" history a history of men. Interest is lively and debate is stimulating and sought after: attendance at the Berkshire Conference on the History of Women rivals the size of the annual convention of the American Historical Association.

While books in women's history are daily increasing in numbers and strength, as in any fast-developing field the scholarly literature in the form of articles is most expansive and up-to-the-minute. All the history journals now publish articles on women's work, domestic settings, family relations, household matters, female politics and organizations and so forth, and new journals have sprung into being to concentrate on such topics. Women's historians publish in numerous regional and thematic history journals as well as in feminist outlets and in journals of other social science disciplines. This series brings together a collection of outstanding articles from the field, almost all written in the past twenty years and more than half published during the 1980s. It brings together, in volumes organized by topic, essays otherwise widely dispersed. These volumes reprint only articles that originally appeared in journals, not chapters of books; review articles are not included. Articles have been chosen for overall quality and for range. Each one was chosen for one or more of the following reasons: because it is the standard authority on its subject matter; represents an important statement on a topic by a recognized scholar; presages an important book to come; provides a first look at new evidence or new methods; or opens an untapped area or new controversy. Older articles have been reprinted if their data or interpretation have not been surpassed or if they marked an important stage in the historiography, even if since superseded.

The historical coverage of the series extends from the Revolutionary era to the 1960s. The articles themselves are dated from the 1940s through 1988. Volumes are organized by topic rather than time period. Within each volume, the articles are ordered chronologically (with respect to substance), so that the whole can be read as an historical overview. The only exception to this ordering principle is Volume One, on Theory and Method, in which the contents are arranged in order of publication. Within each volume there is an attempt to include articles on as diverse kinds of women as possible. None of the volume topics is regionally or racially defined; rather, all volumes are topically designed so as to afford views of women's work, family lives, and public activities which cut across races and regions. Any volume in the series stands on its own, supplying as full a treatment of a designated subject matter as the scholarly literature will provide. Several groupings of volumes also make sense; that is, volumes two through five all center around domestic and family matters; volumes five through nine consider other varieties of women's work; volumes nine through eleven concern uses and abuses of women's bodies; volumes twelve through fourteen look at major aspects of socialization; and volumes fifteen through twenty include organizational and political efforts of many sorts.

As a whole, the series displays in all its range the vitality of the field of women's history. Aside from imbuing U.S. history with new vision, scholarship in this area has informed, and should continue to inform, current public debate on issues from parental leave to the nuclear freeze. By bringing historical articles together under topical headings, these volumes both represent accurately the shape of historical controversy (or consensus) on given issues and make historians' findings most conveniently available for current reference.

Introduction

As the proportion of women in the labor force edged ahead during the nineteenth century, the patterns of women's employments also changed. Domestic service remained the predominant employment recorded for women. Agricultural labor, of course, claimed many women who never were recorded as workers—tenant farmers and sharecroppers, black and white, in the South especially. But as the century moved on a growing proportion of employed women were factory operatives or otherwise engaged in manufacturing. In the last third of the century, when white-collar work and the professions began to bulk larger in the whole economy, women became visible in these occupations. Since 1890, women have composed between a third and a half of the category of "professional and kindred" workers classified by the U.S. Census. This is, surprisingly, a higher proportion than women supplied to any other occupational group except domestic service.

Women occupied such a high proportion of professional jobs because the relatively low-status "female" professions of teaching and nursing demanded so many workers. Like women's industrial wage-earning, women's professional and white-collar employments have been marked by extreme sex-segregation. The traditional "learned professions" of law, medicine, the ministry, and the professoriat, and the modern professions of engineering, architecture, and science, have been highly male-dominated. The less privileged stations of nursing, teaching, social work, and librarianship have been principally female domains. In white-collar occupations, women have clumped in lower-echelon sales and clerical work while men have the lion's share of managerial positions.

Women's rights advocates from the mid-nineteenth century named entry into the male-dominated professions one of their demands for balancing the sexual power in society. Exclusion from leadership in law and medicine, science and the humanities rankled feminists because it appeared not only to reflect but also to shape gender hierarchy. If women lacked power in the social world, the professions embodied the notion that organized knowledge is power. They were thus obvious citadels to conquer as part of women's attainment to education and full citizenship. Indeed, in our own time, women's concerted entry into the male-dominated professions has been regarded as one of the principal markers of feminist success since 1970.

The proportion of women achieving the college and higher degrees requisite for professional training, and entering the male-dominated professions, increased steadily through the nineteenth and early twentieth century to about 1930, but did not continue to ascend steadily after that. There are significant differences among professions—it matters whether one looks at lawyers, doctors, teachers, scientists, college professors, or some other professional group—but the aggregate pattern showed stasis and even decline in women's hold on professional occupations in the mid-twentieth century, not mitigated until about 1960 and then sharply changing for the better after 1970. Many of the articles in this volume consider and discuss the reasons for this pattern, which differs so strikingly from the overall pattern of steady increase in women's participation in the labor force.

While the proportion of professional jobs held by women has shown puzzling ups and downs during the twentieth century, lower-echelon white-collar work has become consistently more identified as "women's work." The place of white collar occupations in the American economy roughly doubled between 1900 and 1950: almost one-fifth of the working population held white-collar jobs at the earlier date, but almost two-fifths did by mid-century. Women's employment even more than men's skewed the picture in that direction. In 1950 less than one-third of employed men, but approximately half of all employed women, were in "non-manual," or white-collar and professional occupations. The increase in clerical jobs—especially for typists and stenographers—was a major reason for the expansion of the white-collar sector, and for women's employment in it. Women composed a quarter of the approximately one million clerical workers of 1900, and almost two-thirds of the seven million such in 1950.[1] Women assumed new white-collar jobs, creating new employment patterns, without significantly altering the ongoing sex segregation in the work force, that is, the fact that "men's" jobs and "women's" jobs rarely were the same. When new employments such as telephone operation, for instance, appeared, and women were hired, these became defined as "women's" work.

The increased demand for women in white-collar work came from the national consolidation, marketing strategies and new technologies of American companies, which required literate and tractable employees to accomplish the greatly expanded work of record-keeping and communications. With compulsory school laws in effect by the early twentieth century, employers could rely on high school to train potential clerical employees adequately. Attendance at high school in fact zoomed up, to meet the changing shape of the economy. Where less than ten percent of teenagers were in school at the turn of the century, more than half were by the 1920s—and more girls than boys.[2]

The historical move of women's employment away from domestic service and agriculture toward manufacture and then white-collar work was, however, racially specific, controlled by the numerical predominance of whites. Black women, constrained to remain in their traditional employments in the household and on the land, did not share the pattern despite being twice as likely as white women to be in the labor force. Virtually barred from jobs in manufacturing until the increased industrial demand of World War I, black women entered factories then (under segregated and inferior conditions), but were denied clerical or sales jobs in white establishments (with few exceptions) until forty or fifty years later. A small stratum of black professional women did appear and persist through the twentieth century, however—doctors, nurses, and especially teachers, who opposed the odds and established models of achievement for young black women to emulate.

This volume, grouping together articles on women in the male-dominated professions and in the female-dominated areas such as teaching, nursing, social work, and white-collar occupations, examines a wide variety of women's career aspirations and work experiences. Questions about women's self-definition, economic independence, and feminist organizing are often in the forefront, along with considerations of occupational experience, work culture, and social service. Together they demonstrate how essential to comprehension of the modern labor force is an understanding of its gender dimensions.

Notes

[1] See Valerie Oppenheimer, *The Female Labor Force in the United States*, (Westport, CT., Greenwood Press, 1970), esp. 149, and Gertrude Bancroft, *The American Labor Force: Its Growth and Composition* (N.Y., Wiley, 1958), esp. 35-37.

[2] Paula Fass, *The Damned and the Beautiful: American Youth in the 1920s* (N.Y., Oxford, 1977), 124-25; Susan B. Carter and Mark Prus, "The Labor Market and the American High School Girl, 1890-1928," *Journal of Economic History* 42 (March 1982), 163-71.

Professional and White-Collar Employments

The Female School Teacher in Ante-Bellum Massachusetts

Richard M. Bernard and Maris A. Vinovskis

Historians have frequently commented that in the age of Horace Mann and Henry Barnard, teaching offered one of the few opportunities for female employment.[1] Yet researchers have investigated neither the extent nor the nature of those opportunities. How many ante-bellum women taught school in the United States? How were these women trained for their chosen work? What problems did they encounter because of their sex? These are the questions this article seeks to answer by examining the nature of the teaching experience for women and the consequences of that experience for those who taught and for the broader society.

In order to counter the lack of standardized national data on ante-bellum teachers, we center on the state of Massachusetts. Admittedly, the results of a single state study provide little authoritative basis for generalizations to the nation as a whole. This is especially true for a study of Massachusetts because of that state's high levels of urbanization and industrialization and of its relatively intense emphasis on education itself.[2] However, due largely to the propaganda of Mann himself, many of the patterns developed in Massachusetts subsequently re-emerged elsewhere. To assist in making future comparisons, the authors have indicated where they have uncovered relevant data for other states.

Despite the implication that teaching was a major source of job opportunities for women, historians have never clearly specified exactly what they mean by that phrase, "major source of job opportunities." If we are concerned about the opportunity that educational jobs provided for women relative to men, then we should ascertain the percentage of teaching positions held by women. If we wish to know the importance of female school teachers as a source of employment for women at a single point in time, then we should determine the proportion of the female population which was teaching school in any particular year. If, on the other hand, we are concerned with the impact of the teaching experience on those women who taught, we should calculate the percentage of females who taught school at some point in their lives. For purposes of clarity, let us examine each possible approach briefly.

In comparison to the employment it afforded men, education was a significant employer of women. Female teachers outnumbered their male counterparts throughout the ante-bellum years. Moreover, the overall increase in the number of teachers that Massachusetts employed between 1834 and 1860 was due directly to the steady and relative rise in female instructors. The absolute number of male teachers actually declined. While in 1834 females comprised 56.3% of the teaching force, their percentage bolted upward to 77.8% by 1860. Education did supply substantially more job opportunities for women than for men.[3]

Although teaching served the female job market better than the male market, at no point during the ante-bellum period did it provide employment to as much as 2% of all white women ages fifteen to sixty. To make matters worse, there was an overall decline in the percentage of women employed in education during our period. Thus, if we limited our scope to static, time-period "snapshots" of the early nineteenth-century, we could properly place little emphasis on school teaching when defining the status of women in society.

But the "snapshot" perspective, even if a series of years were viewed simultaneously, cannot portray the full impact of teaching on American women. For every woman standing at a chalkboard at a given time, there were a number of women who had formerly been teachers but had left the profession. Whether they joined another sector of the labor force or abandoned outside employment for household tasks, they did not just forget their experiences in the classroom. Thus, a very useful framework for studying the effects of teaching opportunities on American society is the percentage of women who at some time had the experience of conducting classes.[4]

The results produced by this approach are quite startling – approximately one out of five white women in pre-Civil War Massachusetts was a school teacher at some time in her life! Moreover, since almost all of the teachers were native-born, probably one out of four Massachusetts females born in this country once taught school. It is also interesting to note that the teaching profession did not have such a major impact on males and that, over the years, the gap between the percentage of males and females who had ever taught widened.[5] Hence, although teaching was not particularly significant to ante-bellum society in terms of employment opportunities available at any one time, the education profession had considerable potential for affecting American society through its female adherents.

Due to the large proportion of women who were teachers or who had been teachers, the nature of the teaching experience becomes considerably more interesting. The initial phase of that experience was training, but the opportunities for extended teacher education offered ante-bellum women were quite restricted. Generally, the teacher or would-be teacher could go beyond her common-school education by attending a college or university, one or more teacher training institutes, or a state normal school which specialized in teacher preparation.

Before the Civil War, very few young people went to college. In the three federal censuses from 1840 to 1860, the percentage of the nation's students enrolled in colleges and universities never rose above 1%. And by no means were all students in higher education studying to become teachers. Moreover, since most colleges admitted only men, the numbers of college-educated female teachers were few indeed.[6]

The roles of teachers' institutes and normal schools are more difficult to interpret because data on these institutions are scattered and usually not comparable from state to state. In Massachusetts, institutes and normal schools emerged quite early and information on them is available.

In 1839 Henry Barnard established the pattern for institutes in Massachusetts when he held the first "teachers' class" in Hartford County, Connecticut. That first meeting set important precedents for an institution that would remain in vogue right up to the Civil War. The sessions originally lasted a few weeks and were designed for young men who wanted to attend normal schools but who could not afford to leave their jobs for long periods of time. Inexpensive to operate, these institutes drew small and predominantly male enrollments in rural areas throughout the 1840's. In Massachusetts, up to 450 people annually attended these sessions during the latter half of the decade with an average meeting attracting about seventy-three teachers. These figures jumped substantially in the 1850's when, according to one author, the institutes' leaders shifted their emphasis from attempts to "awaken" the moral character of the teachers to a "professionalization of education."[7] At the same time, institutes began to appear in urban areas, usually in the evenings, where the sessions were shortened to five nights. Paralleling the rise of the number of women teachers, more females began attending the institutes.

Based only on gross attendance figures, the impact of these institutes appears at first glance to exceed that of either colleges or normal schools. If, however, one makes allowances for teachers who attended more than one institute in a given year and for students from colleges and normal schools whose attendance only supplemented their regular course work, the number of teachers whose only professional training came through the institutes was substantially smaller. No estimates for the number of institutes attended per person have appeared, but at least two institutes in 1850 reported the number of students present from normal schools. Of the 122 persons who gathered in Plymouth County, seventy were from Bridgewater Normal School, and of the 166 persons at Hadley, fifty-two attended Amherst.[8] Doubtless, these figures exaggerate the proportion of students among institute goers since some sessions were miles from the nearest college or normal school. Remember, however, that those who attended the institutes were by no means all females. Finally, whatever the actual number of women teachers who received their formal training from these gatherings, it is doubtful that a five-day training session could have the impact of one, two, or three years of study in a normal school.[9]

In terms of sheer numbers, Massachusetts normal-school graduates did not overwhelm their profession. On the average, between 1840 and 1844, pupils enrolled in normal schools amounted to only .8% of the state's teachers or 1.9% of its annual number of new teachers just entering the classroom. It is noteworthy, however, that these percentages rose substantially to 6.3% and 16.4%, respectively, by 1857.[10] Thus, by the beginning of the Civil War about one new teacher in every six had prepared to teach through the normal-school process.

In 1860 Massachusetts operated four normal schools including coeducational ones at Bridgewater and Westfield and all female establishments at Salem and Framingham. Scattered reporting by these schools makes some student sex ratio comparisons possible. Overall, between 1840 and 1844, 50.2% of those admitted to what was then the only normal school in the state (Bridgewater) were females. In 1846, that figure was 55.1%. By 1854 the state's two normal schools accepted 83.1% females, and the following year with three schools in existence, these institutions reported an only slightly lower percentage of 82.7. In the final year of the period, the percentage of females in all four schools was 85.4.[11]

Students entering normal schools were generally a little older than today's typical freshmen. The average entering age of students at Bridgewater, for example, was an even twenty years in 1846 and only a year younger in 1860. For all but one of the sessions reported before 1860, Bridgewater's entering females were younger than entering males. These differences ranged from two and one-half years to only a few months and form no particular pattern. Young men apparently worked a few years, perhaps taught or worked on the family farm, before applying to a normal school. As future family breadwinners, young men might have hesitated before committing themselves to such a low-paying profession. Young women, whose occupational and wage-rate choices were much more limited, more often seemed to go straight to normal schools from their parents' homes.

Despite their youth, quite a large number of students had some experience teaching before they entered a normal school. Again, comparable figures are elusive but a reasonable guess is that between one-third and one-half of all incoming students had taught before entering.[12] As we might have expected, the percentage seems to have dropped over the period.

Most students selected a normal school in their own county or an adjacent county. Few students came to Massachusetts from other states and very few listed a home residence in a foreign country. As Massachusetts normal schools expanded and matured, they began to draw from a wider area, yet the vast majority of students continued to be state residents. Interestingly, only a very small number of students came from Boston. Suffolk County (Boston) supplied only 4.8% of the state's normal-school enrollment between 1840 and 1844 and only 1.3% of the 1855 total.[13]

Between 1846 and 1860, the four normal schools reported 172 different occupations for the fathers of their students. These occupational titles suffer from the same problems census occupational listings do, and they carry the additional handicap of irregular reporting.[14] For one year, 1859, however, the information on the occupation of the fathers is reasonably usable.

Some 43.1% of the normal school pupils came from farms. The owner-manager and artisan classes combined accounted for 40.2% of the students. The rest spread over professional, laborer, service, and government categories. Only three of the 239 students were themselves the children of teachers.

Sex of the students is difficult to correlate with fathers' occupations. Among the students of coed schools, farmer fathers were significantly more prevalent than among students in all-female schools. Conversely, artisan fathers were more than twice as prominent among female-school pupils as among their mixed peers at other normal schools, and for merchant-managers, the ratio exceeded three to one. The reasons for these differences are equally difficult to determine. Perhaps they are a function of school location. On the other hand, teaching may have provided a more appealing alternative to the family farm for males than for females. Farm families may have been more reluctant to let their daughters go out on their own. Or, farm girls may have grown up with stronger home-orientations than either farm boys or city girls. There are many different possible explanations and a more definitive answer awaits further research.

Table 1. Occupations of the Fathers of Selected Students in Massachusetts Normal School in 1859

	Bridgewater*	Westfield*	Coed Schools Total	% of Coed Schools Total	Framingham**	Salem*	Women's Schools Total	% of Women's Schools Total	Total of All Schools	% of Total of All Schools
Professionals	1	4	5	3.8	2	3	5	4.7	10	4.2
Merchants-Managers	4	4	8	6.1	7	13	20	18.7	28	11.7
Artisans (skilled & semiskilled)	3	22	25	18 9	4	39	43	40.2	68	28.5
Laborers	0	0	0	0	0	4	4	3.7	4	1.7
Farmers	21	58	79	59.8	8	16	24	22.4	103	43.1
Service Workers	4	0	4	3.0	2	5	7	6.5	11	4.6
Government Workers	0	0	0	0	0	3	3	2.8	3	1.3
None or deceased	11	0	11	8.3	1	0	1	.9	12	5.0
Total	44	88	132	100.0	24	83	107	100.0	239	100.0

* All students admitted in 1859
**One-third of total students in attendance in 1859

Source: *Abstract of Mass. School Returns, 1859*

How many of these entering normal-school students actually graduated? The aggregate number of students who graduated in a given year represented anywhere from 20 to 80% of the number who had gained admittance two years earlier. It is interesting, however, that only one out of seven graduating classes reported by coed schools listed more male than female graduates. Perhaps overall as many as four-fifths of all graduates were female. Although the recorded material is useful only impressionistically, it seems likely that women were at least equally persistent with men at the task of getting a normal-school certificate.

Only Bridgewater made any attempt to verify whether its former students did indeed obtain teaching jobs. Of its spring 1855 graduates, all eight men and four of six women immediately assumed positions while of its 1859 graduates, eleven of fourteen men and eighteen of twenty-two women did the same.[15] These numbers are far too small for conclusions about the normal schools' relationship to the job market for teachers, but they do hint that a high proportion of the graduates probably did go into teaching.

Women, therefore, found more opportunities for training as teachers in normal schools than in colleges, universities, or institutes, but even those opportunities failed to reach the majority of female instructors. Most women teachers had only common school educations. They came into the profession young and poorly prepared for their duties. Naturally, they faced problems from the start.

The ages of most women teachers fell between sixteen and twenty-five. They were almost always single and for good reason. A customary part of teachers' salaries was the food and lodging they received by "boarding around" in the homes of their pupils. The constant moving, cramped quarters, and lack of privacy inherent in this system were not conducive to married life for either sex.[16]

Due largely to the attractions of the altar or employment opportunities elsewhere, few women regarded teaching as a permanent career. While 2.1 years was the average tenure for public school teachers in 1845-46, the percentage teaching three or more years was much smaller (21.9 and 2.6% respectively).[17]

Vertical mobility for women in public schools was minimal. Although non-teaching women could sit on school boards, female principals were few and they never had males teaching under them. Female assistant principals, although the primary supervisors over education for younger children and older girls, remained subordinate to their male principals. The administrative ladder for women was generally missing its top rungs.

In the division of classroom duties, women almost always drew assignments to teach younger children and "less difficult" subjects. Male-dominated school boards based this arrangement on nineteenth-century stereotypes of the proper place of women in society.[18] Horace Mann often supported this division of labor in his annual state reports on education:

> All those differences of organization and temperament which individualize the sexes point to the female as the guide and guardian of young children. She holds her commission from nature. In the well developed female character there is always a preponderance of affection over intellect. However powerful and brilliant her reflective faculties may be, they are considered a deformity in her character unless overbalanced and tempered by womanly affections. The dispositions of young children of both sexes correspond with its ordination of Providence.[19]

One of the factors supporting the notion that women should teach only small children was the widespread belief that female teachers were unable to discipline older boys who were prone to disrupting classrooms. Since younger children were more apt to attend schools during the summer sessions and older ones during the winter sessions when they were not needed for farm chores, women usually taught only in summer schools. This situation changed gradually as cost-conscious school boards turned to female teachers for both summer and winter work.

Massachusetts female educators always earned less than did male teachers, about 60% less on the average. Female salaries grew slowly during the antebellum years, but their status relative to male salaries worsened. As the burden of public school education increased, local school boards looked for ways to reduce expenditures. Since teacher salaries were a large proportion of annual school budgets, school committees increasingly hired women for their winter terms in order to reduce costs. Incidentally, as this shift was occurring, administrators also noted that disruptions of winter schools by older boys declined drastically.[20]

The impact of the salary situation on women teachers must have been mixed. For those women gainfully employed for the first time, every paycheck represented a step toward financial independence. The reality of earned income probably outweighed their feelings of resentment over their deprivation relative to male teachers – especially in a society where women were normally subordinated to men outside the home. Moreover, since the cost of living remained fairly constant during the 1834-60 period, female teachers actually experienced an increase in real income. This development enhanced their positions in society both financially and socially. On the other hand, the nagging fact that their services were not as desired as those of men must have upset many women educators. In effect, their employment meant that school boards were willing to settle for what many school committeemen considered second-best in order to save money. Self-respect must have been a difficult ideal for women under such conditions.[21]

A broader conception of the relationship between income and self-worth is possible through a comparison of teaching salaries and wages in alternative forms of employment. The number of employment opportunities for Massachusetts women during the ante-bellum period were limited. Women could and did obtain positions as domestics, but these were very low-paying jobs that greatly inhibited privacy and independence.

The other major competing source of employment for women was manufacturing. During the initial decades of industrialization in Massachusetts, industries recruited women in large numbers to work in the factories. In fact, school committees often lamented that many women were leaving the teaching profession in order to obtain higher wages in the textile mills.[22] Although on the average women's wages in the mills were about the same as those in the schools, women teachers who went into the factories usually gained better positions and higher pay than other women because manufacturers felt that they made more productive and more disciplined workers.[23] Furthermore, there was a considerable difference between the low wages a woman might have earned in many of the rural schools and the wages offered her in industry. As a result, there was a tendency for many teachers to leave for the milltown even though they were giving up a white-collar position for a blue-collar one.[24]

Evaluating the overall impact of the teaching experience on ante-bellum American women remains difficult because of the lack of comparative studies of average, not exceptional, female educators. Essentially, this study is only an initial step toward understanding the impact of teaching on the typical woman instructor.[25]

Although short in duration, the teaching experience was common to a surprisingly large proportion of Massachusetts women. Most of the women who entered teaching did so without adequate preparation. A handful of would-be instructors did obtain such training from colleges, universities, institutes, and normal schools, but only the last institutions offered sustained instruction in how to teach school.

Teachers faced living conditions that often forced a choice between the profession and marriage, and, judging from their short tenure, many women opted for the latter. Opportunities for advancement within education were few as both occupational mobility and faculty roles were sex-determined. It is not, therefore, surprising that some female teachers resigned to accept industrial positions.

The inferior status of women in education thus counterbalanced the independence generated for these young women through their gainful employment. Teaching created for women a limbo between their parents' homes and marriage or other careers. Yet, even in this transitional state, away from the domination of fathers and husbands, women still remained under the watch of male principals and male-dominated school boards. Few could have been unaware of the situation.

University of Wisconsin Richard M. Bernard
University of Michigan Maris A. Vinovskis

Graph No. 1 Annual Number of Different Teachers in Massachusetts Public and Private Schools: 1834 – 1860

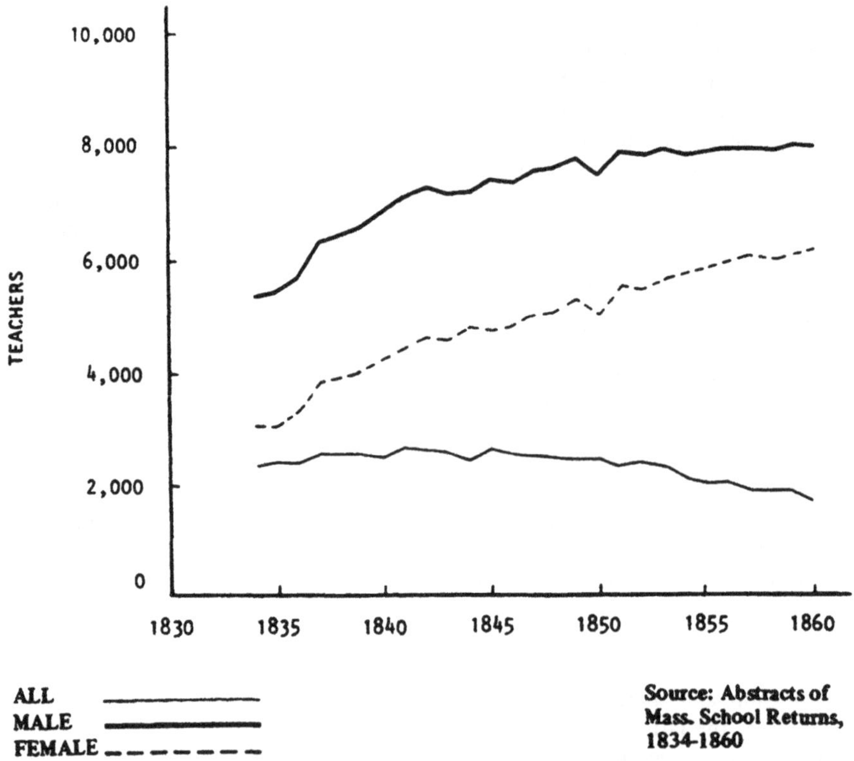

Source: Abstracts of Mass. School Returns, 1834-1860

Graph No. 2 Percentage of Massachusetts White Population Who Were Ever Teachers: 1834 – 1860

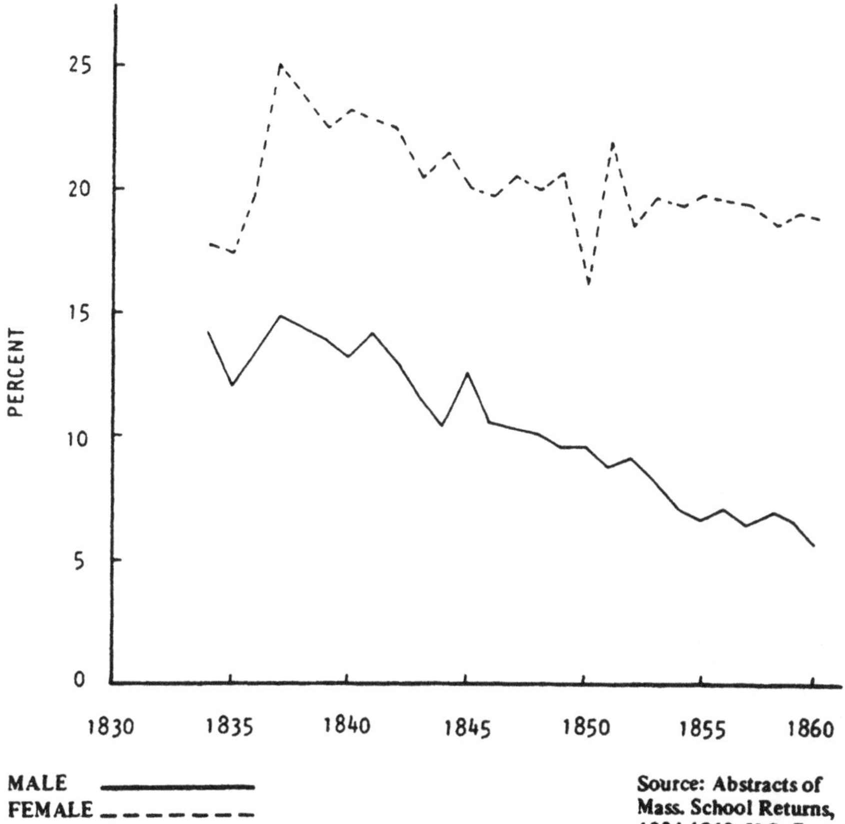

Source: Abstracts of Mass. School Returns, 1834-1860; U.S. Censuses, 1830-1860

FOOTNOTES

An earlier version of this paper was presented at the Berkshire Conference on Women in History at Radcliffe College, October 1974. The authors wish to thank Colin Burke, Carl Degler, Sarah Elbert, Ann Gordon, Tamara Hareven, Deborah Hood, Richard Jensen, Jacqueline Jones, Carl Kaestle, Sheila Rothman, Katheryn Sklar, and Daniel Scott Smith for their helpful comments and suggestions. Any errors remain solely the responsibility of the authors. A statistical appendix detailing the data for the graphs in the text is available upon request from the authors.

1. For example, see Gerda Lerner, "The Lady and the Mill Girl: Changes in the Status of Women in the Age of Jackson," *American Studies Journal*, X (Spring 1969), 5-15.

2. Maris A. Vinovskis, "Trends in Massachusetts Education, 1826-1860," *History of Education Quarterly*, XII (Winter 1972), 501-529. An extensive analysis of the educational development of Massachusetts in 1840, 1860, and 1875 is now underway by Maris Vinovskis and Carl Kaestle.

Graph No. 3 Percentage of Massachusetts Teachers
Attending Teachers Institutes Each Year:
1845 – 1860

Source: Abstracts of Mass. School Returns, 1845-1860

3. Exact figures for the number of male and female public school teachers appeared yearly in the *Abstracts of Massachusetts School Returns, 1834-1860.* The private school figures represent an estimate of two different teachers per incorporated academy annually with male teachers outnumbering female instructors three to one and .8 different teachers per unincorporated academy before 1850 (1.0 thereafter) with four female teachers to every male instructor. The .8 figure for unincorporated academies is an adjustment for the number of public school teachers who also taught in unincorporated private academies during the year. The complete set of data on this issue can be found in our longer version of this paper that was presented at the Berkshire Conference on Women in History at Radcliffe College, October 1974.

In most states the percentage of female teachers increased steadily during the ante-bellum period. Some states such as Pennsylvania and Ohio were slower in this area than other states such as Maine, New Hampshire, and Rhode Island. Thus, the proportion of female teachers in Pennsylvania was only 36% in 1856. See Willard S. Elsbree, *The American Teacher: Evolution of Profession in a Democracy* (New York, 1939), 200-208.

4. Too many scholars have based their analysis of individuals and families on static

Graph No. 4 Average Monthly Wages of Massachusetts Public School Teachers (Including Board): 1837 – 1860

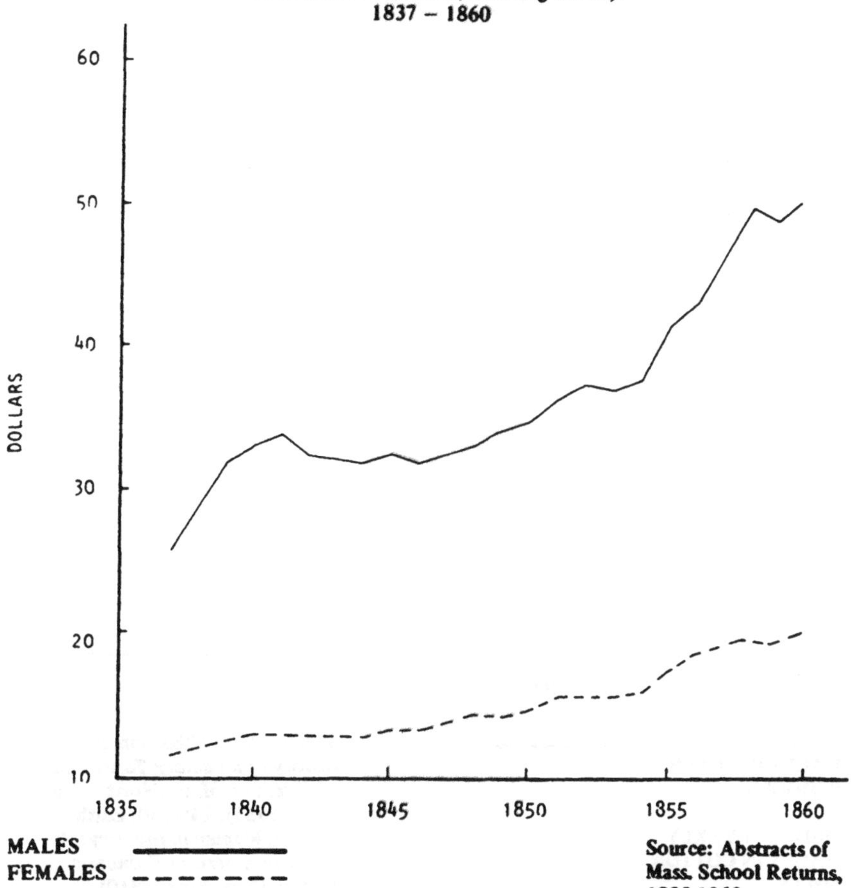

Source: Abstracts of Mass. School Returns, 1835-1860

interpretations of cross-sectional data. For two excellent discussions of an alternative life-course approach, see Glen H. Elder, Jr., "Adolescence in the Life Cycle: An Introduction," in *Adolescence in the Life Cycle*, eds. S. Dragastin and Glen H. Elder (New York, 1975), 1-22; Tamara K. Hareven, "The Family as Process: The Historical Study of the Family Cycle," *Journal of Social History*, VII (Spring 1974).

5. Compiling the number of Massachusetts ante-bellum women who ever taught was an involved task. Essentially, we estimated the number of females who annually entered the profession, and then from that figure, the percentage of women who worked as teachers at some time in their careers. The number of yearly female entries into teaching was itself a composite of three factors: the new teachers replacing other teachers who left their duties, the new teachers filling newly created positions in expanding school systems, and the overall change in the sex ratio of female to male teachers due to these additions.

The crucial problem in estimating teacher replacement or turnover in the pre-war period is the limited data available. Horace Mann's statewide tallies of the teaching experience of public school instructors in 1845-46 provided the only empirical information still remaining for Massachusetts. In the absence of more complete records, we have reluctantly applied his

Graph No. 5 Comparison of Weekly Wages for Women in Massachusetts Public Schools and Cotton Mills: 1840 – 1860

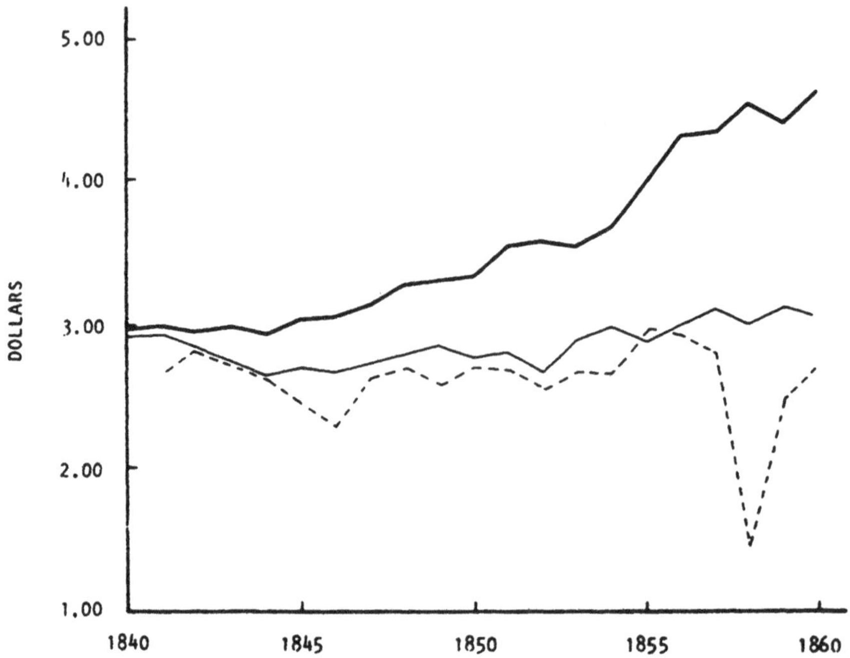

AVERAGE WEEKLY WAGES IN PUBLIC SCHOOLS ————

MEDIAN WEEKLY WAGES IN COTTON MILLS:

COMPANY 'C' IN CHICOPEE - - - - - - -

TWO MASS. MILLS (ABBOTT DATA) ————

Sources: Vera Shlakman, *Economic History of a Factory Town: A Study of Chicopee, Mass.* (Northhampton, Mass., 1935), 249-250; Edith Abbott, *Women in Industry: A Study in American Economic History* (New York, 1910), 290; *Abstracts of Mass. School Returns, 1840-1860*

findings to the whole period. Mann, *Ninth Annual Report of the Board of Education* [Massachusetts] *Together with the Ninth Annual Report of the Board* (Boston, 1846), 39-43; hereafter cited as *Massachusetts Annual School Report.*

The average amount of teaching experience for all teachers, including beginners, was 2.1 years. For determining turnover, however, the crucial figure was 2.6 years – the mean duration of tenure for those who had already begun to teach. The 1845-46 turnover rate for Massachusetts teachers was, therefore, the reciprocal of 2.6, or 38.5%. Unfortunately, we do not have comparable data for private school teachers; nonetheless, a combined replacement rate of 38.5% for all the state's teachers during this period is probably a very reasonable estimate. Elsbree, 293-295, had noted similar rates for Rhode Island and Pennsylvania teachers.

Given the turnover rate, we easily determined the number of new teachers required annually to replace those who retired. Next, we calculated the number of new teachers necessary to staff the expansion of Massachusetts schools during these years (taking into account the fact that the number of female teachers was steadily increasing whereas the total number of male teachers was declining). Having then established the total number of new male and female teachers entering both the public and private schools every year, we estimated the percentage of white women and men in the state who ever taught.

6. For a lengthy discussion of the nature of education for females in ante-bellum America, see our extended version of this paper presented at the Berkshire Conference. For a comparison of male and female school attendance patterns at the household level, see Carl F. Kaestle and Maris A. Vinovskis, "From Fireside to Factory: School Entry and School Leaving in Nineteenth-Century Massachusetts," paper presented at the MSSB Conference on The Family Life Course in Historical Perspective, Williamstown, Massachusetts, July 1975.

7. Paul H. Mattingly, "Educational Revivals in Ante-Bellum New England," *History of Education Quarterly*, XI (Spring 1971), 41-42, 47-49.

8. *Massachusetts Annual School Report*, XIV, 54.

9. In his analysis of American educators in the nineteenth century, Mattingly argues for the importance of the teacher institutes. Paul H. Mattingly, *The Classless Profession: American Schoolmen of the Nineteenth Century* (New York, 1975). Unfortunately, he did not attempt to make any quantitative estimates of the relative importance of teacher institutes to the teaching profession as a whole. Furthermore, the book focuses almost exclusively on male teachers since it studies the members of the American Institute of Instruction – an organization which did not admit females until after the Civil War.

10. Calculated from *Massachusetts Annual School Reports*, VIII, 22-23; XXI, 15-30.

11. Calculated from *Massachusetts Annual School Reports*, VIII, 22-23; X, 7-8; XVIII, 11, 17-18; XIX, 11-14, 24-25; XXIV, 30-35, 39-43.

12. Calculated from *Massachusetts Annual School Reports*, X, 7-8; XV, 14; XVI, 11; XVIII, 11, 17-18; XIX, 12-14, 22-25, XXI, 15-29; XXIV, 33-35, 39-43.

13. Suffolk County had 13.0% of Massachusetts total population in 1840 and 14.5% of the 1850 population.

14. On the problems of using occupational data in the ante-bellum period, see Stuart Blumin, "The Historical Study of Vertical Mobility," *Historical Methods Newsletter*, I (September 1968), 1-13; Clyde Griffen, "Occupational Mobility in Nineteenth-Century America: Problems and Possibilities," *Journal of Social History*, V (Spring 1972), 310-330; Michael B. Katz, "Occupational Classification in History," *Journal of Interdisciplinary History*, III (Summer 1972), 63-88; Theodore Hershberg, et. al., "Occupation and Ethnicity in Five Nineteenth-Century Cities: A Collaborative Inquiry," *Historical Methods Newsletter*, VII (June 1974), 174-216.

15. *Massachusetts Annual School Reports*, XIX, 12-17; XXII, 17-19.

16. The difficulties of being a married teacher were similar to those in many other occupations such as domestic service. Single women who served as domestics also complained about their lack of privacy and often left that position for jobs which offered them more personal freedom. On the demands and rewards of various types of women's work, see Robert W. Smuts, *Women and Work in America* (New York, 1971), 69-109.

In general, relatively few married women worked in nineteenth-century America. For an analysis of the determinants of women entering the labor force, see Karen Oppenheim

Mason, Maris A. Vinovskis, and Tamara K. Hareven, "Women's Gainful Employment and the Life Course in Essex County, Massachusetts, 1880," paper presented to the MSSB Conference on The Family Life Course in Historical Perspective, Williamstown, Massachusetts, July 1975.

17. Calculated from *Massachusetts Annual School Report*, IX, 40-41. Unfortunately, these data do not distinguish between tenure for female and male insturctors.

18. On the nineteenth-century stereotypes of women, see Barbara Welter, "The Cult of True Womanhood: 1820-1860," *American Quarterly*, XVIII (Summer 1966), 151-174.

19. *Massachusetts Annual School Report*, VI, 28.

20. *Ibid.*, 38.

21. An interesting sideline to the wage question is whether the statewide wage differentials for male and female teachers was in part a function of rural and urban pay scale differences. That is, given that city teachers made more money than country teachers, a concentration of female teachers in rural districts could explain their lower wages. A complete exploration of this possibility would entail a district by district comparison of salaries, by sex of teacher. Instead, we have relied on W.R. Burgess's compilation of male-female wage differences for teachers in rural and urban areas between 1841 and 1860. These data suggest that though female teachers were always paid less than male teachers in both rural and urban areas, the differential between male and female wage rates was considerably greater in the cities. W.R. Burgess, *Trends of School Costs* (New York, 1920), 30-45.

22. The state school reports often reprinted portions of local school committee reports. There are numerous references in these local reports to the fact that female teachers often left their positions for factory jobs. For a sampling of such complaints, see *New Hampshire Annual School Reports*, II, v, xxv-xxvi, xxxix, lii.

23. John Clark, superintendent of the Merrimack Mills, in a letter to Horace Mann claimed that 150 former female school teachers who were then working in his mills earned 17.75% above the average wages of all his female workers. He felt that this was due to the fact that they were generally employed in the "higher department" in the mills where the pay was better. *Massachusetts Annual School Report*, V, 97-99. Though there is no reason to doubt that former female school teachers in the mills generally earned higher wages than other female workers, one must be cautious in accepting Clark's testimony since it was prompted by Horace Mann who was trying to demonstrate the economic value of education. Maris A. Vinovskis, "Horace Mann on the Economic Productivity of Education," *New England Quarterly*, XLIII (December 1970), 550-571.

24. Though many local school committees, particularly those in rural areas, commented on the tendency of female teachers to leave in order to work in factories, there has been little effort by labor historians to explore the extent or significance of this shift. As a result, we do not have any good estimates on the percentage of former female teachers who worked in factories. John Clark's letter to Mann suggests that at least twelve percent of his female workers in the Merrimack Mills in 1841 were former school teachers. In the late 1840's and 1850's the situation was reversed. As the wages of female teachers improved relative to female factory workers and as there was an influx of Irish into the mills, native-born female workers in the Merrimack Mills in 1841 were former school teachers. In the late 1840's and women in the factories, see Edith Abbott, *Women in Industry: A Study in American Economic History* (New York, 1910); Caroline F. Ware, *Early New England Cotton Manufacture* (New York, 1931); Hannah Josephson, *The Golden Threads: New England's Mill Girls and Magnates* (New York, 1941).

25. Fortunately, there is work already underway by Deborah Hood of the University of Pennsylvania on the reactions of Massachusetts women to the feminization of the teaching force in that state in the ante-bellum period.

In from the Periphery: American Women in Science, 1830–1880

Sally Gregory Kohlstedt

Women engaged in scientific work throughout much of the nineteenth century, but they remained on the periphery of the scientific community. Their efforts to participate in and be recognized by that community were cautious and sometimes circuitous, a product of the social and intellectual climate of the times. Disapproval of women considered "too learned" was only one aspect of Victorian notions about women which inhibited their participation. Socialization as helpmates and lack of independent credibility meant that many women assisted male researchers, and they rarely achieved recognition commensurate with their skills. Moreover, the scientific community itself, in its conscious effort to professionalize, to establish an international reputation, and to raise the status of American science, formed national specialized or honorary associations and established journals that were not receptive to women. As the scientific community became more professional, it limited the acceptance of all who presented themselves or were perceived as amateur-like.[1] Thus, women doing research and writing remained

A version of this paper was presented at the Berkshire Conference on Women in History, June 1976. I would like to thank Margaret Rossiter, Michele Aldrich, Janet Bogdan, Sandra Coyner, and Sari Knopp Biklin for their interest, criticism, and support. The editors of *Signs*, particularly Domna Stanton, were exceptionally conscientious in helping sharpen and condense the ideas in this essay. Travel assistance was provided by the Syracuse University Fund for Faculty Research.

1. There is a striking absence of women among the groups of leading scientists identified by publication, society membership, or officeholding prior to 1876. See Sally Gregory Kohlstedt, *The Formation of the American Scientific Community: The American Association for the Advancement of Science, 1848–1860* (Urbana: University of Illinois Press, 1976); Clark Elliott, "The American Scientist, 1800–1863: His Origins, Career, and Interests" (Ph.D diss., Case Western Reserve University, 1970); and Robert V. Bruce, "A Statistical Profile of American Scientists, 1848–1876," in *Nineteenth-Century American Science: A Reappraisal*, ed. George Daniels (Evanston, Ill.: Northwestern University, 1972).

[*Signs: Journal of Women in Culture and Society* 1978, vol. 4, no. 1] largely invisible. Indeed, standard accounts of American science have tended to miss the individual women who pursued scientific study throughout much of the nineteenth century.[2] During the period from 1800 to 1864 a substantial number of women produced textbooks and illustrations in science, yet a standard index like the Royal Society's catalog of scientific papers identifies only three American women writers in those years and five more from 1865 to 1874. The increase thereafter was dramatic: from 1874 to 1883 there were 36 women and from 1884 to 1900 there were about 400 women publishing articles.[3] Both the nature of women's efforts in science and the expansion of visible participation need to be examined.

For purpose of analysis, the women scientists from the 1830s through the 1880s who are the subject of this study will be loosely divided into three generations. The first group, the "independents," active through the early decades of the century, are characterized by their individual, unselfconscious, and largely unrecognized efforts. The second generation of mid-nineteenth-century American women remained within their prescribed sphere, working primarily as educators and popularizers (illustrators and disseminators of science). Their successors and students in the third generation were forced to choose between amateur, local club activity and a more rigorous career within the emerging professional modes of post–Civil War America. Regardless of the choices, this third generation formed study or research groups which reinforced their conviction that scientific investigation was appropriate for women. Familiar with women's rights literature, they were the first to challenge stereotypes and worked toward full opportunity for women in science. An increase in relative numbers of women in science and a growing spirit of camaraderie created a positive environment for those who finally found full-time employment and were accepted as professionals in the 1880s. Although individual examples of these three loosely defined styles—independents, disseminators, and group coordinators—can be found throughout the period under investigation, the descriptive categories do provide a way to distinguish the status and activity of women scientists during the critical period of professionalization in American science.

2. See, however, Margaret Rossiter, "Women Scientists in America before 1920," *American Scientist* 62 (May–June 1974): 312–23. For the earlier period, see Joan Hoff Wilson, "Dancing Dogs of the Colonial Period: Women Scientists," *Early American Literature* 7 (Winter 1973): 225–35.

3. These data were provided by Clark Elliott of Harvard University Archives from the Royal Society of London, *Catalogue of Scientific Papers*, 6 vols. (London: C. J. Clay, 1867). Because of problems with non-sex-typed names and initials, this number may not be fully accurate, but the relative increase in involvement throughout the century cannot be accounted for simply by the increasing number of scientific periodicals.

Independent Correspondents

Women interested in science were inconspicuous and unchallenged during the early decades of the nineteenth century because, among other reasons, they worked as independent investigators apparently asking for and receiving no public recognition. There were relatively more women in natural history and agriculture than in the physical sciences, a fact that applied to men as well. Many of them were drawn by the Romantic movement to a sentimental, even religious attachment to the "beauties of nature." Jane Colden provides the earliest example of an independent researcher. She learned botany with her father on their New York estate (since he approved such constructive use of idle time) and eventually corresponded with leading European and colonial botanists. Following the Linneaean system she prepared a "Flora of New York" containing 340 illustrations, a study in the best eighteenth-century tradition which not only described the plants but also reported on their medicinal qualities. Other colonial naturalists, especially John Bartram near Philadelphia and Alexander Garden of South Carolina, encouraged her to gather and identify local New York plants. Typically cited as "Colden's daughter," her own contribution was eventually recognized and she published (in her own name) a brief plant description in an Edinburgh journal. She remained, however, at the outer rim of the natural history circle.[4]

This pattern of private and relatively isolated study, in which women relied almost exclusively on informal ways of learning and exchanging scientific information, remained until well into the nineteenth century.[5] After 1810 some academies for girls had more "modern" curricula, with science and contemporary literature, than did those for boys, but the content was rudimentary.[6] Most often, individual study, interested family members, local lectures, lyceum series, and, later, women's

4. Raymond P. Stearns, *Science in the British Colonies of North America* (Urbana: University of Illinois Press, 1971), pp. 566–67; and Anna Murray Vail, "Jane Colden, an Early New York Botanist," *Contributions from the New York Botanical Garden*, no. 88 (1907), pp. 21–34.

5. Max Meisel, *A Bibliography of American Natural History: The Pioneer Century, 1769–1865*, 3 vols. (New York: Hafner Publishing Co., 1926), 2:114–15, 274.

6. James A. Mulhern (*A History of Secondary Education in Pennsylvania* [Philadelphia: Science Press, 1933]) argues that the sciences, especially natural philosophy, botany, and natural history, were fairly common in women's seminaries by 1829. Also see Willystine Goodsell, ed., *Pioneers of Women's Education in the United States: Emma Willard, Catharine Beecher, and Mary Lyon* (New York: McGraw-Hill Publishing Co., 1931), pp. 87–88. Keith Melder ("Masks of Oppression: The Female Seminary Movement in the Central States," *New York History* 55 [July 1974]: 261–79) stresses the negative side of this alternative education.

clubs provided an introduction to the natural sciences.[7] Inevitably, the women in science came from the upper educated classes and showed most interest in research when they had fewest family responsibilities.

A number of women maintained herbaria or small collections. As the correspondence files of leading botanists like Asa Gray in Cambridge, John Torrey in New York, and William Darlington in Philadelphia confirm, the women's letters deal with exchange of specimens more often than with theoretical or analytical matters. The Darlington manuscripts provide an especially useful view of this informal activity because there are nearly two volumes of letters from women (bound separately!) primarily from the 1840s and 1850s. As early as 1829 Sarah W. Leaton of Washington, D.C., initiated correspondence with Darlington and offered to send rare specimens and thus "solicit a niche in your Temple of Fame by becoming a contributor."[8] Although modest about her ability as a naturalist, Leaton was able to identify plants from her conservatory and to solicit unusual specimens from traveling diplomats for Darlington. In subsequent decades, the number of women writing to Darlington who either were only casually interested in science or pursued systematic study increased rapidly. They sought and apparently received specific help from him (specimens, books, and identification of rare or difficult plants), as well as a certain validation of their interest. Darlington became the center of a network created by women who "shared" him with friends. While many of the women were isolated and dependent on this correspondence, some were teachers, like Abagail Kimber, Martha Beach, Mary P. Thomas, and Emma Musser, who asked for help in choosing textbooks and in arranging plants for educational purposes. Still others belonged to informal groups which aimed to learn "that science [botany] peculiarly appropriate to gentle minds";[9] among the most active was the Female Botanical Society of Wilmington, to which Darlington gave an informal presentation.[10] In their letters, the authors were deferential toward Dr. Darlington and eager to exchange services with him by sending local specimens. They frequently referred to the beauty and inspiration they found in studying the natural world, but some showed unease about their lack of expertise, which they attributed to their inadequate education. Although single women seemed the most active, they joined their married sisters in identifying family responsibilities as a major distraction and a drain on time and energy. Eliza

7. As early as 1800 Dr. John Vaughan gave a lecture in Delaware to a "mixed" audience of men and women and dedicated his published version to "The Female Enquirers of Wilmington." Murphy Smith of the American Philosophical Society Library kindly brought this pamphlet to my attention: *Valedictory Lecture Delivered before the Philosophical Society of Delaware* (Wilmington, Del.: Franklin Press, 1800).

8. Leaton to Darlington, December 7, 1828. William Darlington manuscripts, New York Historical Society Library (hereafter cited as Darlington).

9. Sarah Ann Fell to Darlington, May 7, 1944, Darlington.

10. Letter and report from Mary M'Caulley to Darlington, February 16, 1846, Darlington.

Fell, who corresponded with Darlington from 1848 to 1856, pointed out, "As is often the case of single ladies, who can and want to be useful, I am prone to be ready at the beck and call of many to serve them, thereby I sometimes find I have allowed an unnecessary enfringement upon my time and pleasure [in botany]."[11] Intellectual activity was considered a luxury.

The Morris sisters—Margaretta Hare Morris and Elizabeth Morris—demonstrate the possibilities for women in the early national period and the obstacles they faced. Elizabeth Morris was the more frequent correspondent of Darlington and, through him, met Asa Gray at Harvard.[12] She was eager to make some contribution and offered to prepare sketches for his publications, noting that Thomas Nuttall had praised her work as attractive and "botanically correct"; she also completed at least one set of woodcuts for Darlington. But as she recorded in November of 1845, her study, too, came second to other demands: "All out of doors looks wintry and dreary, and in the house *woman's work* must continue for some time to engross every faculty so completely, that it will be more by good luck than good arrangement if I lose not the little brains I have, and degenerate into a complete household drudge."[13] Her younger sister Margaretta Morris was educated in local schools in Germantown and attended scientific lecture series, including those by Charles John Wister on geology and mineralogy; but she concentrated her own research efforts on entomology, raised insects for study, and worked out the life cycles of several destructive species such as the locust and the so-called Hessian fly. Her results on the fly were presented to the American Philosophical Society (APS) in 1840 (through the "courtesy of a member"), and her observations on the locust were read before the American Association for the Advancement of Science in 1850.[14] After years of unaffiliated status, she was made an honorary (or corresponding) member of the APS as well as of the Academy of Natural Science in Philadelphia, the Boston Society of Natural History, and the New York State Agricultural Society. These associations served as a stimulus to her work and correspondence. In 1853, when she gave Darlington permission to publish her results, Margaretta Morris noted, "I have arrived at that time of life where *fastidiousness* appears wrong when *good may* be

11. Fell to Darlington, November 12, 1854, Darlington. Fell's correspondence became more frequent after a visit to Darlington's herbarium and library in 1851. She often noted that her study of botany was a "solace" to her otherwise busy and sometimes unhappy life.

12. Elizabeth Morris's propriety nearly prevented the correspondence: "Highly as I should prize a botanical correspondence with Dr. Gray I really want courage to obstruce [*sic*] myself upon his notice by opening a communication with a perfect stranger!" (Morris to Darlington, November 15, 1846, Darlington). The problem was resolved when Darlington sent seeds with her name to Gray, who then wrote first to her. See letters of December 12, 1842 and March 18, 1843, Darlington.

13. Elizabeth Morris to Darlington, November 3, 1845, Darlington.

14. Similar entomological work was done by Charlotte DeBernier Scarbrough Taylor of Georgia and published in *Harpers New Monthly* in the 1850s; see *Dictionary of American Biography*, s.v. "Taylor, Charlotte DeBernier."

done so I often shock the more sensitive feelings of those who have not been so much accustomed [to women in science]" and gave Darlington permission to publish her results.[15]

Morris's expanding aspirations suggested that self-confidence and better education would create new patterns for the younger generation of women. Private study and romantic notions about natural history were not sufficient for women as they made contact with men of achievement and the environment of research.

Teachers and Illustrators

The popularization of natural history in the 1820s and 1830s served to spur women's interest. Lyceum lectures (given by men, since only "radicals" like Fanny Wright dared to speak before a mixed audience) were open to women attending with friends or family.[16] Increased education, private and public, gave women further opportunity to learn and to teach. Indeed, as women organized secondary schools for young women and found few materials appropriate to their students, they produced general descriptive textbooks and classroom maps and charts. Although some published aids were based on traditional texts and explained facts that were well established, others attempted to add new descriptions or to organize their books in a format appropriate for classroom teaching.[17] Several early proponents of science education for women—Mary Lyons, Emma Hart Willard, and Almira Hart Lincoln

15. Margaretta Morris to Darlington, February 3, 1853, Darlington. Margaretta Morris published five articles prior to 1863. Her sister Elizabeth apparently wrote a review of Darlington's *Agricultural Botany* for the *American Agriculturalist* but she urged, with bold underline, that "my name must not be known as the author" (Morris to Darlington, December 3, 1848, Darlington). Women may have been among the "anonymous" authors on scientific matters in popular journals. E.g., Darlington's friend, Isabella Ratchelder, admitted (in a letter dated January 5, 1850 [Darlington]) that she was the reviewer of his *Memorial of John Bartram and Humphrey Marshall* in the *North American Review* 70 (January 1850): 210–25. Some geneological details on the Morris sisters are in Robert C. Moon, *The Morris Family of Philadelphia*, 5 vols. (Philadelphia: R. C. Moon, 1898–1909), 2:581–83.

16. E.g., Benjamin Tucker, a teacher at the Young Ladies Academy of Philadelphia, offered a lecture series in chemistry for women and their families which was apparently renewed in subsequent years. See Wyndham Miles, "Public Lectures on Chemistry in the United States," *Ambix* 15 (October 1968): 136–37.

17. The titles suggest the educational intention of most of these textbook authors: James Rennie and Arabella Clark, *Alphabet of Botany for the Use of Beginners* (New York: P. Hill, 1833); Mary A. Holley, *Texas: Observations: Historical, Georgraphical and Descriptive* (Baltimore: Armstrong & Plaskitt, 1833); Lucy Hooper, ed., *The Lady's Book of Flowers and Poetry* (New York: Claxton, Remsec, & Haffelfinger, 1843); Laura Johnson and Amos Eaton, *Botanical Teacher for North America* (Albany, N.Y.: Oliver Steele, 1843); Louisa Johnson, *Every Lady Her Own Flower Garden* (Charleston, S.C.: S. Babcock & Co., 1842); Jane Kilby Welsh, *Familiar Lessons in Mineralogy and Geology* (Hallowell, Me., 1832–33); Mary Swift, *First Lessons in Natural Philosophy for Children* (Hartford, Conn.: W. J. Hamersley, 1955).

Phelps—were friends of Amos Eaton. Eaton had offered natural science courses in Connecticut and in the Albany area, organized popular education at the Troy Lyceum, and subsequently became a special instructor at Emma Willard's seminary. A letter of support in 1817 noted: "As his first class consists chiefly of ladies, and as these branches of learning have not hitherto generally engaged the attention of that sex . . . from this experience we feel authorized to recommend these branches as a very useful part of female education."[18] Since Eaton believed that more science generally should be taught in the schools he encouraged his students to teach rather than do research. His most famous pupil was Almira Hart Lincoln Phelps, who gained a scientific background from the lyceum lectures on science at Brattleboro, Vermont, and the open lectures at the Rensselaer technical institute. Her first textbook, *Familiar Lectures on Botany* (1829), was enormously successful; it went through seventeen editions by 1842 and had sold 275,000 copies by 1872. A review in the leading scientific journal, edited by Benjamin Silliman of Yale, was positive, if patronizing: "The intention of the work is expressed in the title page . . . and it cannot fail of answering the principle intention of its amiable authoress, of engaging persons of her own sex in a study eminently calculated to interest and instruct them."[19] Phelps's textbook, which included history, poetry, and bibliographical sketches along with the descriptions of specific specimens, was a teaching tool, an "aid to inductive reasoning" intended to show the natural order of the physical world without being too technical. Although she became one of the first women members of the American Association for the Advancement of Science, she remained primarily a teacher. Explaining her lack of scientific work, she wrote somewhat apologetically to Darlington, "My pages at present are the hearts and minds of the young."[20] A pioneer in the education of women in the sciences, Phelps was, however, also a product of her own time, who sought not to change women's role by the study of science but to enrich its content. She wished to educate "good women rather than fine ladies" and believed that a lively intellect contributed to a full, happy life.[21] Her aspirations and limitations are

18. "To Whom It May Concern," Northampton, November 24, 1817, Smallwood Collection, Bird Library, Syracuse University (hereafter cited as Smallwood). Signatories were Josiah Dwight, Caleb Strong, Solomon Williams, Elyah H. Mills, Eben Hunt, and David Hunt. William Smallwood, "Amos Eaton, Naturalist," *New York History* 18 (April 1937): 167–88; and with Mable Smallwood, *Natural History and the American Mind* (New York: Columbia University Press, 1935).

19. Quoted in Emma Lycia Bolzau, "Almira Hart Lincoln Phelps: Her Life and Work" (Ph.D. diss., University of Pennylvania, 1936), p. 261.

20. Phelps to Darlington, May 1844 and November 14, 1859, Darlington.

21. Goodsell, *Pioneers of Women's Education* (n. 6 above), pp. 561–62. Phelps's sister, Emma Hart Willard, argued: "Natural Philosophy has not often been taught to our sex. Yet why should we be kept in ignorance of the great machinery of nature, and left to the vulgar notion, that nothing is curious but what deviates from her common course? If mothers were acquainted with this science, they would communicate very many of its principles to their children in early youth."

revealed in a letter to Eaton, her mentor: "... I am afraid you will be severe with me about this book—you were never much in favor of my attempting any thing of the kind; but you know I have long thought that I might do a little towards rendering the sciences more popular among my own sex—I make no pretense at being a *geologist* myself; but I love the science, and want others to do the same."[22] Her concern about the quality of her work is a persistent theme of her letters: "I hope you will find in it [the newest textbook] no gross errors, as I have endeavored to keep under the shadow of good authorities."[23] The textbooks she wrote were built on the work of others and stressed the enjoyment and relevance of science. Her chemistry textbook, for example, showed the uses of that science in housewifery. It must also be noted that, while the young women's seminaries in West Chester, Pennsylvania, and in Ellicott's Mills outside Baltimore, which Philips headed, offered a stronger science curriculum than most schools, many women's institutions by the 1850s included some scientific study.[24]

The debate on the appropriateness of science to women, even teachers, was far from settled. By 1825, New York's state-sponsored *New York Teacher* and the *American Institute of Instruction* encouraged more general education for women in the natural sciences.[25] Still skeptical, the governor of New York wrote more than a decade later that women teachers had "a quality for excellence in all departments of learning except perhaps the physical sciences."[26] Echoing Phelps's position, Dr. Raymond, founding president of Vassar, supported science education for women with the following rationale: "Physiology, chemistry, physics, and the various branches of natural history—have all of them a womanly side, and may be taught throughout, with reference to practical application, in women's acknowledged domain."[27] Even as the debate concerning the appropriateness of science for women took shape, secondary educational training and practical experience permitted the entry of an increasing number of women to science. The discussion of women's roles and of the dedication of women science teachers helped the next generation realize that they had choices beyond private employment by friends or elementary teaching.

Sometimes equipped by seminary training and inevitably socialized as helpmates, a number of nineteenth-century women also worked as

22. Phelps to Eaton, June 21, 1838, Smallwood.

23. Ibid.; also see Phelps to Darlington, July 18, 1838 and March 20, 1852, Darlington.

24. Bolzau, pp. 98–99 and 271–72; Thomas Woody, *A History of Women's Education in the United States*, 2 vols. (New York, 1929), 1:474–80.

25. See, e.g., *American Institute of Instruction, Annual Meeting*, no. 2 (1831), pp. 29–32.

26. Quoted in Paul Monroe, *Founding of the American Public School*, 2 vols. (New York: Macmillan Co., 1940), 1:486.

27. James Orton, ed., *The Liberal Education of Women: The Demand and the Method, Current Thoughts in America and England* (New York: A. S. Barnes & Co., 1973), p. 35.

scientific illustrators or collaborators with relatives or friends. A teacher, Lucy Say, developed an active interest in conchology and assisted her husband's research in New Harmony, Indiana, by "making drawings for the plates and supervising and helping in the coloration."[28] Orra White Hitchcock and Sarah Aiken Hall, although seldom mentioned in histories of American science, also worked creatively as illustrators with their established, professionally recognized husbands.[29] Credit was typically given to the employed member of such a team, but more research in the family papers of scientists is needed to reveal the nature and extent of such coordinate production. Helen Lawson, who was introduced to the world of science by her father, an engraver, learned sufficient natural history to illustrate publications by well-known naturalists, including Samuel S. Haldeman and Amos Binney. Such activities aroused little attention in the 1830s and 1840s because the work was completed privately and in ways deemed appropriate for women.

The Third Generation: Private Study or Professionalism

If the mid-century illustrators and textbook writers attracted little attention, Maria Mitchell's discovery of a comet in 1847 was widely acclaimed as proof of the capabilities of woman scientists.[30] After receiving an award from the King of Denmark, she became the first female member of the American Academy of Arts and Sciences. Feminists noted her achievement: she was acclaimed by Lucretia Mott at the Seneca Falls Convention in 1848 and discussed by the editor of *Godey's Ladies Book*. Mitchell was cautious about what she said and did concerning women in science during the 1850s but became increasingly aware of the uniqueness of her opportunities and the problems faced by aspiring women scientists. Born a generation after Phelps, Mitchell would even-

28. Harry Weiss and Grace Ziegler, *Thomas Say, Early American Naturalist* (Springfield, Ill.: Charles C. Thomas, 1931), pp. 213–20. Lucy Say drew sixty-six of the sixty-eight plates for her husband's book on conchology; five drawings are at the Houghton Library, Harvard. After his death, she continued writing to D. Humphreys Storer, Thaddeas W. Harris, and Samuel S. Haldeman and became a corresponding member of the Academy of Natural Sciences of Philadelphia.

29. Hitchcock is mentioned in the sketch of her husband, *Dictionary of Scientific Biography*, s.v. "Hitchcock, Edward," and some of her work is at the Amherst College Archives. Also see John M. Clarke, *James Hall of Albany, Geologist and Paleontologist, 1811–1898*, 2d ed. (Albany, N.Y., 1923), p. 180. Although Lucy Bakewell Audubon has also been credited with illustrations, Alice Ford's *John James Audubon* (Norman: University of Oklahoma Press, 1964) suggests that the plates were done by her husband (p. 245). Ford elaborates on Maria Martin's contribution to the work of John Bachman. Also see Andrew Rodgers III, (*"Noble Fellow" William Sullivant* [New York: G. P. Putnam's Sons, 1940]) on the role of Eliza Sullivant.

30. Sally Gregory Kohlstedt, "Maria Mitchell and the Advancement of Women in Science," *New England Quarterly* 51 (March 1978): 39–63.

tually lead a movement to help women enter regular scientific occupations.

Educated into the "cult of true womanhood," most women were taught that intellectual achievement for its own sake was not a virtue. Commenting favorably on Mary Treat, a popular botanist, a contemporary male noted with approval that she had a "modesty so shrinking as to make any public recognition of her services painful to her."[31] Even more, the female intellectual was regarded as a decided oddity. One editor suggested that if an educated woman was a curiosity, a woman scientist was nothing less than peculiar; thus, if "an unfortunate female should happen to possess a lurking fondness for any special scientific pursuit she is careful (if of any social position) to hide it as she would some deformity."[32] If interest in science appeared inappropriate, achievement seemed impossible. Experts on human species used arguments from Darwin and Francis Galton to assert that in evolution woman had been "the loser in the intellectual race as regards acquisition, origination and judgment."[33] Faced by these pervasive stereotypes, many women continued to be amateurs when given a choice between private study or professional participation. Of course, participation at meetings, presentation of research papers, and public visibility, increasingly important professional activities, seemed a violation of established social norms. At best, some male scientists in the nineteenth century supported women in adjunct roles. Prominent scientific educators like Eaton in the 1830s, Louis Agassiz in the 1860s and 1870s, and David Starr Jordon in the 1880s encouraged women to be teachers and assistants, but not peers. Discussion about the level of female participation increased, however, as women became more visible and articulate. During the 1850s, the American Association for the Advancement of Science (AAAS), the major forum for science, heard occasionally sarcastic discussions about whether or not women should attend meetings or become members, even though Mitchell's membership in the AAAS made the general question irrelevant.[34] It is not surprising that no woman presented a paper on her own work at annual meetings in the pre–Civil War period. The public, however, appeared more receptive to women scientists than the professional scientific community. The popular *Scientific American*,

31. John W. Harshberger, *The Botanists of Philadelphia and Their Work* (Philadelphia: T. C. Davis & Son, 1899), p. 300. Treat was active as a researcher. See, e.g., her letters to Samuel H. Scudder, December 18, 1876, August 28, 1877, and January 8, 1878. Scudder manuscripts, Museum of Science, Boston, Massachusetts.

32. Quoted in Helen Wright, *Sweeper in the Sky: The Life of Maria Mitchell, First Woman Astronomer in America* (New York: E. P. Dutton & Co., 1966), p. 140. Also see Barbara Welter, "Anti-Intellectualism and the American Women: 1800–1860," *Mid-America* 48 (October 1960): 258–72.

33. George J. Romanes, "Mental Differences in Men and Women," *Popular Science Monthly* 31 (July 1887): 383–401, quotation from p. 385; J. Stall Patterson, "Women and Science" *The Radical* 7 (March 1870): 169–85 and (April 1870): 287–300.

34. Kohlstedt, *The Formation of the American Scientific Community* (n. 1 above), p. 103.

which was read by women, pointed to the specific achievements of women like Mitchell and suggested in editorials women's potential for science and invention.[35] And when Edward Fisk Youmans founded the *Popular Science Monthly* in 1872 he made the magazine a forum for discussion of women's roles, perhaps influenced by his sister Eliza's own efforts in science.

The ongoing interest and achievement of women in science was undeniable. By the 1850s women like Elizabeth Agassiz were not only assisting their husbands but also writing their own texts (although her *First Lesson in Natural History* was published under a pseudonym in 1859).[36] Some women were working as curators and librarians in all-male natural history societies. Cautiously, women were expanding their activities, testing alternative roles, and enjoying new challenges. The discussion did signal the need for women to move to one side or the other of a widening chasm between those who were avocationally involved and those who were engaged in scientific research.

Private Study and Avocation

The organization of small, local, scientific study groups paralleled the general women's club movement across the country and the cooperative tendencies among women in religious and reform efforts. The Dana Society of Natural History of the Albany Female Academy was only one of several such clubs founded in the 1860s under the encouragement of Adrian J. Ebell, professor at Rensselaer Polytechnic Institute. Taken over by local women in Albany, the club's stated purpose was "to awaken in ourselves and in others a growing interest in the study of nature, and increase our knowledge of the natural sciences in both their practical and scientific bearings."[37] Since it reflected an older approach and an alternative to the modern demands of professional science, one member could acknowledge without regret: "We do not claim to have made any original discoveries, nor added to the store of scientific knowledge."[38] Rather, the society stressed self-development by maintaining a small

35. Deborah J. Warner, "*Scientific American* and Women's Rights, 1845–1870." Available from the author, Smithsonian Institution, Washington, D.C.

36. Elizabeth Agassiz was undoubtedly an important force in the subsequent movement for women in science. She published books and pamphlets on science, helped establish a summer school in natural history, became prime mover for the "Harvard Annex," and was first president of Radcliffe College.

37. Janet McNaughton, "A Sketch of the Dana Natural History Society," *Albany Argus* (November 18, 1876); manuscripts are deposited at the Albany Institute and Historical and Arts Society. Also see James M. Hobbins, "The Albany Institute and Vicissitude in the Learned Culture" (paper presented at a symposium of the American Academy of Arts and Sciences, June 1975).

38. McNaughton. Membership varied from thirty to 100 members, although attendance at monthly meetings usually numbered twenty persons.

library and cabinet of specimens and taking numerous summer excursions led by state science employees, including paleontologist James Hall. Similar private and group study was encouraged in the 1880s by the Chatauqua Library and Scientific Circle, whose large membership was dominated by women, and the Society for the Encouragement of Study at Home, which operated out of Boston.[39] Some of these local scientific societies provided an alternative to closed men's groups such as the Botanical Society of Pennsylvania, whose counterpart became the female Philadelphia Botanical Club. Educated, active, but dedicated first to private study and socializing, the members of these societies had little contact with practicing research scientists. A few groups, however, like the Syracuse Botanical Club, undertook publication of local guides to flora and fauna and maintained limited correspondence with scientists describing specimens not previously known to be in their vicinity.[40] Many became involved with animal and land conservation at the end of the century, supporting local parks and zoos. Their efforts also supported the "nature study" movement of Anna Botsford Comstock, which coordinated teachers and community leaders in out-of-door education.[41] Whether the societies assisted other women who sought to do research or gain advanced training remains unclear.

The Professional Alternative

After the Civil War several women reformers and teachers encouraged their best students to pursue employment in science and tried to persuade the scientific community to grant them access. Their efforts were underscored by a number of articles and books. Caroline H. Dall's published lectures on women's education, legal status, and career opportunities were among the first to point out the lack of real employment

39. Charles R. Kniker ("The Chatauqua Literary and Scientific Circle, 1876–1914" [Ph.D. diss., Columbia University, 1969]) suggests that, of the 500,000 members enrolled between 1878 and 1914, approximately two-thirds were women. The *Chautauquan* occasionally published articles on women in science, including Esther Singleton, "Women as Astronomers" 14 (November 1891): 209–12 and (December 1891): 340–42, and Katherine Lee Bates, "Woman as Scholar" 13 (April 1891): 77–79. Science was one of the major component areas of the home study movement, from the 1870s into the 1890s; see Madame Marie Theresa Blanc, *The Condition of Women in the United States A Traveler's Notes*, trans. Abby Langton Alger (Boston: Roberts Brothers, 1895), pp. 115–122.

40. See the folder of undated clippings at the Onondaga Historical Society, Syracuse, New York.

41. Material on this movement is in the Comstock manuscripts at Cornell University Archives. Lydia E. Becker, "On the Study of Science by Women," *Contemporary Review* 10 (April 1869): 386–404; Frances Emily White, "Woman's Place in Nature," *Popular Science Monthly* 6 (January 1875): 292–301; Department of Public Instruction of the State of New York, *Annual Report*, no. 8 (Albany, 1862).

opportunities for women in science.[42] Even more direct was an article by the English feminist, Lydia Becker, who rejected the idea that there were relatively few women in science because "of a natural distaste or capacity for scientific pursuits among women." Becker argued, to the contrary, that society denied women access to scientific learning and discredited their interest, a particularly unfortunate tendency since science stressed structured, systematic approaches to problem solving which women might not otherwise learn.[43] Debate on this issue became an ongoing feature of the new *Popular Science Monthly,* and the discussion was vigorously pursued by the Association for the Advancement of Women.

In some cases, the initiative for educating women in science came from women's reform groups. The philanthropic New England Women's Club, for example, established a horticultural school in 1870. Led by Ednah Dow Cheney, the school was intended to train women in the theory and practice of agriculture in the hope that some graduates would become teachers, while others would simply increase their "taste for gardening and the care of flowers and fruits."[44] Plagued by financial and administrative problems, the school's assets were absorbed by the Bussey agricultural school at Harvard, which agreed to admit women.[45] Similar schools were planned in New York and Chicago, but prospective horticulturists apparently found these schools inadequate, as vocational training and enrollment was not sufficient to sustain the program.

The impetus to provide advanced study of science to women came from individuals as well. Bostonian Lucretia Crocker, whose interest in mathematics and physical science earned her a faculty position first at her own alma mater, West Newton Normal School, then at Antioch College under Horace Mann, and, finally, in the Boston public schools, where she was among the first women elected to the school board, sought ways to improve the education of teachers.[46] Convinced that most

42. Caroline H. Dall, *Woman: The College, the Market, and the Court, or Woman's Relation to Education, Law, and Labor* (Boston: Lee & Shephard, 1867). Also see the review in *The Radical* 3 (January 1868): 353–64.

43. Janice Law Trecher, "Sex, Science and Education,' *American Quarterly* 26 (October 1974): 352–66. American educator Catharine Beecher argued, "Still more unjust is the custom which gives superior advantages to men for the scientific and practical training for a profession by which an honorable independence may be secured and almost none at all are provided for women" (quoted in Kathryn Kish Sklar, *Catharine Beecher: A Study in American Domesticity* [New Haven, Conn.: Yale University Press, 1973], p. 269).

44. The manuscript records of the committee assigned to oversee the horticultural school are in the Social Meetings Record Book, 1869–1871, New England Women's Club manuscripts, Schlesinger Library, Radcliffe.

45. Ibid., October 27, 1871.

46. There is no biography, nor apparently any major manuscript collection, of Crocker. See, however, *Memoirs of Lucretia Crocker and Abby W. May, Prepared for Private Circulation by Ednah Dow Cheney* (Boston, 1893) and "Lucretia Crocker," *Report of the Association for the Advancement of Women, Fifteenth Women's Congress, 1887* (Fall River, Mass.: J. H. Franklin & Co., 1888).

women lacked opportunities to study science, she persuaded Alpheus Hyatt, curator of the Museum of the Boston Society of Natural History, to sponsor evening and Saturday lecture series for the postgraduate education of elementary and secondary teachers.[47] She also organized the science department of the Society to Encourage Studies at Home and was an active honorary member of an informal science club of local women who sought to do research and to publish.[48] By the 1870s Louis Agassiz, a prominent zoologist at Harvard, had also accepted a number of young women assistants in his laboratory and pioneered a summer school near Woods Hole which welcomed women. As Joan Burstyn has demonstrated, this school was enormously important to those thirty women who attended in 1873 and 1874.[49] Most of them returned to teach at colleges and public schools, and their students constituted an important segment of the next generation of zoologists. Similarly, Alpheus Hyatt, a supporter of Crocker's lecture program, determined to use his home at Annisquam as a summer school. While this school was of short duration—partly because of Hyatt's impatience with administration and with the "raw recruits" who took more time than anticipated—his interest led Boston women to establish the Marine Biological Laboratory at Woods Hole.[50] Several other summer schools, which aimed to supplement the education of the normal schools, were also founded in the 1870s and 1880s.[51]

Because these special study groups and summer schools proved insufficient as a career base, it was the women's colleges with women

47. Society sponsorship was nominal; assistant librarian Harriet Biddle took personal responsibility for the circulars and tickets, a number of community women financially underwrote the program, and Crocker herself arranged most of the lectures. For a detailed discussion of the program, see participant Frances Zirngiebel, "Teacher's School for Science," *Popular Science Monthly* 55 (August 1899): 451–65 and (September 1899): 640–52. A typescript summary of Biddle's work from 1885 to 1925 is at the Museum of Comparative Zoology, Harvard University.

48. The club was discussed in a series of letters from Cora Clark to Miss Alexander in the summer of 1882 while Clark was abroad (Alexander manuscripts, Houghton Library, Harvard University). For evidence of Crocker's efforts to assist women applying for positions and seeking society membership, see her notes to Alpheus Hyatt on Feburary 15, 1883, October 21, 1884, and November 3, 1884 in Boston Society of Natural History manuscripts, Boston Museum of Science.

49. Much of this information is derived from a paper by Joan Burstyn and my comment at the Centennial Commemoration of the Founding of the Anderson School of Natural History, August 14, 1973. A revised version of Joan Burstyn's paper was published as "Early Women in Higher Education: The Role of the Anderson School of Natural History," *Journal of Education* 159, no. 3 (August 1977): 50–64.

50. See the Hyatt-Beebee manuscripts, Syracuse University Manuscript and Archives. Parts of the correspondence are reproduced in Ralph W. Dexter, "Views of Alpheus Hyatt's Sea-Side Laboratory and Excerpts from his Expeditionary Correspondence," *The Biologist* 39 (May–September 1956): 5–11.

51. See William A. Smith, *A History of the Summer Session, Cornell University: The First Seventy-five Years, 1862–1966* (private printing, 1974), pp. 1–5.

faculty in the postwar years that offered perhaps the single largest support for women in science. Certain schools took an early lead. Mary Lyon at Mount Holyoke hired naturalist Lydia Marie Shattuck, an expert on the Connecticut Valley region of Massachusetts. She attended Agassiz's Anderson School on Penikese Island in 1873 and made sure that her younger colleague, Cornelia Clapp, had an opportunity to study there as well.[52] Intrepid women, who went on summer excursions with David Starr Jordan and attended national scientific meetings, Shattuck and Clapp were also dedicated scholars. Although Shattuck never became well known outside Mount Holyoke, Clapp was one of the first scholars at Woods Hole and helped support the Naples Zoological Station.[53] No less important, their students maintained an interest in science and, even when they chose religion over science and became foreign missionaries, sent back rare specimens from India and South Africa.[54] At Vassar, students tended to study astronomy and mathematics, thanks to the influence of Maria Mitchell. Through annual reports before the Association for the Advancement of Women which detailed accomplishments of women in science, Mitchell worked to encourage women to study science or support others pursuing a science career. Teaching was the profession of most college graduates, although some astronomers became members of observatory teams and biologists joined private and governmental laboratories.

As women gained qualifications and confidence, they showed interest in joining the associations dominated by men. With few exceptions, the women admitted through the 1860s were, like Margaretta Hare Morris, only "corresponding members," who were not expected to attend meetings or permitted to vote. In the 1870s and 1880s, women gained nominal membership in such local groups as the New York Lyceum and the Boston Society of Natural History, as well as in the newly established disciplinary societies. By the time women were admitted as members many had already worked as librarians, curators, and assistants. The authors of the Boston Society of Natural History's

52. A lively description of Shattuck and of the Penikese school is found in the typescript of an oral history interview with Clapp conducted by Ann Morgan in 1921. Clapp manuscripts, Williston Library, Mount Holyoke College.

53. Shattuck's letterbook indicates that she actively did local research and corresponded with scientists concerning her findings. Even active women could be overlooked, however. Shattuck attended a chemistry meeting in 1874 but was not officially listed in the minutes of the meeting. Also see S. Jean Crawford, "The Association to Aid Scientific Research by Women," *Science* 126 (July–December 1932): 492–93; and Donna Jeanne Haraway, "The Marine Biological Laboratory at Woods Hole" (paper presented at the Symposium on Learned Societies of the American Academy of Arts and Sciences, June 1975).

54. Clapp's "Report of the Zoological Department" (1875) notes that two students hoped to go into medicine. Letters from missionaries are found in both the Clapp and Shattuck manuscript collections, Williston Library, Mount Holyoke College.

guidebook series for teachers, for example, included Jennie Arms Sheldon, Elizabeth Agassiz, and Ellen Swallow Richards.[55] These long-sought affiliations were symbolic, but even a cursory look at the record of several such groups indicates that women largely remained adjuncts rather than fully recognized participants.

The hopes and triumphs of women in the 1880s indicate that they were a "first generation" of public achievers. Their success, however, was built on the persistent efforts of women who had worked quietly in science throughout the century, women who both reflected and expanded contemporary expectations. The female illustrators and textbook writers had not challenged the boundaries of women's sphere, but their work refuted glib assertions about women's capability to understand science. Although educators like Phelps had consciously presented science as compatible with the traditional responsibilities of women, they had also provided the requisite learning for the next generation to achieve some public success. The women working on the periphery provided the foundation that helped gain the third generation access to advanced training and scientific associations. Most important, by their own example, the forerunners demonstrated to those who chose to notice the capabilities of women in science, and they established cooperative networks which would be essential for expanding women's opportunities in science.

Department of History
Syracuse University

55. Sally Gregory Kohlstedt, "The Nineteenth-Century Amateur Tradition: The Case of the Boston Society of Natural History," in *Science and Its Public*, ed. Gerald Holton and William Blanpied (Dordrecht: Reidel Publishing Co., 1756), pp. 183–86.

AMERICAN FEMALE HISTORIANS IN CONTEXT, 1770-1930

Kathryn Kish Sklar

The papers in this volume testify to the present strength of associative activity among American female historians. Selected from the Second Conference on Women's History held in October, 1974, and cosponsored by the Berkshire Conference of Women Historians, this volume's causal origins can be traced to a decision at the Berkshire's forty-second annual meeting in 1972 to sponsor a special conference on women's history in 1973. The success of that conference led the group to commit itself to two others, one represented here, and one planned at Bryn Mawr College in 1976.

Although the oldest association of female historians, the Berkshire Conference is now but one among many such regional groups. Within the past ten years associative activity among female historians has significantly increased. These associations form a distinct subculture within the historical profession. Adopting the Berkshire Conference's concern with the female as well as the professional identity of its constituency, they promote collective consciousness and friendship among female historians, assess the status of women within the historical profession, and gather statistics that have proved to support their conviction that women are far from fully integrated into professional life.[1]

Although historians today are familiar with these female collectivities, most know very little about their history, and even less about how these professional associations compare with the associative structures characterizing eighteenth- and nineteenth-century female historians. Did female historians always form their own groups? If not, why not? Has the experience of American female historians varied significantly over time? If so, what social structures account for this variation? This paper attempts to answer these and other questions about female historians living and working between 1770 and 1930. Concluding with a discussion of the formation of the Berkshire Conference in 1930, it compares the careers of female historians in three distinct periods of American historical writing: the community context of early American history; the Victorian context of nineteenth-century history; and the early professional context of twentieth-century history.

The lives and careers of the twenty-six women listed as "Historians" in the "Classified List of Selected Biographies" in *Notable American Women, a Biographical Dictionary*, edited by Edward James, Janet James, and Paul Boyer, provide us with the most systematic sample of earlier female historians.[2] Based on this sample, this study is biased toward the inclusion of women whose works meet our current professional standards. Nevertheless this sample also embraces the successful amateur and it does permit us to view a century and a half of changing work context for female historians.

For purposes of analysis these twenty-six women have here been divided into three major chronological groups: those born before 1800, those born between 1800 and 1850, and those born after 1850. Given the difficulties strict chronology often poses to the historian, these three chronological categories contain a remarkable degree of internal coherence. Among the first group of four born before 1800, all wrote history within the context of a specific community to which they were committed.[3] Reflecting the local nature of late eighteenth- and early nineteenth-century American life, the lives and works of female historians before 1800 were inseparably linked to their immediate community contexts. In contrast, the careers of women historians born between 1800 and 1850 all took place within the context of the Victorian literary world.[4] This literary network linked the older local tradition with the newer translocal elements in American life and embrace both analytic and fictive writing. The third group of female historians, born after 1850, generally pursued academic or academically related careers.[5] These three chronological groups thus allow us to view and compare three distinct contexts within which female historians have worked in the past: local communities, Victorian letters, and "the academic community."

The life and career of Hannah Adams (1755-1831), author of the first publication by those women born before 1800, *An Alphabetical Compendium of the Various Sects* (1784), introduces us to characteristics general to female historians in all three groups as well as to characteristics specific to the first group alone. Two important themes in her life run through the lives of most of her successors: the need to make a living and a consciousness of gender discrimination.

The primary causal influence behind Hannah Adams' commitment to history was her need to support herself. In her own words, "I wished to exert myself as much as possible to be useful, and to gain a subsistence."[6] Typical of the unmarried women of her generation, she initially sought to support herself through needlework. Like many women in wartime, she experienced some occupational mobility. In her *Memoir* published in 1832, she wrote:

> I was pressed by necessity to make every exertion in my power for my immediate support. During the American Revolutionary War, I learned to weave bobbin lace, which was then saleable, and much more profitable to me than spinning, sewing, or knitting, which had previously been my employment.... But at the termination of the American war, this resource failed, and I was again left in a destitute situation. My health would not admit of my teaching in a school, and I was glad to avail myself of every opportunity of taking any kind of work which I found to do, though the profit was very small, and inadequate to my support.[7]

Meanwhile Adams' religious interests had moved her to study the history of American sectarianism in a systematic way. In her twenty-eighth year, at the edge of utter destitutjon, it occurred to her that she might make some money by publishing her historical materials on religion. "I was not, like my sister, ingenious in all kinds of needle work," Hannah Adams explained in her *Memoir*, "and the difficulty of taking in such kinds of work as I could do induced me, as the last resort, to attend to my manuscript with the faint hope that it might be printed and afford me some little advantage."[8]

In her search for some means of economic self-sufficiency, Hannah Adams resembled the great majority of female historians who came after her. Only six of the twenty-six women considered here were not self-supporting through most of their adult lives. Two in the pre-1800 group, three in the 1800-1850 group, and only one in the post-1850 group were partly dependent on their husband's earnings. Moreover, two of the twenty self-supporting historians also supported a child born during brief marriages that ended either in widowhood or divorce.[9]

More than half of these twenty-six historians initially supported themselves by teaching in primary or secondary schools. In Hannah Adams' life teaching took the form of preparing young men for college. Twenty years later Frances Caulkins (1795-1869) founded female seminaries in Norwich and New London, and taught in them for fifteen years. One-third of the women born between 1800 and 1850, and two-thirds of those born after 1850 taught school. Typically this interlude of teaching preceded their careers as historians, and among the latter group, provided the means for their graduate education.[10] The basic career goal of women historians—economic self-support—has not, therefore, differed significantly from that of their male peers.

Besides her reliance on her work as a livelihood, Hannah Adams was typical of American female historians in another important respect: she was highly conscious of her gender identity and did not always see it as a positive contribution to her career. on this topic she wrote in her *Memoir*:

> The penalties and discouragements attending authors in general fall upon women with double weight. To the curiosity of the idle, and the envy of the malicious, their sex affords a peculiar excitement. Arranged not merely as writers, but as women, their chracters, their conduct, and even their personal endowments, become the object of severe inquisition.[11]

In her awareness of the inequities she suffered because of her sex, Hannah Adams resembled many of the female historians who followed her. Overt feminism among women historians appeared in the mid-nineteenth century and grew steadily throughout the Victorian and early professional period. Mary Booth (1831-1889), first-born among our group of female historians to join a feminist organization, was a friend of Susan B. Anthony's and served as secretary at a women's right's convention in Saratoga, New York, in 1895 and in New York City in 1860. Mary Williams (1878-1944), last-born of our twenty-six historians, exemplified the feminist commitment among early professional women with the following inscription on her tombstone: "Teacher, Historian, Feminist, Pacifist." Nearly half of the women historians born after 1800 were affiliaated with some sort of feminist activity.[12]

Hannah Adams thus introduces us to two characteristics general to American female historians—their need to earn a livelihood, and their consciousness of gender discrimination. Although the proportion of self-supporting women increases across our three chronological time periods from 50 percent to 60 percent to 90 percent, and although overt feminism more frequently characterized women born after 1850 than those born before, the need to earn a living and the awareness of discrimination against them transcend the chronological structures within which we are viewing them.

While revealing many traits general to women historians as a whole, Hannah Adams' life and career also reflect characteristics specific to her time. The most important of these was her characteristic pursuit of her work within a specific community context. For Adams, this context consisted of a community of Boston religious liberals, who, encountering her obscurely published *Alphabetical Compendium of the Various Sects* and admiring its impartial accuracy, urged her to seek a much wider sales potential than she had imagined for her book. The Reverend Joseph Buckminister, a leading proto-Unitarian and the Reverend James Freeman, minister of the Anglican King's Chapel, assisted her in publishing three popular American editions and three English editions under the new title, *Views of Religions*. The income from these publications allowed her to continue her scholarship. When Adams was drawn into a protracted conflict (lasting over a decade) with the religious conservative Jedidiah Morse, this support network of Boston liberals extended to her essential resources and encouragement. During the last twenty years of her life it provided her with an annuity enabling her to continue her work.[13]

Frances Caulkins was similarly sustained in her work by the community context of New London and Norwich, Connecticut. After establishing, directing, and teaching in female seminaries in those towns for fifteen years in the 1820s and 1830s, Caulkins devoted herself to evangelical work for about ten years in New York City, primarily writing books and pamphlets for the American Tract Society. Through this organization her works were distributed by the millions throughout the nineteenth century. Living with her half-brother in New London, by the mid-1840s she became a central figure in the town's associative life. Secretary for twenty years of the Ladies Seamen's Friend Society, for example, and active in a host of related collectivities, Frances Caulkins became an authority on the structures of her community life and how they functioned. It was then that she wrote her histories.

In writing history, Caulkins said she was heeding the scriptural admonition to "remember the days of old and consider the years of many generations," but she was also drawing on the main commitment in her life–that to the region and the people where she lived–and in addition, she was earning a living. Her Norwich work brought her tremendous local recognition. This was followed in 1849 by her election to membership in the Massachusetts Historical Society, the oldest and most prestigious in the United States. For more than a century Caulkins was the only woman admitted to the Society.

If Hannah Adams and Frances Caulkins exemplify the harmonious side of the relationship between female historians and the communities to which they were committed during this early American period of history writing, Mercy Otis Warren (1728-1814) exemplifies the conflicts that could arise out of such community contexts.[14]

In the mid-1770s Mercy Otis Warren lived at the hub of Boston's revolutionary-minded elite. Her father was a justice of the peace, her husband a member of the Massachusetts legislature, and her brother, James Otis, a leading spokesman against writs of assistance. Her home in Plymouth became a meeting place for opponents of royal policy within Massachusetts, and in her sitting room Mercy Otis Warren actively debated political issues with such men as John Adams and Samuel Adams. From 1772-1775 Warren published three satirical political plays, *The Adulateur*, *The Defeat*, and *The Group*. In the last of these, Massachusetts tories were disguised under such names as Judge Meagre, Brigadier Hateall, Sir Spendall, and Hum Humbug. Participating in the public as well as the private political debates of her day, Warren also corresponded extensively on political questions with one of the leading English Whig and anti-Burkeian historians, Catharine Macaulay. Like that of her husband and brother, Warren's political perspective was consistently to the left of such Federalists as John Adams who feared the social revolution that political revolution might trigger. She vigorously opposed this fear (and the Federal Constitution embodying it) in a 1788 pamphlet entitled: "Observations on the Constitution." In 1791 she defended the French Revolution in a preface she wrote for an American edition of Catharine Macaulay's attack on Burke. In 1800 she further outraged Federalist Boston by supporting Jefferson's election.

But not until the 1805 publication of her *History of the Rise, Progress and Termination of the American Revolution* (in three volumes) did the chief member of her Boston community launch an attack against the threat she posed to it from within. To John Adams the threat was especially grave since she had portrayed this "Founding Father" and former president as harboring monarchical political beliefs. Specifically her *History* stated: "Unfortunately for himself and his country, he became so enamoured with the British Constitution and the government, manners, and laws of the nation, that a partiality for monarchy appeared, which was inconsistent with his former professions of republicanism."[15] Adams wrote Warren demanding to know the basis for such allegations. After several pages of irritated prose, however, he nervously admitted that he did remember one time in her Plymouth home when he had: ". . . said jocularly, laughing, in that style of familiarity which had been long habitual between us, 'For my part, I want King, Lords, and Commons.' " Insisting that he had meant "only such a balance of power as the constitution contained," Adams concluded that surely Warren knew he was joking since she had laughed with him at the time.[16]

Warren replied by examining in detail other instances when Adams had expressed the need for a hereditary monarch in the United States. In reply to an assertion by her that the American people could govern themselves, for example, she quoted Adams back to himself: "We are like other people, and shall do like other nations, where all well-regulated governments are monarchic." On this occasion in 1788 in a carriage trip from the Winthrop to the Gerry home, and on another over breakfast at Braintree during that same year when the Warrens had paid the Adams' an extended visit, he had made such monarchical assertions. And as for agreeing with him! "I well remember-ber my own reply," she wrote: "That a limited monarchy might be the best government, but that it would be long before Americans would be reconciled to the idea of a king."[17]

In what Warren described as "ten long letters of accusation and reproach"—letters covering almost one hundred and fifty printed pages when later published by the Massachusetts Historical Society—Adams declared his hostility toward and fear of her

History. At the end of this assault, having made no headway in his campaign to shake her confidence in her work, Adams was driven to the last resort of a gentleman and asserted: "History is not the Province of the Ladies." He wrote Warren that he blushed for her in her unfeminine willingness to discuss matters of obscure moral meaning. Warren replied, "Though I am fatigued with your repetition of abuse, I am not intimidated," and she concluded: "Blush for yourself."[18]

During this onslaught from John Adams, Warren turned to mutual friends to mediate the dispute between them. She tried to maintain her friendship with Abigail Adams, she asked Elbridge Gerry, a signer of the Declaration of Independence, and a trusted friend of Adams, to arrange a personal meeting between her and Adams as the most direct and effective means of clarifying their differences, and she sought Gerry's advice on what she should do if Adams published his letters. Four years later Gerry did mediate a resumption of cordial relations between Warren and Adams. Locks of hair and rings were exchanged, and the dispute was relegated to the status of unmentionable in the community they both continued to share.[19]

The lives and works of female historians born before 1800 reflect an essentially local culture. The community context of this culture might contain an author's harshest critics, but at the same time it constituted an important support system for her work. The second group of women historians, born between 1800 and 1850, found an analogous support sytems in the literary structures of Victorian culture.

Taken as one of the basic measurements of the modernization process, the vast expansion of communication networks in the nineteenth century facilitated the development of specialized reading constituencies whose interests transcended the boundaries of traditional village life.[20] Middle-class women, both urban and rural, constituted one such specialized constituency.[21] Gender, a category that had broken loose from its eighteenth-century moorings in community life, emerged in the mid-nineteenth century as a distinct force in American literary life as well as in American political life.

Perhaps because they sought in the printed page some behavior guidelines to carry them through this period of profound reorientation to economic production and human reproduction, Victorian female readers supported a vast array of prescriptive and other literature relating to modern womanhood and domestic life.[22] Perhaps because the notion of a woman supporting herself by her writings was growing more acceptable, female authorship burgeoned as rapidly as female readership.[23] The unparalleled proliferation of local periodicals and printers gave female authors relatively easy access to nearby publishers, and national periodicals such as *Godey's Lady's Book* and book distributors such as Harper and Brothers gave many the opportunity to address a national audience. The careers of women historians born in the first half of the nineteenth century were shaped by this literary context.

With the exceptions of the first-born and last-born, all women historians during the Victorian period began their careers with a literary rather than an historical work. Most continued throughout their careers to publish fiction, poetry, travel, and translations as well as history. Several were also editors. Female historians who fared best during this period linked their careers closely with the Victorian literary world, and gave considerable attention in their writings to female testimony and domestic experience.

Martha Lamb (1826-1893), for example, after divorcing her husband sometime around 1866, and with the belief that a woman "with any brains or any sort of intellectual capacity," could do interesting work, wrote eight volumes of children's stories, a romantic novel, several Christmas manuals, and magazine articles before she discovered that her true interest lay in writing history. After completing her history of New York City, she purchased the financially ailing *Magazine of American History,* which under her editorship, became one of the first professional historical journals of national scope, publishing articles, original documents, book reviews, notes of historical societies, and a letters section. The importance of Martha Lamb's own historical work as well as her skills as an editor were widely recognized. She was elected to membership in at least a dozen historical societies, and in 1888 a White House dinner was held in her honor. Well established in the popular press before her success as an historian, Martha Lamb exemplifies the extent to which a woman's success as an historian during this era grew out of a prior commitment to the Victorian literary world.

Literary works by female historians ranged from the realistic novels written by Frances Victor (1826-1902) for Beadle's Dime Novels series to the "politely feminist" interpretations of the lives of women painters and Biblical heroines written by Clara Waters (1834-1916), to the aristocratic *Harper's Bazar*, edited for twenty years by Mary Booth. In their content these literary works reflected the experience of the female readership to which they were, in part, addressed. Frances Victor's (1826-1902) novel *Ainzetta, the Guajira: or Creole of Cuba* (1848), and Elizabeth Ellet's (1912-1877) *Practical Housekeeper* (1857) are examples of works of this sort.

Many of the histories written by these women also featured female experience. The central focus of Juliette Kinzie's (1806-1870) *Wau Bun: The "Early Day" in the Northwest*, still a basic source of Chicago's early history, was that classic female frontier experience—Indian captivity. Elizabeth Ellet's histories, written after twenty years of active literary effort, were exclusively about women. Alice Earle (1851-1911), the only member of this second group whose writings were exclusively historical, wrote chiefly about women and domestic life.[24] This distinct strand of self-consciously female writing speaks to the strength of the female constituency within the Victorian literary world. The careers of women historians were structurally linked to this constituency and directly or indirectly assisted by it.

The female historian who fared least well during this period participated only minimally in the Victorian literary world and not at all in the new tendency to separate female experience from community experience. Abby Hemenway (1828-1890), whose career had many eighteenth-century characteristics, began her career as none of her eighteenth-century predecessors had: with a literary work, *Poets and Poetry of Vermont* (1858). A compilation of local tales and sayings, ballads, and verses that Hemenway gathered by advertising in country newspapers, the one hundred and ten pieces included forty-five by women on a wide variety of topics. Based on the success of this work, Hemenway applied the same technique to historical sources, and traveled by stagecoach from town to town compiling town histories and major historical documents relating to Vermont community life. From 1860 to 1882 she gathered material for and published four volumes of local histories as *The Vermont Historical Gazeteer*.

Vermont's provincial elite, however, centered at Middlebury, opposed Abby Hemenway's historical work from its inception. The faculty of Middlebury College judged her project "impractical," and "in any event not suited for a woman."[25] Working at a local level, Abby Hemenway had ignored the importance of trans-local cultural structures, and her work went unsupported. An eighteenth-century localist amid nineteenth-century forces, Hemenway failed to develop a constituency capable of supporting her, and throughout her career as a committed historian she lived in impoverished circumstances, vulnerable to attacks on her not merely as an historian, but also as a woman.

The last years of Hemenway's life are a chronicle of disaster. With the type for the fifth volume ready to be set, but too hounded by creditors to proceed with its publication in Vermont, Abby Hemenway fled to Chicago in 1884, and set the type herself. Two years later, just as finished volumes were rolling off the press, she lost the manuscript, the type, and the finished volumes when the printer's shop was destroyed in a fire in 1886. Hemenway restored the material for this fifth volume and collected enough for a sixth while she was at it, but died before either could be published. Her sister eventually published the fifth volume, and the materials for the sixth were destroyed in a Chicago fire in 1811, just as the Vermont Historical Society was deliberating on purchasing and publishing them.

As Abby Hemenway is an instructive example of eighteenth-century continuities among Victorian female historians, so Frances Victor is an instructive indicator of the shape of the future. Frances Victor, like Abby Hemenway, had initially pursued a literary career. While attending a female seminary in Worceters, Ohio, she and her sister published poems and stories locally as well as in the New York *Home Journal*. In 1848 her novel, *Anizetta*, was published in Boston. That year she and her sister moved to New York City where they were encouraged by editors and critics. In 1850 they jointly published a volume of poetry.

When their father died that year, however, Frances, as the elder sister, returned home to care for their family. While her sister's career flourished happily ever after in New York, Frances, after marrying locally in Ohio, homesteaded in Nebraska, divorced her husband in Nebraska, joined her sister in New York, married her sister's brother-in-law, and emigrated with her new husband to California. After her husband died in a shipwreck, she resumed her literary career, this time with a strong focus on Western experience and lore. She published two excellent local studies before Hubert Howe Bancroft, for whom Berkeley's Bancroft Library is named, offered her a position on the staff of his ambitious project to write a history of the Pacific states. Tempted by the economic security, and interested in the topic, she accepted. Victor worked on this series for twelve years, completing all the work on four of the series' twenty-eight volumes and much of the work on three others. Her contribution remained anonymous because Bancroft claimed authorship of the entire series. Upon leaving Bancroft's employ, Victor sold toilet articles door-to-door in Salem, Oregon. Eventually she received a pension from Bancroft and returned to writing, producing among other things a series of short stories about the hard lot of women on the frontier.[26]

The hard lot of Frances Victor on the frontiers of professional history reveals the extent to which the writing of history had by the 1870s separated from the Victorian literary world and formed a distinct discipline. With the development of modern American universities in the 1880s, history shifted even further from a humanist profession to an academic discipline.[27] The work context of female historians born after 1850 was therefore radically different from that characteristic of authors born before 1850.

Nine of these last thirteen women historians attended graduate school. The exceptions are: Ida Tarbell (1857-1944), whose main career was in journalism; Constance Skinner (1877-1939) who began her writing career in a Victorian modality at the age of 14, but who in her later career published extensively with Yale University Press; Zelia Nuttall (1857-1933), whose training came through travel and archeological experience in Mexico, but who actively participated in professional life through her position on the staff of Harvard's Peabody Museum; and Kate Hurd-Mead (1867-1941) who wrote about the history of women in medicine at the end of a distinguished medical career. With the exceptions of Tarbell, Skinner, and Hurd-Mead, none of these authors wrote in genres other than history, and all held academic or academically-related positions.

Excluding these three latter historians and viewing the main group of ten, we find strong professional commitment among them. Lucy Salmon (1853-1927), for example, was a founding member of the American Historical Association in 1884. Zelia Nuttall was a founding member of the American Anthropological Association. Nellie Neilson, (1873-1947) served as President of the American Historical Association in 1943, the only woman ever elected to that office. A strong force in the founding of the Medieval Academy of America and its journal, *Speculum*, Neilson was for many years the only female Fellow in the Academy and also served as its president. In 1930, Louise Kellogg (1862-1942) was elected president of the Mississippi Valley Historical Association (now the Organization of American Historians). Mary Williams was a major figure in the creation of the field of Latin American history, serving for many years on the editorial board of the *Hispanic American Historical Review* and as secretary of the Conference on Latin American History within the AHA. Her undergraduate text was the basic one in the field for twenty years.

Although these women were well integrated into professional life, they were not well integrated into the academic marketplace. Since women were rarely hired to teach in coeducational institutions or traditionally male institutions during these early professional years from 1880-1930, female historians found only two sources of academic employment—in women's colleges, and in institutions on the margins of academic life. Although eight of these nine academically related historians attended coeducational graduate institutions (Nellie Neilson, the exception, was a Bryn Mawr Ph.D.), only one of them taught in a coeducational college—Mary Barnes at Stanford for the last five years of her career.

Lucy Salmon at Vassar, Katherine Coman (1857-1915) and Mary Barnes (1850-1898) at Wellesley, Annie Abel (1873-1947) at Smith, Nellie Neilson at Mount Holyoke, and Mary Williams at Goucher all remained in their respective institutions throughout the greater part of their careers. Similarly immobile were the women who held positions in institutions at the margins of academic life: Nuttall at Peabody Museum, Louise Kellogg at the State Historical Society of Wisconsin, Helen Gardner (1878-1946) at the Art Institute of Chicago. Only Helen Sumner who moved from the American Bureau of Industrial Research at the University of Wisconsin to the Children's Bureau of the U. S. Bureau of Labor, experienced significant job mobility.

Helen Sumner's career, the exception to this stationary pattern, throws a good deal of light on the gender boundaries within which female historians worked during the early years of professionalization. Graduating from Wellesley in 1898, and completing a doctoral dissertation at the University of Wisconsin in 1909, Helen Sumner worked closely with John Commons and Richard Ely (her professors) in developing the field of labor history. She was one of five coeditors with Commons, of their eleven-volume *Documentary History of American Industrial Society* (finally published just after she received her Ph.D.). With a similar group including Commons, she coauthored a two-volume history of *Labor in the United States*, which included much material from her dissertation, "The Labor Movement in America, 1827-1837," and much from her pioneering study, "Women in Industry in the United States." The latter was also incorporated by the U. S. Bureau of Labor Statistics into its monumental 1910 *Report on Condition of Woman and Child Wage Earners in the United States*, still the major historical source on the topic. Here, then, was a prolific young scholar making contributions central to the field of labor history. But after receiving her Ph.D., Helen Sumner, in the words of her biographer, "did not readily find permanent employment commensurate with her professional training and her outstanding record as an investigator and labor scholar."[28]

Sumner's desire was clear: to continue in some more advanced capacity at the University of Wisconsin, and she wrote Commons to that effect, saying she very much wanted to write what she called "A History of American Industrial Democracy." "I have been looking forward to that for years, and shall never be satisfied until I have realized my dreams. And nothing would please me more than to have the opportunity of working with you as we worked from 1905-1906 when we laid the foundation for the whole study of labor history."[29] Sumner made it clear, however, that she wanted to be an author in her own right and not merely contribute to the works of others. In response, Commons said he could offer her only marginal and temporary employment. After living with her widowed mother in Washington, D.C. for three years Helen Sumner eventually joined Julia Lathrop's staff in the newly created Children's Bureau in 1913. After five years of very productive scholarship growing out of her work as Director of the Bureau's investigations, she married her statistical collaborator in 1918, and left the Bureau, serving thereafter only on special contract projects, and considerably reducing her professional life. She was then forty years old.

The Children's Bureau, in many ways the most positive institution in Helen Sumner's career since it provided work commensurate with her training, was a predominantly female institution. Headed by a woman (Julia Lathrop was the first woman head of a major federal bureau), and supported by a network of pioneering female settlement workers including Jane Addams and Florence Kelley, the Children's Bureau had a female support system similar to that characterizing the women's colleges.[30]

Most of those who taught at women's colleges made a telling impact on their institutions. Katherine Coman, for example, developed departments of economics and sociology at Wellesley, and Lucy Salmon similarly developed Vassar's history department and its research library. Salmon was also responsible for basic reforms of the college's curriculum and administration, transferring much power from autocratic trustees to the faculty.

These women took an active role in the social life of their institutions. Meeting in small classes and even smaller discussion groups outside of class, they shaped social as well as intellectual discourse, and acted as role models for their students. "There was a lovely mature dignity, somewhat awe-inspiring, but alluring, about Katherine Coman," one of her students, Vida Scudder, later recalled.[31] At Mount Holyoke and Goucher, Nellie Neilson and Mary Williams were central to groups of dedicated female teachers who gave those institutions their reputation for scholarship.

Many of these women were active feminists. At Goucher, for example, Mary Williams taught a course on the history of the women's rights movement, and wrote many of the articles on women's rights leaders in the *Dictionary of American Biography*. Annie Able, who taught at Goucher as well as Smith, served as President of the Maryland Branch of the College Equal Suffrage League. Katharine Coman warmly supported the College Settlement Movement, a movement in which Wellesley students played a large role. From 1900-1907 Coman chaired the standing committee of the National College Settlements Association. She also helped create a club for young working women in Boston, and was a founding member and executive committee member of the Massachusetts Consumer's League. Working with the Women's Trade Union League of Chicago in 1911, she chaired the League's Committee on Grievances during the strike negotiations of that year.[32]

Within the context of women's colleges this group found an environment that fostered their growth as teachers, as historians, as women, and as citizens. In 1930, however, half a century into the professional era, female historians met for the first time as a professional group and discussed then the constraints as well as the benefits of their environment. Learning that they had been excluded from a weekend conference of male historians on the grounds that their presence would interfere with the gathering's desired informality, female historians discussed the matter at the AHA's annual convention in 1929 and decided to hold an informal, but gender-specific meeting that spring. Meeting in Lakeville, Connecticut, the group called itself the Lakeville History Conference.[33]

At that meeting an energetic discussion took place "on the subject of the drawbacks faced by women teaching history in colleges."[34] Sixty-seven historians in fifteen predominately female colleges received before the Conference's second meeting a letter that summarized the discussion and put forward a partial solution, saying:

> We all realize that the limited number of positions open to women means that women are likely to remain in the same institutions throughout their teaching careers. They thus miss the refreshment and stimulus coming from variety of experience that men are likely to get, through accepting posts in different places. The idea that a system of exchange professorships might meet this lack has been suggested.[35]

Questionnaires attempting to establish the feasibility of such an exchange accompanied the letter, and were returned with enthusiastic endorsement. Well-launched the association assumed a regional identity in 1934 and renamed itself the Berkshire History Conference. Revitalized in the 1960s by the addition of new members, the association is now stronger than ever and has adopted the name that evolved during that decade–the Berkshire Conference of Women Historians–emphasizing both the female and the professional aspects of its identity.[36]

While female historians in earlier eras relied on community or literary support networks, professional women historians turned to one another for such support. Historians as a whole faced each other more directly than ever before in the early professional era. Female historians facing each other more directly recognized their collective circumstances. Female historians, facing male historians more directly, interacted successfully on a professional level, but were effectively segregated from the mainstream of job competition. Although many found the women's colleges a supportive and positive environment, they found the institutional boundaries between their colleges and those employing most of their male colleagues nearly impassable. In some ways their circumstances compared unfavorably with both earlier contexts of American historical writing, for although these eras exhibited far more overt gender distinctions, they nevertheless contained far less institutional rigidity and thus could not systematically exclude women from their economic mainstream. More rigid than its predecessors, and more self-contained, the professional context also separated women historians from other women authors and from the female reading public in general.

Female historians have over the past two hundred years been persistently sustained by female support networks. Whether indirectly through the Victorian female readership or directly through female professional associations, their ties to other women have been structural ones delineating the circumstances in which they have worked. Judging by the vitality of such associations today, female historians continue to see them as important sources of career support in their increasingly direct encounter with the historical profession.

NOTES

[1]The Coordinating Committee on Women in the Historical Profession lists nine other regional associations of women historians, besides the Berkshire Conference, as affiliates. See the West Coast Association of Women Historians *Newsletter* 5, no. 2 (November 1974), p. 2, for a summary of statistics on the status of women historians in 113 four-year institutions in thirteen western states.

[2]See Anne Firor Scott's review of *Notable American Women*, 3 vols. (Cambridge, Mass.: Harvard University Press, 1971), "Making the Invisible Woman Visible: An Essay Review," *Journal of Southern History* 38 (November 1972): 629-38, for a full evaluation of these biographical sketches as sources for the history of American women.

[3]In this group are: Mercy Otis Warren (1728-1814), Hannah Adams (1755-1831), Deborah Norris Logan (1761-1839), and Frances Manwaring Caulkins (1795-1869).

[4]In this group are: Juliette Kenzie (1806-1870), Elizabeth Ellet (1812-1877), Frances Victor (1826-1902), Martha Lamb (1826-1893), Abby Hemenway (1828-1890), Mary Booth (1831-1889), Clara Waters (1834-1916). Two historians who were born early in 1851 and whose careers resemble the Victorian pattern have been included in this group rather than the post-1850 group: Mariana Van Rensselaer (1851-1934) and Alice Earle (1851-1911).

[5]In this group are: Mary Barnes (1850-1898), Lucy Salmon (1853-1927), Zelia Nuttall (1857-1933), Ida Tarbell (1857-1944), Katharine Coman (1857-1915), Louise Kellogg (1862-1942), Kate Hurd-Mead (1867-1941), Annie Abel (1873-1947), Nellie Neilson (1873-1947), Helen Sunmer Woodbury (1876-1933), Constance Skinner (1877-1939), Helen Gardner (1878-1946), and Mary Williams (1878-1944).

[6]Hannah Adams, *Memoir of Miss Hannah Adams Written by Herself with Additional Notices by a Friend* (Boston: Gray and Bowen, 1832), p. 28.

[7]Ibid., pp. 11-12.

[8]Ibid., p. 12.

[9]Those were: Mercy Otis Warren and Deborah Logan; Juliette Kinzie, Clara Waters, and Alice Earle; Mary Barnes. Supporting children were: Mariana Van Rensselaer and Zelia Nuttall.

[10]Those who taught school were: Hannah Adams, Frances Caulkins, Mary Booth, Martha Lamb, Abby Hemenway, Mary Barnes, Louise Kellogg, Nellie Neilson, Annie Abel, Lucy Salmon, Ida Tarbell, Helen Gardner, Mary Williams.

[11]Adams, *Memoir*, pp. 34-35.

[12]Affiliated with some variety of feminist activity were: Mary Booth, Frances Victor, Mariana Van Rensselaer, Alice Earle, Lucy Salmon, Ida Tarbell, Katharine Coman, Kate Hurd-Mead, Nellie Neilson, Helen Sumner Woodbury, and Mary Williams. Unless otherwise noted, biographical information cited in this paper can be found in the relevant biographical sketches in *Notable American Women*. Such material will not be cited separately, though each article directly quoted will be cited separately.

[13]Adams, *Memoir*, pp. 20-30.

[14]Deborah Logan's experience was very similar to Mercy Warren's and will not be discussed separately. Both of their historical work arose from their commitment to the more radical political factions that developed within Revolutionary Boston and Philadelphia. Both were related through ties of blood and marriage to the leading families of Massachusetts and Pennsylvania, and both experienced exclusion from their elite communities for political reasons.

[15]"Warren Papers," *Collections of the Massachusetts Historical Society* vol. 4, Fifth series (Boston, 1878), "Appendix," p. 497.

[16]Ibid., p. 327.

[17]Ibid., pp. 361-62.

[18]Ibid., p. 456.

[19]Ibid., Appendix, pp. 499-511.

[20]See Richard D. Brown, "Modernization and the Modern Personality in Early America, 1600-

1865: A Sketch of a Synthesis," *Journal of Interdisciplinary History* 2 (1972): 201-28.

[21]See Frank L. Mott, *A History of American Magazines, 1741-1850* (Cambridge, Mass: Harvard University Press, 1930).

[22]For a summary of these productive and reproductive changes, see: Daniel Scott Smith, "Family Limitation, Sexual Control and Domestic Feminism in Victorian America," *Feminist Studies* 1, no. 3/4 (Winter-Spring, 1973): 40-57.

[23]See Helen Papshvily, *All the Happy Endings* (New York: Harper & Row, 1956).

[24]The fact that Earle wrote exclusively in an historical genre argues for her inclusion in the third group, within which she was born, but in other ways her career is congruent with the Victorian pattern.

[25]Quoted in W. K. Jordan, "Abby Maria Hemenway," *Notable American Women* 2, p. 178.

[26]For a full discussion of Bancroft's career, see: Harry Clark, *A Venture in History, the Production, Publication and Sale of the Works of Hubert Howe Bancroft* (Berkeley: University of California Press, 1973). For Victor's years in Salem, Oregon, see her biography in *Dictionary of American Biography* 10, p. 265.

[27]John Higham, *History, Professional Scholarship in America* (Princeton, N.J.: Princeton University Press, 1965), pp. 15-21.

[28]Frederick Olson, "Helen Laura Sumner Woodbury," in *Notable American Women* 3, p. 651.

[29]H.S.W. to John Commons, April 3, 1910, Commons Papers, State Historical Society of Wisconsin. The full text of Sumner's letter makes clear her intention of receiving full recognition for her work in the future, and avoiding the "drudgery and obscurity" that would come from being a "special investigator" without at the same time begin a "teacher" or a "writer." Stating her desire to collaborate with Commons as an equal, she wrote, "I should be perfectly contented and happy to do research work and write monographs with you provided I could clearly see that in the end we would write *history* together. I used to go ahead by faith and not by sight,—but I have come to feel that it is time to get some view of the Promised Land. . . ."

[30]For a description of the Children's Bureau in these terms, see Nancy P. Weiss, "Save the Children, A History of the Children's Bureau," (Ph.D. dissertation, University of California, Los Angeles, 1973).

[31]Vida Scudder, *On Journey* (1937), quoted in Allen F. Davis, "Katharine Coman," *Notable American Women*, 1, p. 366.

[32]In the numbers of children they bore these professional women differed distinctly from their predecessors. Whereas eight children were born to women historians born before 1800, and seventeen born to those women born between 1800-1850, among the last group only one child was born—a daughter to Zelia Nuttall who was divorced from her husband by the time the birth occurred. In this last groups there were two divorces, three late marriages, and two women who spent most of their lives with close female friends. This compares to one divorce, four marriages, and two life-long female friendships in the preceeding group.

[33]Berkshire History Conference Papers, "From Louise Fargo Brown re origin of Conference, written 1951," unpublished ms, Arthur and Elizabeth Schlesinger Library, Cambridge, Mass.

[34]Berkshire History Conference Papers, Vera Lee Brown (Smith College), Louise Roper Loomis (Wells College) and Louise Fargo Brown (Vassar College) letter, March 15, 1931 distributed with questionnaire.

[35]Ibid.

[36]The Berkshire Conference's Constitution of 1975 adopts this name. See Margaret Rossiter, "Women Scientists in America before 1920," *American Scientist* 62, no. 3 (May-June 1974): 312-23 for an analysis of the career patterns of over five hundred women scientists and the discrimination they systematically encountered. The best general discussion of academic women is Jessie Bernard, *Academic Women* (University Park: Pennsylvania State University, 1964), which contains extensive historical material.

"To Barter Their Souls for Gold": Female Clerks in Federal Government Offices, 1862–1890

Cindy S. Aron

"I, being a lady and an entire stranger, shrink from making an appeal to you for work, but necessity compels me to lay aside all modesty and reserve."[1] So

This essay was awarded the Louis Pelzer Award for 1979. Cindy S. Aron is a graduate student at the University of Maryland, College Park, where her adviser is James B. Gilbert. Her research has been supported by the Employment and Training Administration of the United States Department of Labor.

[1] S. S. Kelty to John W. Noble, Feb. 18, 1892, file 1890–2208, Applications and Appointments Files, Appointments Division, Records of the Office of Secretary of the Interior, RG 48 (National Archives). Application files maintained by the Treasury Department in the four post-Civil War decades and by the Department of the Interior from 1879 to 1905 constitute the major sources for this essay. The Department of the Interior (which in the nineteenth century included the Patent Office, Pension Bureau, Census Office, General Land Office, and Bureau of Education, among others) and the Treasury Department were two of the largest federal agencies and the primary employers of women during this period. These application files contain personnel dossiers which document the lives and work histories of thousands of federal employees. Letters written by female applicants not only requested jobs, but also discussed family and financial problems and sometimes delineated the specific situations or crises that brought them into the federal labor market. In describing their qualifications, female job aspirants furnished information on their education and previous work experience, often revealing as well their family background, social status, and perception of what being a clerical worker entailed. This study is based on a reading of more than 2,000 files of such female applicants. The social and demographic profile of these women is based on statistical analysis of all women who applied for clerical jobs in the Treasury Department in 1862/1863 (the years when women first worked in Washington's bureaucracy) and 1870 and all women who applied for clerical jobs in the Interior Department in 1880 and 1890. In 1862/1863 there were 128 women who applied; in 1870 there were 101; in 1880 there were 598; and in 1890 there were 812. (These totals include 115 women who applied for jobs but who may not have been successful in their quest for work. When I examined these women separately I found that they did not differ significantly, in social or demographic characteristics, from the women who clearly did receive jobs.) To augment the data available in the federal application files, I also searched the 1880 District of Columbia manuscript population census schedules for the 598 women who applied for work in 1880. I successfully located 256 of them, and all information on household structure is based on an analysis of these 256 women. The following figures provide a rough indication of how many women clerked in all Washington federal offices in the years 1862/1863, 1870, 1880, and 1890, and indicate what proportion of the total number of female clerks I have accounted for in my analysis. There are only 176 women clerical workers listed in the entire 1863 official register of federal employees. See *Register of Officers and Agents, Civil, Military, and Naval, in the Service of the United States, on the Thirteenth September 1863* (Washington, 1864). The 1870 census reported that 943 women were "Officials and Employees of

wrote Sally Kelty in 1892 as she applied for a clerking job in the United States Census Office. In the three decades after the Civil War, Kelty and thousands of other middle-class women turned away from nineteenth-century norms that restricted a respectable lady to the domestic sphere and became clerical workers in federal government offices.[2] These women created the first large-scale female clerical labor force in the United States.

The first women to enter federal offices, members of America's burgeoning middle class, had imbibed the dominant domestic ideology that prescribed limited female roles and passive female personality traits. When economic and family difficulties impelled such women to take jobs as government clerks, they found themselves forced to contradict conventional rules of behavior. In accommodating to their new positions as government workers these women did not reject, but rather tried to expand, the traditional ideology to fit their changed circumstances. In the process they significantly transformed their own lives and attitudes. By examining in detail who these women were, why they chose to work as clerks, and the effects of work experiences on their attitudes, this essay explores the reciprocal relationship between social reality and ideology in the lives of many nineteenth-century women.

When the Treasury Department first hired female office workers in 1862, clerking was an exclusively male occupation. In the next thirty years, expansion of the federal bureaucracy and growth of the tertiary sector of the economy increased the need for clerical workers and attracted large numbers of women to government and private clerical jobs. By the early 1890s, women held nearly 5,600 of the 17,600 positions in the executive departments in the nation's capital, and at the turn of the century 104,000 comprised 29 percent of the clerks in the United States.[3] The women who worked in federal govern-

Civil Government" in Washington; many of these women probably worked in other than a clerical capacity—as printer's assistants and charwomen, for example. The 1880 census reported 1,412 women clerks in government offices. In 1890 there were, according to the census, 3,741 female clerks, copyists, stenographers, and typists in Washington. Francis A. Walker, *The Statistics of the Population of the United States . . . Compiled from the Original Returns of the Ninth Census (June 1, 1870)* (Washington, 1872), 727; U.S. Census Office, *Statistics of the Population of the United States at the Tenth Census (June 1, 1880)* (Washington, 1883), 801; U.S. Census Office, *Report on Population of the United States at the Eleventh Census: 1890*, (Washington, 1897), Part II, 307-09.

[2] For a discussion of the development of the ideology of separate sexual spheres, see Barbara Welter, "The Cult of True Womanhood: 1820-1860," *American Quarterly*, XVIII (Summer 1966), 151-74; Nancy F. Cott, *The Bonds of Womanhood: "Women's Sphere" in New England, 1780-1835* (New Haven, 1977); Kathryn Kish Sklar, *Catherine Beecher: A Study in American Domesticity* (New Haven, 1973); Carroll Smith-Rosenberg, "The Female World of Love and Ritual: Relations between Women in Nineteenth-Century America," *Signs*, 1 (Autumn 1975), 1-29.

[3] Janet Hooks, *Women's Occupation through Seven Decades* (Washington, 1947), 74-77. It is difficult to ascertain the precise number of female workers in Washington federal offices, for published documents offer varied findings. Lucille Foster McMillin noted that in 1893 there were 3,770 women and 8,377 men employed in the departments at Washington, but she perhaps included only Civil Service employees in this count. Lucille Foster McMillin, *Women in the Federal Service* (Washington, 1939), 12. The larger figures cited in my text were furnished to a congressional commission by heads of the departments in October 1893. U.S. Congress, House of Representatives, *Organization of the Executive Departments and Other Government Establishments at the National Capital, and Information Concerning the Persons Employed Therein*, 53 Cong., 1 sess., 1893, H. Rept. 88, p. 208. These disparate figures refer, moreover, only to em-

ment offices from 1862 to 1900 opened the field of clerical work to other members of their sex.

These pioneering female clerks came from native-born, white, middle-class families: they were the daughters, widows, and wives of doctors, lawyers, ministers, and other government clerks. At least 65 percent of their fathers worked as professionals, white-collar workers, small businessmen, or federal clerks. Less than 7 percent of female clerks' fathers earned their living through manual labor, and nearly all of these were skilled craftsmen such as carpenters, stonecutters, or engravers.[4] Indeed, some of these women came from old, established, and at one time very wealthy families. Others represented families that were becoming members of the new middle classes: men and women who would not only staff the expanding federal bureaucracy but would also fill the growing number of white-collar positions throughout industrializing, urban America.

While the presence of the federal bureaucracy and the absence of heavy industry may have made Washington a city with an unusually high percentage of white-collar workers, the special occupational structure of the city does not explain the social-class background of the women who entered government offices.[5] Forty-three percent of female clerks who assumed their positions

ployees, not to clerical workers. My own count of clerks in the Treasury and Interior Departments listed in the official register of federal employees for 1891 revealed 1,573 women and 3,468 men, indicating that the ratio of female to male clerical workers was about the same as the ratio of female to male employees. *Official Register of the United States, Containing a List of the Officers and Employés in the Civil, Military, and Naval Service on the First of July, 1891* (2 vols., Washington, 1892).

[4] Of the 1,639 women who applied for work in my sample years, there were 279 for whom I could gather information regarding occupation of fathers. Some of these data come from the women whom I traced to the 1880 census and who were living with their fathers. In other cases, however, I learned about the father's occupation only from the applicant's letter. When asking for work, women would sometimes describe their family background and mention their father's position. Since many women entered the labor market after their fathers had died, some of this information refers to previous occupational status of fathers. The exact breakdown on father's occupation is: professional and high white-collar jobs, 34.3 percent; low white-collar jobs (including government clerks), 31.3 percent; skilled manual laborers, 5.7 percent; unskilled laborers, 1.1 percent; unspecified government jobs (most of which were probably clerical positions), 26.2 percent; and farmers, 1.8 percent. The data on occupations of husbands reveal much the same pattern: over 75 percent held professional or white collar positions, and only 5 percent worked in manual jobs. There were, however, only 82 out of 450 ever-married women for whom I could obtain information on occupation of husbands. Female clerks were almost all white; only 7 of 1,639 female clerks who applied in the sample years were black. Data on birthplace of parents come from those women in the 1880 sample year who were located in the 1880 manuscript census schedules. Of the 248 women for whom I have this information, only 14 percent had mothers who were immigrants and 18 percent had fathers who were immigrants. The greatest number of these immigrant parents came from England, Canada, or western Europe.

[5] The occupation tables in the 1870 and 1880 published census reports are unfortunately not broken down by race, and the population of the nation's capital included a large percentage of blacks (33 percent in 1880 and 32 percent in 1870). Therefore, it is not possible to assess accurately the structure of occupations for white men in these years. The 1890 published census reports do, however, simultaneously delineate occupational and racial categories. In 1890 as many as 35 percent of native white men born of native parents worked in unskilled manual occupations in the nation's capital. Thus it is clear that Washington did include a sizable white, working-class population in this period, despite the striking absence of female clerks whose fathers occupied such positions. Walker, *Ninth Census*, 97; U.S. Census Office, *Tenth Census*, 384; U.S. Census Office, *Eleventh Census*, Part II, 544.

between 1862 and 1890 lived someplace other than Washington prior to taking government jobs. Middle-class women flocked to the nation's capital to become clerks. While one of every five had previously lived in the neighboring states of Maryland, New Jersey, New York, Pennsylvania, and Virginia, all other regions of the country, New England, the South, the Midwest, and the Far West also contributed women to the federal clerical labor force.[6]

Education affords an index to middle-class origins that is even more persuasive than fathers' occupation. Federal women clerks had been well educated, most having enjoyed the advantage of a secondary education. Ninety-four percent had remained in school at least through the age of sixteen, and an impressive 13 percent had continued their formal education into their twenties.[7] About one quarter of these women claimed private school tutelage, usually in a seminary or female academy. These figures indicate that the women who worked in government offices came from families that had at one time been able to forgo the wages of female children and in some instances to pay for their daughters' private education as well.

Many federal female clerks had probably grown up without expecting to work for a living, but after the Civil War they found it necessary to enter the paid labor force. The reversals they experienced did not, however, destroy their commitment to middle-class respectability. Lucy Wilson, a clerk in the Pension Office in the mid-1880s, expressed horror at the thought that anyone suspected her true financial plight. In a letter describing the dire state of her finances, she hastened to add: "There is no living soul who knows my condition. I am cheerful in the presence of others, make a respectable appearance and people imagine I have the world on a string. Only *I* know."[8] For these women social class status was as much a product of perception as of income or wealth.

Recognition that women clerks came from middle-class families adds an important dimension to our understanding of women's work in the nineteenth century. Recent historical scholarship on the labor force activities of working-class and immigrant women has explained their wage-earning behavior as contributions to a "family economy." In discussing the middle class, however, historians have emphasized women's exclusion from productive economic functions as those activities moved from the home to the market,

[6] Twenty-one percent had been living in Maryland, New York, Pennsylvania, New Jersey, or Virginia; 3.2 percent came from the southern states of Florida, Georgia, Alabama, Mississippi, North Carolina, South Carolina, Tennessee, Kentucky, and West Virginia; 8.1 percent from the Midwest, including Ohio, Indiana, Illinois, Wisconsin, and Michigan; 4.6 percent from New England; and 5.3 percent from the states and territories west of the Mississippi River.

[7] By comparison, published census statistics on school attendance for the year 1890 reveal that only 42 percent of native whites aged fifteen to nineteen were attending school. The Census Office chose not even to report the percentage of people over the age of twenty attending school, since the numbers were so small. U.S. Census Office, *Eleventh Census*, Part II, xxviii.

[8] Lucy K. Wilson to Col. Keogh, Sept. 25, 1881, file 1881-1847, Applications and Appointments Files, Appointments Division, Records of the Office of the Secretary of the Interior.

their growing participation in reform, educational, and organizational activities, and the importance of their role within an increasingly separate and isolated domestic sphere. Indeed, historians have accepted as real those nineteenth-century standards that declared the presence of non-wage-earning wives and daughters to be the hallmark of middle-class status.[9] While leisure may reflect the ideal to which middle-class women aspired, it does not describe the real-life situations of many nineteenth-century households. The middle-class family frequently placed upon the shoulders of its female members heavy financial burdens which, in the context of late nineteenth-century American society, required that they leave the domestic sphere and enter the paid labor force.

In Washington a great many people with middle-class background and values faced severe family and economic problems. Moments of crisis brought respectable, comfortable, and even established families to the verge of economic disaster and pushed middle-class women into the federal job market. During the three post-Civil War decades, the primary motivation for a woman's entry into the government's labor market remained economic: she and her family needed the wages she could earn. Definitions of need, however, varied widely, ranging from procuring food and shelter to bolstering the middle-class status of parents, siblings, or children.

Economic burdens fell to middle-class women at all stages in their life cycles. When necessary, daughters, sisters, wives, and mothers became federal workers. Not surprisingly, single women comprised the majority of female federal clerks, for families looked first to their unmarried female members for financial assistance. Approximately two-thirds of the women who applied for

[9] For a discussion of the role of working-class women within a family economy, see Louise A. Tilly and Joan W. Scott, *Women, Work, and Family* (New York, 1978). On the lives and work experiences of working-class and immigrant women in the United States, see Virginia Yans-McLaughlin, *Family and Community: Italian Immigrants in Buffalo, 1880–1930* (Ithaca, 1977); Milton Cantor and Bruce Laurie, eds., *Class, Sex, and the Woman Worker* (Westport, Conn., 1977); Daniel J. Walkowitz, *Worker City, Company Town: Iron and Cotton-Worker Protest in Troy and Cohoes, New York, 1855–84* (Urbana, 1978); Carole Turbin, "And Are We Nothing but Women: Irish Working Women in Troy," in *Women of America: A History*, ed. Carol Ruth Berkin and Mary Beth Norton (Boston, 1979); Susan J. Kleinberg, "Technology and Woman's Work: The Lives of Working-Class Women in Pittsburgh, 1870–1900," *Labor History*, 17 (Winter 1976), 58–72; Leslie Woodcock Tentler, *Wage-Earning Women: Industrial Work and Family Life in the United States, 1900–1930* (New York, 1979). For a discussion of the activities of middle-class women see William L. O'Neill, *Everyone Was Brave: The Rise and Fall of Feminism in America* (Chicago, 1969); Barbara J. Berg, *The Remembered Gate: Origins of American Feminism, the Women and the City, 1800–1860* (New York, 1978); Keith E. Melder, *Beginnings of Sisterhood: The American Woman's Rights Movement, 1800–1865* (New York, 1977); Mary P. Ryan, *Womanhood in America: From Colonial Times to the Present* (New York, 1975); Barbara Welter, *Dimity Convictions: The American Woman in the Nineteenth Century* (Athens, Ohio, 1976); and Eleanor Flexner, *Century of Struggle: The Woman's Rights Movement in the United States* (Cambridge, 1959). Daniel Rodgers discusses the image of "idle womanhood," which was held up as the ideal for middle-class women. Daniel T. Rodgers, *The Work Ethic in Industrial America, 1850–1920* (Chicago, 1978), 182–209. For more on the evolution of middle-class women's important role within the domestic sphere, see Sklar, *Catherine Beecher*, and Cott, *Bonds of Womanhood*. For a discussion of the need to reappraise our view of nineteenth-century middle-class women, see Mary Beth Norton, "The Paradox of 'Women's Sphere,'" in *Women of America*, ed. Berkin and Norton.

work in 1862–1863, 1870, and 1880 had never been married, with the proportion increasing to 73 percent in 1890.[10]

Various economic circumstances prompted single women to apply for government clerkships. Young, single women frequently entered the labor force when their fathers lost their jobs, fell ill, or died. For example, Ellen Neale applied for a job in the Department of the Interior in 1890, one month after the death of her father. Nineteen years old at the time, she defended her efforts to secure a federal clerkship: "I am the daughter of the late Judge Neale of Virginia and at his death . . . I was left the sole support of a helpless, invalid mother and invalid sister, with two little sisters and brothers to support and educate. Being a large family we lived up to my Father's income during his life, so that we are left with absolutely nothing, excepting the heritage of his noble name and memory."[11] Unemployment of the father, even if temporary, could result in the same economic disaster as his death or illness. In the Rhea family, sixteen-year-old Lillie, the eldest of six children, sought a job because her father, a bookkeeper, had lost his position in the Census Office. In the meantime her family lacked resources to purchase even "daily necessaries."[12]

Even in families where the male breadwinner had accumulated enough to bequeath a comfortable estate, unforeseen economic reversals could result in penury. The Civil War precipitated financial problems for many among the first generation of women clerks. Cordelia Emmons, who became a clerk in the Treasury Department in 1865, described her unfortunate family's situation: "I . . . have been, during the last four years, reduced from ease and comfort to destitution. I am a Marylander by birth, but have passed half my life in the city of Philadelphia. There my father died, but from time to time before his death, he invested his means advantageously [in] the South. From a part of this I received my maintenance, but with the breaking out of the war my income ceased and it is very doubtful if I ever again [will] derive any benefit from it."[13] With her father dead, and no male wage earner in her family, the sudden loss of a previously secure income brought Emmons into government employ where she remained for more than ten years. Unsuccessful business ventures also created economic hardships and propelled many women into government

[10] The proportion of never-married women who applied for work in each of my sample years was:

Year	Proportion of never-married women (percent)
1862/1863	64.4
1870	61.1
1880	64.7
1890	73.0

[11] Ellen Neale to the Secretary of the Interior, Nov. 12, 1891, file 1890–2075, Applications and Appointments Files, Appointments Division, Records of the Office of the Secretary of the Interior.

[12] Lillie Rhea to Robert Walker, Sept. 17, 1880, file 1880–1886, *ibid.*

[13] Cordelia Emmons to the Honorable Secretary of the Treasury, Dec. 26, 1865, file of Cordelia Emmons, Applications and Recommendations for Positions in the Washington, D.C., Offices of the Treasury Department, 1830–1910, entry 210, Records of the Division of Appointments, General Records of the Department of the Treasury, RG 56 (National Archives).

clerkships. Laura Robinson explained in her 1881 letter of application: "A few years ago I enjoyed all the luxuries of an elegant home, but commercial disaster, which as you know has ruined so many men, compels me now to seek assistance from strangers."[14] Such situations reveal the precarious financial status of many middle-class nineteenth-century families—comfortable and successful one year, reduced to poverty the next.

The picture of an insecure middle class emerges more sharply in an examination of the single women who became government clerks even when they resided with fathers who were healthy and employed. Twenty-seven percent of the single women who applied for jobs in the Department of Interior in 1880 shared households with an employed father. Many of these men held jobs that placed them on the lower edge of the middle class, positions as clerks or bookkeepers drawing salaries insufficient to support families adequately in high-cost Washington.[15] Some fathers called upon their daughters, usually in their late teens or early twenties, to become government clerks and contribute to the support and education of younger children. Mamie Sandidge, for example, began clerking in 1890 while her father also worked for the government. She wanted to help her parents rear and educate her siblings.[16]

Financial difficulties sometimes required that even young, single women from more comfortably placed middle-class families become wage earners. Some women whose fathers held better-paid or more prestigious jobs claimed they needed government positions in order to help extricate the family from a difficult, but temporary, economic crisis. Ada Collins's father, an editor of the *Washington Evening Star*, wrote to the secretary of the interior in 1880 asking employment for his daughter to "relieve me from a temporary but uncomfortable financial squeeze."[17] Similarly, twenty-year-old Mary McKee, daughter of the assistant librarian of the Senate, applied for work in 1889. An influential friend, intervening on her behalf, noted that "in a recent campaign [McKee's father] published and practically gave away his book called 'Protection Echos,' which was very much used by the Committee and speakers during the campaign. He is now financially embarrassed, growing out of this publication, and desires to get a position for his Daughter in your Bureau. He only desires a place for a short time for her." McKee worked in the Census Office for four years to help her father overcome his "financial embarrassment."[18]

[14] Laura Robinson to Mrs. Hayes, n.d., file 1880-725, Applications and Appointments Files, Appointments Division, Records of the Office of the Secretary of Interior.

[15] All information on structure of households is based on women whose applications were found in the records of the Interior Department in the year 1880 and then located within the 1880 manuscript census. An analysis of the 201 single women within this group revealed that 54 lived with fathers who were gainfully employed. Of these 54 fathers, 24 percent held professional or high white-collar jobs, 56 percent held low white-collar jobs or were small businessmen (this group included men who were government clerks, who represented 30 percent of the entire 54 men), 15 percent were skilled manual laborers, and 4 percent were unskilled laborers.

[16] John J. Heard to Robert Porter, Jan. 9, 1890, file 1890-1543, Applications and Appointments Files, Appointments Division, Records of the Office of the Secretary of the Interior.

[17] W. R. Collins to Gen. F. A. Walker, Dec. 16, 1886, file 1880-2420, *ibid.*

[18] Wm. W. Dudley to Hon. R. P. Porter, July 1, 1889, file 1890-2234, *ibid.*

The labor of a daughter could allow her family to maintain its respectable economic and social standing, or an unmarried woman's employment might enable her family to improve its status. The income from a daughter's salary sometimes permitted the family to purchase property or accumulate savings. When Maggie Loftus faced possible loss of her $720 per year job in the Census Office she appealed, stating that "my father was a Union soldier having served his country faithfully in the late war, and we have but recently purchased a little home, and if I am deprived of my position this we must lose."[19] Maggie's salary allowed the Loftus family the added security and status of property ownership. In other instances an adult daughter assumed financial responsibilities so that a brother might attend college or professional school. Gertrude Bourne, for example, described her family's situation in 1890: "I am twenty years of age and am anxious to earn something for my support and to assist my family. My father was recently a sergeant in the 2nd Rhode Island Regiment and has recently obtained employment at the Springfield armory. He has a large family to support—there are nine of us—and the pay he receives barely provides the necessaries of life. I also have a brother in the War Department but he is over twenty-one years of age and is studying law, so the principal help he can give us at present is in relieving my father of the cost of his support; and I am anxious to be employed in Washington so as to be near him and do what I can do to help educate my brothers and sisters."[20] In these families the promise of intergenerational upward mobility rested on the earning power of single women clerks.

Despite nineteenth-century rhetoric that cast sons in the role of providers and daughters in the category of those "provided for," economic burdens fell upon young women as well as young men. Unmarried daughters worked along with sons to help support the family or took over the role of breadwinner when their brothers proved unable, or unwilling, to do so.[21] Among the female clerks who shared households with adult brothers in 1880, as many as 30 percent worked in federal offices while at least one brother remained unemployed.[22] Take, for instance, the case of Marion Porter who in 1885, at the age of eighteen, graduated from a private seminary in Washington. Her father worked in the Adjutant General's Office, but in early 1889 he allegedly suffered a severe mental breakdown and deserted Marion, her mother, and three siblings, leaving them nearly destitute. That summer Marion began to work for the government. Her seventeen-year-old brother, however, "continued studying for the University, friends having secured him a scholarship and are supporting him." The other daughters remained "absolutely without support save from Miss Marion's salary."[23]

[19] Maggie Loftus to Hon. A. F. Childs, Oct. 7, 1890, file 1890-3472, *ibid.*

[20] Gertrude Bourne, April 25, 1890, file 1890-1583, *ibid.*

[21] See, for example, Hattie Wood to Carl Schurz, March 1880, file 1880-1322, and G. H. Ourty to Mr. Teller, May 10, 1882, file 1880-812, *ibid.*

[22] Seventy-six percent of the women applicants to the Interior Department in 1880 who were located within the 1880 manuscript census did not have adult brothers. Of the sixty-one women who did have adult brothers, eighteen of these women had one or more unemployed adult brothers.

[23] Mr. Hill, June 12, 1894, file 1890-2080, Applications and Appointments Files, Appointments Division, Records of the Office of the Secretary of the Interior.

Many of the same circumstances that brought single women into the federal labor market also pushed widows into government clerkships. From 1862 to 1890 widows comprised between 13 percent and 28 percent of the government's clerical labor force.[24] The death of a wage-earning husband, like the loss of a father, created severe crises for middle-class women and often reduced them from comfortable situations to penury. Mrs. William Pemberton's distress, although more eloquently expressed than most, was typicial:

> I like many others although surrounded by poverty and its blasting effects, was neither born nor reared in poverty, nor was my early married life seared by such a curse. I never knew want or never had a wish ungratified. . . . I have sacrificed piece after piece of furniture (which was very dear to me from association) to pay rent and to buy bread. Now to day finds me even worse off. I have neither money, coal or wood, and nothing to eat but mush without meat or butter, what is left for me to do. I will not beg, I cannot steal, I cannot depend on what the world calls friends for help, they might for a while aid me, but how soon would they too grow weary. I never until now thought there was an excuse for women to barter their souls for gold, it is such an hour as this when the strongest become weak, make one fearful leap accepting the present, postponing the future. What is sadder than widowhood.[25]

The hope of securing their families within the middle class impelled less desperate widows to become clerks just as it had driven young single women into the work force. Many widows recognized that maintaining the status of the family often required that they try at all cost to keep their children in school. Amanda Doty, for instance, worked in the Census Office in 1881 but lost her job within the year. In 1882 she asked to be reinstated, saying "I have been waiting for more than a year for a position. . . . I have been dependent on the charity of friends since my husband's death three years ago. I have three children to educate and provide for." Without employment, she noted, she could not purchase the necessary Latin and Greek books to help her son prepare for Princeton.[26] These widows held fast to their middle-class values and struggled valiantly to maintain their families' social status.

Federal clerking jobs also attracted married women, but it is difficult, if not impossible, to determine their numbers with much certainty. It appears that some women concealed their marital status. Societal norms questioning the propriety of married women's employment, as well as departmental restrictions against hiring more than one member of a family, prompted many wives to apply for jobs as single women. Rumors in the Patent Office in the mid-1870s hinted that many of the allegedly unmarried women workers were wives of clerks in the same office. Mrs. Whittlesey, the wife of a clerk R. H. Whittlesey, apparently had accepted her $900 per year job under the name of Miss E. M. Fisk. The official who investigated the scandal reported that "Mr. Whittlesey says that his wife signs this name although it is the name of her sister.

[24] Of the 1,639 women in my sample, 16.9 percent of those in the 1862/1863 group were widows, 28.3 percent of the 1870 group were widows, 18.2 percent of the 1880 group were widows, and 13.1 of the 1890 group were widows.

[25] Mrs. Wm. Pemberton to Hon. Henry M. Teller, April 23, 1882, file 1879–758, Applications and Appointments Files, Appointments Division, Records of the Office of the Secretary of the Interior.

[26] Mrs. Amanda Doty to Wm. Dudley, Sept. 13, 1882, file 1881–203, *ibid.*

He also says that it was placed on the roll at the suggestion of the Commissioner [of Patents] who thought it would be better to appear by that name than to have it appear that two in the same family were drawing pay from the office."[27] Anonymous letters sent to Treasury Department officials in the 1860s and 1870s suggest that this practice was not limited to the Patent Office.[28] Since there is no way to know how many women lied, the data on married women are inexact: married female clerks represented at a minimum 6 percent and perhaps more than 13 percent of the women in federal clerical jobs during this period.[29]

Married women who desired government clerkships encountered problems that did not so significantly affect their unmarried coworkers. Although all middle-class women faced prohibitions against entering the public sphere, married women who relinquished their domestic roles received special condemnation. Besides deserting their homes, married working women were indicted for depriving widows, orphans, or male breadwinners of jobs. An anonymous accuser enumerated a litany of such charges against Mrs. Swan, an employee in the Treasury Department in the mid-1870s: "1st. Her husband is in the Navy Department and is competent to care for her and family. 2nd. She has an infant at home about one year old which requires the care of a mother. 3. Her husband owns the property which they occupy at present. 4. Children four in number growing up without the care of either parent during the day. 5. All the cares of her house including washing and ironing etc. imposed on her husband's mother an old lady 65 years old. 6. She holds her place in the Office against her husband's will."[30] Intense competition for government jobs in Washington added economic justification to the widespread moral and social sanctions against the employment of married women.

In the mid-1870s various departments responded to such complaints by prohibiting the employment of more than one member of a family. The government did not, however, specifically exclude married women from its work force. Instead the judgment, or whim, of a particular department head or

[27] A. Bell to Z. Chandler, Dec. 23, 1876, Miscellaneous Letters Received, Appointments Division, Records of the Office of the Secretary of the Interior.

[28] Mrs. Anna Sander et al. to Appointments Clerk, Feb. 12, 1876; "Justice" to G. S. Boutwell, Dec. 6, 1869; and Anonymous to Secretary of Treasury, Oct. 19, 1874, Correspondence of the Division, entry 208, Records of the Division of Appointments, General Records of the Department of the Treasury.

[29] In addition to the problem of women lying about their true marital status, there are other variables which make these figures inexact. Although only 6 percent of the women responded "married" in their applications to the Treasury Department and the Interior Department in these years, another 5 percent signed their letters "Mrs." but never mentioned their marital status. Some of these women were undoubtedly widows, but since describing oneself as a widow was a definite advantage and increased the chances of getting a job, there is a great likelihood that many of these women were in fact married with husbands still living. Moreover, some women who were single, widowed, or divorced when they began to work continued in government employ after marrying. The figure of 13 percent represents all of these women combined with the 6 percent who responded "married." Examination of these figures at each point in time reveals that in 1862/1863 there were 18.6 percent who worked at some time while they were still married; in 1870 the figure dropped to 8 percent, then rose to 15.3 percent in 1880 and dropped to 11 percent in 1890.

[30] "Justice" to Secretary of the Treasury, Oct. 24, 1874, Correspondence of the Division, Records of the Division of Appointments, General Records of the Department of the Treasury.

bureau chief determined whether or not a married woman could be hired. In many offices married women were the first to lose their jobs in case of a reduction of the work force, and single women often found their positions in jeopardy if they married. This was especially true in the 1860s and 1870s. The third auditor wrote to the secretary of the treasury in 1877 reporting that Emma Fuller, a highly paid, $1,600 per year clerk in his office, had married a clerk in the Patent Office and "being further advised that it is not Miss Fuller's intention to resign, I have the honor to recommend her removal." Under threat of dismissal, Fuller quit her job a few days later.[31] But not all officials were so eager to fire married women, and some women continued to work after marriage. Widow E. A. McPheeters feared in 1868 that if she remarried she would lose her job, but when she explained to Treasurer Francis Spinner that her future husband could not afford to educate her sons, "[he] advised me to marry promising that my name should be changed on the payroll and my place secured."[32] Throughout the four post-Civil War decades the government's ambiguous policy, rather than outright prohibition, made job hunting difficult for married women.

Although married women faced unique problems, their motivations for working in many cases paralleled those of unmarried women. Like single clerks and widows, financial crises within the family compelled many married women to exchange roles as full-time childrearers and housekeepers for positions within the clerical labor force. Most married women who entered government offices did so when their husbands became ill or unemployed. For example, Nellie Grant was twenty-seven years old when she began to work in the Census Office in August 1890. She lost her job in a reduction of the work force ten months later and within a year applied for reinstatement on the following grounds: "My husband is in Ill health having consumption and heart disease and is not able to work . . . but little. . . . as a wife it is my duty to help him which compels me to seek work to help support us."[33] A husband's business reversals or chronic unemployment could also precipitate a wife's entering the labor force. In some cases couples came to Washington initially to seek work for the husband but found job opportunities for the wife instead. Other women had worked for the government before marriage and reentered federal employ when their husbands fell ill or lost their jobs.[34]

Dire financial stress does not entirely account for the presence of married women in clerical jobs. The relationship between work and marriage appears to have been complex, with various factors inducing married women to work. In some situations the ultimate financial success of a middle-class man rested on the ability of his wife to become a government worker. Sometimes the wife

[31] J. W. Grew to John Sherman, Dec. 17, 1877, file of Emma Fuller, Applications and Recommendations, Records of the Division of Appointments, General Records of the Department of the Treasury.

[32] E. A. McPheeters to Hugh McCulloch, Oct. 6, 1867, file of Mrs. E. A. McPheeters, *ibid.*

[33] Nellie Grant to J. W. Noble, July 15, 1892, file 1890-3267, Applications and Appointments Files, Appointments Division, Records of the Office of the Secretary of the Interior.

[34] See, for example, Viola Hunter to Sec. Kirkwood, July 9, 1881, file 1881-1255, and E. W. Leavenworth to F. Walker, Sept. 26, 1880, file 1881-124, *ibid.*

took on the responsibilities of supporting the family during those lean years while her husband was establishing himself within a profession. Mary Whitehead, for example, had worked in the General Land Office for ten years when in 1892 she married an attorney. She argued that although now married, she could not afford to lose her $1,000 per year job because her husband "is laboring to build up a practice that we hope will, in time, enable me to resign my position."[35]

Many married women worked in government offices not to help husbands or children, but to provide financial assistance to parents, siblings, or more distant relatives. Marriage did not necessarily relieve middle-class women of the economic burdens of their families of origin. Mrs. M. A. Naylor, dismissed in 1868 from a $900 per year job in the Register's Office, petitioned for reappointment. She contended that although her husband worked in the Pension Office she needed her position: "[My] mother and five children are left without support since the death of my father in 1867 [and] look to us for assistance. My salary since entering the department has been exclusively devoted to them, by my discharge their support is cut off."[36] Emma Whelply worked in the Treasury Department for more than nine years during which time her husband also clerked in the Pension Office. She explained that she "applied for the position in order to provide for my [widowed] Sister and her children and my entire salary has been applied to their support—being their only legitimate means."[37]

Husbands were not necessarily more likely to assume a wife's personal debts than to undertake her family's support. Financial obligations incurred while still single kept some middle-class women in the labor force after they had married. Kate Wing, daughter of a judge, had worked in the Treasury Department for eight years when she married a Mr. Hunter in 1891. A senator intervened on her behalf: "she asked [me] if she should marry—if it would prevent her holding her position—and was told it would not. She was somewhat in debt—and desired to retain her position long enough to enable her to pay said debts—and expected to do so. . . . If she had not been told she would retain her place, she would have *postponed* her marriage till she could have paid off her debts—which were caused by the long and severe sickness of her sister."[38]

A married woman's decision to enter the federal clerical labor force could precipitate major changes in the life of her family. Some couples even lived separately so that the wife could obtain a government job. The opportunities for employment of middle-class women in Washington induced more than one married woman to leave her husband in another city and journey to the nation's capital to find work. Both Emily Cilley and Martha Hutcheson lived

[35] Mrs. Gourick to S. W. Lamoreus, April 13, 1893, file 1880-440, *ibid.*

[36] Mrs. May Naylor to D. H. Browning, Dec. 3, 1868, file of Mrs. M. Naylor, Applications and Recommendations, Records of the Division of Appointments, General Records of the Department of the Treasury.

[37] Emma Whelply to Hugh McCulloch, Nov. 4, 1867, file of Emma Whelpy, *ibid.*

[38] Francis B. Stockridge to A. B. Nettleton, Oct. 4, 1891, file of Kate Wing Hunter, *ibid.*

and worked in Washington while their ailing husbands maintained residences in Ohio.[39] Some nineteenth-century couples apparently considered temporary separation an acceptable, if undesirable, solution to economic problems.

Other married women entered federal offices with an entirely different motivation—to gain sufficient financial independence to separate permanently from their husbands. The $900 average annual salary paid to female clerks, while still below what most male clerks earned, represented one of the highest salaries available to women in this period. Female public schoolteachers in the District of Columbia earned by comparison between $400 and $700 per year, with a few making as much as $800.[40] A thrifty woman could live respectably, but not luxuriously, on her government salary. To women trapped in unhappy marriages, federal employment held out the possibility of self-support and the option of separation or divorce. Twenty-four-year-old Charlotte Cross, for example, applied in 1866 for a job in the Treasury Department. Her husband had joined the army in 1863, and she had spent the war years teaching school in Buffalo, New York. When he returned at the end of the war, she found he had changed: "Warm-hearted, social, and easily influenced he proved too susceptible to the temptations and many allurements of camp life, and like many of our brave and noble soldiers yielded to the demon intemperance, rendering him unfit for work, for society, and too soon unworthy of a wife's care, forgiveness, or endurance." She decided to leave "home, friends, position and occupation to rid myself of him. . . . I have become fully convinced that while I live with him I shall have him to support, and this I can never think my duty. I should feel unworthy the name of woman, to support a husband who is able and capable to support himself and wife, and shall never do so, even though I should come to beggary, no never." Cross journeyed to Washington where she began a fifteen-year stint as a government clerk.[41] In a variety of circumstances married women thus chose to enter the federal labor force. Marriage did not necessarily constitute the end of a middle-class woman's wage-earning experience in the nineteenth century.

Whether married, single, or widowed, middle-class women risked the potential opprobrium of society when they became government clerks. The ideology of separate sexual spheres, which had developed in the first half of the ninteenth century, dictated a specific, limited role for native, respectable, middle-class women. Woman's sphere revolved around her home. Her primary responsibilities were to care for the physical, moral, and religious needs of her family and to make her home a safe, quiet, Christian refuge from the competitive, aggressive, public world. The job of teacher, seen as an extension of

[39] See, for example, Matthia Martin, John G. Rinehard, A. W. Thurman, and Joseph Olds to Joseph Outhwaite, Sept. 27, 1893, file 1890–3366, and Emily Cilley to Robert Porter, Dec. 10, 1889, file 1890–280, Applications and Appointments Files, Appointments Division, Records of the Office of the Secretary of the Interior.

[40] Board of Trustees of the District of Columbia, *Third Report: 1876–1877* (Washington, 1877), 28–31, 174–80.

[41] Charlotte Cross to Capt. Johnson, Feb. 4, 1868, file of Charlotte Cross, Applications and Recommendations, Records of the Division of Appointments, General Records of the Department of the Treasury.

women's natural domestic role, was by the late 1830s considered an acceptable occupation for genteel, unmarried women who did not yet have children of their own. By the post-Civil War era this domestic ideology allowed women to participate in certain other public arenas, such as the church, charity or settlement house work, and moral reform. Respectable middle-class women were warned, however, not to venture beyond the household, classroom, or church.[42]

The women who became government clerks had imbibed these values and had tried to conform to these standards. Prior to government employment many had engaged in other, more acceptable occupations. A large number had previously taught school, but had found the wages inadequate. At the age of eighteen Rosalie Mace left home to accept a teaching job in a private seminary. Within a year she applied for a federal job saying that the school had paid her such a meager salary that she found herself "unable to do more than pay my expenses." She needed higher wages in order to help her ailing father support the family.[43] Similarly, married women and widows had taken in boarders, thus remaining safely within the domestic sphere while attempting simultaneously to earn some money. This too, however, proved an unstable livelihood. Fanny Smith, a widow with three daughters, wrote in 1880: "I have been treated so badly by [boarders] going off without paying that I had to give it up and am now in debt with no means of getting out except by having employment. My children and myself are in need of actual necessities in the way of clothing."[44] Social class background prohibited these women from seeking employment either in factories or as domestic servants, areas which had by the 1860s become predominantly the domain of working-class, immigrant women.[45] Having exhausted the limited options, middle-class women hazarded society's disapproval and ventured into the public sphere as government clerks.

Societal attitudes confirmed many women's worst fears. Almost immediately after the Treasury Department hired its first female office workers in 1862, rumors began to fly about the immoral women in the departments in Washington. Allegations of immorality derived partly from the fact that in these offices men and women worked in close physical proximity, a situation unlike other middle-class work experiences. In his 1869 book *The Sights and Secrets of the National Capital*, John B. Ellis discussed the "treasury courtesans," and although the author admitted that the "black sheep are greatly in the minority," he maintained that they "are still believed to be numerous."[46] Throughout the rest of the century many women in federal offices faced charges (often made by anonymous accusers) of being strumpets, keeping or

[42] See Cott, *Bonds of Womanhood*; Sklar, *Catherine Beecher*; Flexner, *Century of Struggle*; O'Neill, *Everyone Was Brave*; Ryan, *Womanhood in America*; Welter, *Dimity Convictions*.

[43] Rosalie Mace to Robert Porter, Sept. 21, 1889, file 1890–1447, Applications and Appointments Files, Appointments Division, Records of the Office of the Secretary of the Interior.

[44] Mrs. Fanny C. Smith to General Francis A. Walker, April 21, 1880, file 1880–1216, *ibid*.

[45] See Yans-McLaughlin, *Family and Community*; Walkowitz, *Worker City*; Kleinberg, "Woman's Work."

[46] John B. Ellis, *The Sights and Secrets of the National Capital* (Chicago, 1869), 387.

frequenting houses of ill repute, and engaging in adultery with male coworkers. This image of immoral female clerks persisted in the public mind. According to historian Constance McLaughlin Green, during the Wilson administration city officials attempted to clean up Washington's notorious red-light district. When a well-known madame was called before the judge and asked how she pleaded, she responded: "Your Honor, everybody knows I run the second best house in the city. . . . the Treasury runs the best."[47]

Female clerks realized that in becoming government employees they had crossed the boundary of what many considered to be acceptable behavior. Consequently, nearly every woman's job application contained repeated assurances that the candidate was "of good moral character" and from a "respectable and worthy" family. Besides emphasizing virtue and purity, applicants took great pains to demonstrate the requisite amount of passivity, reserve, and helplessness demanded of well-bred, nineteenth-century ladies. Miss M. L. Burroughs wrote in 1879: "If you only knew how long I've been trying for a position, without success, and still persevering, I am sure you would through pity and compassion help me—It is so embarrassing (at least I find it so) for a girl to be compelled to seek employment alone. I sometimes wish that my eyes could close in silent death."[48] Similarly Martha J. Brooks portrayed herself as a helpless female in her 1890 letter of application: "I . . . battling all alone and failing in strength because of sacrifices too harrassing to mention, fall on my knees today imploring the coveted privilege to work in your great 'bee hive'. . . . Help me! I'll work with a soul of iron to shield my best of good mothers. . . . throw around hungry-hearted, helpless me the wide mantle of your protection."[49] Various factors could account for the continued use of this rhetoric. Statements that echoed the dominant nineteenth-century concept of "true womanhood" may have reflected genuine feelings, or they may have been a means of compensating for an unorthodox, and by definition unwomanly, entry into the public arena. Alternatively, applicants might, with good reason, have felt that a shy, helpless, needy female stood a better chance of getting a job than a coarse, aggressive one. In fact, all these interpretations are probably valid. Women undoubtedly knew which characteristics were most likely to win them jobs, and they were also genuinely concerned for their reputations as moral, upright ladies.

Women clerical workers were products of a culture that defined women as domestic, submissive, and passive, and they had for the most part assimilated these values. They struggled, therefore, to minimize the contradictions between their roles as respectable middle-class wives, daughters, and mothers and their roles as government clerks by presenting clerical work as an extension of domestic responsibilities: they worked to help their families. Many women tried to stretch the domestic ideology as far as possible by claiming that the needs of their families justified even so bold an action as entering government

[47] Constance McLaughlin Green, *Washington: Capital City, 1879–1950* (Princeton, 1963), 168.

[48] M. L. Burroughs to Mr. Clark, March 24, 1879, file 1879–1041, Applications and Appointments Files, Appointments Division, Records of the Office of the Secretary of the Interior.

[49] Martha J. Brooks to Gen. John W. Noble, Sept. 22, 1891, file 1890–1993, *ibid.*

offices. In pushing the domestic ideology to its limits, these women exposed one of its major contradictions. It was becoming increasingly difficult even for some middle-class women to care for their families without entering the public sphere.[50]

The contradictions inherent in the domestic ideology became more apparent after women began to work in federal offices. Success as clerks required women to exhibit, not passivity and reserve, but assertiveness, competence, and skill in nontraditional areas. Female office workers met these challenges, and in the process new attitudes emerged side by side with their old justifications and protestations of female virtue. The women became proud of their abilities, achievements, and ambitions for success. Julia Henderson described her years in federal employ this way: "I gradually rose from grade to grade, until . . . I was promoted to $1,200, having previously been made an Examiner of accounts of Indian agents . . . and endorsed by the then Chief of my Division . . . as 'possessing the qualities of reliability, accuracy, quickness, and application'. . . . For years I worked faithfully. . . . the work being brain work of a character that requires a knowledge not only of the rulings of this Department, but also those of the Treasury, Second Auditor, Second Comptroller, and Revised Statutes; demanding the closest and most critical attention, together with a great deal of legal and business knowledge."[51] Other women pointed proudly to their reputations for performing routine clerical tasks with speed and accuracy. Alice Harvey, for examply, asked in 1891 if she could be transferred to a different division within the Census Office. She complained that her supervisor's refusal to rectify certain records was "injuring my standing as a good clerk. . . . Last week my average in tabulation was 591 per day giving me the first standing in the room, and third in the division, this week it is 636 and I am told I am a first class tabulator."[52] For many women the experience of work led to the emergence of proprietary attitudes toward their jobs and signalled the beginnings of a new career mentality. Female clerks began to see themselves, not as temporary wage earners, but as permanent employees.

Like other workers, women clerks displayed anger and resentment when denied recognition of their skills or services. Female office workers were frequently passed over for promotion, dismissed without cause, or reduced in pay, and these actions drew angry responses from the women. The same

[50] Jane Addams phrased a similar argument in the early 1900s: "There is no doubt . . . that many women to-day are failing properly to discharge their duties to their own families and households simply because they fail to see that as a society grows more complicated it is necessary that woman shall extend her sense of responsibility to many things outside of her own home, if only in order to preserve the home in its entirety." She argued that as society assumed many functions previously performed by the family, women must participate in the world outside the home to have a voice in how their children were educated, whether their families would be able to have uncontaminated food, and if the environment in which they lived would be clean and disease free. See Jane Addams, "Women's Conscience and Social Amelioration," *The Social Applications of Religion* (Cincinnati, 1908), 41-60; and Christopher Lasch, ed., *The Social Thought of Jane Addams* (Indianapolis, 1965), 143-261.

[51] Julia Henderson to Hoke Smith, Oct. 4, 1893, file 1879-1718, Applications and Appointments Files, Appointments Division, Records of the Office of the Secretary of the Interior.

[52] Alice Harvey to A. F. Childs, April 11, 1891, file 1890-440, *ibid.*

Martha Brooks who in 1890 begged that "helpless me" might be given a position wrote again exactly one year later, but now she used a quite different tone. Complaining bitterly that her salary had been cut from $900 to $720 per year, she asked that her former salary be restored. "I feel constrained to believe that you will say I shall have what I justly deserve—for great fire, I know my average and record as far as *correctness*, diligence, conscientiousness, and faithful observance of every regulation in office is concerned is second to none. The comparers pronounce my work good, and I never have a piece brought back to me for correction. I could not send in a soiled or careless sheet, but strive every day to improve on the last."[53] Wilhelmine Smith, after being ranked thirteenth out of 226 men and women competing in the civil service examination, received a temporary $900 per year position in the Pension Office. Although the appointment lasted only three months, she managed to be reinstated later that year, but at a lower salary. She explained that "returning to the offices, the humiliation to which I was subjected, could only have been endured for the sake of my children."[54]

While much of these women's anger undoubtedly stemmed from their acute need for wages, the case of Elizabeth Stoner shows that egos as well as pocketbooks suffered when a female clerk received unfair treatment. In 1862 Stoner filled one of the first four positions ever offered to a woman in the Treasury Department. She worked for thirty-two years, supporting two invalid sisters during much of this time. In 1894 Stoner lost her job, learning after her dismissal that charges of dereliction had been made about her performance as clerk. She immediately wrote to the secretary of the treasury asking that these charges be removed from her record. "I beg leave to say that I have been misrepresented on my record. . . . As to not attending to the duties of my office when present . . . I did the work assigned me accurately and well and was current and my desk was clear every evening. I was in the room under eight of Mr. Bradley's predecessors—and as far as I know gave satisfaction. . . . I did not know, until a few days ago that my record was the cause of my dismissal. I was told it was long service under Republican influence. . . . I beg most earnestly that my record be re-adjusted, it means so much to me—and I ask it in the name of simple justice."[55] Even with financial concerns no longer relevant, pride in work well done and her reputation as an efficient clerk remained important to Stoner.

The career of Jane M. Seavey offers an excellent example of the way in which the older values associated with nineteenth-century domesticity continued alongside new attitudes produced by the work experiences. When the Civil War broke out, Seavey was thirty-two years old and teaching in a small woman's college in a "secessionist neighborhood" in Tennessee. She desired to leave immediately for the North, "but the pecuniary embarrassment of

[53] Martha J. Brooks to John W. Noble, Sept. 26, 1892, file 1890-1993, *ibid.*

[54] Mrs W. M. Easby Smith to C. Schurz, Feb. 1, 1881, file 1880-262, *ibid.*

[55] Elizabeth Stoner to Mr. Van Sanden, Oct. 26, 1894, file of Elizabeth Stoner, Applications and Recommendations, Records of the Division of Appointments, General Records of the Department of the Treasury.

those who had charge of my means prevented me." The war and Union blockade contributed to the collapse of the college, and with it Seavey's source of income. In 1862 she finally arrived in Boston but found herself "entirely without the means of support, dependent on the kindness of friends, and most keenly feel[ing] the necessity of obtaining remunerative employment."[56]

In January 1863 Seavey received an appointment in the Internal Revenue Bureau at $600 per year. Within six months she had been put in charge of the recording room within the bureau and wrote complaining that the "duties . . . have become more than one person can faithfully perform." She requested that a friend be appointed assistant superintendent. Furthermore she asserted that her own work had become "arduous and exceedingly responsible, yet the salary had [remained] only that of a recording clerk." She therefore requested that her wages be increased to $1,200 per year and that her assistant be paid $1,000.[57] Seavey remained in the Internal Revenue Bureau for thirty-one years during which time she was promoted to the highest classified clerkship, a $1,800 per year position. During her years in office Seavey introduced a new system of organizing the work in her section, a method of filing adopted throughout the Treasury Department and used as a model for other agencies as well.

In 1894 Seavey lost her job, ostensibly because of a change in the appropriations for her office. Some evidence suggests, however, that complaints regarding her "domineering" and "overbearing" behavior might have caused her to be discharged. Seavey's dismissal bought protests from numerous people, including former Treasury officials, and four years later she was reinstated at a salary of $1,200. It is significant that these protests stressed not only her excellent record as an employee, but also the fact that she had over the years contributed "substantial assistance to some of her relatives who still look to her for assistance," and that consequently she is "currently without the means of support."[58] In 1906 Seavey still worked in the department, but the commissioner of internal revenue asked that her salary be reduced to $1,000. He insisted that this recommendation was "made upon the request of Miss Seavey and at her earnest desire. She feels that, while her health is reasonably good and she is still able to perform her official duties in a creditable manner, yet at her advanced age (78) she cannot handle the same class of work nor accomplish as much as when she was in her prime. She therefore wishes that some one younger than she, in years and service, performing a higher and better class of work, should receive the compensation accorded her. Miss Seavey has been and still is a valued and honored clerk in this bureau."[59]

Although Seavey's career was undoubtedly longer and more successful than that of most female clerks during the late nineteenth century, it mirrored the experiences and attitudes of many of her co-workers. Her class background and

[56] J. M. Seavey to Joseph Holt, Oct. 11, 1862, file of Jane M. Seavey, *ibid.*
[57] J. M. Seavey to J. J. Lewis, June 8, 1863, *ibid.*
[58] Horatio King to John G. Carlisle, Dec. 3, 1894, *ibid.*
[59] John M. Yerkes to Sec. of the Treasury, May 3, 1906, *ibid.*

the conditions under which she entered government employ were typical. Once in the job she very quickly acquired managerial and clerical skills and simultaneously became dedicated, ambitious, and proud of her work. Nevertheless, at the end of her long and successful career, she still displayed the altruism and reserve reminiscent of the older nineteenth-century standards of female virtue.

What began for many women as a desperate attempt to preserve their families' social and economic positions within the middle class became the beginnings of new, unplanned careers as government clerks. As members of the middle class, these women had been schooled in traditional nineteenth-century norms which closely circumscribed proper female behavior. Most had ventured no further from the domestic sphere than its extension, the classroom. Yet, when the need arose, women of this class left that sphere and entered the public, wage-earning world. In many cases, women worked as clerks for only a year or two; in other instances careers in government offices lasted a decade or more.

As important as the time spent in offices was the transformation in attitudes that even a short experience as a clerical worker could begin to effect. In the last half of the nineteenth century these attitudes did not so much displace as merge and coexist with the women's previous values. The strong tenets of domesticity with which these women had been imbued were not discarded in a few short years. Even at their most militant, women clerks often couched their demands in terms that reflected the old views of female propriety: Stoner "begged" and did not "insist" that her thirty-year record as an excellent clerk be set straight. Nevertheless women clerks began to embrace a new self-image. However strongly influenced by the prevailing notion that genteel, respectable women should remain passive, dependent, and helpless, they soon began to recognize their ability to succeed in what had previously been a man's world. While continuing to hold fast to their positions as proper, respectable middle-class ladies, they simultaneously developed and asserted an important sense of themselves as competent, dedicated, resourceful workers.

The Duty or Right to Care? Nursing and Womanhood in Historical Perspective

Susan M. Reverby

The vivid television images of closed emergency rooms in local hospitals and abandoned elders in overcrowded nursing homes viscerally sear in our mind's eye what appears to be a growing societal crisis in caring. As such images remind us almost daily, the problems of caring have left the supposed quiet of domestic life or the hospital bedside and intruded into public consciousness and political discourse. Nowhere is this public "talk" about caring louder than in the widespread media coverage of what is labelled the "nursing shortage" and women's seeming abandonment of this most traditional of the so-called women's occupations (Aiken and Mullinix 1987). In many of the commentaries on this "problem" the underlying assumption is that caring was always central and unproblematic in both women's and nurses' lives, surfacing only recently as a dilemma as feminism and changing structures in our capitalist economy have transformed women's work.

In the last decade, however, scholars from many different disciplines within Women's Studies and nursing have analyzed the many meanings of the term *caring* and suggested its problematic status is not a new one (Blum et al. 1976; Chodorow 1978; Dalley 1988; Finch and Groves 1983; Gilligan 1982; Leininger 1981; Noddings 1984; Watson 1979). Much of this literature, however, runs the danger of universalizing caring as an element in female identity, or as a human quality, separate from the cultural and structural circumstances that create it (Benner and Wrubel 1989). But as the editors of this volume and policy analyst Hilary Graham have argued, caring is not merely an identity; it is also work. As Graham notes, "caring touches simultaneously on who you are and what you do" (Graham 1983:13). Because of this duality, caring can be an unbounded act, difficult to define, even harder to control.

Graham's analysis moves beyond seeing caring as a psychological trait, but her focus is primarily on women's unpaid labor in the home. She does not fully discuss how the forms of caring are shaped by the contexts under which they are practiced. Caring is not just a subjective and material experience, it is also an historically created one. Particular circumstances, ideologies, and power relations thus create the conditions under which caring can occur, the forms it will take, and the consequences it will have for those who do it.

The basis for caring also shapes its effect. Nursing, since the Nightingale-inspired reforms, has been organized under the expectation that its practitioners would accept a duty to care, rather than demand a right to determine how they would satisfy this duty. Nurses were expected to act out of obligation to care, taking on caring more as an identity than as work, and expressing altruism without any thought for autonomy either at the bedside or over control of their profession. Thus nurses, as with others who perform what is defined as "women's work" in our society, have contended with what appears as a dichotomy between the duty to care for others and the right to control their own activities in the name of caring. Nursing is still searching for what philosopher Joel Feinberg argued comes prior to rights, that is, being "recognized as having a claim on rights" (1980:41). The duty to care, organized within the particular, political, and economic context of nursing's development, has made it difficult, although not impossible, for nurses to obtain this moral, and ultimately, political, standing.

Because nurses have been given the duty to care, they are caught in a secondary dilemma: forced to act as if altruism (assumed to be the basis for caring) and autonomy (assumed to be the basis for rights) are separate ways of being, even human characteristics distributed along gender lines. Nurses are still searching for a way to forge a link between altruism and autonomy that will allow them to have what philosopher Larry Blum (1976:223) and others have called "caring-with-autonomy," or what psychiatrist Jean Baker Miller (1976:71) labelled "a way of life that includes serving others without being subservient." Viewed from the nursing perspective, our contemporary crisis in caring can thus be seen as a consequence of the efforts by nurses and other women to create the conditions for such a life.

In this chapter, I argue that while caring has always been essential to nursing work and often to women's sense of self, it has been far from unproblematic and not merely psychological. Indeed, the crucial dilemma of American nursing has been the order to care in a society that refuses to value caring. This article is an analysis of the historical creation of that dilemma and its consequences for nursing (Reverby 1987). To explore the meaning of caring for nursing, it is necessary to unravel the terms of the relationship between nursing and womanhood as these bonds have been formed over more than a century.

Most of the writing about American nursing's history begins in the 1870s when formal training for nursing was introduced in the United States.

But nursing did not appear *de novo* at the end of the nineteenth century. As with most medical and health care, nursing throughout the colonial era and most of the nineteenth century took place within the family and the home. In the domestic pantheon that surrounded "middling" and upper-class American womanhood in the nineteenth century, a woman's caring for friends and relatives was an important pillar. As a form of caring, nursing was often taught by mother to daughter as part of female apprenticeship, or learned by a domestic servant as an additional task on her job. Embedded in the seemingly natural or ordained character of women, it became an important manifestation of women's expression of love of others, and thus integral to the female sense of self (Reverby 1987; Young 1983). In a society where deeply-felt religious tenets were translated into gendered virtues, domesticity advocate Catherine Beecher declared that the sick were to be "commended" to a "woman's benevolent ministries" (1846:214).

The responsibility for nursing went beyond a mother's duty for her children, a wife's for her husband, or a daughter's for her aging parents. It attached to all the available female family members. At any time the family's "long arm" might reach out to a woman working in a distant city or mill, pulling her home to care for the sick, infirm, or newborn. No form of women's labor, paid or unpaid, protected her from this demand. "You may be called upon at any moment," Eliza W. Farrar warned in *The Young Lady's Friend*, "to attend upon your parents, your brothers, your sisters, or your companions" (1837:35). Nursing was to be, therefore, a woman's duty, not her job. Obligation and love, not the need of work, were to bind the nurse to her patient. Caring was to be an unpaid labor of love.

Even as Farrar was proffering her advice, pressures both inward and outward were beginning to reshape the domestic sphere for women of what was then called the middling classes. Women's obligations and work were transformed by the expanding industrial economy and changing cultural assumptions. Parenting took on increasing importance as notions of "moral mothering" filled the domestic arena as other productive labor entered the cash-nexus. Female benevolence similarly moved outward as women's charitable efforts took increasingly institutional forms. Duty began to take on new meaning as such women were advised they could fulfill their nursing responsibilities by managing competently those they hired to assist them. Bourgeois female virtue could still be demonstrated as the balance of labor, love, and supervision shifted (Beecher 1876; Hale 1844; Strasser 1982).

An expanding economy thus had differing effects on women of the various classes. For those in the growing urban middling classes, excess cash made it possible to consider hiring a nurse when circumstances, desire, or exhaustion meant a female relative was no longer available for the task. Caring as labor, for these women, could be separated from love.

For older widows or spinsters from the working classes, nursing became a trade they could "profess to" relatively easily in the marketplace. A widow who had nursed her husband till his demise, or a domestic servant who had cared for an employer in time of illness, entered casually into the nursing trade, hired by families or individuals unwilling, or unable, to care for their sick alone. The permeable boundaries for women between unpaid and paid labor allowed nursing to pass back and forth when necessary. For many women, nursing thus beckoned as respectable community work.

These professed or "natural-born" nurses, as they were known, usually came to their work, as one Boston nurse put it, "laterly" when other forms of employment were closed to them, or when the lack of any kind of work experience left nursing as an obvious choice. Mehitable Pond Garside, for example, was in her fifties and had outlived two husbands—and her children could not, or would not, support her—when she came to Boston in the 1840s to nurse. Similarly, Alma Frost Merrill, the daughter of a Maine wheelwright, came to Boston in 1818 at age nineteen to become a domestic servant. After years as a domestic and seamstress, she declared herself a nurse (Home for Aged Women 1850).

Women such as Garside and Merrill differed markedly from the Sairy Gamp character of the Dickens' fiction *Martin Chuzzlewit*. Gamp was portrayed as a merely besotted representative of lumpen-proletarian womanhood, who asserted her autonomy by daring to question medical diagnoses, to venture her own opinions (usually outrageous and wrong) at every turn, and to spread disease and superstition in the name of self-knowledge. If not Gamps, nurses such as Garside and Merrill were also not the healers of some more recent feminist mythology that confounds nursing with midwifery, praising the caring and autonomy these women exerted, but refusing to consider their ignorance (Ehrenreich and English 1972). Some professed nurses learned their skills from years of experience, demonstrating the truth of the dictum that "to make a kind and sympathizing nurse, one must have waited, in sickness, upon those she loved dearly" (Penny 1863:420). Others, however, blundered badly beyond their capabilities or knowledge. They brought to the bedside only the authority their personalities and community stature could command: neither credentials nor a professional identity gave weight to their efforts. Their womanhood, and the experience it gave them, defined their authority and taught them to nurse.

Nursing was not limited, however, to the bedside in a home. Although the United States had only 178 hospitals at the first national census in 1873, it was workers labelled "nurses" who provided the caring. As in home-based nursing, the route to hospital nursing was paved more with necessity than intentionality. In 1875, Eliza Higgins, the matron of Boston's Lying-In Hospital, could not find an extra nurse to cover all the deliveries. In desperation, she moved the hospital laundress up to the nursing position, while a recovering patient took over the wash. Higgins's diaries of her trying years at the Lying-In suggest that such entry into nursing was not uncommon (Higgins 1889).

As her reports and the memoirs of other nurses attest, hospital nursing could be the work of devoted women who learned what historian Charles Rosenberg has labelled "ad-hoc professionalism," or the temporary and dangerous labor of an ambulatory patient or hospital domestic (Rosenberg 1977, 1987). As in home-based nursing, both caring and concern were frequently evinced. But the nursing work and nurses were mainly characterized by the diversity of their efforts and the unevenness of their skills.

Higgins's memoirs attest to the hospital as a battleground as nurses, physicians, and hospital managers contested the realm of their authority. Nurses continually argued their right to control the pace and content of their work, to set their own hours, and to structure their relationships to physicians. Aware that the hospital's paternalistic attitudes and practices toward its "inmates" were attached to the nursing personnel as well, they fought to be treated as workers, "not children," as the Lying-In nurses told Higgins (July 11, 1876; July 1, 1876), and to maintain their autonomous adult status.

As with home-based nursing, hospital nurses had neither the formal training nor class status upon which to base their arguments. But their sense of the rights of working-class womanhood gave them the authority to press their demands. The necessity to care, and their perception of its importance to patient outcome, also structured their belief that demanding the right to be relatively autonomous was possible. However, their efforts were undermined by the nature of their onerous work, the paternalism of the institutions, class differences between trustees and workers, and ultimately, the lack of a defined ideology of caring. Mere resistance to those above them, or contending assertions of rights, could not become the basis for nursing authority.

Much of this was to change with the introduction of training for nursing into the hospital world. In the aftermath of Nightingale's apparent triumph over the British army's medical care system in the Crimea, similar attempts by U.S. women during our Civil War, and the need to find respectable work for the daughters of the middling classes, a model and support for nursing reform began to grow. By 1873, three nursing schools in hospitals in New York, Boston, and New Haven were opened on the model of the Nightingale School at St. Thomas's Hospital in London.

Nightingale had envisioned nursing as an art, rather than a science, for which women needed to be trained. Her ideas linked her medical and public health notions to her class and religious beliefs. Accepting the Victorian idea of divided spheres of activity for men and women, she thought women had to be trained to nurse through a disciplined process of honing their womanly virtue. She stressed character development, the laws of health, and strict adherence to orders passed through a female hierarchy structured like an upper-class household with a mistress and retinue of servants of various statuses (Summers 1988). Nursing was built upon a model that relied upon the concept of duty to provide its basis for authority. Unlike other feminists at the time, Nightingale spoke in the language of duty, not rights.

Furthermore, as a nineteenth-century sanitarian, Nightingale never believed in germ theory, in part because she refused to accept a theory of disease etiology that appeared to be morally neutral. Given her sanitarian beliefs, Nightingale thought medical therapeutics and "curing" of lesser importance to patient outcome, and she willingly left this realm to the physician. Caring, the arena she did think of great importance, she assigned to the nurse. In order to care, a nurse's character, tempered by the fires of training, was to be her greatest skill. Thus to "feminize" nursing, Nightingale sought a change in the class-defined behavior, not the gender, of the work force (Reverby 1987; Rosenberg 1979).

To forge a good nurse out of the virtues of a good woman and to provide a political base for nursing, Nightingale sought to organize a female hierarchy in which orders passed downward from the nursing superintendent to the lowly probationer. This separate female sphere was to share power in the provision of health care with the male-dominated arenas of medicine. For many women in the Victorian era, sisterhood and what historian Carroll Smith-Rosenberg (1975) has called "homosocial networks" served to overcome many of the limits of this separate but supposedly equal system of cultural division. Sisterhood after all, at least in its fictive forms, underlay much of the female power that grew out of women's culture in the nineteenth century. But in nursing, commonalities of the gendered experience could not become the basis of unity because hierarchical filial relations, not equal sisterhood, lay at the basis of nursing's theoretical formulation (Roberts-Gersh 1987).

Thus unwittingly, Nightingale's sanitarian ideas and her beliefs about womanhood provided some of the ideological justification for many of the dilemmas that faced American nursing by 1900. Having fought physician and trustee prejudice against the training of nurses in hospitals in the last quarter of the nineteenth century, American nursing reformers succeeded only too well as the new century began. Between 1890 and 1920, the number of nursing schools jumped from 35 to 1,775, and the number of trained nurses from 16 per 100,000 in the population to 141 (Burgess 1926:36–37). Administrators quickly realized that the opening of a "nursing school" provided their hospitals, in exchange for training, with a young, disciplined, and cheap labor force. Thus, often no difference could be found between the hospital's nursing school and its nursing service. The service needs of the hospital continually overrode the educational requirements of the schools. A student might, therefore, spend weeks on a medical ward if her labor was so needed, but never see the inside of an operating room before her graduation.

Once the nurse finished her training, however, she was unlikely to be hired by a hospital because it relied upon either untrained aides or nursing student labor. The majority of graduate nurses, until the end of the 1930s, had to find work in private duty in a patient's home, as the patient's employee in the hospital, in the branches of public health, or in a few hospital staff positions. Beyond their hospital school, trained nurses still had to compete with the thousands of professed or "practical" nurses who continued to ply their trade in an overcrowded and unregulated marketplace. The title *nurse* began to take on very ambiguous meanings (Reverby 1982, 1984). Nor was the phrase *trained nurse* a uniform designation. As nursing leader Isabel Hampton Robb lamented in 1893, the title "'trained nurse' may mean then anything, everything, or next to nothing" (quoted in James 1979:229).

In the hospital-based schools, the exigencies of nursing increasingly acutely ill or surgical patients required the sacrifice of coherent educational programs. Didactic, repetitive, watered-down medical lectures by physicians or older nurses were often provided the students, usually after they finished ten to twelve hours of ward work. Training emphasized the "one right way" of doing ritualized procedures in hopes that the students' adherence to specified rules would be least dangerous to patients (Ashley 1976; Reverby 1987). Under these circumstances, the duty to care could be followed with a vengeance and become the martinet adherence to orders.

Furthermore, because nursing emphasized training in discipline, order, and practical skills, it made possible the rationalization of the abuse of student labor. And because the work force was almost entirely women, altruism, sacrifice, and submission were expected, encouraged, indeed demanded. Exploitation was inevitable in a field where, until the early 1900s, there were no accepted standards for how much work an average student should do, how many patients she could successfully care for, or any mechanisms through which to enforce such standards. After completing her exhaustive and depressing survey of nursing training in 1912, nursing educator M. Adelaide Nutting bluntly pointed out: "Under the present system the school has no life of its own" (1912:49). In this kind of environment, nurses were trained. But they were not educated.

It would be a mistake, however, to see the nursing experience as only one of exploitation and the nursing school as a faintly concealed reformatory for the wayward girl in need of discipline. Many nursing superintendents lived the Nightingale ideals as best they could and infused them into their schools. The authoritarian model could and did retemper many women. It instilled nurses with idealism and pride in their skills, somewhat differentiated the trained nurse from the untrained, and protected and aided the sick and dying. It provided a mechanism for virtuous women to contribute to the improvement of humanity by empowering them to care.

For many of the young women entering training in the late nineteenth and early twentieth centuries, nursing thus offered something quite special: both a livelihood and a virtuous state. As one nursing educator noted in 1890: "Young strong country girls are drawn into the work by the glamorer [*sic*] thrown about hospital work and the halo that sanctifies a Nightingale" (Wells 1890:98). Thus, in their letters of application, aspiring nursing students expressed their desire for work, independence, and womanly virtue. As with earlier, nontrained nurses, they did not seem to separate autonomy and altruism, but rather sought its linkage through training. Flora Jones spoke for many such women when she wrote the superintendent of Boston City Hospital in 1880, declaring: "I consider myself fitted for the work by inclination and consider it a womanly occupation. It is also necessary for me to become self-supporting and provide for my future" (Boston City Hospital Training School Records 1880). Thus one nursing superintendent reminded a graduating class in 1904: "You have become self-controlled, unselfish, gentle, compassionate, brave, capable—in fact, you have risen from the period of irresponsible girlhood to that of womanhood" (Snively 1904:838). For women such as Jones, and many of nursing's early leaders, nursing was the singular way to grow to maturity in a womanly profession that offered meaningful work, independence, and altruism (Armeny 1984a).

For many, however, as nursing historian Dorothy Sheahan has noted, the training school "was a place where... women learned to be girls" (1981:2). The range of permissible behaviors for respectable women was often narrowed further through training. Independence was to be sacrificed on the altar of altruism. Thus, despite the hopes of aspiring students and promises of the training school superintendents, nursing rarely united altruism and autonomy. Duty remained the basis for caring.

Some nurses were able to create what they called "a little world of our own." But nursing had neither the financial nor the cultural power to create the separate women's institutions which provided so much of the basis for women's reform and rights efforts (Freedman 1979; Tomes 1978). Under these conditions, nurses found it very difficult to make the collective transition out of a woman's culture of obligation into an activist assault upon the structure and beliefs that oppressed them. Nursing remained bounded by its ideology and its material circumstances.

In this context, one begins to understand the difficulties faced by the leaders of nursing reform. Believing that educational reform was central to nursing's professionalizing efforts and clinical improvements, a small group of elite nursing reformers attempted to broaden its scientific content and social outlook. In arguing for an increase in the scientific knowledge necessary in nursing, such leaders were fighting against deep-seated cultural assumptions about male and female "natural" characteristics as embodied in the doctor and nurse. Such sentiments were articulated in the routine platitudes that graced what one nursing leader described as the "doctor homilies" that were a regular feature at nursing graduating exercises (Dock 1912:136).

Not surprisingly, such beliefs were professed by physicians and hospital officials whenever nursing shortages appeared, or nursing groups pushed for higher educational standards and defined nursing as more than assisting the physician. As one nursing educator wrote, with some degree of resignation, after the flu pandemic in 1920: "It is perhaps inevitable that the difficulty of securing nurses during the last year or two should have revived again the old agitation about the 'over-training' of nurses and the clamor for a cheap worker of the old servant-nurse type" (Stewart 1920:183).

The nursing leadership, made up primarily of educators and supervisors with their base within what is now the American Nurses Association and the National League for Nursing, thus faced a series of dilemmas as they fought to raise educational standards in the schools and criteria for entry into training, to register nurses once they finished their training, and to gain acceptance for the knowledge base and skills of the nurse. They had to exalt the womanly character, self-abnegation, and service ethic of nursing while insisting on the right of nurses to act in their own self-interest. They had to demand higher wages commensurate with their skills, yet not appear "commercial." They had to simultaneously find a way to denounce the exploitation of nursing students and make political alliances with hospital physicians and administrators whose support they needed. While lauding character and sacrifice, they had to find a way to measure it with educational criteria in order to formulate registration laws and set admission standards. They had to make demands and organize, without appearing to be "unlady-like." In sum, they were forced by the social conditions and ideology surrounding nursing to attempt to professionalize altruism without demanding autonomy.

The seemingly higher claim of duty also continually undermined a direct assertion of the right to determine that duty. Whether at the bedside or at a legislative hearing on practice laws, the duty to care became translated into the demand that nurses merely follow doctors orders. The tradition of obligation made it almost impossible for nurses to speak about rights at all. By the turn of the century, as necessity and desire were pulling more young women into the labor force and the woman's movement activists were placing rights at the center of cultural discussion, nursing's call to duty was perceived by many as a somewhat antiquated language to shore up a changing economic and cultural reality. Nursing became a type of collective female grasping for an older form of security and power in the face of rapid change. Women who might have been attracted to nursing in the 1880s as a womanly occupation that provided some form of autonomy were, by the turn of the century, increasingly looking elsewhere for work and careers.

In the face of these difficulties, the nursing leadership became increasingly defensive and turned on its own rank-and-file. From their vantage point as educators and supervisors, many in the leadership lost touch with the pressing concerns for their constituencies in the daily work world of nursing and the belief systems such nurses continued to hold. Yet many nurses, well into the twentieth century, shared the nineteenth-century vision of nursing as the embodiment of womanly virtue. A nurse named Annette Fiske, for example, although she authored two science books for nurses and had an M.A. in classics from Radcliffe College before she entered training, spent her professional career in the 1920s arguing against increasing the educational standards. Rather, she called for a reinfusion into nursing of spirituality and service, assuming that this would result in nursing receiving greater "love and respect and admiration" (1920:8).

Other nurses, especially those who trained in the smaller schools or were raised in families that held to working-class ideals about respectable behavior in women, shared Fiske's views. They saw the leadership's efforts at professionalization as an attempt to push them out of nursing. Their adherence to nursing skill measured in womanly virtue was not merely a conservative and reactionary stance. Rather, it was a belief that seemed to transcend class and educational backgrounds to place itself in the individual character and workplace skills of the nurse. It grounded altruism in supposedly natural and spiritual, rather than educational and middle-class, soil. For a nurse such as Fiske and many others, nursing was thus still a womanly art requiring inherent character in its practitioners and training in practical skills and spiritual values in its schools. Their beliefs about nursing did not require the professionalization of altruism, nor the demand for autonomy either at the bedside or in control over the professionalization process.

Still other nurses took a more pragmatic viewpont that built upon their pride in their workplace skills and character. These nurses also saw the necessity for concerted action, not unlike that taken by other American workers. Such nurses fought against what one 1888 nurse, who called herself Candor, characterized as the "missionary spirit...[of] self-immolation" that denied that nurses worked because they had to make a living (pp. 167–68). These worker/nurses saw no contradiction between demanding decent wages and conditions for their labors and being of service for those in need. Indeed, they were also unconsciously trying to redefine societal understandings of a woman's work of caring. But the efforts of various groups of these nurses to turn to hours' legislation, trade union activity, or mutual aid associations were criticized and condemned by the nursing leadership. Their letters were often edited out of the nursing journals, and their voices silenced in public meetings as they were denounced as being "commercial," or lacking in proper womanly devotion (Ashley 1976; Melosh 1982).

In the face of continual criticism from nursing's professional leadership, the worker/nurses took on an increasingly angry and defensive tone. Aware that their sense of the nurse's skills came from the experiences of the workplace, not book learning or degrees, they had to assert this position in the face of continued hostility toward such a basis of nursing authority (Armeny 1984b; Reverby 1987). While the position of women such as Candor helped articulate a way for nurses to begin to assert the right to care, it did not constitute a full-blown ideological counterpart to the overwhelming power of the belief in duty.

By mid-century, the disputes between worker/nurses and the professional leadership began to take on new forms, although the persistent divisions continued. Aware that some kind of collective bargaining was necessary to keep nurses out of the unions and in the professional associations, the American Nurses Association reluctantly agreed in 1946 to let its state units act as bargaining agents. The nursing leadership has continued to look at educational reform strategies, now primarily taking the form of legislating for the B.S. degree as the credential necessary for entry into nursing practice, and to changes in the practice laws that will allow increasingly skilled nurses the autonomy and status they deserve. Many nurses have continued to be critical of this educational strategy, to ignore the professional associations, or to leave nursing altogether.

In their various practice fields nurses still need a viable ideology and strategy that will help them as they are increasingly caught between the continual demands of more acutely ill patients and an ever-more bureaucratized, cost-conscious, and rationalized work setting. For many nurses, even those who work as practitioners in the more autonomous settings of health maintenance organizations or public health offices, it is still in an ideological sense the nineteenth century. In the face of shortages, some administrators have tried a variety of methods to keep nurses: increasing primary nursing responsibilities, improving the hours and nursing's control over shifts, and offering competitive wages. But even these approaches have failed to confront the problem of the valuing of caring in a meaningful way.

Armed with a sense of obligation, nurses have tried in various ways to articulate a series of rights that will allow them to care and to force our society to revalue caring. The acknowledgment of responsibilities, however, so deeply ingrained in nursing and American womanhood, as nursing school dean Claire Fagin has noted, usually drowns out the nurse's assertion of rights (Fagin 1975:82). Nurses are continuing to struggle to obtain the right to claim rights. Nursing's educational philosophy, ideological underpinnings, and structural position have often made it difficult to create the circumstances within which to gain such recognition. However, it is not so much a lack of vision that thwarts nursing as it is, and often continues to be, the power to give that vision substantive form (Smith-Rosenberg 1985:296).

Much has been transformed in nursing in the last forty years, and the current cry about shortages suggests this may also be a crucial time for change. The severing of nursing education from the hospital's nursing service has finally occurred as the majority of nurses are now educated in colleges, not trained in hospital-based diploma schools. Many hospitals, in the face of shortages, are experimenting with numerous ways to organize the nursing service that provide the nurse with more responsibility and sense of control over the nursing care process. The increasingly technical and machine-aided nature of hospital-based health care has made nurses feel more skilled.

In many ways, however, very little has changed. Nursing is still divided over what counts as a nursing skill, how it is to be learned, and whether a nurse's character can be measured in educational criteria. Technical knowledge and capabilities do not easily translate into power and control. Hospitals, in search of cost-cutting measures, have forced nurses to play "beat the clock" as they run from task to task in an increasingly fragmented setting (Boston Nurses' Group 1978; Hull 1985). In turn, nurses have responded by often refusing to work in situations that are dangerous and life-threatening to patients, and where they themselves are undervalued and underpaid. Many hospital administrators, however, are still more willing to blame nursing, and women, for abandoning caring than to think about what it will cost, financially and politically, to value the caring of nurses.

Nursing continues to struggle with the basis for, and the value of, caring. The fact that the very first legal case on comparable worth was brought by a group of Denver nurses suggests nursing's ongoing role in the political effort to have caring revalued. As in the Denver case, contemporary feminism has provided some nurses with the grounds upon which to claim rights from their caring (Bullough 1978). Feminism, in its liberal form, appears to give nursing a political language that argues for equality and rights within the given order of things. It suggests a basis for caring that stresses individual discretion and values, acknowledging that the nurse's right to care should be given equal consideration with the physician's right to cure. Just as liberal political theory undermined more paternalistic formulations of government, classical liberalism's tenets applied to women have much to offer nursing. The demand for the right to care questions deeply held beliefs about gendered relations in the health care hierarchy and the hierarchy itself.

Many nurses continue to hope that with more education, with explicit theories to explain the scientific basis for nursing and even caring itself, with new skills, with a lot of assertiveness training, and with the increasing demand for their services, nursing will change. As nurses try to shed the image of the nurse being ordered to care, however, a nursing school dean had to remind a graduating class "not to undervalue [their] particular ability to care" (Fahy quoted in Witcher 1985). Unable to find a way to "care with autonomy" and unable to separate caring from its valuing and basis, many nurses find themselves forced to abandon the effort to care or to abandon nursing altogether. More ominously, nursing is having increasing difficulty attracting young women or men into the field.

These dilemmas for nurses suggest the constraints surrounding the effectiveness of a liberal political strategy to address the problems of caring, and therefore of nursing. The individualism and autonomy of a rights framework often fail to acknowledge collective social need, to provide a way for adjudicating conflicts over rights, or to address the reasons for the devaluing of female activity (Eisenstein 1981; Jaggar 1983; Petchesky 1984; Schneider 1986). Thus, nurses often reject certain forms of liberal feminism, not just out of oppression and "false consciousness," but because of some deep understandings of the limited promise of equality and autonomy in a health care system they see as flawed and harmful. In an often inchoate way, such nurses recognize that those who claim the autonomy of rights often run the risk of rejecting altruism and caring itself.

Nurses, as have others in similar positions in our society, may have to find a way to use the language of rights in a communal rather than an individual sense. Nursing needs to share in the rethinking of rights as "infused with values of community, compassion and solidarity," and not merely as a "zero-sum game" in which the gain of nursing rights is measured in the loss for others (Lynd quoted in Schneider 1986:612). In making a cultural claim for the right to care, nursing must, as attorney Martha Minow has suggested for other struggles, focus on a "right to connection" by emphasizing "the social and economic preconditions for rights" (1986:24).

Just as Candor and her sister nurses tried to articulate a different political understanding of the caring work of nursing in the 1880s, late twentieth-century nurses will have to redefine the rights involved in doing caring work. In order to redefine this rights discourse, nurses will have to find ways to create the conditions under which it is possible to value caring and to understand that the empowerment of others does not have to require self-immolation. To achieve this, nurses will have to develop both a new political understanding for the basis of caring and find ways to gain the power to implement it.

Nursing can do much within itself to have this happen through research on the importance of caring on patient outcome, studies of patient improvements in nursing settings where the right to care is created, or by implementation of nursing control of caring through a bargaining agreement. Transforming the political discourse around caring might be possible only now as individuals in our society slowly come to terms with the personal cost of ordering nursing to care.

Nurses, however, cannot make this kind of change alone. The dilemma of nursing is too tied into the broader problems of gender, race, and class in our society to be solved solely by the political or professional efforts of one occupational group. Nor are nurses alone in benefitting from such an effort. If nursing can achieve the power to practice altruism with autonomy, all of us have much to gain. Nursing has always been a much-conflicted metaphor in our culture, reflecting all the ambivalences we give to the meaning of womanhood (Fagin and Diers 1983). Nursing may now be able to give this metaphor, and ultimately caring, new value in all our lives. But this will happen only if we acknowledge the problems created by nursing's history and the undervaluing of caring as we work collectively to make possible a different future.

DOCUMENTATION

Author's Note

This article is a revised version of "A Caring Dilemma: Womanhood and Nursing in Historical Perspective," *Nursing Research* 36 (January–February 1987):5–11, and is based upon material found in my book, *Ordered to Care: The Dilemma of American Nursing* (New York: Cambridge University Press, 1987). I am grateful to Joan Lynaugh, Karen Buhler-Wilkerson, Diana Long, Nancy Fraser, and my colleagues in the Philosophy Department at Wellesley College for their help on previous drafts.

References

Aiken, Linda, and Connie Mullinix (1987) "The Nurse Shortage: Myth or Realty," *New England Journal of Medicine* 317 (September): 641–45.

Armeny, Susan (1984a) "'We Were the New Women': A Comparison of Nurses and Women Physician's, 1890–1915." Paper presented at the American Association for the History of Nursing Conference, University of Virginia, Charlottesville, Va., October.

______ (1984b) "Resolute Enthusiasts: The Effort to Professionalize American Nursing, 1880–1915," Ph.D. diss., University of Missouri, Columbia.

Ashley, Jo Ann (1976) *Hospitals, Paternalism and the Role of the Nurse* (New York: Teachers' College Press).

Beecher, Catherine (1846) *Domestic Receipt-Book* (New York: Harper and Brothers).

______ (1876) *Miss Beecher's Housekeeper and Healthkeeper* (New York: Harper and Brothers).

Benner, Patricia, and Judith Wrubel (1989) *The Primacy of Caring* (Reading, Mass.: Addison-Wesley).

Blum, Larry, Marcia Homiak, Judy Housman, and Naomi Scheman (1976) "Altruism and Women's Oppression," in *Women and Philosophy*, eds. Carol Gould and Marx Wartofsky (New York: G. P. Putnam's Sons), pp. 222–47.

Boston City Hospital (BCH) Training School Records (1880) Box 4, Folder 4, Student 4, February 14. BCH Training School Papers, Nursing Archives, Special Collections, Mugar Library, Boston University, Boston, Mass.

Boston Nurses' Group (1978) "The False Promise: Professionalism in Nursing," *Science for the People* 10(May/June):20–34.

Bullough, Bonnie (1978) "The Struggle for Women's Rights in Denver: A Personal Account," *Nursing Outlook* 26(September):566–67.

Burgess, May Ayers (1985; orig. 1926) *Nurses, Patients and Pocketbooks* (New York: Garland Publishing Co.).

Candor (1888) "Work and Wages," Letter to the Editor, *Trained Nurse and Hospital Review* 2(April):167–68.

Chodorow, Nancy (1978) *The Reproduction of Mothering* (Berkeley: University of California Press).

Dalley, Gillian (1988) *Ideologies of Caring, Rethinking Community and Collectivism* (London: Macmillan).

Dickens, Charles (1965; orig. 1865) *Martin Chuzzlewit* (New York: New American Library).

Dock, Lavinia L. (1912) *A History of Nursing* (Vol. 3) (New York: G. P. Putnam's Sons).

Ehrenreich, Barbara, and Deirdre English (1972) *Witches, Nurses, Midwives: A History of Women Healers* (Old Westbury, N.Y.: Glass Mountain Pamphlets).

Eisenstein, Zillah (1981) *The Radical Future of Liberal Feminism* (New York: Longman).

Fagin, Claire (1975) "Nurses' Rights," *American Journal of Nursing* 75(January):82.

______ and Donna Diers (1983) "Nursing as Metaphor," *New England Journal of Medicine* 309(July 14):116–17.

Farrar, Eliza (1837) *The Young Lady's Friend—By a Lady* (Boston: American Stationer's Co.).

Feinberg, Joel (1980) *Rights, Justice and the Bounds of Liberty* (Princeton, N.J.: Princeton University Press).

Finch, Janet, and Dulcie Groves, eds. (1983) *A Labour of Love: Women, Work and Caring* (London: Routledge and Kegan Paul).

Fiske, Annette (1920) "How Can We Counteract the Prevailing Tendency to Commercialism in Nursing?" *Proceedings of the 17th Annual Meeting of the Massachusetts State Nurses' Association*, Massachusetts Nurses Association Papers, Box 7, Nursing Archives, Mugar Library, Boston University, Boston, Mass.

Freedman, Estelle (1979) "Separtism as Strategy: Female Institution Building and American Feminism, 1870–1930," *Feminist Studies* 5(Fall):512–29.

Gilligan, Carol (1982) *In a Different Voice* (Cambridge, Mass.: Harvard University Press).

Graham, Hillary (1983) "Caring: a Labour of Love," in *A Labour of Love: Women, Work and Caring*, eds. J. Finch and D. Groves (London: Routledge and Kegan Paul), pp. 13–30.

Hale, Sarah Josepha (1844) *The Good Housekeeper* (7th ed.) (Boston: Otis Brothers and Co.).

Higgins, Eliza (1889) "Matron's Journals, 1873–1889," Boston Lying-In Hospital, Rare Books Room, Countway Medical Library, Harvard University Medical School, Boston, Mass.

Home for Aged Women (1850) Cases 2 and 18, "Admissions Committee Records," Volume I, Box 11, Home for Aged Women Collection, Schlesinger Library, Radcliffe College, Cambridge, Mass.

Hull, Jennifer Bingham (1985) "Hospital Nightmare: Cuts in Staff Demoralize Nurses as Care Suffers," *Wall Street Journal* (March 27).

Jaggar, Alison M. (1983) *Feminist Politics and Human Nature* (Totowa, N.J.: Rowman and Allanheld).

James, Janet Wilson (1979) "Isabel Hampton and the Professionalization of Nursing in the 1890s," in *The Therapeutic Revolution*, eds. Morris Vogel and Charles E. Rosenberg (Philadelphia: University of Pennsylvania Press), pp. 201–244.

Leininger, M. M. (1981) *Caring: An Essential Human Need* (Thorofare, N.J.: Charles B. Slack).

Lynd, Staughton (1984) "Communal Rights," *Texas Law Review* 62:1417–18.

Melosh, Barbara (1982) *"The Physician's Hand:" Work Culture and Conflict in American Nursing* (Philadelphia: Temple University Press).

Miller, Jean Baker (1976) *Toward a New Psychology of Women* (Boston: Beacon Press).

Minow, Martha (1986) "Rights for the Next Generation: A Feminist Approach to Children's Rights," *Harvard Women's Law Journal* 9(Spring):1-24.

Noddings, Nel (1984) *Caring* (Berkeley: University of California Press).

Nutting, M. Adelaide (1912) *Educational Status of Nursing*, Bureau of Education Bulletin 7, Whole 475 (Washington, D.C.: Government Printing Office).

Penny, Virginia (1863) *The Employments of Women: A Cyclopedia of Women's Work* (Boston: Walker, Wise and Co.).

Petchesky, Rosalind Pollack (1984) *Abortion and Women's Choice* (Boston: Northeastern University Press).

Reverby, Susan (1982) "'Something Besides Waiting': The Politics of Private Duty Nursing Reform in the Depression," in *Nursing History: New Perspectives, New Possibilities*, ed. Ellen Condliffe Lagemann (New York: Teachers College Press), pp. 133-156.

_____ (1984) "'Neither for the Drawing Room nor for the Kitchen': Private Duty Nursing in Boston, 1873-1920," in *Women and Health in America*, ed. Judith Walzer Leavitt (Madison: University of Wisconsin Press), pp. 454-466.

_____ (1987) *Ordered to Care: The Dilemma of American Nursing* (New York: Cambridge University Press).

Robb, Isabel Hampton (1949) "Educational Standards for Nurses," in *Nursing of the Sick, 1893* (New York: McGraw Hill), pp. 5-11.

Roberts-Gersh, Cathy (1987) "'On a New Quest': Daughter Writing, a Biographer's Journey in Search of Connection through the Maps of Her Mother's Lives," Senior Honors Thesis, Women's Studies Program, Wellesley College.

Rosenberg, Charles E. (1977) "'And Heal the Sick': The Hospital and the Patient in 19th Century America," *Journal of Social History* 10(June):428-47.

_____ (1979) "Florence Nightingale on Contagion: The Hospital as Moral Universe," in *Healing and History*, ed. Charles E. Rosenberg (New York: Science History Publications), pp. 116-35.

_____ (1987) *The Care of Strangers* (New York: Basic Books).

Schneider, Elizabeth M. (1986) "The Dialectic of Rights and Politics: Perspectives from the Women's Movement," *New York University Law Review* 61(October):589-652.

Sheahan, Dorothy (1981) "The Influence of Occupational Sponsorship on the Professional Development of Nursing." Paper presented at the Rockefeller Archives Conference on the History of Nursing, Rockefeller Archives, Tarrytown, N.Y., May.

Smith-Rosenberg, Carroll (1975) "The Female World of Love and Ritual," *Signs: Journal of Women in Culture and Society* 1(Autumn):1-30.

______ (1985) "The New Woman as Androgyne: Social Disorder and Gender Crisis, 1870-1936," in *Disorderly Conduct* (New York: Alfred E. Knopf), pp. 245-296.

Snively, Mary Agnes (1904) "What Manner of Women Ought Nurses to Be?" *American Journal of Nursing* 4 (August):838.

Stewart, Isabel M. (1920) "Progress in Nursing Education During 1919," *Modern Hospital* 14(March):183-85.

Strasser, Susan (1982) *Never Done: A History of Housework* (New York: Pantheon).

Summers, Anne (1988) *Angels and Citizens, British Women as Military Nurses 1854-1914* (London: Routledge and Kegan Paul).

Tomes, Nancy (1978) "'Little World of Our Own': The Pennsylvania Hospital Training School for Nurses, 1895-1907," *Journal of the History of Medicine* 33(October):507-30.

Watson, Jean (1979) *Nursing: The Philosophy and Science of Caring* (Boston: Little Brown).

Wells, Julia (1890) "Do Hospitals Fit Nurses for Private Nursing?" *Trained Nurse and Hospital Review* 3(March):98.

Witcher, Gregory (1985) "Last Class of Nurses Told: Don't Stop Caring," *Boston Globe* (May 13):17-18.

Young, Iris Marion (1983) "Is Male Gender Identity the Cause of Male Domination," in *Mothering: Essays in Feminist Theory*, ed. Joyce Trebilcot (Totowa, N.J.: Rowman and Allanheld), pp. 129-46.

Professionalism, Feminism, and Gender Roles: A Comparative Study of Nineteenth-Century Medical Therapeutics

Regina Markell Morantz and Sue Zschoche

Some historians have argued that nineteenth-century medicine reflected a belief system that oppressed women and that doctors' cultural prejudices biased both treatment and the doctor-patient relationship. Nineteenth-century physicians have been accused of administering harsh and painful therapies to punish and control female patients who were unresponsive to the dictates of "true womanhood." Doctors allegedly practiced a form of medicine that attempted to reinforce childlike dependency in women, defined females as inherently weak and sickly, and discouraged excessive mental or physical exertion which might have turned a woman's attention to pursuits beyond her sphere.

This interesting thesis, which has caught the imagination of many contemporary critics of the present-day male medical establishment, deserves careful examination. Medical practice does reflect and has in the past mirrored larger cultural and social ideologies.[1] We know, for example, that many standard nineteenth-century medical texts described puberty, menstruation, menopause, and pregnancy as critical periods in women's health when innate physiological weaknesses involving the reproductive system could cause permanent and serious damage if not properly managed. Many male physicians vociferously opposed the higher education of women on the grounds that it threatened female health. Indeed, the confluence of medical opinion and cultural attitudes concerning woman's role has been one of the most in-

Regina Morantz is assistant professor of history at the University of Kansas. Sue Zschoche is instructor in history at Kansas State University.

[1] Probably no single example better illustrates the cultural dimension of nineteenth-century medicine than physicians' attitudes toward masturbation. Because Victorian culture disapproved of any form of sexuality divorced from reproduction, doctors, who were representative Victorians, took to defining masturbation as a disease, complete with specific etiology and a catalogue of symptoms. Physicians, however unwittingly, thus used science to create rewards and sanctions for a sexually repressive ideology. See H. Tristam Englehardt, Jr., "The Disease of Masturbation: Values and the Concept of Disease," *Bulletin of the History of Medicine*, 48 (Summer 1974), 234–48.

triguing aspects of recent investigations into the social history of nineteenth-century medicine.[2]

Although nineteenth-century women physicians rarely criticized their male colleagues for overt oppression of female patients, they did believe themselves far more capable of treating women and children than their male colleagues. They took particular pride in their attention to preventive medicine, a concern that they often chided the men for neglecting. The medical literature reveals that most women physicians viewed women and children as their primary constituency, and they busied themselves in teaching and in practice primarily with definitions of female health and disease. Ella Ridgeway wrote in her 1873 thesis at the Woman's Medical College of Pennsylvania that women had been called upon to "supply a deficiency" in medicine "in regard to the diseases of women." There were many questions about the subject that "no doubt" have arisen in the "mind of every woman student which are not answered either by our professors or the books. One of these is why do women generally suffer so much more from ill health than men?"[3] Anna Longshore-Potts also displayed pique at her male colleagues when she wrote that their opinions about women were "cut and dried" and if women had pursued medicine earlier, "today women would have had more healthy bodies."[4] Female medical educators spoke constantly of medical women's humanizing effect on medical practice. "Educated medical women," observed Eliza Mosher, "touch humanity in a manner different from men; by virtue of their womanhood, their interest in girls and young women, both moral and otherwise; in homes and in society."[5]

The effect of such attitudes on actual therapeutic practice has been hotly contested by historians. Some have argued that in this realm women physicians made a wholesale ideological attack against male-defined and male-dominated medicine, unanimously rebelling against the contention that women were innately weak and sickly. The medicine that women physicians practiced has been pictured as deliberately and consciously feminist, concerned less with "restoring" women to good health (the shortsighted goal of their male colleagues) than with controlling future definitions of female health and reworking the medical ideology that kept women sequestered by attributing the causes of female ill health to the inherent defects in female physiology.[6]

[2] See Ann Douglas Wood, " 'The Fashionable Diseases': Women's Complaints and Their Treatment in Nineteenth-Century America," *Journal of Interdisciplinary History*, IV (Summer 1973), 25-52; Charles Rosenberg and Carroll Smith-Rosenberg, "The Female Animal: Medical and Biological Views of Woman and Her Role in Nineteenth-Century America," *Journal of American History*, LX (Sept. 1973), 332-56; Carroll Smith-Rosenberg, "The Cycle of Femininity: Puberty and Menopause in 19th Century America," *Feminist Studies*, 1 (Winter 1973), 58-72; Carroll Smith-Rosenberg, "The Hysterical Woman: Sex Roles and Role Conflict in 19th-Century America," *Social Research*, 39 (Winter 1972), 652-78.

[3] Ella Ridgeway, "The Causes of Uterine Diseases," (M.D. thesis, Woman's Medical College of Pennsylvania, 1873). All Woman's Medical College theses may be found in the Medical College of Pennsylvania Archives, Philadelphia.

[4] Anna Longshore-Potts, *Discourses to Women on Medical Subjects* (San Diego, 1897), 122.

[5] Eliza Mosher, "The Value of Organization—What Has It Done for Women?" *Woman's Medical Journal*, 26 (June 1916), 1-4.

[6] See Virginia Drachman, "Women Doctors and the Women's Medical Movement: Feminism and Medicine, 1850-1895" (Ph.D. diss., State University of New York at Buffalo, 1976).

Because many nineteenth-century women physicians expected their own practice to differ from that of their male teachers and colleagues, it is hardly surprising that historians have actually believed this to have been the case. Yet taking the statements of women physicians at face value may be naive. What women physicians thought to be true need not have actually reflected reality. Such claims must be verified. How accurately did women physicians' pronouncements reflect accounts of their own behavior, and how much did they reflect ideology or merely wishful thinking? How close was their self-image to the reality of their daily care? Did the majority practice a different kind of medicine, and if so, how different, and in what ways?

In this study we propose to examine the hypothesis that female physicians practiced medicine differently from their medical brethren. We have compared late-nineteenth-century records of obstetrical cases at two Boston hospitals, one male-staffed and one female-staffed, in an attempt to examine several historical issues. First, we hope to clarify the relationship between women physicians and the medical profession as a whole. Second, we will seek to obtain further insight into the complex process of patient-physician interaction. Finally, underlying these two problems is a more basic question: when they received similar professional training and education, did women generally behave like men, or were their responses more often shaped by considerations of gender?

Historians have often depicted the views of nineteenth-century male and female physicans toward childbirth as polarized. On the one hand, male physicians treated pregnancy as a disease and therefore tended to be interventionist. Female physicians, on the other hand, supposedly accepted birth as a natural physiological process and remained cautious in the use of instruments.[7] One comparative study of the management of obstetrical cases at the female-run New England Hospital for Women and Children and the male-run Boston Lying-In Hospital found male physicians more careless about infection, more eager to use forceps and other types of intervention procedures, and more callous toward patients.[8] We attempted to test this hypothesis

[7] For the medicalization of childbirth, see Jane Bauer Donegan, "Midwifery in America, 1760–1860: A Study in Medicine and Morality" (Ph.D. diss., Syracuse University, 1972); Catherine Scholten, " 'On the Importance of the Obstetrick Art': Changing Customs of Childbirth in America, 1760–1825," *William and Mary Quarterly*, XXXIV (July 1977), 426–45; Richard W. Wertz and Dorothy C. Wertz, *Lying-In: A History of Childbirth in America* (New York, 1977). For a more extreme view of doctors' culpability, see Mary Roth Walsh, *"Doctors Wanted: No Women Need Apply": Sexual Barriers in the Medical Profession, 1835–1975* (New Haven, 1977), 76–105; Drachman, "Women Doctors," 121–26; and Patricia Branca, *Silent Sisterhood: Middle Class Women in the Victorian Home* (London, 1975), 62–73.

[8] This was the contention of Laurie Crumpacker, "Female Patients in Four Boston Hospitals of the 1890s," a paper delivered at the Berkshire Conference on the History of Women, Oct. 1974 (copy on deposit at the Schlesinger Library, Cambridge, Mass.). In some cases historians have merely assumed the accuracy of nineteenth-century statements when critics of male midwifery insisted that women were more willing to "wait on nature." For an example of the contention that men interfered more than women, see Samuel Gregory, *Man-Midwifery Exposed and Corrected* (Boston, 1848), 12–13. Occasionally even physicians deplored the enthusiasm of their colleagues for instruments. G. S. Bedford, professor of midwifery at the New York University, warned his class not to take part in the "indiscriminate and unpardonable use of instruments"

in two ways. First, we examined the medical literature for evidence of differences in theoretical approach between male and female doctors. Second, we made a statistical comparison of obstetrical cases at the aforementioned Boston hospitals in order to compare ideology with actual practice.

Any extensive examination of nineteenth-century medical literature reveals that the historian's assumption of medical unanimity on any subject is risky. Neither male nor female physicians exhibited a consensus on any of the crucial topics regarding female health. Women internalized many "male" values, and men were sometimes advocates of "female" positions.

An excellent example of such diversity may be drawn from the obstetrical literature. The persistent reader of medical journals appearing in the last third of the nineteenth century will likely discover that a debate raged among obstetricians over whether childbirth was a natural event requiring the obstetrician to "wait on nature" or a pathological crisis demanding active and vigorous intervention. Prominent male physicians distributed themselves on both sides of the issue. The debate crystallized in the pages of the *American Journal of Obstetrics and Diseases of Women and Children* for 1888, where William T. Byford, esteemed teacher in Rush Medical College and president of the Chicago Gynecological Society, and A. F. A. King, president of the Washington, D.C., Obstetrical and Gynecological Society, warmly contested "The Physiological Argument in Obstetric Studies and Practice." King's article had a familiar ring. Though childbirth perhaps should be natural, "in the present age, and among civilized communities," he wrote, a case of natural labor can only be "hypothetical." The bad habits of modern life had exacted their toll on parturient women. Byford, on the other hand, scorned King's distorted picture of American womanhood. The doctor's patients were not representative: "Let the author look elsewhere than in Washington and in large cities and he will find plenty of healthy women in physiological labor—he might indeed have found plenty in Washington. . . ." Byford's positive approach to female health led him to decry passionately the "meddlesome practices" of some of his colleagues.[9]

Just as male physicians lacked unanimity on many medical issues, women physicians also differed significantly among themselves. As females struggling to strike a balance between science, professionalism, and their own womanhood, they were bound to develop individual solutions to the problems of female health. There was no "party line" among these women on how to

which he believed "generally prevailed." *Ibid.*, 31. Because midwives did not use instruments and rarely administered drugs, contemporaries mistakenly assumed that women physicians would follow suit. Here they underestimated the impact of professional training, a matter about which historians of female professionalism are still in conflict. For the differences in practice between physicians and midwives at parturition see Janet Bogdan, "Care or Cure? Childbirth Practices in Nineteenth Century America," *Feminist Studies*, 4 (June 1978), 92–99.

[9] A. F. A. King, "The Physiological Argument in Obstetric Studies and Practice," *American Journal of Obstetrics and Diseases of Women and Children*, XXI (April 1888), 372; Henry T. Byford, "The So-called Physiological Argument in Obstetrics," *ibid.*, XXI (Sept. 1888), 899. See also H. M. Cutts, "The Necessity of Preparatory Treatment for Child-Bed," *ibid.*, XIX (Aug. 1886), 796–801; T. P. White, "The Normal Puerperal State," *ibid.*, XIX (Nov. 1886), 1191–1205; Thomas Opie, "Is the Frequent Use of Forceps Abusive?" *ibid.*, XXI (Oct. 1888), 1088–92.

treat, diagnose, or prevent illness. Yet they did share a common approach. What drew them together was the conviction that women had a right to good health, that their own role should facilitate that right, and that better health among their contemporaries and future generations of women was indeed possible. Even when a woman physician advised caution during the physiological crises of puberty, childbirth, and menopause, her concern was to determine the reasons for ill health during these times and develop fresh methods for managing female problems. The female doctor who believed it was woman's fate to suffer because of her physiology was a rare exception. Nevertheless, a careful study of journal articles and medical school theses by women suggests that in theory female physicians approached childbirth much as their male colleagues did. That is to say, their overall opinions reflected professional and scientific trends, and their divergences among themselves were similar to those of male doctors.

The theses on childbirth at the Woman's Medical College of Pennsylvania, for example, reflected the thinking of the medical profession at large. In the early decades, from the 1850s to the 1870s, the theme was deference to nature, limited interference, and patience in delivery.[10] By the end of the century, however, when doctors began to worry that excessive civilization had complicated delivery for middle-class women, the women's theses reflected this change. Pregnancy, wrote Phoebe Oliver in 1869, though a physiological condition, "has the peculiarity of being in some susceptible constitutions, pathological." She recommended moderate interference, including some drugging, rather than "waiting on nature," especially when there were spasms. Other students noted the dire effects of advancing civilization on the ability of women to give birth easily.[11] Lucy R. Weaver believed that the way in which the physical system changes during pregnancy "may easily become pathological, for it borders so closely on disease." Mary Jordan Finley chided old-fashioned obstetricians reluctant to use forceps. She warned that much serious damage could be prevented by the "timely" use of both forceps and ergot to ease pain, secure the child, and conserve the strength of the mother. "A timid or incompetent practitioner," she complained, "sits by the patient waiting for nature to accomplish the delivery until the life has been crushed out of some point in the soft tissues." The result: vesico-vaginal fistula, caused not by the forceps, but by the hesitation of the physician to use them.[12]

[10] Jane S. Heald, "Obstetrics" (M.D. thesis, Woman's Medical College of Pennsylvania, 1855); Phoebe Wilson, "Disquisition on Parturition" (M.D. thesis, Woman's Medical College of Pennsylvania, 1857). For a general overview, see Wertz and Wertz, *Lying-In*.

[11] Phoebe Oliver, "Eclampsia" (M.D. thesis, Woman's Medical College of Pennsylvania, 1869); Katharine D. Perry, "Puerperal Troubles" (M.D. thesis, Woman's Medical College of Pennsylvania, 1887); Louise Schneider, "Anaesthesia in Natural Labor" (M.D. thesis, Woman's Medical College of Pennsylvania, 1859).

[12] Lucy R. Weaver, "Symptoms of Puerperal Peritonitis" (M.D. thesis, Woman's Medical College of Pennsylvania, 1879); Mary Jordan Finley, "On Vesico Vaginal Fistula" (M.D. thesis, Woman's Medical College of Pennsylvania, 1880). See also Margaret Hoeflich, "Eclampsia" (M.D. thesis, Woman's Medical College of Pennsylvania, 1872–1873); Laura V. Gustin, "A Thesis on Interference in Natural Labor" (M.D. thesis, Woman's Medical College of Pennsylvania, 1873).

Articles on childbirth in the *Woman's Medical Journal*, established in 1893, also reflected prevailing wisdom. While old-timers such as Marie Zakrzewska reminded young practitioners that childbirth was "the most natural process in a woman's life" and decried "meddlesome interference," other women physicians shared the attitude of Agnes Eichelberger. Childbirth may be a physiological function, she conceded, but "from the moment of conception to the end of the lying in state, our patient is in danger and it is our duty to protect her."[13]

Eliza Root recommended wide experience in the use of forceps in teaching obstetrics because of the frequency of faulty development of the reproductive system caused by modern civilization. Other women doctors were actually innovative with certain surgical procedures. Anna E. Broomall, who ran the obstetrical service at the Woman's Hospital of the Woman's Medical College of Pennsylvania, was one of the first surgeons of either sex to recommend episiotomy as a safe and justifiable procedure. When she presented her findings to the Philadelphia Obstetrical Society in 1878, she was criticized by the men for too much interference and for needlessly exposing the patient to septic poisoning.[14]

It is important to point out here, however, that both the "natural" and the "medicalized" view of childbirth could be and in fact were used to justify both feminist and antifeminist positions. For example, the women who advocated certain types of interference did so on the grounds that such interference could be liberating—either from pain itself or from male incompetence. The Twilight Sleep movement in the early part of the twentieth century presents an excellent case in point. In this instance women physicians and other feminists campaigning for woman's relief from birth pain pressured the medical profession into using a technique of anesthesia which at the turn of the century had been rejected by male doctors as unreliable and unsafe. In contrast, antifeminist physicians often used intervention as a means of asserting control over the birth process and keeping women in their places.[15]

Even when women physicians remained critical of accepted therapies, they were occasionally confronted with demands from female patients who expected the same heroic dosing performed by the most respected male practitioners. Although the following example does not involve the management of childbirth, it eloquently illustrates this larger point. Soon after she set up

[13] Maria E. Zakrzewska, "Report of One Hundred and Eighty-Seven Cases of Midwifery in Private Practice," *Boston Medical and Surgical Journal*, CXXI (Dec. 1889), 557–60. See also Frances Rutherford, "The Perineum and Its Care during Parturition," *Woman's Medical Journal*, 2 (Feb. 1894), 29–33; Mary Whery, "The Prevention of Lacerations of the Perineum," *ibid.*, 13 (Jan. 1903), 5–6; Agnes Eichelberger, "Prophylaxis in Obstetrics," *ibid.*, 11 (July 1901), 255–58; Eliza Root, "The Study and Teaching of Obstetrics," *ibid.*, 9 (Oct. 1899), 324–28; Prudence Saur, *Maternity: A Book for Every Wife and Mother* (Chicago, 1889), 218–20; Sarah Hackett Stevenson, *Physiology of Woman* (Chicago, 1882), 91.

[14] Root, "Study and Teaching of Obstetrics," 324–28. Anna E. Broomall, "The Operation of Episiotomy as a Prevention of Perineal Ruptures during Labor," *American Journal of Obstetrics and Diseases of Women and Children*, 11 (July 1878), 517–27.

[15] See Wertz and Wertz, *Lying-In*, 150–54, 164–73.

practice in New York City in the 1850s, Elizabeth Blackwell wrote to her sister Emily, who was then studying medicine in Europe:

a lady called on me today three weeks returned [from Paris]. . . . This lady had had the red hot iron applied to the uterus by Jobert, for ulceration, (so she said) and felt so much better that she thinks there is nothing like it, and means to advise all her friends to be scorched—she came to me hoping that I would apply it to a sister-in-law! So Milly you must be prepared to cut and burn, and practice every conceivable abomination, for it is perfectly evident to me that the more unnatural the applications, the more the women like it. This lady was frizzled twice, the smoke filled the room and she is only desirous now to find some one who will practice as Jobert did.

Though historians have accused nineteenth-century surgeons of performing gynecological surgery unnecessarily, there is occasional evidence to suggest that surgeons were often pressured by female patients. Zakrzewska, writing to Elizabeth Blackwell in 1891, noted that women came to the New England Hospital begging for operations "on the slightest cause." Married women "between 28 & 40 years" came in asking for ovariotomes "because causing [*sic*] dismenorrhea & children were not desired." When surgeons were thus tempted, she mused, "do you wonder . . . [that they] go the whole length of disregard for Nature?"[16]

Lay pressure notwithstanding, our study of the medical literature on childbirth suggests that men and women physicians showed no significant theoretical differences in their approach to parturition. Though women physicians expected to take an especial interest in female health, and though this interest led them to reject the most extreme positions on woman's innate physiological infirmity, they nevertheless reflected in their thinking the influence of professional trends and shifts of opinion in generally the same degree as their medical brethren.

Though gender played a small and relatively insignificant part in the theoretical approach of men and women physicians to treatment, it is now necessary to turn to the actual clinical records. Nineteenth-century Boston offers a unique opportunity for the study of the treatment of women. Many hospital records have been preserved and are still available for study. Boston also boasted one of the first hospitals for women and children staffed by women physicians. The New England Hospital, founded by Zakrzewska in 1862, became a showplace for quality medical care in the latter third of the nineteenth century. Ambitious women doctors longed to receive clinical training there, and its teaching program was rigorous and demanding. Standards reflected the very highest of the day. Fortunately, medical, surgical, and obstetrical records for this institution are virtually intact, and if used along with comparable records for the Massachusetts General Hospital and the Boston Lying-In—both teaching factilities for Harvard Medical School—some interesting comparisons can be made.

Although case histories vary in completeness from hospital to hospital, even

[16] Elizabeth Blackwell to Emily Blackwell, Nov. 27, 1854, Blackwell Manuscripts (Library of Congress, Washington); Maria Zakrzewska to Elizabeth Blackwell, March 21, 1891, Blackwell Manuscripts (Schlesinger Library).

carelessly marked records allow the researcher to ask three basic questions. How frequently were certain medical procedures used; did the patients' medical histories dictate any specific treatments; and what was the social profile of the patients receiving such treatment? Without evidence to the contrary, we must assume that the use of any medical procedure was predicated on the patients' medical history. The patients' condition was surely also affected by environmental factors such as housing or diet. This information can be at least partially inferred from the social data available on case records. Data pertaining to the patients' condition and social situation are an invaluable source of control variables.

Our objective was to determine whether women in childbirth were likely to receive treatment from women physicians different from that given by men and to test in as statistically sophisticated a manner as possible the thesis that childbearing women received better care from female physicians. A systematic sequential sample was drawn from maternity cases at the female-run New England Hospital for the period 1873–1899 and Harvard's Boston Lying-In for the period 1887–1899.[17] Three broad areas of medical treatment and outcome were recorded: the incidence of complications among patients, the use of drugs, and the use of physical intervention techniques, particularly forceps. We assumed that any significant differences between hospitals in these areas could be attributed to the sex of the physicians involved if inherent differences in patient population and other non-gender-related institutional differences could be statistically controlled.

This qualification is critical. Nineteenth-century hospitals were institutions of the urban poor, who were by no means a homogeneous group. Nor did nineteenth-century sensibilities perceive the poor as such. This distinction in perception was reflected in the development of two different types of hospitals. On the one hand stood the free municipal hospital, a medical almshouse which represented a refuge of last resort for the chronically ill and indigent. The private or "voluntary" hospital, in contrast, ministered to a paying clientele or to the "industrious and worthy" poor who came to fill its endowed beds.[18] Though Boston Lying-In and New England Hospital were both voluntary institutions, evidence reveals that there were important differences in their clienteles.

Hospital records and annual reports indicate that the "worthiness" of patients was an appreciably more significant factor in New England Hospital admissions policy than at Boston Lying-In. New England Hospital patients generally paid at least a nominal fee for the medical services they received. At Boston Lying-In, only 23 percent were paying patients. Like the male-run Boston Lying-In, the female-run New England Hospital normally refused obstetric service to unwed mothers bearing their second illegitimate child. Unlike Boston Lying-In, the proportion of single mothers at New England Hospital declined throughout the time period studied. One of the hospital's

[17] Case records are available only after 1887 for Boston Lying-In Hospital.

[18] Charles E. Rosenberg, "And Heal the Sick: The Hospital and the Patient in 19th Century America," *Journal of Social History*, 10 (June 1977), 428–47.

senior physicians, Emma Call, referred to this trend when she noted that after the hospital moved to suburban Roxbury in 1871, "the class of patients was . . . a much better one, and we have never had any number of the most undesirable cases, which inevitably gravitate to an institution located in the midst of a dense population."[19]

This concern with the "worthiness" of patients corroborates impressionistic evidence gathered from other sources that women physicians showed a greater interest than the male physicians at Boston Lying-In in moral reform and in providing a Christian atmosphere for erring patients. These women preferred to treat the respectable poor because they were amenable to change. One is tempted to speculate that the male physicians viewed their role in the hospital from a narrower perspective. As Charles Rosenberg has recently pointed out, hospital internships were plums for the ambitious and economically secure and were procured only with difficulty. Young men of good family and appropriate social connections vied for the opportunity to gain prestige and essential clinical experience.[20] Though women physicians also came to the New England Hospital to gain needed clinical experience, internship was not for them a ticket to a prestigious medical practice. In fact, they realized that their scope and power within the larger profession would always be circumscribed. Perhaps such circumstances freed them to view patients as more than just clinical material and to seek personal fulfillment in a more holistic approach.

Whatever the explanation for these differences, clearly discernible here is a conflict between old and new concepts of professionalism. In the middle of the nineteenth century, doctors of both sexes believed in the medically curative powers of morality and natural living—a belief that technocratic male physicians increasingly abandoned after the 1880s. The differences in approach suggest that male doctors surrendered their concern with morality more quickly than did the women. One can only speculate why female physicians clung to traditional values, although we strongly suspect that it had much to do with Victorian culture's identification of women as the moral guardians of society.[21]

Whatever the reasons, the patient selectivity on the part of New England Hospital means that other differences between the hospitals will be partially obscured by inherent differences in the patient populations. Both groups of

[19] Emma L. Call, "The Evolution of Modern Maternity Technic," *American Journal of Obstetrics and Diseases of Women and Children*, LVIII (Sept. 1908), 392–404. For an explicit statement of Marie Zakrzewska's philosophy concerning the hospital's admission practices, see her comments in New England Hospital, Annual Report (1868), 9–21, (Sophia Smith Collection, Smith College Archives, Northampton, Mass.). Virtually every New England Hospital annual report contains rather self-conscious testimony concerning the advantages of the hospital's Christian atmosphere. For examples, see New England Hospital, Annual Report (1873) 5–7; *ibid.* (1880), 5–9.

[20] Rosenberg, "And Heal the Sick," 488.

[21] See Regina Markell Morantz, "'The Connecting Link': The Case for the Woman Doctor in 19th Century American Medicine," in *Sickness and Health in America: Readings in the History of Medicine and Public Health*, ed. Judith Walzer Leavitt and Ronald Numbers (Madison, Wisc., 1978), 117–28.

patients were undoubtedly poor, but Boston Lying-In's were poorer. There was a substantial social distance between doctor and patient at both hospitals, but probably less of one at a hospital staffed by women physicians, many of whom were upwardly mobile and of a lower status than the elite physicians of Boston Lying-In.

This socioeconomic difference in patient populations also indicated that New England Hospital patients should have had an advantage, however slight, in their general medical condition. The sex of the physician in this case has introduced something of a tautological pattern into the data. That is, women physicians attracted a somewhat different type of patient, with somewhat different medical and social problems, which in turn affected the type of medicine women doctors practiced.

The sheer amount of information on the hospital records implies another broad difference between Boston Lying-In and New England Hospital. The latter's records appeared consistently more complete. In addition to the record of actual treatment, they provided a greater amount of information regarding patients' medical backgrounds (for example, general physical condition, number of prior miscarriages) and more complete information regarding social status.

This relatively meticulous record keeping reveals the self-conscious professionalism typical of women physicians, but it also indicates a "leveling" process at work in the Boston Lying-In. The women doctors at New England Hospital made an attempt to know who they were treating and distinguished, at least in their records, between various levels of poverty. The lack of similar distinctions at Boston Lying-In implies that poor women treated in an often overcrowded teaching facility may very well have represented a single category to the male physicians. Interestingly enough, case records were scrupulously complete when male Boston Lying-In physicians presided at the home deliveries of middle-class women.[22]

The impression that male physicians lumped the poor together finds support in the fact that the maternal recuperative period at the Boston Lying-In was a standard two weeks with very little variation. The hospital's annual reports indicate regret that overcrowding made this policy necessary. However unavoidable, it stands in marked contrast to New England Hospital practice. New England Hospital patients remained under care for from four days to three months and were, on the average, under medical supervision over one week longer than their Boston Lying-In counterparts, even during the identical time period (1887–1899). Perhaps this variation can be attributed to a greater sensitivity to individual physical considerations coupled with the availability of space. But the evidence also suggests social considerations. Single mothers normally remained under medical care longer, perhaps because they had nowhere else to go or because the women doctors of New England Hospital felt such patients required more of the hospital's meliorative moral influence. Bits

[22] See Boston Lying-In Hospital, outpatient records (Countway Library, Harvard Medical School, Boston).

and pieces of evidence suggest that we must consider the medical variables with the recognition that women physicians were concerned with their patients' social situations. This factor alone implies a very different subjective experience for each group of patients.

We may assume that a parturient woman's concerns centered on the medical outcome for herself and her child. Regarding infant mortality, the rates at the two hospitals are roughly comparable: 6 percent at the woman-run New England Hospital and 8.5 percent at the male Boston Lying-In. This slight difference is not significant, though there is an idiosyncratic, and presently inexplicable, pattern at Boston Lying-In. Over three-quarters of the infant deaths in the sample occurred in 1895 or later.

As far as maternal outcome is concerned, only two deaths were reported in each hospital's sample. Of greater interest was the relative incidence of delivery-related complications. For the purposes of comparison, we divided maternal complications into types: those labeled infection or systemic complications such as fever, pain, general infection, and puerperal infection, and those categorized as traumas or injuries such as ruptured perineums, fistulas, or lacerations. When the complications for hospitals are compared for the identical time period, there is no statistical difference in the success of each hospital's therapeutics. (See appendix, Table 1.) The state of the medical art, rather than the sex of the physicians, seems to be the logical determinant of the outcome for the obstetric patient.

This analysis, however, confronts the issue of complications only in general terms. We next asked whether any particular group of women was more likely to suffer. In particular, we were concerned with the impact of nationality and marital status on the patient's care. Accordingly, we compared the complication rates among American single, American married, foreign single, and foreign married women (Table 2). Analyzed in this fashion, a distinctive pattern emerges. At Boston Lying-In, we found no significantly higher complication patterns among any of the four groups of women. This information appears consistent with either the observation that Boston Lying-In doctors recognized no particular nuance of social status among their patients or the possibility that there was objectively little difference in the patients' social circumstances. For patients at New England Hospital, however, the complication rate among foreign single women is nearly double that of any other group.

The explanation for this pattern is more likely to be found in social than in medical factors. Single foreign women were twice as likely to be admitted in the New England Hospital's earlier period—that is, prior to 1887—than later. Furthermore, these women suffered a disproportionate number of systemic or infection types of complications. Such complications are as likely to be caused by the patient's prior state of health as by medical treatment per se. Given the fact that over 90 percent of these women worked at menial tasks, the probability exists that environmental factors such as diet and cleanliness were of significance in their medical outcomes. It should be noted that this group of women fared considerably better in the second half of the time period when the state of medical art had improved. But significantly, they and working women in general were a smaller proportion of the hospital's population at the end of the century. We are left with the conclusion that the New England Hospital was indeed drawing, if not a "better," at least a healthier class of women—that is, more homemakers of any nationality and fewer domestics and factory operatives.

Did the sex of the physicians have any bearing on the medical outcome for their patients? The answer is that it did, but only to a small extent and only in an indirect manner. On the issue of complications, the difference between male and female physicians lies less in their medical practice than in the types of hospital and patient populations with which they worked.

A second concern was the treatment offered patients after delivery, particularly prescriptions for relief. In this instance, a strong pattern of differences emerged which can be more directly related to medical policy within the two hospitals.

By the 1870s heroic medicine was on the decline. Large doses of painful and life-threatening therapies were generally avoided by the physician conscious of changing medical trends. Nevertheless, drugs were often deemed necesary. We surmised that drugs would be given in direct proportion to the severity of the complaint, and that women physicians, who had often decried heroic procedures, would be more conservative in their prescriptions. The hospital records revealed precisely the opposite pattern.

We calculated the proportion of women at each hospital receiving certain types of medication, ranging from supportive types such as beef tea to strong and "heroic" types of medication[23] (Table 3). Nearly two thirds of all Boston Lying-In patients received no medication whatsoever from their male physicians, and the statistical correlations revealed that the use of drugs was strongly predicated on the occurrence and severity of complications. At the New England Hospital, every patient was given some form of medication by the women doctors, usually in the range of what was classified as mild to strong pharmaceuticals. Moreover, the prescription of drugs at the New England Hospital did not correlate decisively with any discernible medical factors, meaning that drug prescriptions for postdelivery women were simply standard procedure among women physicians. In short, the male Boston Lying-In physicians followed an objective model: drug prescription was dependent on the physical symptoms. The implied corollary here is that women physicians dispensed medication for less codifiable and nonphysical reasons.

However, an alternative explanation is also possible. While it may be that most of the Boston Lying-In patients were protected from needless medication, it is also possible that they were virtually ignored after delivery. The scanty medical charts certainly suggest this to be the case. At the least, New England

[23] In this sample, "heroic" medicine was defined as any dosage of extremely harsh remedies, such as calomel or opium.

Hospital's medication policy implies an alternative ethos concerning the needs of postdelivery women, and the greater prescription of medication by women doctors may be the objective indicator of more patient-doctor contact. If this speculation is correct, then the female physicians were exhibiting a concept of professionalism which deemed supportive therapy as important to the patient as purely technical concerns.

The third factor under consideration was the relative use of intervention techniques, particularly forceps, upon parturient women. This area is easily the most controversial since it is one of the main issues on which recent historians have based their case that male physicians were arrogantly insensitive to the needs of maternity patients. In particular, the use of forceps is symbolic of the definition of childbirth as a doctor-controlled medical crisis. Hypothetically, women physicians, because they were women, were more sympathetic to the concept of childbirth as a natural process and hence were less prone to resort to instrumental interference in delivery.

Examined over the entire time period, the data revealed no dramatic difference in the relative willingness of doctors at either hospital to resort to intervention techniques. At New England Hospital roughly 18 percent of the patients received anesthetic, forceps, or both. The comparable figure for Boston Lying-In is 20 percent. When we consider only forceps, the rate at New England Hospital is 9.5 percent; at Boston Lying-In it is 13.5 percent. Neither difference is statistically significant.[24]

In addition, medical criteria for forceps use were similar at both hospitals. The labors of those women involved in forceps deliveries were significantly longer than the average, probably because most were bearing their first child. Moreover, these women tended to receive stronger medication in the recuperative period. Finally, the use of forceps increased gradually at both hospitals in the last decade of the nineteenth century. This fact suggests that once sepsis could be controlled forceps deliveries became more likely.

There is, however, a notable difference in the two hospitals' relative success with the forceps. While both institutions resorted to instrumental deliveries with roughly the same frequency, the forceps patients at Boston Lying-In experienced a higher complication rate than did other women at the hospital. No such differential pattern emerged at New England Hospital (Tables 4 and 5). There are at least two possible explanations for this situation. The New England Hospital doctors may have handled forceps cases more carefully than their male counterparts. Or the Boston Lying-In forceps patients might have been in relatively poorer health than their New England Hospital counterparts.

On the issue of puerperal fever, several historians have charged male physicians with negligence in correcting their role in transmitting the dreaded

[24] Our choice of statistical methods was dictated to some degree by the relative paucity of data on the Boston Lying-In case records. We limited our direct comparisons between hospitals to tests for significant differences in the frequency of occurrence for which chi square tests of independence were used. For analyses of data within each hospital, we used a variety of methods. In all instances where a significant difference is either claimed or rejected, a probability level of .05 was the minimum level accepted.

disease. It is true that Boston Lying-In had more difficulty controlling puerperal infection than did New England Hospital. Before the introduction of successful antiseptic techniques there in 1885, the hospital had been forced to close three times because of epidemics, in contrast to once at New England Hospital. More lives were lost at the male-run hospital. Why did this occur, and can it in any way be attributed to differences in approach by male and female physicians? One researcher claimed that Boston Lying-In's comparatively poorer record in preventing sepsis stemmed from the staff's stubborn reluctance to accept the nurses' and physicians' role as possible sources of infection, whereas women physicians at New England Hospital were more willing "to view themselves as fallible."[25]

An examination of the annual reports of the two hospitals suggests that their divergent records on the fever may not be directly related to the sex of the physicians in charge, but rather may originate in complex causes relating to hospital architecture and finances, the personalities and experience of the resident physicians, and blind luck. Although New England Hospital did not institute successful antisepsis until 1884 and Boston Lying-In until 1886, the doctors at both hospitals experimented vigorously with different methods for several years prior to those dates. The annual reports of Boston Lying-In make it clear that sepsis remained a grave problem which was dealt with vigorously, if not always effectively.[26] W. L. Richardson, chief of obstetrics, outlined the hospital's frustrating search for an effective method in an article published in 1887. The procedures used at New England Hospital paralleled those at the other hospital, except that New England Hospital instituted the use of bichloride of mercury, which ultimately proved the most effective, two years before Boston Lying-In. This method, ironically enough, probably came to the attention of the women physicians earlier because many were forced, because of discrimination, to seek postgraduate training in Europe, where more advanced opinions regarding the bacterial nature of infection prevailed.[27]

Yet before 1884 the New England Hospital had a demonstrably superior mortality rate from puerperal sepsis. Why? The answer seems to lie primarily with both Zakrzewska's ideas about maternity care and her greater power to implement them. Before coming to America, Zakrzewska studied clinical midwifery with J. H. Schmidt at the Royal Charité, Berlin's largest and most prestigious lying-in hospital. In 1853, her outstanding work led to her ap-

[25] This argument was made by Crumpacker, "Female Patients." See also Branca, *Silent Sisterhood*, 86–90; Walsh, *Doctors Wanted*, 93–95.

[26] See New England Hospital, Annual Report (1879), 8–9; *ibid.* (1880), 7–13; *ibid.* (1885), 7; *ibid.* (1886), 7–8; *ibid.* (1888), 8–9; W. L. Richardson, "The Use of Antiseptics in Obstetric Practice," *Boston Medical and Surgical Journal*, CXVI (Jan. 1887), 73–79; Boston Lying-In Hospital Annual Report (1874) (Countway Library), 5–6; *ibid.* (1879), 7–8; *ibid.* (1881), 7.

[27] Call, "Evolution of Modern Maternity Technic," 392–404. Zakrzewska wrote, "Our best women physicians have been educated there [Switzerland] as well as in Germany and in France—for even these two latter countries have received women into their schools more on an equality with men than has America." She said they returned "with a higher standard of scientific learning" than in America. See Agnes C. Victor, ed., *A Woman's Quest: The Life of Marie E. Zakrzewska, M.D.* (New York, 1924), 359.

pointment as accoucheuse-en-chef, a position that required teaching both midwifery candidates and medical students. Here she had an opportunity to develop strong opinions regarding proper delivery and efficient means of avoiding sepsis. Thus, although the woman's hospital was no more enlightened on the actual source of infection in the years before the discoveries of bacteriologists, it implemented Zakrzewska's prejudices, which happened to be empirically, if not necessarily scientifically, sound.[28]

In the annual report for 1868, she discussed her ideas concerning the proper organization of lying-in hospitals. Experiments had been conducted in Europe, she wrote, but so far no one knew exactly how to avoid the fever. She advised caution. Lying-in institutions should be small, spread throughout the city, and retain separate wards for isolation cases. She then detailed the ideal set-up—a room for women in labor, two rooms for delivery used alternatively, and still another for convalescents—thus keeping women at different stages of childbirth separated from each other. She also proposed isolation procedures, including requiring nurses and physicians treating fever cases to be disqualified from the normal deliveries.[29] Zakrzewska may have been ignorant of germ theory, but she did everything she could think of in the area of prevention. When the new hospital buildings were completed in Roxbury at the end of 1872, the lying-in facilities followed her plan.

In practice these procedures could not consistently be followed to the letter. Demand for space usually exceeded the supply, partly because New England Hospital, in contrast to Boston Lying-In, did not always release patients after the standard two weeks. And even with all their precautions, New England Hospital was not immune from epidemics of puerperal fever. In 1872 the lying-in wards temporarily closed because of a scourge which killed four patients.[30] Yet for severe problems New England Hospital at least owned an isolation cottage, something Boston Lying-In never had.

The trustees of Boston Lying-In wrote in 1874 of the desirability of small contiguous dwellings and isolation wards. Yet their cautious financial policies, which probably derived from the fact that the hospital had been forced to close in the 1860s because the trustees had overextended themselves financially with an ambitious building program, never allowed them to implement these goals.[31] Boston Lying-In functioned primarily on income from investments, whereas New England Hospital depended mostly on donations. Although their budgets were roughly comparable, New England Hospital exhibited a boldness in management which reflected more active and more consistent support from wealthy subscribers. At the very least, the two hospitals' funding practices represented entirely different philosophies regarding financial management.[32]

[28] For an account of the staff's ignorance of theory and the hit-and-miss approach before bacteriology, see Call, "Evolution of Modern Maternity Technic," 392–404.

[29] New England Hospital, Annual Report (1868), 12, 18.

[30] *Ibid.* (1872), 11.

[31] Boston Lying-In Hospital, Annual Report (1874), 5–6.

[32] New England Hospital, Annual Report (1879), 19–23; Boston Lying-In Hospital, Annual Report (1879), 13.

Boston Lying-In's failure to implement in practice what its medical staff recognized in theory was suggested by Zakrzewska in her autobiography. She claimed that the women physicians were given much more power to carry out policy decisions:

> Our Hospital is utterly different from all hospitals carried on by the City or the State or by private individuals and endowments.
>
> In these latter there exists either a need to provide for the helpless who are dependent on the Commonwealth, or benevolent persons wish to provide a charity and so they establish hospitals. In both conditions, the staff of physicians is employed by those who manage the institutions and, consequently, either money or thanks are due to such physicians as serve.
>
> With us, it is entirely different. None of our original directors wanted a hospital; none of them was inspired by charity or had the means to provide such charity. I, the representative of an idea in its earliest evolution—I sought those Directors that they might serve the purpose of carrying out that idea.
>
> They served then and in the future the women physicians connected with the Hospital. They never dictated as to the number of physicians or internes; they never proposed to enlarge the work; this has always been done by the professional staff. *We* thank *them* for their generous aid, but they cannot thank us for doing much or little.
>
> Of course, the Directors are the corporate body, and they represent us legally before the public; but they carry out our ideas, not we theirs. They simply stand ready to support the principle of giving to women physicians full opportunity to manifest their skill and judgment.[33]

Thus, although sources indicate that physicians at Boston Lying-In made every attempt within the limitations of their knowledge to control infection, their success was hampered by financial burdens and a decentralized system of authority on policy decisions such as hospital structure that may have been crucial before antisepsis. Perhaps if the male physicians had taken the problem more to heart, they would have been better able to assert pressure on the trustees successfully. In contrast, it seems likely from the history of New England Hospital that the degree of control exercised by the women physicians there derived at least in part from a shared feminist ideology, which of course was conspicuously absent at Boston Lying-In.

This comparative study of male and female physicians' clinical behavior has revealed that as far as the mechanics of obstetric practice are concerned, the complication rates and frequency of forceps use within each hospital indicate a rough parity between the therapeutics of male and female physicians. Drug prescription, in fact, represented the only discernible difference between the two hospitals that can be directly attributed to the sex of the physicians.

Physicians' social attitudes also influenced their medical practice. Our findings suggest that male and female physicians' attitudes toward their professional roles may well have been diverging. As men embraced a more modern, technocratic approach to their patients, women physicians continued to cling to traditional holistic orientations. Thus New England Hospital sought a different type of patient from the Boston Lying-In: the "worthy poor." Its annual reports consistently emphasized the women's concern with the

[33] Vietor, ed., *A Woman's Quest*, 449–50.

hospital's Christian atmosphere. That the obstetric care at the two hospitals was therapeutically similar suggests that the impact of such attitudes remained indirect.

Letters, diaries, written literature, and hospital records have served to illuminate the differences between male and female physicians in their approach to medical care. We see a picture certainly more penetrating than that revealed by what women physicians said and wrote about themselves. The therapeutic similarities remind us that the staff members of New England Hospital were not only women, but doctors as well. As doctors, the New England Hospital staff operated under the dictates of their profession: they viewed themselves as full-fledged health professionals, they read the same journals as the men, and they subscribed to theories that represented the collective wisdom of their group.

Nevertheless, the gender of the physician may well have mattered in more subtle ways. One wishes to believe that some, perhaps most, parturient women were comforted by the attendance of a professional physician of their own sex. Certainly women physicians never forgot that they were women, and it is clear that their interests within medicine as well as their affective behavior as doctors were influenced by that fact. Our study suggests that women physicians probably exhibited a different orientation toward patient care. Thus men and women doctors acted alike in most therapeutic situations, but for very different reasons and with meanings both different to themselves and to their patients. The hospital records offer a final valuable insight into this complex and as yet dimly understood relationship between attitudes and therapeutic behavior. Such evidence suggests that future researchers would do well to at least modify the polarized perspective with which they have hitherto approached the subject of medical treatment for women.

Appendix: Notes on Methodology

Our sample of the case records of the two hospitals is best described as a systematic sequential sample; that is, we drew a random sample of the case records from alternate years. For New England Hospital, this included a sample from the odd-numbered years, 1873–1899, with a total n of 171. For Boston Lying-In, the sample included the alternate years 1887–1899, with a total n of 305. We attempted to codify virtually every piece of information that was available from the case records. One group of variables may be said to be related to the patient's social position and included: marital status, nationality, race, place of residence, and kind of employment (if any). The second group of variables provided the patient's medical profile and included: age, number of living children, miscarriages, stillbirths and/or abortions, general physical condition, the birth presentation of the fetus, length of labor, use of anesthetics or forceps, type of postpartum complication, drugs used after delivery, length of hospital stay, and maternal and infant mortality. We also noted whether the woman paid for hospital services. We attempted to codify the type of comments that the physicians occasionally wrote on the charts, but there were too few to be of any use.

As reported in footnote 24, our ability to analyze the hospital data using multiple regression was hindered by the fact that Boston Lying-In case records were relatively less complete. In particular, we had to exclude from comparison the impact of a woman's prior health condition and the impact, if any, of the patient's employment status, since Boston Lying-In did not usually include such data on their records.

The most obvious discrepancy in our samples is the difference in the time periods studied. As we have noted, data from Boston Lying-In were available beginning with the year 1887. We were concerned whether the New England Hospital data remained consistent throughout the time period or whether we could only legitimately use the data after 1887. Accordingly, we compared the New England Hospital data before 1887 with those from 1887 and later. With two important exceptions, both discussed in the text, the data remained consistent, and we therefore concluded that we could appropriately use the entire sample. The first exception was the aggregate change in the patients' employment status. The number of employed women treated at the New England Hospital declined dramatically from the first half of the sample to the second. In 1873, only 11 percent of the maternity cases in our sample were listed as housewives; by 1899, 63 percent were so listed. Supporting our conclusion that the condition of the patients did improve at the New England Hospital toward century's end, 44 percent were listed in poor condition in 1873; by 1899 only 12 percent were so listed.

The second change over time was the decline in the complication rate at the New England Hospital from 1887 on. This decline is most dramatically shown by comparing the first year of our sample with the last. In our 1873 sample, all patients are listed as having some type of postpartum complication; in 1899, 87 percent are complication-free. Although our decision to compare com-

TABLE 1

Proportion of Patients Suffering Complications, Boston Lying-In versus New England Hospital

	Boston Lying-In Hospital 1887-1899 n = 305	New England Hospital 1873-1899 n = 171	New England Hospital 1873-1885 (n = 72)	New England Hospital) 1887-1899 (n = 99)
Proportion of Patients with No Complications	73.4%	68.4%	59.7%	74.7%
Proportion of Patients with Complications	26.6%	31.6%	40.3%	25.3%
.Proportion with Iniuries!	(7.5%)	(12.3%)	(16.7%)	(9.1%)
.Proportion with Infections)	(19.0%)	(19.3%)	(23.6%)	(16.2%)

Comparison of Boston Lying-In with New England Hospital for the years 1887-1899:

chi square = .066
degrees of freedom = 1
no significant difference

TABLE 2
Proportion of Patients Suffering Complications
by Marital Status/Nationality Groups

	New England Hospital 1873-1899		Boston Lying-In 1887-1899	
	number of women in group	proportion with complications	number of women in group	proportion with complications
Single American Patients	18	27.8%	55	36.4%
Married American Patients	54	24.1%	58	25.9%
Single Foreign Patients	29	55.2%	80	26.2%
Married Foreign Patients	65	27.7%	107	21.0%
Total cases	166	—	300	—
Aggregate complication rate	—	31.3%	—	26.7%

Comparison of differences in the frequency of complications among groups within each hospital:

New England Hospital	*Boston Lying-In*
chi square = 9.39	chi square = 3.59
degrees of freedom = 3	degrees of freedom = 3
probability < .05	no significant difference

TABLE 3
Post-Delivery Drug Prescription,
New England Hospital versus Boston Lying-In

	New England Hospital 1873-1899		Boston Lying-In 1887-1899	
	number of patients	proportion of patients	number of patients	proportion of patients
No Medication Prescribed	0	0%	194	63.6%
General Supportive Treatments	1	.6%	5	1.6%
Mild Pharmaceuticals	89	52.0%	60	19.7%
Strong Medication	74	43.3%	42	13.8%
Heroic Medication	6	3.5%	4	1.3%
Combination of Above	1	.6%	0	0%
Total Cases	171	100.0%	305	100.0%

Comparison of the frequency of drug prescription at the New England Hospital and Boston Lying-In:

chi square = 189.86
degrees of freedom = 5
probability < .05

plication rates from 1887 on was dictated by the availability of Boston Lying-In case records, we feel that the time demarcation is less arbitrary than it first appears. Since successful antisepsis was instituted at both hospitals in the mid-1880s, we were able to compare directly the complication rates during a period immediately after a significant improvement had just been made in obstetrical therapeutics.

Tables 1, 2, and 3 compare the complication rates and drug usage at the two hospitals. To analyze the differences in frequencies we used a chi square test of

TABLE 4
Frequency of Complications among Patients with Different Intervention Treatments, New England Hospital, 1873-1899

	number of patients	number suffering complications	proportion with complications
Patients with No Intervention Treatment	139	45	32.4%
Patients with Intervention Treatment	31	8	25.8%
(Anesthetic Only)	(15)	(4)	(26.7%)
(Forceps Only)	(5)	(1)	(20.0%)
(Both)	(11)	(3)	(27.3%)

Comparison of the frequency of complications between the group of patients with no intervention treatment and the group with one or both types of intervention:

chi square = .51
degrees of freedom = 1
no significant difference

TABLE 5
Frequency of Complications among Patients with Different Intervention Treatments, Boston Lying-In Hospital, 1887-1899

	number of patients	number suffering complications	proportion with complications
Patients with No Intervention Treatment	244	58	23.8%
Patients with Intervention Treatment	61	23	37.7%
(Anesthetic Only)	(20)	(7)	(35.0%)
(Forceps Only)	(20)	(8)	(40.0%)
(Both)	(21)	(8)	(38.1%)

Comparison of frequency of complications between the group of patients with no intervention treatment and the group with one or both types of intervention:

chi square = 4.86
degrees of freedom = 1
probability < .05

independence which has the advantage of correcting for an unequal number of cases.

In order to analyze the relationship between complications and drugs within each hospital, we computed the correlation between the two. We scaled the complications from least to most severe. In ascending order of severity they were: (0) no complications; (1) pain in groin; (2) fever and chills; (3) lacerations of vulva; (4) other—constipation, ulcerations; (5) ruptured perineum; (6) hemorrhaging; (7) vaginal fistula; (8) puerperal fever. In similar fashion, drugs were scaled from mildest to strongest prescription: (0) no drugs; (1) general supportive (teas, rubs); (2) mild pharmaceutical; (3) strong; (4) heroic; (5) combination of the preceding. We admit that the scaling is open to debate. However, the scaled variables did in fact correlate significantly at both hospitals though there was an enormous difference in the relative predictive values of the correlations. When we attempted a multiple regression on drug usage at New England Hospital, we could explain only 4.5 percent of the variance in drug prescription on the basis of complications (multiple R = .21375). In comparison, the same regression performed on the Boston Lying-In data revealed that 38 percent of the variance could be explained solely on the severity of the complication (multiple R = .61691). In neither regression did any other variable add much to the explanation of the variance in a direct—that is, logically causal—way. In this regard, we would have liked to pursue the question of whether complications were related to the patient's prior medical history and/or her socioeconomic status; the gaps in the Boston Lying-In data precluded this line of analysis.

Tables 4 and 5 analyze the differences in complication rates between the group at each hospital that received neither forceps nor anesthetics and the group that received one or both intervention treatments. Once again, a chi square test of independence was used to test for significant differences in frequency of complications.

Finally, by using the scaled complications and a t-test for differences in means, we were also able to calculate whether any intervention group suffered more severe complications than those patients that received neither anesthetic nor forceps.

At New England Hospital there was no significant difference in mean complication severity among the intervention groups. At Boston Lying-In the mean complication for the groups that received forceps or both forceps and anesthetic was significantly higher. For the group labelled "no intervention," the mean on the severity scale was .9. For "anesthetic only," "forceps only," and "both," the means were 1.2, 1.7, and 1.8 respectively. The latter two means are significantly higher at the .05 level. Thus we concluded that at Boston Lying-In, patients who were delivered by forceps were more likely to experience complications and, moreover, were likely to have more severe complications than other patients.

FEMINISM, PROFESSIONALISM, AND GERMS: THE THOUGHT OF MARY PUTNAM JACOBI AND ELIZABETH BLACKWELL

REGINA MARKELL MORANTZ
University of Kansas

ON CHRISTMAS DAY, 1888, DR. MARY PUTNAM JACOBI SAT AT HER DESK TO write a long, frank, and remarkably revealing letter to Elizabeth Blackwell. Although Blackwell was several years her senior, both women belonged to the pioneer generation of women physicians. Blackwell, the first woman to receive a medical degree in the United States, had founded both a hospital and a medical school for women—the New York Infirmary for Women and Children—where Jacobi had been an attending physician and professor of materia medica and therapeutics since 1870. Yet the two women never knew each other well. In 1869, shortly after she established the Woman's Medical College of the New York Infirmary, Blackwell left America and took up permanent residence in England, where she believed she could accomplish more in behalf of women physicians. She consigned the school to the competent administration of her sister Emily (also a physician), and an able faculty, which included Jacobi, a handful of recent graduates, and a few young but sympathetic male physicians.

Both women had fine reputations and were recognized leaders among the rapidly expanding ranks of women physicians. Yet though they admired each other deeply, it is also clear that their cordiality and mutual respect was enhanced rather than hampered by the geographical distance between them. No two temperaments could have differed more profoundly. Jacobi had not a trace of sentimentality about her. Her quick and penetrating intellect cut to the core of things with a rapidity that left lesser minds bewildered. No one valued rational thinking more highly; no one remained more frustrated with mushy generalities that could not be grounded in empirical investigation and factual analysis. Jacobi chose medicine out of a love for scientific rationalism. She adored chemistry and pursued medical study with the joyous abandon of a mind comfortably at home with its rigors.

While attending the Ecole de Medicine in Paris she once sheepishly confessed to her mother that "immersion in technical studies is like arsenic eating,—once begun, you must go on, and at a continually increasing dose. I am really astonished to find how this absorption grows upon me."[1]

Blackwell, in contrast, was nothing if not sentimental. She entered medicine with a perfectionist conception of morality and her own role in the moral universe. Believing that the realm of medicine and health must be a fundamental area of concern for the reformer, she wrote in 1889, "The progress and welfare of society is more intimately bound up with the prevailing tone and influence of the medical profession than with the status of any other class of men."[2] Indeed, Victor Robinson, a younger physician who knew and admired her, called her a "Swedenborgian-theosophical-theological-Christian-metaphysician, instead of just an unadulterated scientist."[3]

To the amused Robinson such failings could be tolerated in great pioneers. But, as Jacobi formulated her thoughts on Christmas morning in 1888, she realized that Blackwell's thinking raised her "antagonistic hairs" particularly because the woman was a pioneer. Sentimentality hurt the cause. Blackwell's preoccupation with the abstract struggle to make a place for women in medicine, Jacobi complained, never allowed her to descend from her vision "into the sphere of practical life within which, that vision if anywhere must be realized. You left that for others to do." What rankled Jacobi most was Blackwell's dominant "mental habit,—principle,—or method, . . . the well known Transcendental method of arriving at conclusions by the force of meditative insight, and then refusing to submit these to tests of verification. Indeed," Jacobi continued upon further reflection,

> it is the latter omission I really object to: the Transcendental vision probably always comes first in all large generalizations. . . . But whether these are to stand as effective truths or not depends upon how far they can bear the tests of close conflicts with facts, with innumerable details: how they can sustain the onslaught of argument and criticism. Your sex, your age, and your cast of mind render all this difficult. . . . You resemble your sister Anna sufficiently to prefer to remain within the sphere of large, often half mystical assertion.

What mystified and frustrated Jacobi was Blackwell's inattention to clinical medicine. "You have always disliked, ignored and neglected medicine!"

[1]Jacobi to Victorine Haven Putnam, 13 Jan. 1870, *Life and Letters of Mary Putnam Jacobi*, ed. Ruth Putnam (New York: G. P. Putnam, 1925), 233.

[2]Elizabeth Blackwell, "The Influence of Women in the Profession of Medicine," in Blackwell, ed., *Essays in Medical Sociology* (1902; rpt. New York: Arno Press, 1972), II, 5–6, 12.

[3] Victor Robinson, *Pathfinders in Medicine* (New York: Medical Life Press, 1929), 673–74.

she wrote, and the "one real occasion where from your position you should have shown me much, yet failed to show me anything, was when I began to study medicine under your direction in New York." Jacobi could sympathize with the "immense" obstacles in the way of Blackwell's reading and being taught medicine at mid-century, but she confessed she had always suspected that her friend's "greatest real difficulty" was "your own intense indifference to the work."[4]

The differences between the two women were partly temperamental. Yet in the last third of the nineteenth century they also reflected tensions within the medical profession created by the new discoveries in immunology and bacteriology. In the decade or so between the time that Blackwell received her medical degree in 1849 and Jacobi entered the Woman's Medical College in Philadelphia in 1864, medicine as an occupation began to merge with medicine as a science. Certainly Jacobi's exposure to the new ideas as a student rather than as a young practitioner may account for the younger woman's greater openness to change. Yet the debate over the role of the physician in specific areas of reform—a debate intensified by findings in the laboratory—was never wholly generational, nor was it ever confined solely to the female portion of the profession.

Yet Jacobi and Blackwell disagreed not only over bacteriology; they also represented variant traditions among women physicians, and their divergences led them on occasion to view the role of the woman physician from slightly different perspectives as well. For both these reasons their lives will be explored in this essay. Women physicians, by nature of their being physicians, ranged themselves on different sides of the controversies shared by their medical brethren. Yet by virtue of their being women, they also faced dilemmas from which their male colleagues were spared. Most of these centered around the fact of their womanhood and its meaning with regard to their larger connection with the profession.

* * *

One of the most bewildering controversies to twentieth-century observers remains the reluctance of many nineteenth-century physicians and public health advocates to accept the discoveries of the bacteriologists. How could such men and women persist in speaking of "effluvia," "miasma," and "filth" when the precise experimentation of Pasteur, Koch, and their followers had, by reproducing various diseases in the laboratory and identifying various "germs," ushered in the concept of "specific etiology?"

[4]Jacobi to Blackwell, 25 Dec. 1888, Blackwell Manuscripts, Library of Congress, Washington, D.C.

To make sense of the sanitarians' objections we must remember that bacteriological concepts called into question an older and deeply internalized view of disease which was holistic in its scope, moralistic in its implications, and fundamentally religious in its point of departure. In the minds of many sanitarians, Elizabeth Blackwell included, health was the natural order of things, a gift to be enjoyed by people if they governed their lives wisely and well. Disease was neither the arbitrary visitation of an angry God nor the quixotic outcome of blind fate, but rather the inevitable result of one's violation of the laws of nature made manifest by a benevolent deity. Disease, so often equated in their cosmology with sin, was permitted by God to exist, but conscience and revelation on the one hand and reason and science on the other were the tools provided by Him for men and women to combat these evils. The task of medicine was to reveal and teach the laws by which people could ensure the proper balance between environment and individual behavior.

From our perspective, nineteenth-century sanitarians may have been scientifically naive, but their ideas exhibited an internal consistency that linked together a perfectionist world view with the more personal concerns of men and women interested in active and dramatic social reform. They reasoned that since disease was always accompanied by ugliness, want, and pollution, health could be achieved by replacing these modern blights with the pure food, air, water, and pleasant surroundings enjoyed in the preindustrial age.[5]

To be sure, the tension between environmentalism and the concept of specific etiology, which agitated the medical community at the end of the nineteenth-century both in America and abroad, generally represented different points of view on a continuum rather than a conflict between two opposing camps. As early as the 1840s and 1850s individual physicians spoke of "germs," and used the term to identify a cause of disease that defied mere cleanliness and purity and suggested further that conscience and clean living were not always enough.[6] Enlightened American physicians like Lemuel Shattuck or Henry Ingersoll Bowditch, for example, carefully balanced traditional sanitation theory, with its emphasis on filth, against new concepts pointing to a specific microbial invader. Nevertheless, the social implications of the two poles of thought can be usefully contrasted. Blackwell,

[5]See Rene Dubos, *Mirage of Health* (New York: Harper and Row, 1959), 117–18.

[6]See Barbara Rosenkrantz, *Public Health and the State* (Cambridge: Harvard Univ. Press, 1972), 74–96, 177–85; Charles Rosenberg, *The Cholera Years* (Chicago: Univ. of Chicago Press), 1962, passim; and Rosenberg, "Florence Nightingale on Contagion: The Hospital as a Moral Universe," in Rosenberg, ed., *Healing and History; Essays for George Rosen* (New York: Neale Watson, 1979), 116–36.

perhaps because her scientific opinions exhibited none of the subtlety of contemporaries like Shattuck, Bowditch, or Mary Putnam Jacobi, stands as an appropriate representative of an older, more conservative tradition, still unmoved by the startling new discoveries of laboratory experimentation.

One clue to Blackwell's thinking lies in the fact that her interest in moral reform antedated her attraction to medicine. In part this was due to her remarkable family background. The children of the abolitionist Samuel Blackwell immersed themselves in the traditions of Christian perfectionism and reformist activity. Elizabeth's brothers, Henry and Samuel, supported antislavery and women's rights: the former married the feminist Lucy Stone and the latter married Antoinette Brown, the first formally ordained woman minister in the United States. Sister Emily also became a physician, and another sister, Anna, a poet and translator. Several family members dabbled in spiritualism. Blackwell's approach to medical issues confidently bore the stamp of her family's progressive tendencies.

The idea of studying medicine did not come easily to Blackwell, for she admitted in her autobiography that as a young adult she "hated everything connected with the body" and "the very thought of dwelling on ... its various physical ailments filled me with disgust." Yet other circumstances pushed her toward her life's work. One was her burning desire for engrossing, ennobling activity. When a close friend dying of what was probably uterine cancer urged upon Blackwell the thought that her worst sufferings would have been alleviated had she been treated by a woman physician, Elizabeth could no longer "put the idea . . . away." She knew even then that the term "female physician" referred primarily at that time to abortionists, the most notorious of whom was New York's Madame Restell. Such misuse of female power directly offended her growing mystical fascination with what she later termed "the spiritual power of maternity." The Madame Restells of the world represented "the gross perversion and destruction" of womanhood, and "utter degradation of what might and should become a noble position for women." With determination she concluded to do what she could to "'redeem the hells, ... especially the one form of hell thus forced upon my notice.'"[7]

·Blackwell seems to have consciously chosen a life that would protect her from marriage and intimacy with men. Her autobiography reveals that her

[7]For a fascinating view of the effects of Blackwell's family life on her psychology, see Margo Horn, "The Effect of Family Life on Women's Role Choices: The Case of the Blackwell Women," paper delivered at the Fourth Berkshire Conference on the History of Women, Mount Holyoke College, 23–25 Aug. 1978. See also Elizabeth Blackwell, *Pioneer Work in Opening the Medical Profession to Women* (1895; rpt. New York: Schocken, 1977), 27; and Nancy Sahli, "Elizabeth Blackwell, M.D.: A Biography," Diss. Univ. of Pennsylvania 1974.

choice of career came in part from her susceptibility to the "disturbing influence exercised by the other sex." Although she was constantly "falling in love," she shrank from the implications of those feelings, "repelled" by the idea of intimacy and a "life association." Soon after seizing upon the idea of medical practice, she confided to her journal:

> I felt more determined than ever to become a physician, and thus place a strong barrier between me and all ordinary marriage. I must have something to engross my thoughts, some object in life which will fill this vacuum and prevent this sad wearing away of the heart.[8]

Blackwell often used a traditionally religious vocabulary to articulate these goals. She turned for aid "to that Friend with whom I am beginning to hold true communion," and shortly after she began preparing for her future course her fears and doubts were dispelled by a mystical experience which left her confident that her individual work was divinely inspired and "in accordance with the great providential ordering of our race's progress."[9] This conversion of religious impulses into paths of professional activity was characteristic of many sanitarians during the antebellum period, both in America and in England.[10]

Similar themes pervaded Blackwell's writings as she formulated her two major concerns, the role of the physician in society and the place of women in the profession. Because her approach to disease was holistic, she argued that the physician had more to do than cure. She constantly spoke of the union of the spiritual and the physical, warning her students frequently against the dangers of materialism. "True science," she wrote, "supports the noblest intuitions of humanity, and its tendency is to furnish proof suited to our age of these intuitions." When "the recognition of the higher facts of consciousness is obscured, and the physician is unable to perceive life more real than the narrow limits of sensation," she warned, the loss to practical medicine was "immense."[11]

The bacteriologists obscured "the higher facts of consciousness" because bacteriology *appeared* to develop at the expense of sanitation, hygiene, preventive medicine, and most important, morality itself. By equating dis-

[8]Blackwell, *Pioneer Work*, pp. 28.

[9]Ibid., 35.

[10]Lloyd Stevenson, "Science Down the Drain: On the Hostility of Certain Sanitarians to Animal Experimentation, Bacteriology and Immunology," *Bulletin of the History of Medicine*, 29 (Jan-Feb 1955), 1-26; Charles Rosenberg and Carroll Smith-Rosenberg, "Pietism and the Origins of the American Public Health Movement: A Note on John H. Griscom and Robert M. Hartley," *Journal of the History of Medicine*, 23 (Spring 1968), 16-35.

[11]Blackwell, "The Influence of Women," 26-27.

ease with a specific microbial invader, laboratory scientists seemed to be challenging the older view of health as equilibrium and threatening the work of those reformers who supported massive sanitary measures to remove the filth, want, and pollution that they believed caused disease. The traditional art of medicine, whose monistic pathologies bid the physician treat only after a careful balance of emotional, environmental, and physio-psychological factors, was rendered obsolete. Not laboratory experimentation, dissented Blackwell, but "pure air, cleanliness, and decent house-room secured to all ... form the true prophylaxis of small-pox."[12] "The arbitrary distinction," she continued elsewhere, "between the physician of the body and the physician of the soul ... tends to disappear as science advances."[13]

Blackwell continued to explore these themes when she turned her attention to the role of women in the profession. In 1889 she wrote that the sense of right and wrong must constantly govern medical research and practice, "the Moral must guide the Intellectual, or there is no halting-pace in the rapid incline to error." Because she believed that women innately exhibited a higher moral sense than did men, she saw the role of medical women as integral to the proper and healthy progress of the profession as a whole. Indeed, a "distinguishing characteristic" of the nineteenth century, she argued, was the "increasing devotion of women to the relief of social suffering" through the "spiritual power of maternity." By this she meant

> the subordination of self to the welfare of others; the recognition of the claim which helplessness and ignorance make upon the stronger and more intelligent; the joy of creation and bestowal of life; the pity and sympathy which tend to make every woman the born foe of cruelty and injustice.

Women were accomplishing great deeds. Such "spiritual mothers of the race," she judged "often more truly incarnations of the grand maternal life, than those who [were] technically mothers in the lower physical sense."[14]

Women physicians, she argued, had to monitor medical progress so that it did not violate moral truth. "Whatever revolts our moral sense as earnest women," she reminded her students, "is not in accordance with steady progress . . ." and "cannot be permanently true." It was through the "moral,

[12]Elizabeth Blackwell, "Why Hygienic Congresses Fail," in *Essays on Medical Sociology*, II, 73.

[13]Blackwell, "The Influence of Women," 5–6. See also Blackwell, "The Human Element in Sex," in *Essays in Medical Sociology*, I, 69.

[14]Blackwell, "The Influence of Women," 10, 13, 21.

guiding the intellectual," that the "beneficial influence of women in any new sphere of activity" would be felt.[15]

Bacteriology and its penchant for vaccination offended Blackwell because its concept of specific etiology undermined her sense of the moral order. A concomitant of modern laboratory science, animal experimentation represented something much worse: the triumph of the intellect over morality. Blackwell probably opposed vaccination primarily because early in her practice she lost a young child whom she had vaccinated against small pox. Vivisection, however, represented to her an attempt to do good by evil means. Animal experimentation, she felt, hardened the heart, blunted the moral sense, and injured the "intelligent sympathy with suffering" which was the mark of a good physician. Ultimately it led to the dangerous habit of treating the poor and helpless with indifference, by regarding them merely as "clinical material." Blackwell regretted this tendency particularly among younger physicians, and she felt it the responsibility of women doctors to discourage such inhumane practices. In 1891 she addressed a letter of protest to the Alumnae Association of the Woman's Medical College of the New York Infirmary in which she opposed their endowment of a new experimental laboratory. She reminded her female colleagues of their "duty" as potential mothers to oppose the cruelty and narrow materialism of which, to her mind, the new laboratory was symbolic.[16]

Blackwell even connected the corruption of the moral sense resulting from "unrestrained experiment on the lower animals" to the increase in gynecological surgery at the end of the century. To her, ovariotomy represented "mutilation" and was especially heinous because it rendered women incapable of having children. Again she looked to women physicians to remind the profession that "moral error may engender intellectual error," and talked often of returning to the United States to rally women's attention on these issues.[17]

Fascinated and energized by recent events in laboratory medicine, Mary Putnam Jacobi could muster little enthusiasm for Blackwell's views. In her private life she too confronted the moral dilemmas of the reformer, and she enthusiastically supported numerous meliorist efforts, including the Consumer's League, woman's suffrage, and the reform of primary education in

[15]Ibid. See also Blackwell, "Why Hygienic Congresses Fail," passim.

[16]Ibid. On antivivisection, see Richard D. French, *Antivivisection and Medical Science in Victorian Society* (Princeton: Princeton Univ. Press, 1975); James Turner, *Reckoning with the Beast: Animals, Pain, and Humanity in the Victorian Mind* (Baltimore: Johns Hopkins Univ. Press, 1980). Also see Elizabeth Blackwell, "Scientific Method in Biology," in *Essays in Medical Sociology*, II, 119, 90.

[17]Blackwell, "Scientific Method in Biology," II, 119, 90.

the direction of manual training and physical culture. Yet though she understood that the pursuit of truth could never be divorced totally from moral life, she approached the acquisition of medical knowledge as something quite independent of morality. Believing in science with an earnestness that was almost religious, she nevertheless remained uncomfortable with Blackwell's traditional religious vocabulary, and she viewed scientific research as an absolute good because it added to the fund of human knowledge.

As a young medical student, Jacobi had written her mother that her vision of Heaven was "simply the Region of Pure Thought" emancipated from "the overwhelming dominion of personal emotion and instinct." Her desire to pursue a scientific career developed early and she hesitated only when deciding whether to concentrate on medical practice or laboratory research. The oldest daughter of the publisher George Palmer Putnam, Jacobi, like Blackwell, received considerable support from her family. Although the Putnams were not active reformers, they were nevertheless New Englanders who remained sympathetic to the meliorist causes of the day. Mary's Aunt Elizabeth Peabody, for example, kept her in touch with every new social "ism." Yet Mary remained too hardheaded and practical to identify herself with trends and fads. She once wrote to her mother, "I detest vulgarity, pretention, . . . inanity, twaddle, insipidity and pretention in velvet. I will have none of either. No homeopaths, no spiritualists, few 'female' orators. . . ."[18]

The Putnams were not pleased with their daughter's choice of career, but their disappointment did not hinder their providing emotional and material support. Jacobi's father considered medical science to be a "repulsive pursuit," but nevertheless took great pride in Mary's success. He begged only that she shun the company of "strong-minded women! . . . (your self-will and independence . . . are strong enough already)," and that she preserve her "feminine character." "Be a lady from the dotting of your i's to the color of your ribbons," he wrote to her in 1863, soon after she began her studies at the Woman's Medical College of Pennsylvania, "and if you must be a doctor and a philosopher, be an attractive and agreeable one."[19]

Jacobi appreciated and respected her parents' advice because she understood the significance of their liberalism with regard to her aspirations. "You have always been such a dear good father . . . ," she once wrote to George Putnam. "The more I see of other people's way of doing, the more highly I value the large liberty in which you have always left me. It has occasioned

[18]Jacobi to Victorine Haven Putnam, 17 Aug. 1869, *Life and Letters*, 216.
[19]George Palmer Putnam to Jacobi, undated letter, 1863, *Life and Letters*, 67.

certain mistakes, but on the whole, the advantage has infinitely outweighed the disadvantage. I do not see how I could have lived without it."[20]

Their tolerance of her plans was indeed remarkable for Victorian parents. Jacobi was headstrong, and she spent long years stubbornly pursuing her goals—years that the oldest girl of an upper middle-class New York family might have passed making more of a contribution to home life as daughter, sister, and, eventually, wife. After receiving a degree in 1863 from the New York College of Pharmacy, Jacobi attended the Woman's Medical College of Philadelphia and was graduated a year later, the only student in the history of the school to write her thesis in Latin. She spent the next several months studying clinical medicine with Marie Zakrzewska and Lucy Sewall at the New England Hospital for Women and Children. Yet neither experience satisfied her thirst for formal medical training, and in 1866 she left the United States for France, where she hoped to be admitted to the Ecole de Medicine in Paris. Looking back on this decision in 1871, she wrote to her mother,

> I cannot do a thing half way. When I was in Boston, Lucy Sewall considered me stupid, because I could not do things without having studied them, and could not accept her methods without question. In Paris, I am considered one of the most successful students, because I have been able to "go the whole horse." Explain it as you may, I always find the whole of a thing easier to manage than the half.[21]

Jacobi's time in Paris testified to her persistence and determination. Although she immediately began attending hospital clinics, lectures, and laboratories, it took her two years of dogged perseverance to achieve her goal of admission to the Ecole. Characteristically, she passed her examinations with high honors and won a bronze medal for her graduating thesis in 1871.

In Paris, Jacobi pursued the most advanced medical science of her day. Soon after her arrival there she wrote enthusiastically to her mother, "I have a fair prospect here of becoming a thoroughly educated physician," adding that "unless I am, I certainly will never undertake to practice medicine." Her commitment to the laboratory made it natural that she would welcome the discoveries of the bacteriologists and seek to stay abreast of their findings. She perceived early that opportunities for medical study in America did not begin to compare with those abroad. In another letter to her mother she spoke of New York City's inadequacies:

[20]Jacobi to George Palmer Putnam, 1 Feb. 1867, *Life and Letters*, 110.

[21]Jacobi to Victorine Haven Putnam, 11 March 1871, Jacobi Manuscripts, Schlesinger Library, Radcliffe College.

> I have already sufficient terror of the demoralization imminent from the atmosphere of New York, with its very slack interest in medical science or progress, its deficient libraries, badly organized schools and hospitals, etc. I am doing my best to accumulate a sufficient fund of original force to make headway against these adverse influences, and to subordinate them to my purposes, instead of allowing them to subordinate me.

Yet at the same time Jacobi shunned opportunities for practicing medicine that would take her out of the mainstream, as inadequate as it was. She would not even consider teaching at the Woman's Medical College in Philadelphia, which she believed to be sincere, but deficient, and when offered the position of resident physician at one of the women's colleges she remarked that such isolation from the medical world would be "suicidal."[22]

In 1871 Jacobi returned to New York to join the faculty of the Woman's Medical College of the New York Infirmary as professor of therapeutics and materia medica. She also set up private practice, feeling satisfied that "few young physicians could have a better opening." Family considerations and a sense of duty determined the subordination of chemistry—her first love—to private practice. As she explained to her mother, "After all the sacrifices you have made ... I see more chance of satisfying you if I am a practical physician than if, without fortune, I try to become a scientific chemist."[23]

Plunging herself into the world of New York medicine, Jacobi fulfilled her ambitions to become a first-rate physician and scientist. She became the first woman to be admitted to the New York Academy of Medicine and later chaired their section on neurology. She gained admission to numerous other medical societies as well and sustained her interest in research by publishing 9 books and over 120 medical articles. The respect of her male colleagues was never in doubt. One younger member of the Pathological Society, for example, remembered her as a woman

> whose knowledge of pathology was so thorough, whose range of the literature was so wide and whose criticism was so keen, fearless and just that in our discussions, we felt it prudent to shun the field of speculation and to walk strictly in the path of demonstrated fact."[24]

Perhaps Jacobi's successes in the male professional world were due at least in part to her willingness to accept men as equals—no more, no less. Certainly Jacobi did not share Blackwell's ambivalence toward romantic attachments to men, and her private correspondence never reveals the

[22]Jacobi to Victorine Haven Putnam, 22 April 1867, 13 Jan. 1870, *Life and Letters*, 125, 233–34.
[23]Jacobi to Victorine Haven Putnam, 22 Dec. 1867, 13 Nov. 1866, *Life and Letters*, 157, 100–01.
[24]Dr. Allan Wyeth, quoted in *Life and Letters*, 325.

mistrust of marriage characteristic of many accomplished women of her generation. Nevertheless, she sought in a mate a rare thing in the nineteenth century—an intellectual and spiritual companion who could fully support her commitment to her work. Although she had a passionate nature, she was prepared to forgo marriage if she did not find such a man and broke two engagements before she joined the ranks of New York's professional medical elite. While still in Paris she had written on the subject of marriage to her mother:

> I have no particular desire to marry at any time; nevertheless, if at home, I should ever come across a physician, intelligent, refined, more enthusiastic for his science than me, . . . I think I would marry such a person if he asked me, and would leave me full liberty to exercise my profession.[25]

Fortunately, Jacobi did meet such a man. In 1873 she became the wife of Dr. Abraham Jacobi, a German-Jewish refugee from the revolutionary upheavals of 1848. Jacobi was already one of the most distinguished physicians in America and has often been called the father of modern pediatrics.[26] The couple shared common medical interests and collaborated occasionally. Although the marriage was often stormy, it remained a relationship of equals, despite Jacobi's assuredly ironic remark to her students that "it is desirable that every woman remain as inferior to her own husband as may be feasible and convenient."[27]

Jacobi's personal and professional history made her understandably impatient with Blackwell's rigid theorizing, and glimpses of irritability appear in her comments concerning Blackwell's proposed trip to America. On Blackwell's antivivisectionism she remarked coolly, "Of course . . . you know . . . I should oppose you," adding with humor and a touch of wistful regret that a campaign among women physicians would be useless because "I am tolerably confident that I am the only woman in the United States who experiments on animals!"

As for the "problem" of gynecological surgery, Jacobi was less polite: "When you shudder at 'mutilation,'" she wrote,

[25]Jacobi to Victorine Haven Putnam, 29 May 1867, *Life and Letters*, 141.

[26]Indeed, Dr. Herbert C. Miller in his 1981 Abraham Jacobi lecture to the American Academy of Pediatrics has called Mary Putnam Jacobi the "mother of American pediatrics." See "Intrauterine Growth Retardation: An Unmet Challenge," presented April 1981, in Washington, D.C. Reprints available at the Dept. of Pediatrics, Univ. of Kansas Medical Center, Kansas City, Kan.

[27]Mary Putnam Jacobi, "Shall Women Practice Medicine?" in The Women's Medical Association of New York City, eds., *Mary Putnam Jacobi, Pathfinder in Medicine* (1882; rpt. New York: G.P. Putnam, 1925), 390.

it seems to me you can never have handled a degenerated ovary or a suppurating Fallopian tube—or you would admit that the mutilation had been effected by disease,—possibly by the ignorance or neglect of a series of physicians, before the surgeon intervened. You always seem so much more impressed with the personalities,—sufficiently faulty,—of doctors, than with the terrific difficulties of the problems they have to face. . . . There has been much reprehensible malpractice. But I do not see that malpractice which may render a woman incapable of bearing children differs . . . from the malpractice which may result in the loss of a limb or of an eye. *There is not such special sanctity about the ovary*!

To Blackwell's suggestion that women physicians ought to avoid performing gynecological surgery she retorted, "And why should not women be delighted if they succeed in achieving a difficult and useful triumph in technical medicine," adding that she did not feel women physicians should be urged to strike out for independent views until they had "demonstrated an equality of achievement in the urgent practical problems,—*not of sociology but of medicine*."[28] The chief task of women physicians, she believed, was not the fostering of morality ("sociology"), but "the creation of a scientific spirit" among them.[29]

* * *

In the end, their divergent attractions to the potentialities inherent in medical practice led Blackwell and Jacobi to differ most intensely on the question of the role of women in medicine. Historians have long maintained that much of the rhetoric mustered in defense of women's medical education fell into two broad categories which occasionally contradicted each other. The first set of arguments, which paralleled Jacobi's brand of feminism, emphasized woman's right to self-development and her ability to make a contribution to clinical medicine equal to any man's. Proponents downplayed the physical and psychological handicaps allegedly endured by the female sex and openly challenged the tenet of Victorian culture that relegated woman to the private and the family spheres. No longer were all women necessarily hampered by family responsibilities; a select few could practice medicine in lieu of family and career. These arguments drew their strength primarily from abstract concepts of justice and equality.[30]

[28]Italics mine. See Jacobi to Blackwell, 25 Dec. 1888, *Life and Letters*.
[29]Mary Putnam Jacobi, "Specialism in Medicine," *Pathfinder in Medicine*, 358; Jacobi, "Inaugural Address at the Opening of the Woman's Medical College of the New York Infirmary, October 1, 1880," Ibid., 334; Jacobi "Annual Address Delivered at the Commencement of the Woman's Medical College of the New York Infirmary, May 30, 1883," Ibid., 293; Jacobi "Shall Women Practice Medicine?" Ibid., 373.
[30]See Aileen Kraditor, *The Ideas of the Woman Suffrage Movement, 1890–1929* (New York: Columbia Univ. Press, 1965).

Blackwell's thought derived from a second, more popular set of beliefs emphasizing not the essential identity between men and women, but their differences. This approach adapted itself more readily to Victorian mythology regarding separate sexual spheres. Women should become physicians because they exhibited unique qualities that would allow them to make a distinct contribution to the profession.

Indeed, a central theme in the story of women in medicine—the tension between "feminism" and "morality" on the one hand and "professionalism" and "science" on the other—has plagued women physicians up until the present day. Nor have other women professionals escaped such conflicts. In a society that has continued to emphasize woman's primary maternal role, the stepping out of prescribed avenues of endeavor has inevitably involved for its participants some explanation of purpose. Did women have the right to pursue professional goals, usually considered masculine, with the same vigor as their male colleagues and for similar reasons of self-interest and personal fulfillment? Was the goal of equality legitimate for women, or need they contribute as well to some higher female mission? What obligations did women professionals have to other women, or to "female values" in general? Must women emulate the professionalism of men, or seek to temper dominant male values by asserting their uniquely feminine characteristics?

Blackwell's writings underscored the singular capabilities of women as physicians and led to a peculiar kind of female chauvinism. The purpose of teaching women medicine was not to convert them into "physicians rather inferior to men," but to occupy "positions which men cannot fully occupy," and exercise "an influence which men cannot wield at all." Those positions had mainly to do with women, children, and the family. Women physicians must bring science to bear on daily life. This could be done best as family physicians, obstetricians, public health advocates, and teachers of preventive medicine and hygiene, because it was in these areas that women could excel. Other branches of medicine reeked to Blackwell of the tyranny of male authority unmitigated by the dictates of conscience. She cautioned her students against the "blind acceptance of what is called 'authority' in medicine," which she equated with the "male intellect." "It is not blind imitation of men, nor thoughtless acceptance of whatever may be taught by them that is required," she wrote. Women students, she regretted, were as yet too "accustomed to accept the government and instruction of men as final, and it hardly occurs to them to question it." They must be taught that "methods and conclusions formed by one-half of the race only, must necessarily require revision as the other half of humanity rises into conscious responsibility."[31]

[31]See Notes, Elizabeth Blackwell, "On the Education of Women Physicians," Blackwell Manuscripts, Library of Congress; Blackwell, "The Influence of Women," 27–29, 19–20, esp. where she denounces the "narrow and superficial materialism which prevails so widely amongst scientific men."

In advocating this position Blackwell voluntarily set herself and women physicians apart from the mainstream of professional developments. Rather than assimilate women into the larger group, she preferred to give them special responsibilities in order to achieve what she believed was a higher social and moral purpose. Women physicians were to be "in" the profession, but not "of" it.

This stress on the primacy of the maternal qualities of sympathy and instinct troubled Jacobi because she objected to female-centered, moralistic, and separatist standards for women. Her concern for objective science and the centrality of intellectual endeavor remained fundamentally universalist and assimilationist. For Jacobi, the physician dwelt in two realms, the intellectual and the practical. Although she admitted that moral considerations occasionally entered into the equation, she hailed the liberation of science from the mystic and demonic influences of the past and believed that the physician should deal with rational concepts based on objective knowledge. Ideally his business was to "take conditions which science has abstracted for the purpose of thought and to recombine them for the purpose of life. In the absence of the physician there would be no one to do this. . . ." Thus the physician was the link between theory and practice. Moral issues were often beside the point. The intrinsic difficulty in medicine, she wrote, was not moral, but remained "the great mass of facts which it is necessary to know" and "the variety of sciences which must be understood in order to interpret these facts."

Where Blackwell emphasized sympathy and compassion and identified such qualities with women, Jacobi spoke rarely of exclusively feminine contributions to medical practice. Having a sympathetic nature, she argued, did not necessarily make one a good physician. He or she must be interested primarily in the facts. In the end, she wrote, unless "the interest in the disease be not habitually greater than the interest in the patient," the patient would surely suffer. She saw women participating in the profession, not as a distinct entity unto themselves, but as separate individuals united with men by objective, demonstrable, and professional criteria in the search for truth. "Indeed," she cautioned her students in 1883, "you are liable to be so much and so frequently reminded that you are women physicians, that you are almost liable to forget that you are, first of all, physicians."[32]

Jacobi did not reject entirely the notion that women had special strengths, although it is apparent that she believed such characteristics were acquired rather than innate. She admitted, for example, that "it is impossible to deny that women are intrinsically more suitable than men to take charge of insane women," because of their "superior kindness and conscientiousness." She quarreled little with the common wisdom that "tact, acuteness, and sympa-

[32]Jacobi, "Specialism in Medicine," 358; Jacobi, "Shall Women Practice Medicine?" 373; Jacobi, "Commencement Address," 392.

thetic insight [were] natural to women." Indeed, while stressing the importance of first-rate training she graciously conceded that "the special capacities of women as a class for dealing with sick persons are so great, that in virtue of them alone hundreds have succeeded in medical practice, though most sufficiently endowed with intellectual or educational qualifications."[33]

Yet despite women's unique skills, Jacobi insisted that they be fully integrated into the profession. She deplored the tendency of women doctors "to nestle within a little circle of personal friends and to accept their dictum as the ultimate law of things." Their role must not be supplementary or distinctive; inevitably skilled women physicians should displace inferior men. There was nothing earthshaking about women competing with men: "Since society is, numerically speaking, already supplied with quite enough doctors," she wrote, "the only way in which women physicians can possibly gain any footing is by displacing a certain number of men." In order to do so, of course, they needed to be either equal or superior, and this meant receiving a better medical education than had yet been possible.

While Blackwell urged women to specialize, Jacobi continuously cautioned women not to concentrate in obstetrics and gynecology, but to devote themselves to a "liberal study of the whole field." Treating women and children should be used only "as a stepping-stone to general medicine." If women "do not obtain a foothold" there, if they "content themselves with claiming this little corner," she warned, "they will never really gain a high place even there. . . ."[34]

Although Jacobi remained suspicious of separatism, she also conceded that since the "opposition to women students and practitioners of medicine has been so bitter, so brutal . . . so multiple in its hypocrisy," women did have common interests as an oppressed class. She repeatedly prescribed grit and hard work in the face of discrimination: "I have always advised you . . . to so saturate and permeate your consciousness with the feeling for medicine," she told the graduating class of the Woman's Medical College of the New York Infirmary in 1883, "that you would entirely forget that public opinion continued to assign you to a special, and on the whole, inferior" position. She even urged students to forget that they "have in any way braved public opinion." "Acclimate," she implored, "as quickly and as thoroughly as possible" to your "new place," and don't "keep dawdling on the threshhold to forever remind yourselves and everyone else that you have just come in." Medicine remained too demanding a profession for conscientious doctors to

[33]Mary Putnam Jacobi, "Female Physicians for Insane Women," *Medical Record*, 37, 10 May 1890, 543; Jacobi, "Woman in Medicine," in Annie Nathan Meyer, ed., *Woman's Work in America* (New York: Henry Holt, 1891), 177.

[34]Jacobi, "Inaugural Address," 352, 348, 354.

allow themselves to be concerned with problems of "social status." If you do not find the facts of medicine more interesting than any other facts," she cautioned, "you are not fit to be physicians."[35]

Yet if Jacobi lost her patience with those who "dawdled on the threshold," the "monopoly" that excluded "one half of the race [from] the advantages of education and the facilities of increased life which that confers" rankled even more. She was not naive; she knew such opposition could be removed only after "much effort, individual and collective, persistent, patient, far-sighted, indomitable." Thus she devoted considerable time and effort to examining the practical difficulties involved in assimilating women into the male professional world. For her the most obvious problem remained what she knew was "the most delicate": "actually raising to an equality the class which hitherto has been really inferior."[36]

In acknowledging and working to overcome women's shortcomings, Jacobi and Blackwell remained of one mind. Indeed, one suspects that however substantial were their disagreements on theoretical points, practical issues of strategy continuously drew them together. Both women deplored women's inferior preparatory education, an education that rendered them deficient in intellectual initiative, dependent on authority, and apathetic—all qualities that Jacobi perceptively labeled characteristics of the subordination of "colonial life." In order to rectify such disadvantages, she wrote, medical women must combine as a class to remove the obstacles that have blocked their progress. Their first task was to create among themselves a "scientific spirit," by improving medical education for women and encouraging "free, self-sustained, self-reliant intellectual activity." Jacobi hoped that this "gradual progress in mental culture" would improve "mental initiative" in women and hopefully render them equal to men "in every work that both undertake."[37]

Blackwell had no quarrel with these points. She agreed that the barriers to women's equal access to quality medical education must be removed as quickly as possible, and she understood that only thorough scientific training would promote women's success. Both women hoped that the unique opportunities offered by the Woman's Medical College of the New York Infirmary would begin to alleviate some of these difficulties. The two stood united as well in the battle to widen women's opportunities for clinical experience and professional association, and both, for different reasons,

[35] Jacobi, "Commencement Address," 392–93, 397, 400.
[36] Ibid.
[37] Jacobi to Blackwell, 25 Dec. 1888; Jacobi, "Commencement Address," 401; Jacobi, "Shall Women Practice Medicine?" 390.

enthusiastically welcomed the advance of medical coeducation. Yet where Jacobi's brand of feminism strived to minimize the differences between men and women and to integrate female physicians into the profession as rapidly as possible, Blackwell adhered to the very end to a vision of the woman doctor's unique contribution. This was true at least in part because her concept of disease was linked to her notions of morality and her belief that authentic moral understanding depended on female intuition. Such assumptions allowed her to equate bacteriology with male science and its triumph with the victory of the male principle over the female. That such a victory would lead inevitably to the denigration of intuition and morality in medicine was deplorable enough, but the final and most egregious consequence would be that women would be deprived of their power, purpose, and unique advantage in the profession—and this at the very moment when civilized society was beginning at long last to afford them a role appropriate to their highest capacities.

Blackwell's suspicions of "ignorant male domination" caused her to worry that women physicians accepted male models uncritically. "The only disappointment which comes to me now, as I draw towards the close of a life full of joy and gratitude," she mused in 1889,

> is the surprise with which I recognize that our women physicians do not all and always see the glorious moral mission, which as women physicians they are called on to fulfill. It is not by simply following the lead of male physicians, and imitating their practices, that any new and vitalizing force will be brought into the profession.[38]

* * *

As first-generation women physicians, Jacobi and Blackwell shared similar goals as well as the common experience of being pioneers. Their differences on the issue of women appear in retrospect less pronounced than their broad areas of agreement. Each struggled defiantly in her own way with the humiliating effects of discrimination, while holding fast to an objective that sought to broaden the sphere of constructive activity for all women. Both saw the role of women in medicine idealistically, in the sense that they rejected its pursuit on the grounds of self-interest and emphasized instead the physician's larger social responsibilities. Jacobi, for example, once declared to her mother that "I look upon a rich physician with as much suspicion as a

[38]Mary Putnam Jacobi, "Social Aspects of the Readmission of Women into the Medical Profession," in *Papers and Letters presented at the First Woman's Congress of the Association for the Advancement of Women, October, 1873* (New York, 1874), 134; Elizabeth Blackwell, Letter to the Editor of the *Philanthropist*, Feb. 1889, rpt. in Blackwell Manuscripts, Radcliffe Women's Archives.

rich priest." In 1889 Blackwell wrote in the same vein, "I say emphatically that anyone who makes pecuniary gain the chief motive for entering upon a medical career is an unworthy student: he is not fit to become a doctor." Both women believed that the success of women in the profession had immense importance for the general success of women "in every other department of society."[39] On questions of strategy too, they were usually of one mind: both struggled to widen the access of medical women to superior scientific training and to increase their professional and clinical opportunities. Nevertheless, the two women represented distinct approaches to the problem of women in medicine, and their differences were passed on to succeeding generations of professional women.

Versions of Blackwell's argument remained the most popular in the public and private rhetoric of women physicians. However committed privately were later generations of women doctors to abstract concepts of equal justice, the Blackwellian tradition, with its glorification of woman's uniqueness, meshed more easily with familiar cultural verities. Male supporters, too, felt more at ease with the idea that women would not so much compete with them as concentrate their energies in what came to be known as "feminine preserves"—public health and social morality, child hygiene and maternal care, institutional work, industrial medicine, and public school and university teaching and counseling.

In 1926 the Woman's Medical College of Pennsylvania issued a pamphlet designed to encourage women to pursue a medical career. Its very title, *Natural Guardians of the Race,* illustrates how little the arguments had changed since Blackwell first spoke of the "spiritual power of maternity." Women "will always be necessary in medicine" the pamphlet maintained, because of "their special qualifications for definite fields of practice." Such fields were "child care," the "care of women, foreign medical missionary work," and "the field of research," for which "women have displayed peculiar aptitude" because of their "natural bent for painstaking accuracy and detail."[40]

This bulletin and others like it suggest that until well into the twentieth century women physicians needed extraordinary reasons to justify their deviation from social norms, and still viewed themselves as a special group within the medical establishment. Not until the profound cultural changes of the 1960s brought about by the black and women's liberation movements did abstract concerns for equality and justice in the rhetoric of medical women

[39]Jacobi to Victorine Haven Putnam, 13 Jan. 1870, *Life and Letters;* Blackwell, "The Influence of Women," 5; Jacobi, "Social Aspects," 173.

[40]Pamphlet is in the Archives of the Medical College of Pennsylvania, Philadelphia, Pa. The quotes can be found on 5–7.

take equal place beside the Blackwellian emphasis on women's unique capabilities.

Although the fact of their womanhood was central to them both, Jacobi and Blackwell differed in the final analysis on medical issues that went well beyond questions of gender. The achievements of the bacteriologists and the introduction of the concept of specific etiology have been among the most constructive forces in modern medicine for almost a century. Yet the scientific medicine that has flourished since 1900 has done so increasingly at the expense of a holistic approach to the problem of illness. In many respects the worst fears of Elizabeth Blackwell concerning the neglect of psychological, environmental, social, and personal factors have come to pass. Doctors no longer treat the whole patient; they concentrate merely on the disease. Medical science has become increasingly and aggressively masculine. The nurturant aspects of nineteenth-century practice, with its heavy emphasis on intuition, sympathy, and art, have all but disappeared. From the perspective of the nineteenth-century, Jacobi's enthusiasm for laboratory science and her identification with the most revolutionary and dramatic achievements of her profession seem progressive and refreshing. Blackwell's ideas, heavy with religious overtones and convoluted personal idiosyncrasies, appear reactionary, uninformed, and annoyingly short-sighted. Yet the passage of time has gradually revealed to us the shocking limitations of laboratory science. Once again we must return full circle to deal with factors in disease causation that cannot be measured, recorded, or re-created in an experimental setting.

To be sure, the contemporary interest in holistic approaches to disease is something very different from the kind of position Elizabeth Blackwell occupied a century ago, and could, in fact, have come about only after the supremacy of scientific reductionism in medicine. However, in the midst of such an about-face, Blackwell's vision seems almost prophetic as she mused to a friend in 1853:

> I hope some day to arrange a hospital on truer principles than any that we have yet seen—but in thinking of this subject, I feel continually the want of the *Science* of reform, which I believe is as yet unknown—I should want my hospital to be a center of Science, and of moral growth—in the scientific department I should be puzzled to know how far I ought to unite men and women—In the future I have no doubt that the two sexes, in varying proportions, will unite in every act of life—but now there are difficulties both in their separation and their combination. . . . I should want also in my Hospital to cure my patients spiritually as well as physically, and what innumerable aids that would necessitate! I must have the church, the school, the workshop . . . to cure my patients—a whole society, in fact. . . .[41*]

[41]Blackwell to Lady Byron, 5 Aug. 1852, Blackwell Manuscripts, Library of Congress, Washington, D.C.

*I am indebted to Rosalind Rosenberg, Judy Leavitt, Barbara Rosenkrantz, Martin Pernick, Joyce Antler, and William Leach for reading and criticizing this manuscript.

DOCTORS OR LADIES? WOMEN PHYSICIANS IN PSYCHIATRIC INSTITUTIONS, 1872–1900*

Constance M. McGovern

In the early 1890s at the Norristown State Hospital for the insane in Pennsylvania, Dr. Lilian Welsh, then a member of the medical staff, invited a woman doctor friend to accompany her on weekly rounds. As they reached the last ward housing the most excitable patients, one of the more troubled inmates, "planted herself firmly" in their way and inquired of the visiting doctor, "Say, are you a doctor or a lady?" Thus, mused Dr. Welsh, "out of the mouths of babes and defectives" come "current social opinions."[1]

Lilian Welsh was only one of the nearly two hundred women physicians who had decided to serve in psychiatric institutions in the last three decades of the nineteenth century. The experiences of these women who chose to take on two male-dominated professions simultaneously are worthy of exploration for these doctors did not correspond to Victorian expectations about the ideal woman and did not even adhere to the much-debated virtues of the "new woman."

Expected to be the preserver of culture and the mother of civilization according to the prescriptive literature, the ideal nineteenth-century woman could best perform these duties by maintaining a submissive and controlled demeanor. Rightfully and properly in her place in the home, she could influence moral attitudes and behavior in her roles as wife and mother. Commentators noted that woman's "chief work" was related to the "future of the world," and facetiously asked, "why should we spoil a good mother by making an ordinary grammarian?" But not everyone, especially in the latter part of the century, adhered to such a conservative view. Some could, and did, acknowledge a new sphere for women; but they were no revolutionaries. If women emerged from the home and participated in volunteer and professional activities, they must still act "in a feminine manner." There was room for the "new woman," but she must acquiesce to a male colleague's advice, rely on his strength and expertise, and always conduct herself in a properly demure manner. Thus, at best, these doctors, as profes-

* Research for this paper was funded in part by a grant from the Penrose Fund of the American Philosophical Society and by a grant from the University of Arizona Foundation.

[1] Lilian Welsh, *Reminiscences of Thirty Years in Baltimore* (Baltimore: Norman Remington, 1925), pp. 44–45.

BULLETIN OF THE HISTORY OF MEDICINE Vol. 55 Pp. 88–107
0007-5140/81/0551-0088 $01.00

sional women, could expect a reserved tolerance, at worst, hostility and the label of "mannish maidens."[2]

The difficulties which beset the paths of women entering medicine in the late Victorian era are well-documented. The mere logistics of obtaining a medical education raised barriers which were nearly insurmountable for all but the most stout-hearted. Women's medical schools came in and out of existence with great frequency; nineteen schools for women had been founded in the nineteenth century, but by 1895, eleven had already disbanded and even those which survived offered little opportunity for any significant clinical practice and most general hospitals did not accept female interns. Only three co-educational medical schools existed and the finest of these, Johns Hopkins, required a B.A. for admission—another difficulty to be overcome by the would-be woman doctor.[3]

The public was equally unfriendly. Women doctors were deemed "unsexed" or at least believed to have some "peculiar underlying reasons" for entering the professions. Gossip usually had it that any woman who took up medicine "must have done so from some profound emotional disturbance, some secret grief, presumably a disappointment in love." Attempts to rent office space met with cries of "no women doctors" and "no signs," even if the sign were "no bigger than a postage stamp." Owners expressed fears that renting to a doctor, would place "such a stigma on the house that they could never rent it again." Success at establishing an office usually meant renting on "Scab Row" or in "bachelors' apartments" and leaving one's self open to ridicule, laughter, and remarks about "bachelors' apartments and old maids livin' in them!" Always considered "somewhat of a curiosity," even professional acknowledgment of women physicians did not necessarily result in social acceptance. For instance, the "Ladies' Committee" of the American Medical Association meeting in Baltimore in 1895 questioned whether the women doctors should be invited to their reception and "finally decided with great reluctance to include them."[4]

[2] The virtues of the Victorian "ideal woman" have been described in the now classic article by Barbara Welter, "The cult of true womanhood," *Amer. Quart.*, 1966, *18*: 151–174. Although scholars have lately pointed out that much of Welter's evidence is prescriptive and normative (see especially Carl Degler, "What ought to be and what was: Women's sexuality in the nineteenth century," *Amer. Hist. Rev.*, 1974, *79*: 1467–1490), other scholars have applied Welter's description in their studies. For the quotation on "ruining a good mother," see T. S. Clouston, "Female education from a medical point of view," *Pop. Sci. Monthly*, 1884: 224. For a discussion of the virtues of the "new woman," see John S. Haller and Robin M. Haller, *The Physician and Sexuality in Victorian America* (Chicago: University of Illinois Press, 1974), pp. 39–40 and 77–78.

[3] The most recent and definitive study of the difficulties experienced by women in their search for a medical education and the barriers raised by the profession itself is Mary Roth Walsh, "*Doctors Wanted: No Women Need Apply*" (New Haven: Yale University Press, 1977). Other standard sources are Mary Putnam Jacobi's chapter, "Woman in Medicine," in Annie Nathan Meyer, *Woman's Work in America* (New York: Henry Holt, 1891), Thomas Woody, *A History of Women's Education in the United States* (New York: Science Press, 1929), especially volume 2, and the voluminous testimony of the women themselves.

[4] I have taken the illustrations of difficulties faced by women doctors from the autobiographies of both Welsh, *Reminiscences*, pp. 43–46, and Bertha Van Hoosen, *Petticoat Surgeon* (Chicago: Pellegrini & Cudahy, 1947), p. 59; since both of them served as women physicians in psychiatric institutions early in their careers. Thus their accounts, besides being fairly typical, seem particularly apropos.

Attitudes of fellow medical students were no better. For the groundbreaking women students some form of hazing seemed to be the normal, although not always expected, experience. Mary Bates who, in 1881, became the first Cook County Hospital female intern, was carried off in the midst of the night, mattress and bedding and all, to the gynecological ward "to be entered as an interesting case" by the male interns. Other women, as medical students, had to put up with being called "hen-medics" or being "clucked at, bombarded with paper wads and thrown kisses."[5]

Heckling and ridicule did not stop even with the attainment of the medical degree. Almost every novice female physician met with expressions of disbelief and periods of testing from her male colleagues. These ranged from relatively harmless practical jokes and medical students boycotting clinical classes taught by women to incidents bordering on sexual harassment. Bertha Van Hoosen, while working in a Chicago clinic, described her feelings in an encounter with a "short, dapper young physician," who walked in, locked the door, and pocketed the key, as those of an "old bay mare moving slowly from side to side in the pasture lot to avoid the advances of the jumping stallion." Van Hoosen was given to barnyard descriptions, nevertheless she was probably more frank about her experiences than most women.[6]

Even salaried positions had limitations. Both Goucher College and Bryn Mawr, for instance, allowed women doctors to practice only preventive medicine. If a student became ill, a male doctor treated her because her "parents might not be satisfied to feel" that she was in the care of a woman physician. Further, when women finally started out on their own voluntary projects, such as evening dispensaries for the poor, these were usually the first to have funds rescinded, sometimes under the guise that "women physicians for women patients represented a specialty" and were therefore not eligible for public support. The problems seemed endless, but they were minimal compared to the additional difficulties met by those women who chose to serve in psychiatric institutions.[7]

Removed from the protection of all those images placing the woman on a pedestal and confronted with questions about their respectability and their physical and intellectual stamina, some women doctors still took on this double burden of proving their worth to both the medical and psychiatric professions. The more difficult to convince would prove to be psychiatry because, with few exceptions, psychiatry in the nineteenth century was still practiced within the asylum walls and stringently controlled by one of the

[5] Van Hoosen, *Petticoat Surgeon*, pp. 52 and 57–58. Also see the account of Van Hoosen in "Opportunities for medical women interns," *Med. Woman's J.*, 1926, *33*: 282 for the "raid" on Mary Bates.

[6] For instance the seven male doctors at the Kalamazoo State Hospital convinced Van Hoosen that it was her duty to extract the teeth of the patients. She went on for weeks before learning of the joke. As newly-appointed Professor of Clinical Gynecology at the Chicago College of Physicians and Surgeons, Van Hoosen also had her first lecture boycotted. See Van Hoosen, *Petticoat Surgeon*, pp. 83, 140–143, and 127–128.

[7] Welsh, *Reminiscences*, pp. 5 and 50.

most long-standing professional organizations—the Association of Medical Superintendents of American Institutions for the Insane (later renamed the American Psychiatric Association). Breaking down brick and mortar walls, as well as emotional and professional ones, proved to be a formidable task.[8]

In only one respect did the would-be woman psychiatrist have an advantage over her sister general practitioner—public opposition was minimal. Treatment of the mentally ill was not an issue of prime public attention in the late nineteenth century. Earlier in the century, some had crusaded for the humane treatment of all types of down-trodden and unfortunate people. But the general post-war cynicism arising from disillusionment with humanitarianism and the growing pessimism of the psychiatric profession itself left few outraged at the mere custodial care of the insane. Many were grateful to have those felt to be defective removed from their view, and most were simply indifferent or uninformed about what occurred in public institutions. Thus, although the women did not enjoy the support of the public, neither did they have to brook its opposition.[9]

Within the psychiatric profession, the prospect of women physicians in mental institutions generated intense discussion. At least one asylum superintendent and his board of trustees welcomed the appointment of a woman and, without hesitation, awaited the "result with confidence," fully expecting that her work would "increase the usefulness of the asylum." Those who favored this innovation stressed the issue of modesty, the modesty of the patients. The theory that women would be more open about their problems and more willing to agree to treatment, either local or surgical, from a doctor of their own sex was constantly discussed in the late nineteenth century and provided a persuasive argument.[10]

Another even more effective argument concerned the sexual behavior of the female patients. The pervading sexual mores, according to the normative literature of the period, and the frequent remarks about the sexual behavior of female patients by the psychiatrists seem to indicate on the part of some both a fascination with and an unspoken fear of female sexuality, at least as expressed through the uninhibited actions of mentally ill women. Unlike the rest of society, which believed masturbation to be fairly common (although not acceptable) in single men but rare in women, the hospital

[8] For a discussion of the problems facing women who entered the profession, see Barbara J. Harris, *Beyond Her Sphere: Women and the Professions in American History* (Westport, Connecticut: Greenwood Press, 1978).

[9] For background on the way in which this crusade, and the waning of it, applied to the psychiatric profession, see Gerald Grob, *The State and the Mentally Ill* (Chapel Hill: University of North Carolina Press, 1966) and *Mental Institutions in America* (New York: Free Press, 1973), and David Rothman, *The Discovery of the Asylum* (Boston: Little, Brown, 1971).

[10] *Sixteenth Annual Report of the Trustees of the Willard Asylum for the Insane* (Buffalo: Baker, Jones, 1885), p. 6. See arguments about modesty in Virginia Penny, *The Employments of Women* (Boston: Walker, Wise, 1863), pp. 24–26; G. C. Paoli and James G. Kiernan, "Female physicians in insane hospitals," *Alienist and Neurologist*, Jan., 1887, *8*: 21–29; Edward N. Brush, "On the employment of women physicians in hospitals for the insane," *Amer. J. Insanity*, Jan., 1891, *47*: 323–330; *Eighth Annual Report of the Committee on Lunacy of the Board of Public Charities of Pennsylvania* (Harrisburg: Edwin K. Meyers, 1890), pp. 30–31; and Mary Putnam Jacobi's letter to the editor, *Medical Record*, May 10, 1890: 543–544.

doctors daily faced the manifestations of this "perversion," this "secret" cause of insanity, in their encounters with women patients. Moreover, despite the general belief that women seldom experienced sexual pleasure, these doctors recorded the remarks of women who reported that they felt "very erotic," that "sexual matters chiefly occupied" their thoughts and they noted patients whose behavior they attributed to "an infatuation for the male sex" or "strongly developed" amativeness.

Particularly unsettling were the sexual delusions of female patients. A number of medical superintendents had observed that insanity in these patients was "tinctured" by sexual delusions about the male physicians, the examining doctors. Some seemed to need a "manifestation of affection" from the doctor and others, in a disturbed state, would recite accounts of "immoral relations" between hospital employees, were willing themselves to go off on an escapade of carnal pleasure, and even accused the officers of attempting to rape them. The situation was often uncomfortable and thus some doctors were quick to advocate the appointment of women assistant physicians because the "female insane," they believed, were "peculiarly susceptible" to any influence which might weaken the "restraints" which society had developed "around the passions." Many responded readily to this argument.[11]

Other doctors, in response to changes in medical theory, attributed women's emotional and mental illnesses to their reproductive systems and became convinced that either local treatment or, especially, the surgical removal of uteri and ovaries would restore mental health to some suffering women. In the 1870s and early 1880s this was a convincing argument with the rise of both gynecology and surgery as specialties, and in the wake of the publicity accruing around Battey's "normal ovariotomy." Robert Battey, an obscure Georgia physician, had added the surgical technique and rationalization whereby non-diseased ovaries also might be removed in order to relieve purely neurotic conditions. The vogue for ovariotomy and the resultant optimism did not last long, but the initial fervor, coupled with the growing idea that women doctors could more properly treat female patients both psychologically and surgically, was enough to help break down the first barriers to women physicians in psychiatric institutions.[12]

[11] See especially, W. B. Goldsmith, "A case of moral insanity," *Amer. J. Insanity*, Oct., 1883, *40*: 162–177 (quotation on p. 171) and the discussion of this article in the "Proceedings of the thirty-ninth annual meeting of the Association of Medical Superintendents of American Institutions for the Insane," *Amer. J. Insanity*, Jan., 1884; *40*: 280–285; E. D. Bondurant, "Two cases of oophorectomy for insanity," *Amer. J. Insanity*, Jan., 1886, *42*: 342–345, (quotations on pp. 343 and 344); S. G. Webber, "Cases of hysteria treated by hypnotism," *Amer. J. Nerv. Ment. Dis.*, September, 1890: 585–596; Allan McLane Hamilton, "The abuse of oophorectomy in diseases of the nervous system," *New York Med. J.*, 1893, *57*: 180–185; and, Paoli and Kiernan, "Female physicians," pp. 21–22. See physician's remarks on cases in the 1882–1884 Case Book for the women's wards at Harrisburg State Hospital, Harrisburg, Pennsylvania. (Hereinafter referred to as the HSH Case Book). Refer also to John Duffy, "Masturbation and clitoridectomy," *JAMA*, Oct. 19, 1963, *186*: 246–248 and Charles Rosenberg, "Sexuality, Class, and Role," in *No Other Gods* (Baltimore: The Johns Hopkins University Press, 1976).

[12] Scores of articles appeared in a variety of professional journals in the late Victorian era which assumed this connection. See especially, W. H. Baker, "Removal of the uterine appendages for nervous disease," *Boston*

A few superintendents, moreover, had hired women doctors for their staffs in the 1870s. Merrick Bemis of the Worcester (Massachusetts) Asylum, "having comprehended the difficulties insuperable by men physicians in the care and treatment of insane women patients," was the first and, in 1869, he employed Mary Stinson as assistant physician in the department for women. Others, like the administrators of the hospitals at Augusta, Maine, and at Kalamazoo and Pontiac, Michigan, also considered women's "services beneficial to patients." As these individual efforts became known, some realized that the "limited avenues for women physicians" made it "easy to get a woman" and "easier to keep her" and that she could be of "great help to the morale of the hospital" because she could more comfortably treat the "special illnesses of female employees." But these were only individual appointments and subject to change with the end of the term of office of each superintendent. Most hospital administrators remained adamantly opposed to the employment of women doctors in public institutions until their presence was required by statute.[13]

The first successful struggle for obligatory staff appointments for women doctors took place in Pennsylvania in 1878–1879. Dr. Hiram Corson, who earlier had waged a campaign in the Pennsylvania State Medical Society for more than a decade to gain recognition for graduates and faculty of female medical schools, now launched a fight for that society to petition the legislature to assure that every psychiatric institution in the state of Pennsylvania would have a woman physician in charge of the care of incarcerated females. A dedicated crusader for justice for women in medicine (some would say a fanatic), Corson could be persuasive and rational, although sometimes overbearing, and was not above using emotionalism. Thus, in 1878, he asked the members to "fancy, if you can, your own mother or daughter taken to a hospital for the insane.... are these sad mothers, these loved sisters, these unhappy daughters likely to reveal aught of their condition" to an inexperienced male staff doctor? The appeal was a standard

---

Med. Surg. J., March 7, 1895: 224–228; Bondurant, "Two cases of oophorectomy," pp. 342–345; Carlos C. Booth, "Report of a few cases of laparotomy: melancholia successfully treated by the removal of the ovaries," *Cleveland Med. Gaz.*, 1896: 209–211; and Joseph Meyer, "A case of insanity, caused by diseased ovaries, cured by their removal," *Amer. Assoc. Obst. and Gyne.* 1895: 503–504. Also see Robert Battey, "Normal ovariotomy," *Atlanta Med. Surg. J.*, September, 1872. B. J. Barker-Benfield, in "The spermatic economy: a nineteenth-century view of sexuality," *Feminist Studies*, 1972, *1*: 45–74 and in *The Horrors of the Half-Known Life* (New York: Harper and Row, 1976) argues that "castration" of women by surgeons and gynecologists was widespread both over time and in numbers. Hard evidence is lacking, however, and, within a very short time, the medical profession itself cried out against the abuse. Battey himself gave warning. For a more balanced view see Regina Morantz, "The Lady and Her Physician," in Mary S. Hartman and Lois Banner, eds. *Clio's Consciousness Raised* (New York: Harper and Row, 1974), pp. 38–53. See also Lawrence D. Longo, "The rise and fall of Battey's operation: a fashion in surgery," *Bull. Hist. Med.*, 1979, *53*: 244–267.

[13] See biographical file of Mary Henderson Stinson at the Florence A. Moore Library, Medical College of Pennsylvania (formerly known as the Woman's Medical College of Pennsylvania and hereinafter referred to as WMCP), Philadelphia, Pennsylvania. Stinson was the woman doctor Bemis hired. See also Mary M. Wolfe, "The present status of women physicians in hospitals for the insane," *Proc. Amer. Medico-Psych. Assoc. at the Sixty-Fifth Annual Meeting*, 1909, pp. 350 and 354–356; Eveline P. Ballintine, "Women physicians in public institutions," *Woman's Med. J.*, April, 1908: 79; and "The employment of women physicians in state hospitals," *Woman's Med. J.*, May, 1912: 116–117.

one by now and Corson cited all the usual arguments: women's reluctance to reveal gynecological infirmities, doctors' aversions to pursuing such questions, "moral and mental delusions" produced by the peculiar female organic susceptibility, and women doctors' innate "devotion and self-sacrifice" and "gentleness and care."[14]

Positions as staff doctors were one thing, but Corson also urged the placement of women as superintendents in complete charge of all the business of the female wards. He scoffed at the objection that it had never been done before and dismissed physical weakness and inexperience as straw man arguments: male superintendents were not chosen for their strength and male staff doctors (the ones who dealt with patients on a daily basis) were equally unqualified when hired. The only objection to which Corson gave credence was that of the untested managerial skill of women. Did they have executive talent? Never one to be unprepared, in reply Corson cited at length the organizational abilities and dedicated work on behalf of the insane of Elizabeth Fry in England and Dorothea Dix in America, threw in a few remarks about the stamina of Elizabeth Blackwell, and then plunged into his most convincing evidence. At that moment, he reported, Sarah J. Smith was heading the Indiana Reformatory for Women and Girls which housed 184 "fallen, vicious, and criminal females" and Eudora Atkinson was directing the Massachusetts Reformatory Prison for Women (416 women and 45 children as inmates), and both had received testimonials from all parts of the country hailing their rehabilitative work and administrative skill. Thus Corson tapped every responsive chord in his audience. Ill women needed understanding, they would respond with confidentiality, and their natural timidity would disappear in the face of the talented, "kind, consoling, sympathizing" women doctors who could alleviate, even possibly eliminate, their sufferings and the cause of their illnesses.[15]

Despite having the support of some hospital doctors, Corson was aware of the possibility that "great opposition" might arise from others. It was not long before his suspicions were verified. His report had passed the Medical Society and the House of Representatives at the state capital. To almost everyone's surprise, however, the Senate committee brought it out with a negative recommendation. The superintendents of hospitals had indeed been at work. Thomas Kirkbride, head of the Pennsylvania Hospital for the Insane for thirty-nine years, and original founder and "grand old man" of the American Psychiatric Association, had written to the governor, lieutenant governor, members of the House and Senate and had circulated his own petition in the Philadelphia area (garnering sixty signatures of doctors and hospital administrators) in opposition to the proposed law. John Curwen,

[14] See the report of the Committee on the "propriety of having a female physician for the female department of every hospital for the insane, which is under the control of the State" in Hiram Corson, *A Brief History of Proceedings in the Medical Society of Pennsylvania to procure the Recognition of Women Physicians by the Medical Profession of the State* (Norristown, Pa.: Herald Printing, 1894), pp. 27–36, for Corson's wide-ranging arguments.

[15] Corson, *A Brief History*, pp. 29–35.

superintendent of the Harrisburg Hospital, who had earlier supported Corson in his struggle to gain recognition for women doctors, now viewed Corson as a troublemaker and ungentlemanly adversary. Even John Gray, the editor of the prestigious and powerful *American Journal of Insanity* and administrator of the Utica (New York) Hospital, denigrated Corson and his followers, calling Corson "malicious and blackhearted" for his criticism of the psychiatrists' resistance to women doctors as administrators of female wards.[16]

The opposition of the superintendents was not an across-the-board disagreement with the idea of women doctors on staffs, but an objection to the placing of women in offices of independent authority within the institutions, thus creating two separate positions of control. Corson had already illustrated that the male and female wards were run quite separately anyway and that a steward as business manager and a male doctor in charge of the medical care of men and a female one for women would be an even more efficient arrangement. Unsympathetic to psychiatrists' worries about divided authority and loss of power, Corson mounted a counter campaign in the Senate and succeeded in having his bill passed. The only drawback was that the wording had been changed and the law, instead of *requiring* the appointment of women physicians, merely suggested that state institutions "may" appoint a woman. Undeterred, the trustees of the state hospitals at Harrisburg and Norristown immediately established women doctors as the heads of their female departments. In the 1880s, a few other states besides Pennsylvania passed more limited legislation (requiring women as assistant physicians but not as autonomous heads of departments) and opened doors to women doctors.[17]

The women did not receive a wholehearted welcome. Initial reactions within the profession ranged from strong and friendly encouragement through mild surprise at the women doctors' competency to cool disregard and outright hostility. Some superintendents made clear that in hiring women doctors they were merely complying with the decisions of their boards—decisions with which they did not agree. (One of these superintendents, however, did express some satisfaction that the woman physician would relieve him from the burden of conducting the training school for attendants.) Other superintendents, at least in their official reports, simply ignored the first appointees, mentioning everyone on the staff by name except the woman physician. One of the more extreme reactions was that of John Chapin, who resigned the superintendency of the Willard Asylum in

[16] Corson, *A Brief History*, pp. 25 and 41–43. Thomas S. Kirkbride to Gov. Hugh (n.d.); to Lieut. Gov. Stone (n.d.); to the Senate and House of Representatives of the Commonwealth of Pennsylvania (n.d.); John Curwen to Thomas S. Kirkbride, May 12, 1881; and John P. Gray to Thomas S. Kirkbride, March 11, 1881, Thomas S. Kirkbride MSS, Pennsylvania Hospital, Philadelphia, Pennsylvania. John Curwen's votes on the issue of the Pennsylvania State Medical Society's recognition of women in medicine are cited in Corson, pp. 14, 21, and 23.

[17] Letters of Thomas S. Kirkbride cited above; Corson, *A Brief History*, pp. 40–41; Minutes of the Board of Trustees, Harrisburg State Hospital, Harrisburg, Pennsylvania, (Hereinafter referred to as HSH Trustee Minutes), July 10, 1879; and "By-Laws" in *The Hospital for the Insane for the South Eastern District of Pennsylvania: Acts of Assembly, By-Laws, and Rules and Regulations Governing It* (Philadelphia: Reen & Trump, 1880), p. 7.

New York in 1884 just as its trustees appointed a woman, and took over the administration of the Insane Department of the Pennsylvania Hospital—where no woman physician was appointed until he retired in 1912![18]

Once ensconced in hospital positions, women faced the further obstacles of the ambiguous expectations others had both about their behavior and about their work within the institutions. Clearly, these were professional women and did not fit the Victorian mold of submissiveness and domesticity, yet they were expected to "keep their place." One superintendent remarked that he was satisfied with the way in which the "first incumbent" had performed her duties under the "requirement of the statute" because among her virtues, she exhibited "feminine self-adjustment" and was always "in the right place at the right time." This practice she "maintained" as a "sensible habit," although, he warned, this was "by no means invariably the case in practice elsewhere." Let the woman who could not adjust to the demands and expectations of the male-dominated institutions beware.[19]

Devotion, fidelity, earnestness, and service were other preferred qualities, and not unlike the desirable characteristics expected in the male assistants. Crossing these lines, however, and asserting one's self, even for the sake of the patients, brought only personal discomfort and possible dismissal for a woman physician. For example, one of the Illinois Commissioners on Charities asked for the resignation of Harriet C. B. Alexander in 1885 when she complained about the quality of the institutional food at the Chicago State Hospital. The Commissioner had asked the cook if the food was always good. Hearing the cook's affirmative answer, Alexander had "held up an iron-ringed, unwashed snout of a pig suffering from catarrh, and asked if that was a specimen of the good food." Apparently the superintendent was equally taken aback by Alexander's outspokenness, for he later described her as having a "bad moral influence on the discipline of the institution." Although he acknowledged that she was perhaps "conscientiously unselfish," that made her even more of a "danger" because she might become involved with "some association of determined advocates of feminine ascendancy." He was right: Harriet Alexander stayed at the hospital for only one year and then pursued a highly successful practice in Chicago, regularly publishing articles illustrating her ongoing concern with the care of mentally ill women, and becoming a strong supporter of and active worker for the Medical Women's National Association.[20]

[18] See *Forty-Eighth Annual Report of the Managers of the Utica State Hospital at Utica* (Albany: James B. Lyon, State Printer, 1890), p. 56; *Friends' Asylum for the Insane, Reports, 1895* (Philadelphia: William K. Bellows, 1895), pp. 6 and 26–27; *Fifty-Third Annual Report of the Trustees of the Worcester Lunatic Hospital* (Boston: Wright & Potter, 1886), pp. 8 and 18; this is a clear pattern if one follows the career line of John B. Chapin, especially since Chapin was the superintendent who ignored the woman physician in his annual report.

[19] *Forty-Ninth Annual Report of the Managers of the Utica State Hospital at Utica* (Albany: James B. Lyon, State Printer, 1892), p. 29.

[20] These qualities are gleaned from the phrases used to describe both the male and female assistants in numerous reports of superintendents throughout the last three decades of the nineteenth century. Alexander's experience is cited in Paoli and Kiernan, "Female physicians," pp. 26 and 28–29. See also Harriet C. B. Alexander, "Paranoia in the female," *Alienist and Neurologist*, July, 1887, *8*: 360–365.

Other women exhibited more perseverance on the institutional scene, but many of them eventually gave up and entered private practice or pursued their interests in psychiatry by establishing their own sanitaria. A woman like Margaret Cleaves, at the Harrisburg Hospital in Pennsylvania, seemed to be in an ideal position with full automony over the women's wards. One of the early women graduates of the medical school of Iowa State University (1873), Cleaves had been assistant physician at the Mt. Pleasant State Hospital in Iowa, a member of the board of trustees of that institution after she resigned her staff appointment, and was practicing in Davenport, Iowa, when the Harrisburg trustees recruited her for their new position. But Cleaves lasted only three years, 1880–1883, at Harrisburg. Although her male counterpart believed that it was the "inalienable right of women" to do the work among insane women, it is clear that some resentment about the reorganization remained. Each of her annual reports made specific reference to this problem.[21]

Cleaves encountered other difficulties as well, some of her own making. She was too optimistic. She entered upon her duties with such "intense interest," "conviction," and "love for the work" that she promptly set out to establish a new program of treatment which in turn led her to radical speculation as to the causes of insanity in women. As her theories evolved, even in those three short years, she challenged a number of long held beliefs. Using her annual reports as her forum, she questioned the relationship of utero-ovarian disease to insanity. At first, in 1881, she believed that such disease "may sustain the relation of cause to effect." But within a year, Cleaves felt that mental and physical improvement after local treatment was perhaps only coincidental and, after a "certain point," further gains were impossible, although patients could at least be made "more comfortable." This uncertainty about causal relationships loomed large in her last report. Acknowledging that in a very small proportion of cases diseased reproductive organs did act as a "causative influence," Cleaves quickly pointed out that the "undermining effect upon the general health" was the real culprit. Finally, she stated flatly that her experience convinced her that the percentage of recoveries would not increase as a result of "such special treatment." Women would remain insane, but they would do so in greater physical comfort.[22]

Her discussion of other issues also reflected her growing pessimism. Stressing heredity factors in the causality of insanity, Cleaves suggested that the formerly insane should "cease to assume the responsibilities of father or motherhood," otherwise the "grand work of prevention" would never

[21] Cleaves' career line is evident from the information in Polk's *Medical and Surgical Registers* (Detroit: R.L. Polk, 1890, 1898, and 1900); Henry M. Hurd, *The Institutional Care of the Insane in the United States and Canada*, 4 vols. (Baltimore: The Johns Hopkins Press, 1916), 3: 434; *Biennial Reports of the Trustees, Superintendents, and Treasurers of the Iowa State Hospital for the Insane at Mt. Pleasant* (Des Moines: R.P. Clarkson, 1874–1880); and HSH Trustee Minutes, July 8, 1880 and August 5, 1880. See also "Report of Physician-Female Department" in the 31st, 32nd, and 33rd annual reports of the Harrisburg Hospital.

[22] "Report of Physician-Female Department" in the 31st, 32nd, and 33rd annual reports of the Harrisburg Hospital.

begin. Deciding that the circumscribed social roles of women contributed to their mental illness, Cleaves decried the "endless monotony of the lives of the majority of women," the "never ceasing routine of work," and the "too frequent child bearing." Thus Cleaves weakened the rationale which underlay her appointment. Gynecological treatment she deemed ineffective in lessening the causality of mental illness in women; she raised the controversial issue of sterilization; and attacked the very warp and woof of the social fabric—the role of women. There was little she could do about the propensity of her patients to have too many children too close together, except lament the unhappy circumstances. Cleaves had other reasons for giving up as well and, in 1883, she left the asylum and returned to private practice concentrating on the treatment of neurasthenic women. Private practice would free her from institutional constraints and, at least with these women, of a different class from that of her patients at the state hospital, she might have some success in convincing them that their ways of "social dissipation" had led them into illness. They might listen and reform their way of living.[23]

Shortly after Cleaves resigned, the trustees changed the administrative structure of the institution "because of friction between the superintendent and the women physicians." Cleaves' successor, Jane Garver, no longer had control over personnel in the women's wards and had to report directly to the superintendent, as did the first assistant in the men's wards. Garver took the hint and her reports were short, without personal comment or innovative professional suggestions. Although she continued the gynecological work, she turned over much of the follow-up care to nurses and, after more than a decade of service, referred to the patients as a "stagnant mass of humanity" and made remarks about their "obstreperous character." When Garver died in 1902, the trustees under the guise of "greater efficiency," once more tightened up the administrative structure so that the formerly autonomous and theoretically powerful "woman physician" at Harrisburg became nothing more than a second or third assistant with at least two male doctors always outranking her in authority. The same two women doctors

[23] See Cleaves' annual reports, 1880–1883, and HSH Case Book, 1882–1884. Two-thirds of Cleaves' patients were married (or widowed) and for the fifty on whom she recorded usable data, they averaged a child birth every 2.1 years (and if miscarriages are included, a pregnancy every 1.9 years). The average number of children born was 6.42 and this statistic obscures even more trying individual cases like the woman who bore twelve children in twenty years or the one who in seven years gave birth to three infants, suffered three miscarriages, and the death of one of her children. See *Autobiography of a Neurasthene: As Told By One of Them and Recorded by Margaret A. Cleaves, M.D.* (Boston: Richard G. Badger, The Gorham Press, 1910) for other reasons for Cleaves' resignation. The internal evidence makes it clear that this is the autobiography of Cleaves herself. Her long battle with neurasthenia and her frequent remarks about "blows received upon my head at the hands of insane patients" (pp. 63 and 84), indicate that the roots of her problem were existent before her actual attack. See also Cleaves' articles: "Neurasthenia and its relation to diseases of woman," *Proceedings of the Thirty-Fourth Annual Session of the Iowa State Medical Society*, May 19–21, 1886: 164–179; in the "Asylum Notes" section, "Can the gynaecologist aid the alienist in institutions for the insane," *J. Nerv. Ment. Dis.* July, 1891: 472–475; and the report of her work in the "Abstracts and Extracts" section of the *Amer. J. Insanity*, July, 1888: 163–164.

served until the 1920s and their therapeutics slipped into regular sedation of patients and routine medical care without any gynecological specialization.[24]

Alice Bennett of the Norristown Hospital in Pennsylvania was of a different character. A woman of incredible energy, she had earned the tuition for her medical education at the Woman's Medical College of Pennsylvania by teaching school. Receiving her degree in the spring of 1876, she worked in a Philadelphia dispensary for the poor until her appointment as demonstrator of anatomy at her alma mater that fall. For the next four years she taught anatomy and other courses, maintained a private practice, and worked toward her Ph.D. degree at the University of Pennsylvania. In 1880, when the trustees of the Norristown Hospital were searching for their first woman doctor-administrator, Alice Bennett was one of the most likely candidates. Unlike Margaret Cleaves who had taken an original approach and ended up, through her own actions, questioning therapeutic procedures and social mores. Bennett almost immediately fitted into many of the male patterns of professional behavior and conformity. She took up all the causes of her male colleagues: expressing dissatisfaction with the classification of the causes of insanity, noting the effects of heredity, and complaining of overcrowded conditions.[25]

But because she was untouched by the pessimism of many of those who had labored in the field for years and inspired by the educational milieu of her medical training, Bennett brought a refreshing attitude to her task. She reinstituted and gave new life to the educational and occupational aspects of the traditional moral therapy regime. Not content with the idea that her responsibility ended when she discharged patients, she made regular follow-up contacts with them through visits and letters. She became worried also about the efficacy of drugs. Suggesting that work therapy was "not inferior to drugs" and urging that a "change *out* of the hospital" might be equally effective, she waged a campaign against unnecessary sedation.[26]

In keeping with the expectations of her role in the asylum, she carried on her gynecological work. Year after year, she increased the proportion of patients examined and treated for gynecological disorders, extending and

[24] Hurd, *The Institutional Care of the Insane*, 3: 434–435; HSH Trustee Minutes, August 30, 1883; "Report of the Physician-Female Department" in *Forty-Fifth Annual Report ... Harrisburg*, p. 15 and *Forty-Seventh Annual Report ... Harrisburg*, p. 16; HSH Trustee Minutes, October 16, 1902 (in which for the first time there is no report by a female physician; nor is there again); and HSH Case Book, 1904–1918.

[25] For Bennett's early career, see Minutes of the Faculty, January 13, 1877, January 27, 1877, January 12, 1878, February 7, 1878, January 1, 1879, January 11, 1880, January 30, 1880, and July 3, 1880; Board of Corporators Minutes, September 30, 1879; and Treasurer's Report, April 27, 1879 to February 29, 1880, WMCP. Also consult biographical material in the file of Alice Bennett, Alumnae Files, WMCP, the Philadelphia *Ledger*, May 5, 1896, and biographical sketch by Stanley I. Kutler in Edward T. James, ed., *Notable American Women* (Cambridge: Belknap Press of Harvard University Press, 1971). For Bennett's years at the Norristown Hospital, see the "Department of Women-Report of the Resident Physician," First through Seventeenth (1880-1896) *Annual Reports of the State Hospital for the South-Eastern District of Pennsylvania at Norristown, Pa.* (Allentown: Allen W. Haines, 1880–1896).

[26] For Bennett's remarks on the follow-up of patients, see especially her 1881 annual report and for her concern about drugs, see her 1882–1894 reports.

systematizing the work until it became a "large and laborious part of the medical work of the department." As she proceeded, Bennett observed that since most of the conditions occurred as a result of childbirth, they were not diseases in and of themselves nor were they causal elements in insanity. Moving increasingly further from the thought of some of those who had supported the employment of women doctors in asylums, she searched for other explanations and ultimately decided that insanity itself was not a true disease but simply a symptom of general ill health. Nevertheless, Bennett continued to relieve her patients' physical discomfort.[27]

For ten years, everything went smoothly. Then Bennett found herself under siege from the Pennsylvania press, the editors of the *American Journal of Insanity*, and the state Commissioners on Lunacy. Bennett allegedly set aside a special building in which to perform "illegal" ovariotomies on a large number of non-consenting insane women either, as her detractors claimed, with the misguided goal of curing insanity or of moving up the "ladder of fame." Bennett did not perform the operations, however. Dr. Joseph Price and Dr. Marie B. Werner did them in the presence of at least six other doctors. The trustees, the superintendent, and Bennett as Female Physician had all concurred in the decision to carry out the gynecological surgery in the most severe cases. But only six operations were performed and in each case there were obvious pathological conditions. Furthermore, Bennett had obtained the permission of the nearest relatives.[28]

Many rallied to support Bennett. The editor of the *Philadelphia Press* praised Bennett's fine reputation and argued that the Lunacy Commission was interfering with the discretionary rights of a physician, and possibly depriving poor women of quality care. Dr. Price dismissed the charge that the operations were experimental and constituted "inhuman and brutal treatment," stating there was "no more unselfish and conscientious woman filling public place" than Alice Bennett. Despite this support, Bennett reacted with dismay at the ferocity of the attack, and withdrew from the public limelight. No longer did her annual reports contain references to gynecological work (although she continued it), instead she took up other, safer,

[27] See especially Bennett's 1882, 1883, and 1884 reports on gynecological treatment.

[28] See the *Philadelphia Press* of January 9, 1893; Thomas G. Morton, "Removal of the ovaries as a cure for insanity," *Amer. J. Insanity*, January, 1893, 49: 397–401; the "Notes and Comment" section, pp. 497–499 and the "Correspondence" section, pp. 512–515 of the same journal. Morton, and the editor of the journal (John P. Gray), were responding to an "extract in advance" from the *Tenth Annual Report of the Committee on Lunacy of the Board of Public Charities of Pennsylvania, 1892*, which supposedly stated that "several patients have already had their ovaries extirpated." After an inquiry by the Board of Trustees at Norristown and their whole-hearted backing of Bennett, that section of the reports was withdrawn and never appeared in print. See Bennett's reports, 1893–1896; "Correspondence" section of the 1893 issue of the *Amer. J. Insanity*, January, 1893: 514–515; and "In the Matter of Certain Charges against the Management of the State Hospital for the Insane for the South-Eastern District of Pennsylvania," *Proceedings before the Legislative Committee*, (Norristown: Hospital Press, 1895). It is fairly clear from the published transcript of the hearings that Dr. Marie Werner had brought a complaint against Bennett because Bennett refused to allow Werner to continue "experimental surgery." Werner perceived it as experimental and Bennett, worried about that aspect of it, discontinued the service of Werner although she allowed four operations by Price later.

causes, such as the state's neglect of the chronic insane and the means of combating tuberculosis.[29]

Paradoxically, it was in this very same year that the American Psychiatric Association devoted a large part of its annual meeting to a discussion of the use of surgical methods in the treatment of insanity. George Rohe, superintendent of the Maryland Hospital for the Insane, led the discussion. Having polled 120 medical officers of asylums on the question of the relationship of the removal of ovaries and uterine appendages to insanity, he had difficulty tabulating the data because some doctors, he said, had performed the operations not only for mental conditions, but also for physical problems. Nevertheless, he himself had operated on fourteen women in the last ten months with some success and even delayed the discharge of four of his "cured" cases for the members to observe. His offer to perform an operation when they toured his institution met with a round of applause. Further discussion illustrated that the members generally approved of the removal of ovarian tumors for the mental welfare of the patient. Some disagreed, and Bennett later found herself the butt of those who not only opposed surgery but who had also remained adamant against having women physicians in the asylums. When questions about the so-called experimental surgery arose again in an 1895 legislative investigation, Bennett finished out her last three-year contract at Norristown in 1896 and returned to her hometown.[30]

Many of the American Psychiatric Association members did remain opposed to women in the profession, especially if there was some question that these women doctors might rise to positions of authority. Already beleaguered by decades of attack for inflexibility, stiff competition from other professional groups, and rumblings of reform from within, some members were particularly sensitive about the possibility of further weakening their position by giving in to female incursions. The request from Margaret Cleaves merely to *attend* the 1881 meeting at Toronto had created such petty quibbling that Cleaves was not seated as a member although her male counterpart at Harrisburg, J. Z. Gerhard, was. The question was not brought up for another decade and a half and, by that time, the Association had changed its name, its rules for membership, and most of the "old guard" had died.[31]

[29] See the *Philadelphia Press*, January 10 and 12, 1893. See the Fourteenth through Seventeenth (1893–1896) *Annual Reports*. Bennett does not mention gynecological work and her last reports are merely perfunctory.

[30] See "Proceedings of the forty-eighth annual meeting of the Association of Medical Superintendents of American Institutions for the Insane," *Amer. J. Insanity*, July, 1892, *49*: 216–306. Among the doctors who both opposed the use of surgery and the presence of women physicians in the institutions were the lukewarm superintendent of the Utica (New York) Asylum, G. Alder Blumer, and none other than John Chapin, who had moved from the Willard (New York) Asylum to the Pennsylvania Hospital in order to avoid appointing women. See "Correspondence" section of the January, 1893, issue of the *American Journal of Insanity* and "Proceedings of the forty-eighth annual meeting."

[31] For evidence of the precarious position of the psychiatric professional organization in the last half of the nineteenth century see Hurd, *The Institutional Care of the Insane*, especially volume 1; Albert Deutsch, *The Mentally Ill in America* (New York: Columbia University Press, 1949); John Burnham, "Psychiatry, psychology and the Progressive movement," *Amer. Quart.* 1960, *12*: 457–465; Grob, *The State and the Mentally Ill*; and

The passing of the founders and their protégés was crucial, for it had been they who, from the 1840s on, had determined the nature of the psychiatric profession, argued psychiatric theory, established therapeutic procedures, and wrested the control of the treatment of the mentally ill from the hands of the poorhouse steward and jail keeper. Although some dissent was tolerated, where the line was to be drawn was always uncertain. Alice Bennett, despite her attempts to remain within the boundaries of her male colleagues' expectations, crossed that line.[32]

Mechanical restraint (the use of physical means or contraptions to control patients) had long been a controversial question among the psychiatrists and the Association never sanctioned total non-restraint. Bennett did, however, justifying it in her reports, boasting annually that not a patient had been restrained, and even delivering a paper on the subject before the Medico-Legal Society of New York. For this she might have been forgiven, but she also joined the National Association for the Protection of the Insane and the Prevention of Insanity, which had the aims of scrutinizing more carefully and controlling the administration of state psychiatric institutions. Outraged by implications of incompetency, the American Psychiatric Association not only scorned, but denigrated, the new organization and helped to bring about its early demise. But Bennett (as well as Cleaves) had been one of the original members and had served on the editorial board of its journal. This was too much for many of her colleagues and although she retained membership in the American Psychiatric Association, she never attended meetings. Indeed, few women attended and not one delivered a paper or took part in discussions. As the representative, at least in a symbolic way, of the entire profession of psychiatry, the Association was on record in opposition to any significant role for women doctors.[33]

What of the other women who were in less powerful positions than either Cleaves or Bennett? By the nature of their appointments they did not

---

Charles Rosenberg, "The Crisis in Psychiatric Legitimacy: Reflections on Psychiatry, Medicine, and Public Policy" in George Kriegman *et al.*, eds., *American Psychiatry: Past, Present, and Future* (Charlottesville: University Press of Virginia, 1975). See "Proceedings of the thirty-seventh annual meeting of the Association of Medical Superintendents of American Institutions for the Insane," *Amer. J. Insanity*, Oct., 1881, *38*: 174–177.

[32] That the psychiatrists themselves recognized the power of their organization is clear in John Curwen's account, *History of the Association of Medical Superintendents of American Institutions For the Insane* (Harrisburg: Theo. F. Scheffer, 1875) and in those of later historians. See Deutsch, *The Mentally Ill in America*; Hurd, *The Institutional Care of the Insane*, vol. 1; Grob, *Mental Institutions*.

[33] See Alice Bennett, "Mechanical restraint in the treatment of the insane," *Medico-Legal J. New York*, 1884, *1*: 285–296. A possible added area of sensitivity in Bennett's case may be that she had also served on the Philadelphia committee to raise the $100,000 donation for Johns Hopkins to assure that the university would accept female medical students in their newly opened medical department. See Welsh, *Reminiscences*, pp. 32–36. See the remarks on the history of the National Association for the Protection of the Insane and the Prevention of Insanity in Deutsch, *The Mentally Ill in America*, pp. 311–314 and in J. K. Hall, ed., *One Hundred Years of American Psychiatry, 1884–1944* (New York: Columbia University Press, 1944), p. 351; the seven issues of the *American Psychological Journal* (Oskar Diethelm Library, The New York Hospital); and such articles as Orpheus Everts, "The American system of public provision for the insane, and despotism in lunatic asylums," *Amer. J. Insanity*, Oct. 1881, *31*: 113–139; and "Rights of the insane," *Amer. J. Insanity*, April, 1883, *33*: 411–432. After 1885 (when women were allowed to attend because membership rules were changed to include assistant physicians) until the turn of the century only nine women made an appearance. Only one came back a second time.

run into the same kinds of difficulties and, in many ways, were little different from the male doctors in institutions who held similar subordinate positions. Like many young male doctors, the women frequently entered asylum service directly from medical school and stayed only a short time (an average of four years for both sexes). The asylum offered an opportunity to observe and treat a variety of physical and mental ailments—an experience that was not readily available elsewhere, especially for women. Economic security also played a part. The asylum provided room and board, plus a salary, and this was, at least initially, attractive to neophyte physicians. Upon leaving institutional service, many, both male and female, established practices in nearby areas—illustrating that another function of asylum service was the making of contacts or reputation in the interest of building up a future clientele. Although marriage while in service was out of the question (the by-laws of nearly every asylum required that assistant physicians remain single), social intercourse did not prove impossible. At least two dozen of these aspiring women doctors married men who were serving on the medical staffs at the same time they were.[34]

There were significant differences, however, in the professional treatment of women within the institutions. Regularly passed over for promotion, women must have felt the ramifications both in the lessening of personal and professional self-confidence and in their lower salaries. Many male assistants received superintendencies and other men were hired as first or second assistants at salaries of $300—$700 more than the woman (as third or fourth assistant) who had served for a number of years. Some of this spilled over into quibbling about titles. One woman always designated herself as the "woman physician," while her superiors insisted on listing her as merely "second assistant physician." Some of it was immortalized in the by-laws of asylums. In most sets of regulations, among the duties of male assistants was that of taking over the administration of the hospital in the absence of the superintendent; women assistants could only take over his medical duties. Thus women tended to move from hospital to hospital more frequently than men, perhaps in search of recognition, and ultimately opted for private practices.[35]

[34] The average tenure of both male and female assistant physicians is derived from the listings in Hurd, *The Institutional Care of the Insane*, vols. 2 and 3. The places where assistants set up private practice are sometimes listed in Hurd, vols. 2 and 3, in the narratives of each hospital. Others are traced through the various editions of *Polk's Medical and Surgical Registers* (Detroit: R. L. Polk, 1886, 1890, 1898, and 1900), (Title varies). Marital information is derived from tracing the women doctors in Hurd, vols. 2 and 3. Since many of these married women retained both their maiden and married names, they are fairly easy to trace, especially in the cases where a future husband served in the same institution during the same time period. Some were traced back from the listings in the *Census of Women Physicians, November 11, 1918* published by the American Women's Hospitals under the auspices of the Council of National Defense.

[35] This was evident, for instance, at the Medfield (Massachusetts) Insane Asylum where the female assistant physician was regularly passed over for promotion for the first nine years. Even newly-hired male assistants were listed ahead of the woman and some men were promoted from third assistant to first with the resultant increase of salary from $800 to $1500. The Medfield practices were not unique. See First through Tenth *Annual Reports of the Medfield Insane Asylum at Medfield, Massachusetts* (Boston: Wright & Potter, 1896—1905). See particularly the experience over titles of Laura Hulme in the *Sixth Annual Report of the State*

In certain respects, women did not differ much from their male colleagues. For instance, both while at the asylums and later in private practice, their medical and psychiatric theories generally followed the same lines as those of their male contemporaries. Most had had neither the opportunity nor the authority to carry out experimental programs as Margaret Cleaves and Alice Bennett had done. When they did establish their private offices they very clearly and purposely chose sites, especially in large cities, where male doctors had been successful. In Chicago, the majority of women doctors clustered in the "Loop" area and in Philadelphia most settled on Spruce, Pine, Walnut, Chestnut and Broad Streets.[36]

Women doctors were not without their own resources, however. It seems clear that certain support systems were devised by the early practitioners and used by the younger women. One pattern which emerged was that of co-practice, that is, a number of women doctors practicing at the same address. A closer look reveals that these women had either served in the same public institution (although not necessarily at the same time), that they had attended the same medical school, or that some were in the same graduating class as a woman who had served in an institution with one of the partners. The emotional and psychological support that this system offered is obvious, but the practice also resulted in women doctors being clustered in large cities and in particular neighborhoods—restricting themselves geographically as well as by their tendency to treat only women and children.[37]

It had taken most women only a few years to realize the intellectual and professional constrictions of institutional service. Although some, like Bertha Van Hoosen, reacted as if the whole experience had been somewhat of a lark, remarking that in a year and a half she "never made a note" on any patient; others could attribute their "tale of woe" to the blows received "at the hands of insane patients." Most, it appears, had assessed their possible professional future in the asylums and had moved on.[38]

Whether primarily motivated to alleviate the sufferings of insane women or using their institutional positions for other reasons, there is no doubt these would-be psychiatrists and women physicians faced multifarious forms of sexism. Not unlike other women entering the professions, these doctors strove to overcome barriers which emerged from deep-seated feelings about traditional sex roles and societal judgments about the intellectual and emotional limitations of women who pursued professional careers. As they circumvented each barrier, new ones appeared. By the end of the century,

Asylum for the Chronic Insane of Pennsylvania (Lebanon, Pa.: Report Publishing, 1895) and for administrative duties, see the *Reports of the Trustees, Resident Officers and the Visiting Committee of the Maine Insane Hospital* (Augusta: Burleigh & Flint, 1888), pp. 11 and 12.

[36] Addresses of practices were derived from the 1886, 1890, 1898, and 1900 editions of *Polk's Medical and Surgical Register* and from the 1918 *Census of Women Physicians*.

[37] Information on service in psychiatric institutions is found in Hurd, *The Institutional Care of the Insane*, vols. 2 and 3 and that on medical school attendance from the 1918 *Census of Women Physicians* and *Polk's Medical and Surgical Registers*.

[38] Van Hoosen, *Petticoat Surgeon*, p. 87 and Cleaves, *Autobiography of a Neurasthene*, pp. 63 and 84.

medical education was available, many medical societies had dropped their exclusive male membership policies, and general hospitals accepted some female interns. But individual and organizational reservations had not completely disappeared, particularly in the psychiatric profession. Thus as some of the more perceptive and innovative women proceeded they faced a dilemma of such proportions that they withdrew from institutional service rather than continue to confront the almost unabated professional hostility toward them and their work.[39]

There had originally been utopian expectations of these women. The very idea of requiring women physicians in public institutions had been promoted on the grounds that they would be the saviors of the female insane. This specialized treatment would result in lower death rates, it would eliminate all sexual delusions, and causes of insanity peculiar to women would disappear. Yet they could not singlehandedly do away with sexual delusions. They might only relieve the stress these delusions engendered among the male medical staff. They could, and did, deal effectively with some gynecological problems, but they could not eliminate them as a cause of insanity. When they attempted to, they were caught up in intraprofessional disputes about the use of surgery and, if they questioned whether reproductive organs, either diseased or healthy, actually did cause insanity, they were reprimanded professionally for undermining long held, and cherished, beliefs.

Questions, however, remain both about these women doctors and about the nearly two hundred others who served in similar positions in other institutions in the first decades of the twentieth century. Given the paucity of internships and residencies for women, did they use these appointments as virtually their only opportunity and then perceiving the limitations, move on? Or were many of them opting for a less rigorous speciality: one which offered more regular hours? Unlike surgery, or even general medicine, a private practice in psychiatry allowed for accommodation with marriage and family life. But, at the same time, did this choice unintentionally fulfill the popular assumptions about the innate limitations of women in the professions?

What of those who stayed? Did they work out viable strategies for avoiding conflict and thereby win the confidence of their male critics and still manage to demonstrate their competency? It would seem that in many cases they did, but not without sacrifice. Pockets of sexism, not unlike that experienced by Harriet C. B. Alexander, remained. In the 1880s, Alexander's performance had illustrated the "desirability of female physicians" to one of her male superiors, but she appeared insubordinate and a "bad moral

[39] For further discussion of the two-fold type of barriers professional women faced in the Victorian era and the overcoming of barriers followed by the raising of new ones, see the essay by Richard Shryock, "Women in American Medicine," in *Medicine in America* (Baltimore: The Johns Hopkins Press, 1966) and Harris, *Beyond Her Sphere*. For other obstacles, see Frank Stricker, "Cookbooks and law books: the hidden history of career women in twentieth century America," *J. Soc. Hist.*, 1976, *10*: 1–19.

influence" to another. In the early twentieth century, administrators still referred to the "weaker side of woman's nature" as a handicap or remarked that women worked out well only when they were the "right kind of women." After 1900, the tenure of many of the women assistant physicians was longer than that of their predecessors. This may be explained partially by their adjustment to the realities of institutional constrictions. They were, of course, not in positions to initiate or direct new programs of treatment and thus they were not so likely to come in conflict with traditional ideas about bureaucratic authority, psychiatric therapy, or feminine behavior and roles. The adaptation necessary for becoming the "right kind" of woman may have eased the living and working conditions of these women, but not without checking opportunity for meaningful and innovative contributions on their part.[40]

The inability to maintain and submit to discipline, a lack of executive skill, and the absence of ambition in women were other frequent complaints. One superintendent criticized women doctors because "their likes and dislikes were too pronounced" and, furthermore, their "jealous nature" frequently surfaced. Another thought that they required "more waiting on" than men, and that patients did not "consider them as real doctors." There was little realization that if women doctors were kept in subordinate positions, given no chance to exercise authority or experiment, and looked upon by their superintendents as inferior and troublesome, then the women themselves might react in such a way as to fulfill the dire prophecies about their innate unworthiness and incompetency. The lack of executive talent was a moot question. Few of these women were in situations which allowed them to exercise any authority or exhibit managerial ability. Of the approximately 270 state, county, city, corporate, and private psychiatric hospitals founded by 1914, only one-third employed women as assistant physicians. Besides the woman at Norristown, only one other headed a county hospital; three women ran their own private sanitaria.[41]

If women appeared less ambitious than men it was simply because they had little by way of reinforcement to preserve their zeal. Except in institutions like the Government Hospital for the Insane in Washington, D.C., the Kanakee (Illinois) Hospital, and the Worcester (Massachusetts) Asylum, all of which were headed by sympathetic and supportive male superintendents, there was little room for women to participate in progressive scientific work or to advance in administrative hierarchies. The Norristown Hospital was the only state hospital which left untouched the autonomous position of the "Female Physician." It took a rare soul indeed who could maintain her

[40] Paoli and Kiernan, "Female physicians," pp. 26 and 28–29. In the same article Paoli and Kiernan discussed Alexander and came to opposite conclusions about her work and effect on the institution. See also, Wolfe, "Present status," p. 352.

[41] Wolfe, "Present status," pp. 352 and 355–356 for complaints about women physicians and Hurd, *Institutional Care*, vols. 2 and 3 for the assessment of the numbers of institutions by 1914 and for those which employed women doctors in any capacity.

ambitions in the face of non-existent opportunity. Thus the failure of an appreciable number of states to require the appointment of women, the continued resistance on the part of many institutional psychiatrists, and the plethora of dead-end positions had limited the success of women doctors in psychiatric institutions and nearly precluded them from carving out a new area of endeavor. Moreover, these trends may well have lessened the desire of others to enter the profession.[42]

It appears that, like so many other women's crusades, many of these women doctors in psychiatric institutions fell prey to the very forces which promoted their cause. In many ways the good they supposedly were to accomplish was to rise from their very femininity, from the nature of their sex, not from their professional acuity. Thus they were faced with fitting the Victorian mold of submission and quiet dedication to prescribed duties or, if innovative and truly professional, they provoked the ire of their colleagues and society in general and were labeled as "dangers" and failures, in an unfeminine manner, at adjusting to "place and time." In other words, they were "unsexed." If they were to accomplish professional miracles yet remain "ideal" women, in the eyes of Victorian society and the psychiatric profession (and, perhaps, in their own), they failed.

[42] Jacobi, "Female physicians for insane women," pp. 543–544; "The reason why," *Woman's Med. J.* April, 1896: 100; Ballintine, "Women physicians in public institutions," pp. 79–80; Wolfe, "Present status," p. 352; "The employment of women physicians in State Hospitals," pp. 116–117; and Bertha Van Hoosen, "Annual Report of Committee on Medical Opportunities for Women," *Med. Woman's J.*, August, 1929: 216–217.

From Hospital to College: Black Nurse Leaders and the Rise of Collegiate Nursing Schools

Darlene Clark Hine, *Associate Professor of History and Vice Provost, Purdue University**

The high mortality sustained by both northern and southern troops during the Civil War underscored the critical need for trained professional nurses. Motivated in part by these excessive deaths, medical men and civic leaders had established, by 1890, thirty-five hospitals equipped with nurse training schools. In so doing they also created a major new outlet for women with professional or career aspirations. The nurse training schools quickly became significant institutions whereby women, most of whom were poor, could receive an education while simultaneously acquiring marketable skills. For many women the nurse training schools represented a welcome alternative to a life in domestic service.[1]

Although black women had long worked as untrained nurses, they encountered virtually insurmountable obstacles when they attempted to enter the professional nursing schools. In spite of the difficulties, however, some black women did manage to secure nursing training and were, therefore, enabled to take advantage of the new career opportunities and become leaders. Indeed, by the end of the Second World War there existed a number of articulate, well-educated, determined black women nurses such as Estelle Massey Riddle Osborne, the first black woman nurse to earn a

*The author wishes to thank the Rockefeller Archive Center for a grant used to complete the research for this paper and Dr. Patricia Sloan of Hampton Institute for her assistance.

[1]See: Muriel Elizabeth Chapman, "Nursing Education and the Movement for Higher Education for Women: A Study in Interrelationships, 1870–1900" (New York: Unpublished Ed.D dissertation, Columbia University, 1969); David M. Katzman, *Seven Days a Week: Women and Domestic Service in Industrializing America* (New York: Oxford University Press, 1978), p. 53; Mary M. Roberts, *American Nursing: History and Interpretation* (New York: The Macmillan Company, 1954), p. 5.

masters of arts degree; Mable Keaton Staupers; the executive secretary of the National Association of Colored Graduate Nurses, who led the campaign to integrate black women into the U.S. Armed Forces Nurse Corps during World War II; Rita Miller, the force behind the creation of the Dillard University Division of Nursing Education; and M. Elizabeth Carnegie, Dean of the Florida Agricultural and Mechanical College School of Nursing.[2]

The emergence of these resourceful leaders was propitious for they became prominent at a moment when the white nursing leadership had become convinced that nursing education belonged on college campuses and not in the hospitals. Barred from most colleges and universities, black women would have been frozen into the lowest strata of nurse professionals had it not been for the talented leadership of Osborne, Staupers, Miller and Carnegie. This essay uses the dynamic interplay between racism and the professionalization of nursing as a backdrop against which to illuminate the efforts of a few black nurses to establish collegiate schools of nursing for black women. Particular attention is paid the work of Dr. M. Elizabeth Lancaster Carnegie who, with the financial backing of the General Education Board (GEB) of the Rockefeller Foundation and the strong moral and professional support of her friends Riddle, Miller, and Staupers, helped to create and direct the Florida A & M College School of Nursing from 1945 to 1951.

The professionalization of nursing and the entrenchment of segregation and discrimination against black Americans both occurred during the decades between the end of the Civil War and the advent of World War I. The process which elevated nursing to the status of a profession entailed the establishment of nurse training schools, the creation of a special pedagogy, production of a body of scholarship and textbooks, development of profesional organizations, journals, and the emergence of an elite cadre of leaders who pressed for the implementation of higher admission criteria in nursing schools, and the adoption of uniform licensing and registration standards. In tandem with the professionalization of nursing came the institutionalization of practices which excluded black women because of their race. Thus, in the formative stage, as many of the nursing schools emerged, black women, with few exceptions were denied admission. The charter for the New England Hospital for Women and Children, one of the pioneer nurse training schools in the country, expressly stipulated, for example, that only *one* Negro and

[2]Darlene Clark Hine, "Mabel K. Staupers and the Integration of Black Women in the Armed Forces during World War II" in John Hope Franklin and August Meier (eds.), *Black Leaders of the Twentieth Century*, (Urbana: University of Illinois Press, 1982), pp. 241–257.

one Jewish student each year would be accepted. On August 1, 1879, Mary E. Mahoney became the first black women to graduate from this institution.[3]

The late nineteenth century convergence of the professionalization of nursing and intense racial segregation worked to limit even more severely the already meager educational opportunities available to black women. Restricted access to the vast number of nursing schools would have denied a significant proportion of black women the chance of ever entering into professional nursing careers had it not been for two developments: the rise of black advocates of the ideology of self-help and the increased willingness of major white philanthropists to put money into black education. During the 1890s, therefore, black self-help initiatives buttressed by white philanthropy resulted in the establishment of several separate schools of nursing for black women that off-set many of the educational inequities racism had wrought. Between 1890 and 1900, a crucial decade in nursing education history due to the sheer proliferation of schools, nine of the top ten black schools came into existence. It is illustrative to note that by this time there existed 432 schools for white women while in 28 states black women possessed no training facilities whatsoever. The white and the ten black training schools were founded and operated in conjunction with hospitals where the student nurse provided, free of charge, the primary nursing and maintenance service in return for instruction and experience. By 1928 the top ten out of thirty-six functioning black nursing schools had 2,238 graduates, accounting for 80.3 percent of the total 2,784 black women nurses.[4] The ten schools were as follows:

- Provident Hospital and School of Nursing, Chicago, IL (1891)
- Dixie Hospital and Nurses Training School, Hampton, VA (1891)
- Tuskegee Institute School of Nursing, Tuskegee, AL (1892)
- Freedmen's Hospital and School of Nursing, Washington, D.C. (1894)
- Lincoln Hospital and Nurse Training School, New York, NY (1896)
- St. Agnes Hospital and Nurse Training School, Raleigh, NC (1896)

[3]"Mary Eliza Mahoney, First Negro Nurse" *Journal of the National Medical Association*, 46 (July, 1954), 299; M. Elizabeth Carnegie, "Are Negro Schools of Nursing Needed Today," in Herbert M. Morris, *The History of the Negro in Medicine* (Washington, D.C.: ASNLH, 1967), pp. 254–259.

[4]Adah Thoms, *Pathfinders: A History of the Progress of Colored Graduate Nurses* (New York: McKay Company, 1929), pp. 12–13; *The Crisis*, 32 (June, 1926), 84; Roberts, *American Nursing*, p. 5; Joyce Ann Elmore, "A History of Freedmen's Hospital Training School for Nurses in Washington, D.C. 1894–1909" Master of Science in Nursing Thesis, Catholic University of America, June, 1965); Elliot M. Rudwick, "A Brief History of Mercy-Douglass Hospital in Philadelphia" *Journal of Negro Education* 20 (1951), 50–66.

- Phillis Wheatley Sanitarium and Nurse Training School, New Orleans, LA (1896); (Renamed Flint-Goodridge Hospital and School of Nursing of Dillard University, 1943)
- The Hospital and Nursing Training School, Charleston, S.C. (1897)
- Hubbard Hospital and School of Nursing, Meharry Medical School, Nashville, TN (1900)
- Mercy Hospital and School of Nursing, Philadelphia, PA (1907)

World War I was one of the first turning points in the history of the nursing profession in America. After the war, nurses had enjoyed increased public esteem for the services they had provided to the sick and wounded. Yet, as nurses basked in the glow of warm public appreciation their leaders raised questions challenging the continued location of nurse training schools within the confines of hospitals. Throughout the 1920s and 1930s nurse leaders engaged in often heated debates with hospital administrators and physicians over the advisability of separating nurse training programs from the actual operation of hospitals. Nursing educators believed that the status of nursing as a profession suffered to the extent that the power to set admission standards, schedules, develop curriculum, and to control student nurses' duties and time and the financial affairs resided in the hands of non-nurses.[5]

Black nurse leaders paid particular attention to this controversy. In 1939 the *National News Bulletin,* official organ of the National Association of Colored Graduate Nurses which black women had founded in 1908 to fight against their exclusion from membership in the American Nurses' Association, published an essay written by Isabel M. Stewart (white), Director of Nursing Education, Teacher's College, Columbia University. Steward had gone to the heart of the issue. In an article entitled "Next Step in the Education of Nurses" she concluded that, "many schools don't know whether they are primarily educational institutions or service departments of hospitals."[6] Stewart advised that the tightly woven threads of service and education be unraveled as a prerequisite for the advancement of the nursing profession.

Similarly, black nurses spoke strongly in favor of the necessity to extricate nursing education from the domination of hospitals and physicians. In 1940 Rheva A. Speaks, Superintendent of Nurses at the Freedman's Hospital and School of Nursing, declared that, "in

[5]Bonnie Bullough and Vern L. Bullough, *The Emergence of Modern Nursing* (New York: Macmillan Company, 1964), pp. 168–171; Estelle Massey Osborne, "Status and Contribution of the Negro Nurse," *Journal of Negro Education*, 18 (June, 1949), 364–369.

[6]Isabel M. Stewart, "Next Step in the Education of Nurses," *National News Bulletin*, 13 (December, 1939). Copies found in the Schomburg Library, New York City.

fact, hospitals should not be expected to finance nursing schools—since the two have separate and distinct purposes: the one, that of caring for the sick; the other that of educating nurses." She applauded the recent trend of locating schools of nursing at educational institutions where the emphasis was placed on education and college affiliation. She predicted that the trend toward developing endowed schools and the charging of fees would spur on the separation of nurse students from the hospital. Speaks advanced that black nurses should adopt the goal and ascribe to the position that nurse training schools should be independent, autonomous and endowed and that more careful consideration should be paid the selection of students.[7]

Clearly, by the 1940s the spirit of reform had affected all nurse leaders regardless of race. Major nurse leaders shared Stewart's and Speaks' conviction that nursing education belonged in an academic setting, far removed from the control of hospital administration. They persuasively argued that nurses should pursue, or at least have the choice to earn, bachelor of science degrees in colleges and universities. To be sure, hospital training schools would remain on the scene for decades, producing a constant flow of ward and private duty nurses. Although the demise of the hospital training school was anything but eminent, many agreed that the future educators, administrators, nurse supervisors and leaders of the nursing profession would come from the ranks of those armed with bachelor's and master's degrees.[8]

In 1943 Rita E. Miller, former superintendent of nurses at Mercy-Douglass Hospital in Philadelphia and part-time consultant for the United States Public Health Service reported on the existing educational opportunities for black women in nursing. She pointed out that of the 27 Negro accredited nursing schools, 21 of them were located in the South. She asserted that the faculty in the majority of the black nursing schools suffered from excessively heavy teaching loads, and that too many of the schools were characterized by underprepared teachers and poor selection of students.[9] Miller declared that sound public policy and planning mandated the need to upgrade the quality of the black hospital nursing schools by

[7]Rheva A. Speaks quoted in *National News Bulletin*, 13 (April, 1940).

[8]Ibid.

[9]Rita E. Miller's remarks were included as part of the "Report of National Conference of Hospital Administrators," Norfolk, Virginia, November 19–20, 1943, prepared by Mary Elizabeth Lancaster, Acting Chairman of Department of Nursing, Hampton, Institute. Copy of this document is in the Dixie Hospital Manuscript Collection in Hampton Institute Archives. Papers are unprocessed, thus there are no box or folder numbers. Also see: Rita E. Miller, "Negro Schools of Nursing in the South," November, 1943, Box 548, Folder 5864 (General Education Papers, Rockfeller Archives Center, Pocantico Hills, New York).

establishing new collegiate programs in nursing education if the black woman was to avoid suffering an intellectual and economic disadvantage in the profession.

Miller's remarks fell on receptive ears for the prevalence of racial exclusion as practiced in the white colleges and universities had already aroused the concern and apprehension of black women nurses. The leaders appreciated the fact that the ascendency of collegiate schools of nursing held significant implications, for it portended the development of increased stratification within the profession along educational lines. Those who possessed bachelor's and master's degrees would be able to command higher wages, leadership positions, and better promotions than graduates from unfunded and ill-staffed diploma granting hospital training schools. In short, racial discrimination and elevated standards threatened to loosen the black woman's tenuous position in the nursing profession. To retain even a small amount of ground they had no alternative but to establish separate black collegiate nursing schools while continuously challenging the exclusionary or racial segregation policies of the white schools of nursing.[10]

The black collegiate nursing schools that arose during the 1940s were located in the South and incorporated into older established educational institutions. They were directed largely by black women, although there were exceptions, as at Hampton Institute, and were subsidized by white philanthropists. The programs at Dillard University in New Orleans and at Florida A & M in Tallahassee flourished because the directors of the nursing divisions were women who enjoyed the support of the university presidents, and the endorsement of officials in philanthropic foundations. Although a couple had come into existence earlier, the five institutions with schools or divisions of nursing education were: Tuskegee Institute, Hampton Institute, Howard University, Dillard University, and Florida A & M College.

The Nursing Education Division at Dillard, under the guidance of Rita Miller, gained widespread attention as a prototype or model of the ideal black collegiate nursing school. Others would imitate (or emulate) her successes. Miller did more than simply speak to the issues concerning black women nurses, she acted quickly to ensure that they would not be left out. During the early 1940s Nurse Miller, with the wholehearted support of Albert Dent, president of Dillard University and former superintendent of the Flint-Goodridge Hospital in New Orleans, created one of the most successful

[10]Osborne, "Status and Contribution of the Negro Nurse," pp. 365–366; Carnegie, "Are Negro Schools of Nursing Needed Today?" pp. 254–255.

black collegiate divisions, or schools, of nursing education. The refurbished Flint-Goodridge Hospital of Dillard University had previously operated a nurse training school. Unable to meet minimum accreditation standards of the National League of Nursing Education and the Louisiana Board of Nurse Examiners, the hospital's nurse training school closed in 1932. For the next ten years Dent, although hampered by lack of funds, pursued the dream of reopening the nurse training component.[11] At Miller's insistence, however, he would soon abandon the idea that the nursing school, if reopened, should be a part of the hospital.

By 1942, Miller, who had an M.A. degree from Teachers College, Columbia University, needed no introduction to the General Education Board (GEB) officials. Although Dent described her as, "one of the best qualified nursing educators from the standpoint of educational background, experience and temperament" they knew her as one of the vocal leaders in black nursing.[12] As she addressed the GEB officials, Miller wasted little effort on ceremonies, devoting all the time to stressing the need for GEB funds to underwrite the opening of a collegiate division of nursing at Dillard University. After Miller's speech, the GEB consulted Mary Elizabeth Tennant (white), nursing advisor on the staff of the International Health Division of the Rockefeller Foundation, and asked her to review the situation. Tennant's subsequent favorable report persuaded both the GEB and the Julius Rosenwald Fund to invest considerable sums in the project. GEB officials concurred with Tennant's recommendation that Miller be named professor of nursing and director of the division.[13] In September, 1942 the Nursing Division of Dillard University opened with thirty students and Miller at the helm. Within a very short while, Tennant exulted that the Dillard Nursing Division was, "one of the most interesting developments in nursing education in the country, irrespective of race." She declared that it was, "the best there is in the South."[14]

Much of the credit for the success of the Dillard Nursing Division belongs to the hard working Miller. Almost single-handedly, from scratch, she recruited a nursing faculty characterized by bright, ambitious, aggressive young women. Miller aided in their professional development by arranging for several of them to receive GEB graduate study fellowships. Indeed, by 1948 all of her nursing instructors, with one exception, had earned masters degrees. GEB

[11] "The History of Flint-Goodridge Hospital of Dillard University" *Journal of the National Medical Association*, 61 (November, 1969), p. 533ff.

[12] Notes in Mary E. Tennant's Diary, August 5 and 6, 1942. Box 548, Folder 5864. GEB papers.

[13] Ibid.

[14] Robert D. Calkins, Interoffice Memorandum, March 4, 1948. Box 548, Folder 5864. GEB papers.

officials consistently expressed their delight with Miller's leadership. Tennant applauded Miller's effort noting that she had "assembled an unusually fine nursing staff, probably one of the best in the colored schools of nursing in the country."[15]

As soon as she had organized the faculty, Miller focused on upgrading the curriculum and on raising admission standards to the Division. Intent on preparing the students for the general practice of nursing, Miller devised a five-year bachelor of science degree course. During the first two years in the course a typical student took more general academic subjects, including a course on the history of nursing. The final three years were spent at the adjoining Flint-Goodridge Hospital or in the affiliated public institution, Charity Hospital. Flint-Goodridge provided nursing experience in surgery, operating room, diet kitchen, and out-patient service while Charity Hospital permitted experience and gave instruction in communicable disease, obstetrics and pediatrics.[16]

In 1947, Miller revised the curriculum so that anatomy and physiology replaced general biology. Moreover, she introduced a course in the nursing applications of physics which was taught by the science and nursing arts instructor. Finally, bowing to the demands of fourth and fifth year students, Miller instituted a nursing seminar whereby the students could engage in spirited discussions on current trends, issues, and concerns in nursing and in related health care professions. By 1948 the Nursing Division boasted 20 graduates. Three years later Miller's hard work bore special fruit when the Collegiate Board of Review of the National Nursing Accrediting Service conferred full accreditation on the Dillard University Division of Nurse Education.[17]

Miller's success had depended upon the right mixture of institutional support, white philanthropy, and her own clarity of vision, determination and organizational skill. Her pioneering work at Dillard University would serve as a model and inspiration for the development of other black collegiate nursing schools, most notably the one that came into existence at Florida A & M.

In 1948, M. Elizabeth Lancaster Carnegie summarized the rationale and process which had influenced the transformation of nurse training to nursing education at Florida A & M College. She recalled the feeling that, "since the nurse copes with so many problems of

[15]Ibid. Tennant's Diary, January 23, 1944. Box 548, Folder 5864, GEB papers.

[16]Rita E. Miller, "Report on the Development of the Dillard University Division of Nursing, September 15, 1942 to November 22, 1943." Box 548, Folder 5864, GEB papers.

[17]Miller, "Report of Division of Nursing, 1947–1948"; Albert Dent to Calkins, February 14, 1948, Box 548, Folder 5864, GEB papers.

humanity, she should have a broad general background of education."[18] While Carnegie pointed out that Florida A & M College had allegedly established the first baccalaureate school of nursing for Negroes in the country, this observation was only part of a much larger and complex story. The school's shortcomings were legion, so much so that by 1945 the administration acknowledged that drastic reorganization was critical if the nursing program was to keep abreast of the times. Actually, as we shall see, there was quite a bit more involved in the modernization of nursing education at Florida A & M than is readily apparent.

Florida A & M's nursing school opened initially in 1911 in conjunction with the College's student hospital. For over three decades the nursing program remained unaccredited and its graduates were prohibited from registering in the state as both the physical plant and the quality of nursing instruction left much room for improvement. In the early 1940s, President William H. Gray requested from the General Education Board sums to aid in the construction of a new hospital. Gray's description of existing conditions at the hospital understated the urgent need for renovation of the building and modernization of nursing education. The forty-five-bed hospital, which regularly accommodated twice as many patients than was comfortable, was the only such facility for blacks within a 200-mile radius. While the hospital's primary responsibility was to care for the 1,000 students enrolled at the college it, nevertheless, catered to the demands for health care of thousands of poor black Floridians.[19]

In response to Gray's request, GEB official A. R. Mann visited the institution. Although Mann's observation confirmed Gray's depiction, he elaborated that, "all parts are fully used and the gross inadequacies are readily apparent. The frame building with wooden floors, doors, and partitions is also a serious fire hazard."[20] The chief administrator in charge of the hospital and nursing training was Dr. L.H.B. Foote, a graduate of the Howard University Medical School who had come to Florida A & M in 1928. Dorrie M. Mack and Eunice Johnson provided nursing education and two members of the local county public health office pitched in to round out the staff. The student nurses performed all the work necessary to maintain the hospital.[21]

[18]M. Elizabeth Lancaster Carnegie, "Nurse Training Become Nursing Education at Florida A & M College," *Journal of Negro Education*, 17 (1949), 200–204.

[19]Alma E. Gault to William H. Gray, Jr., April 23, 1946. Box 548, Folder 5867-9, GEB papers.

[20]A. R. Mann to William H. Gray, Jr., October 21, 1944; Interoffice Memorandum, January 12, 1945. Box 548, Folder 5867-9, GEB papers.

[21]Interoffice Memorandum, A Summary of Interviews between Mann and Dr. L. H. B. Foote, at Tallahassee, January 12, 1945. Box 548, Folder 5868, GEB papers.

In spite of the fact that several GEB officers appreciated Gray's dilemma, the foundation, nevertheless, voted against his requests for money. Instead, R. A. Lambert, for one, advised that Gray be dissuaded from building a large new hospital and persuaded to concentrate on improving the nurse training program. Lambert declared, "a hospital is a costly appendage to any institution and its operating deficit can easily become a handicap in the development of other functions of the college." That a new hospital was what Gray wanted did not alter Lambert's conviction. Lambert insisted, "any aid GEB would give would be strictly on the educational side, that is a contribution toward the nursing school."[22] In informing Gray of the Board's rejection, Mann did not close the door completely but intimated that the foundation was very much interested in improving nursing education. He tactfully advised Gray to investigate the nursing program at Dillard University, adding, "the program there appears to be well considered and it might merit your careful examination if you are considering modifications in your program."[23]

Undoubtedly the GEB directors relished the possibility of a duplication of the Dillard success. The GED had poured thousands of dollars into the Dillard school expecting that it would become the model for other efforts. Thus, partly because it did seem like an opportune chance to test the Dillard model, the GEB officers dispatched Mary Elizabeth Tennant to Tallahassee to survey conditions and to recommend appropriate actions. The outcome was predictable as Tennant's report echoed many of the suggestions she had made regarding Dillard's early development. She observed that, "the weakness of the basic nursing course at Florida A & M College is its limited direction by qualified nurses." She added, "it is my impression that the basic course is not well planned in coordinating the science classes with medicine and nursing instruction and practice."[24] Likewise, when black nurse Estelle Massey Riddle was asked her opinion of Florida A & M she responded that, "there was a complete lack of coordination between the nursing school and the college. . . ."[25]

In short, all observers agreed that what Florida A & M needed in order to become a modern black collegiate school of nursing was a well-trained tenacious nurse leader. The GEB officials did not

[22]Robert A. Lambert to A. R. Mann and Mary E. Tennant, August 29, 1945, Box 548, Folder 5868, GEB papers.

[23]Mann to Gray, October 21, 1944, Box 548, Folder 5868, GEB papers.

[24]Mary Elizabeth Tennant to Dr. M. Don Clawson and Miss Alma Gault, May 3, 1945, Box 548, Folder 5868, GEB papers.

[25]Estelle Massey Riddle, Consultant, National Nursing Council for War Service, to Tennant, March 8, 1945, Box 548, Folder 5868, GEB papers.

have far to look as they had already primed M. Elizabeth Carnegie for just such a leadership position. The GEB had financed her advanced training at the University of Toronto and in the process had let her know that she would be expected to serve for a while in an administrative capacity in a black school. To her credit, Carnegie welcomed the opportunity to create a new and better educational program for black women. Gray, in turn, convinced that the only way he could secure GEB funds was to upgrade the nursing training program, consented to employ Carnegie.

Mary Elizabeth Lancaster Carnegie was born on April 19, 1916, in Baltimore, Maryland. She received a diploma in 1937 from the Lincoln School for Nurses in Washington, D.C., and in 1942 she earned a B.A. degree from the West Virginia State College. In the summer of 1943 she took courses at Teachers College. From 1944 to 1945, Carnegie attended the University of Toronto on a GEB Fellowship. Her employment history reflects a variety of experiences. She worked as a general duty nurse at the Veterans Administration in Tuskegee, a school nurse at West Virginia State College, a clinical instructor at the St. Philip Hospital in Richmond, Virginia and as assistant director of the Division of Nurse Education at Hampton Institute before her appointment in 1945 as Dean of Division of Nursing Education at Florida A & M College. In 1951, Carnegie applied for and received another fellowship to attend the master's degree program at Syracuse University. Later, she accepted the position as assistant editor of the *American Journal of Nursing* (1953–1956) before moving on to a position of associate editor of *Nursing Outlook*. In 1970 she was promoted to editor of the magazine. While pursing her editorial career, Carnegie enrolled parttime, in 1967, in the New York University and subsequently received a doctorate degree in 1972, after completing a dissertation entitled "Disadvantaged Students in R.N. Programs." In 1973 she was named editor of *Nursing Research*. While Carnegie's illustrious twenty-five year editorial career certainly warrants detailed comment, it is her Florida years and experiences that shed light on the development of collegiate nursing education for black women.[26]

As eager as she was to help provide better education for black women and to advance her own career, it was with some trepidation that the twenty-nine-year-old Carnegie traveled to Florida to confront what she later termed "a *real* challenge" (emphasis hers). Dr. Foote and Nurse Mack greeted her arrival cooly, but their reserve

[26]Biographical material summarized from documents regarding M. Elizabeth Carnegie, Box 548, Folder 5868, GEB papers. For more detailed information see the lengthy interview of Dr. M. Elizabeth Carnegie by Dr. Patricia Sloan at the Carnegie Nursing Archives at Hampton Institute in Hampton, Virginia.

was initially lost on a Carnegie who was struck by the delapidated physical conditions of the hospital. Carnegie confided her first impression to Riddle, "the things that I have observed actually brought tears to my eyes, such as, the nursing arts laboratory with one bed in it and a handfull of supplies; the library with only seventeen nursing books, some of which date back to 1898, plus one bound volume of the *American Journal of Nursing;* the condition of the hospital as a whole, . . ." As she inventoried the surroundings a realization of the magnitude of her tasks descended upon her and she confessed, "I shudder to even think of it." The only moment of levity she relished occurred when she asked Nurse Mack whether she was familiar with Dillard's program and Mack had replied, " 'Dillard copied *this* program ' " (Emphasis hers). Carnegie laughingly noted that, "I thought that was a big joke and must tell Miss Miller when I write."[27]

Thus, it was in a climate mixed with humor and pathos that Carnegie commenced her struggle to overcome the three problems which would have undone a less determined individual. First, she had to develop a sound curriculum. Second, she had to find a new institution with which to affiliate in order to supplement the resident requirement as dictated by the Florida State Board of Nursing Examiners. Third, she had somehow to gain control of nursing education from the domineering Dr. Foote and simultaneously soothe hurt feelings of the intractable Nurse Mack, who deeply resented having been overlooked for the position of Dean. After one year of tremendous effort, Carnegie knew that she would achieve some of her objectives while others would forever elude resolution.

Carnegie revised the curriculum so that the sixty enrolled students could complete the program of studies within four years and three summers, instead of the usual five years. Borrowing liberally from Nurse Miller's program at Dillard, Carnegie instituted many other significant changes. Within nine months she had organized a nursing school faculty, adopted psychometric tests as a means of screening freshmen students, won control over her own budget, held monthly meetings with the student body, instituted clinical instruction, ordered a new supply of reference and textbooks, shortened hours on duty for student nurses, and initiated the maintenance of League·records, daily time and procedure books.[28]

Despite success with her curriculum innovations and winning budgetary control, Carnegie lamented that the reorganization meant little as long as she lacked "educational control" of nursing. She

[27]Carnegie to Riddle, September 19, 1945. Box 548, Folder 5868, GEB papers.
[28]Carnegie to Tennant, May 13, 1946. Box 548, Folder 5868, GEB papers.

declared that, "I will not be satisfied until the school of nursing becomes a division of the college. . . . I would like to see this school have the same organization as Dillard."[29] She elaborated,

> I am often reminded of the two basic principles of administration of nursing schools that I learned in the University of Toronto, namely, financial independence and educational control. With the budget approved for next year, we will have financial independence, but with the organization remaining as is we will not have educational control.[30]

Indeed, on this point Carnegie enjoyed the support of the Florida State Board of Examiners of Nurses which had recommended, in 1946, that Florida A & M suspend all admissions to the School of Nursing until, "the nurse in charge of the school be made Dean of the Division of Nursing *responsible directly to the President of the College and not to the medical director of the hospital*" (emphasis mine). Florida A & M's arrangement clearly violated Policy IV (b) of the State Board of Nurse Examiners.[31] Of course, Gray neither suspended admissions nor did he remove the deeply entrenched Dr. Foote. Likewise, appeals to the GEB officials evoked only a cautionary response as Jackson Davis, Director and Vice President, pointed out that, "it would be very difficult to replace Dr. Foote with anyone better at the present time."[32] Recognition that she would have to live with the existing organizational structure for a while longer did not deter Carnegie from making changes which aroused Dr. Foote's ire. Actually, the relations between Dr. Foote and Carnegie threatened to erupt into a full fledged war over the question of affiliation for student nurses. Dr. Foote jealously guarded his position as Director of Nursing Training and consequently was determined to protect and preserve the 1936 affiliation agreement he had arranged with Provident Hospital in Baltimore, Maryland.[33] Affiliations were essential to the survival of small, understaffed, limited service hospital training schools. Such schools often entered into contractual agreements whereby the larger institution provided a one year broad clinical experience to enable students to meet the minimum residence standards for registration upon graduation. In exchange, the larger institution received uncompensated student labor, both inside and outside the hospital.

In reality, these long distance affiliations could, and frequently did, risk and conceal abuse and exploitation of the student nurse. In early 1946 Carnegie made a brief visit to Provident Hospital in

[29]Ibid.

[30]Ibid.

[31]Kathryn R. Gutwald, Secretary, Florida State Board of Nurse Examiners to Gray, June 19, 1946. Box 548, Folder 5868, GEB papers.

[32]Jackson Davis, Interoffice Memorandum, October 18, 1946. Box 548, Folder 5868, GEB papers.

[33]Mann to Riddle and Carnegie, January 2, 1946. Box 548, Folder 5868, GEB papers.

Baltimore to investigate complaints and allegations regarding the blatant "exploitation of Florida students." She was shocked by the actual depth of abuse and shared with Riddle and GEB officials that, "the girls going to Provident have received very little training and have been excessively exploited." Furthermore, she asserted, that, "the degrees hitherto conferred at Florida upon students completing the nurse training course have been without educational significance."[34]

The only remedy to the Provident/Baltimore fiasco was, as Carnegie maintained, to sever relations and immediately contract an affiliation with another hospital. On this point she proved so unyielding that eventually Gray and GEB officials overruled Dr. Foote's strong opposition and gave her the cue to proceed. After talking with a number of institutions Carnegie urged Gray to work out an agreement with the Duval county Hospital in Jacksonville, Florida.

The affiliation document stipulated the duties and obligations of both parties. Florida A & M agreed to provide a full-time clinical instructor and some additional supervisory personnel and to donate the free services of twelve student nurses. The Duval County Hospital, on the other hand, agreed to provide, via its professional staff, fifteen lectures in obstetrics, pediatrics, and communicable diseases such as tuberculosis, as well as ten lectures in gynecology and urology, skin and veneral disease and orthopedics. To facilitate the implementation of the affiliation agreement, the GEB officials voted to appropriate $5,100 to Florida A & M in order to rent a house for the student nurses and to pay the salaries of the clinical instructor and dietitian-matron. This sum was a harbinger of more to come. Finally, Carnegie somewhat appeased Nurse Mack by endorsing her appointment as the resident instructor at the Duval County Hospital. All concurred that Mack was, "just the right person for the place . . . a native of Florida who fit in perfectly." Significantly, the affiliation won approval from the Florida State Board of Nurse Examiners."[35]

Carnegie summed up the overriding objectives of the Division of Nursing and charted the agenda for the future. The objectives were: (1) to give the student a wider scientific, social, and technical background necessary for the care of the sick, prevention of disease, and the conservation of health; (2) to provide educational enrich-

[34]GEB interoffice Memo, January 2, 1946. Box 548, Folder 5868, GEB papers.

[35]"Tentative Agreement Between the Duval County Hospital and Florida A & M College Concerning Affiliation of Student Nurses," June 14, 1946; Gray to Gault, April 30, 1946; Jackson Davis to Gray, July 26, 1946; "A Request for Assistance in Developing an Affiliation Program for Nurses Between Florida A & M College and the Duval County Hospital." Box 548, Folder 5868, GEB papers.

ment so that the graduate nurse is equipped to meet her needs as a citizen; (3) to maintain the wholesome relationship that she had started between Duval County Hospital and Florida A & M College; (4) to establish an affiliation between Leon County Health Department and Florida A & M College so that the student's experience may be rounded out with a picture of the community health needs of blacks in the area.[36]

The General Education Board continued to demonstrate interest in the Florida nursing program throughout Carnegie's tenure as Dean of the Division. In 1947 the GEB awarded $50,000 to the Board of Control of the State Institutions of Higher Learning of Florida, "for equipment principally for the School of Nursing Education at Florida A & M." This sum buttressed the $700,000 appropriated by the State legislature, the city of Tallahasse and the Federal Government to erect a modern 100-bed hospital on the school's campus.[37] The dream of a modern hospital and a modernized collegiate division of nursing education had become a reality. Indeed, the GEB's Education Board's chief nursing consultant considered Florida A & M's School of Nursing one of the best of the Negro nursing programs. By 1951 it belonged in the company of the Dillard University, the Meharry Medical College, and the Medical College of Virginia (Richmond) nursing education programs.[38]

With her major objectives realized, Carnegie decided to return to school to pursue an advanced degree. GEB officials conceded that she had done a good job at Florida A & M under what were trying conditions, both personally and professionally. In her endorsement of Carnegie's fellowship application to the GEB, Mary Tennant enthused that she was, "one of the most able Negroes likely to be found at this time in her field." Thus, at age thirty-four Carnegie received one of the last two fellowships the GEB offered for, "the training of Negro instructors in southern schools of nursing."[39]

The discussion of Carnegie's and Miller's leadership in the development of collegiate nursing divisions in black colleges sheds much needed light on the role black women have played in the education of black women. It is a departure from traditional studies in one significant respect. While scholars have devoted considerable

[36]M. E. L. Carnegie, "Report of Activities of Division of Nursing, Summer, 1946" (September 14, 1946) in Box 548, Folder 5868, GEB papers.

[37]W. W. Brierly to J. J. Diamond, December 6, 1946. Box 548, Folder 5868, GEB papers.

[38]Calkins's Interview with Miss M. Elizabeth Tennant, March 5, 1951. Box 548, Folder 5868, GEB papers.

[39]Interoffice Memorandum, Robert W. July, April 20, 1951; Robert D. Calkins, Director and Vice President, Grant In Aid" May 23, 1951. Box 548, Folder 5868; July "GEB Fellowship Applicants in Nursing," January 26, 1951. Box 548, Folder 5868, GEB papers.

attention to the roles of black women as educators and as founders of colleges and institutes, little work has been done on black women's leadership in creating professional educational programs and schools. By the twentieth century, nursing had become one of the major women's professions in America along with teaching and, later, social work. Without the determination, intelligence and commitment of nurses such as Carnegie and Miller the participation of black women at all levels in the nursing profession would have been severely reduced due primarily to the effects of racial segregation and discrimination. Thus, these women working in a segregated environment with critical support from philanthropic foundations, nevertheless, managed to create and build reputable collegiate programs which provided increased educational opportunities for thousands of black women. Only now, with the advantage of hindsight, can we begin to appreciate fully the value and significance of their struggles and contributions.

BARRED FROM THE BAR: WOMEN AND LEGAL EDUCATION IN THE UNITED STATES 1870-1890*

D. KELLY WEISBERG**

One of the paramount concerns of any skilled profession is the regulation of access to the profession. As Chroust has pointed out, in colonial America any person desiring to be admitted to the legal profession had four major avenues of entry.

> "He might, by his own efforts and through self-directed reading and study, acquire whatever scraps of legal information were available in books, statutes, or reports; he could work in the clerk's office of some court of record; he could serve as an apprentice or clerk in the law library of a reputable lawyer, preferably one with a law library; or he could enter one of the four Inns of Court in London and receive there the 'call to the bar.' "[1]

Chroust's use of the masculine pronoun above is not entirely without significance. "Any" person in colonial America did have four avenues of legal education open to him, provided that that person was male. The first hundred years of American legal education were characterized by a glaring absence of woman lawyers. This paper shall deal historically with women's entry into the legal profession after the Civil War in terms of their admission to law schools and to the bar.

The struggle for women to gain entrance to the legal profession began in the late 1860's with Ada Kepley the first woman to graduate from the Union College of Law (now Northwestern) in 1870[2] and Arabella Mansfield the first woman to be admitted to the bar of any state (Iowa, 1869). However, the battle was by no means over: in reality it had just begun.

Scarcely two months after Arabella Mansfield was admitted to the Iowa bar, Myra Bradwell passed an examination for the Chicago bar, but the Illinois Supreme Court refused to grant her a license to practice law on the grounds of her sex. When the case was taken on a writ of error to the United

* Special acknowledgement is made of the assistance of Professor Egon Bittner, Brandeis University, and of Leonard Klein, Senior Reference Librarian, Harvard University Law Library, for facilitating the access to rare materials.

** Ph.D., Brandeis University.

[1] Chroust, The Rise of the Legal Profession in America 173(1965).

[2] Several women attended some of the nation's law schools for brief periods prior to this date; however, Ada Kepley was the first woman both to attend and graduate from a school of law. Paradoxically, Mrs. Kepley was barred from the bar of Illinois upon first application by the adverse *Bradwell* decision cited infra.

States Supreme Court, she was once again unsuccessful.[3] In other landmark cases Lavinia Goodell was refused admission to the Wisconsin bar in 1875,[4] Lelia Josephine Robinson was refused admission to the bar of Massachusetts in 1881,[5] and Belva Lockwood, although admitted to the District of Columbia bar and admitted to practice before the United States Supreme Court, was still refused admission to the Virginia bar in the 1890's because of her sex.[6]

Even after the turn of the century when women were admitted to the bar of almost every state,[7] the battle continued for women's admission to law school. Columbia University first admitted women law students in 1929, Harvard University in 1950 (although women had first applied to Harvard in the 1870's,[8] the University of Notre Dame in 1969, and the last male bastion, Washington and Lee University in 1972.

In order to understand better the century of discrimination against women in terms of their access to the legal profession, it is helpful to examine the legal and social rationale utilized for the exclusion of women from the profession. Often the legal and social rationale cannot be separated, as will be seen in the court decisions of this period barring women. The legal rationale for denying women access to the profession may be seen to include the following:

The Fight Over the Masculine Pronoun or Women as Non-Persons

In most states admission to the bar was controlled by statutes. These statutes provided for the admission of "persons" or "citizens," or for specifically "male" persons or citizens. The language of the statutes was framed similar to the following:

> "The Superior Court may admit and cause to be sworn as attorneys such *persons* as are qualified therefore agreeably to the rules established by the judges of said court, and no other person than an attorney so ad-

[3] Bradwell v. The State, 16 Wall. 130 (1872); 55 Ill. 535 (1869).

[4] *In Re* Goddell, 39 Wis. 232 (1875).

[5] *Ex parte* Robinson, 131 Mass. 375 (1881).

[6] *In re* Lockwood, 154 U.S. 116 (1893). Virginia and Georgia still did not admit women to the bar in 1914. Cottle, "The Prejudice Against Women Lawyers: How Can It Be Overcome?" 21 Case and Comment 372 (1914).

[7] By 1900, 34 states admitted women to the legal profession. Pettus, "The Legal Education of Women," 61 Alb. L.J. 330 (1900).

[8] When M. Fredrika Perry and Ellen Martin applied to the Harvard Law School in the 1870's, the reason given for denying their applications for admission was that "it was not considered practicable to admit young men and young women to the Law Library at the same time, and it was not considered fair to admit to the Law School without giving the privileges of the Library." Martin, "Admission of Women to the Bar," 1 Chic. L.T. 83 (1886). The story of the admission of women to Columbia Law School may be found in Goebel, A History of the School of Law, Columbia University 290, 473 (1955). In 1924 the Columbia faculty unanimously resolved that "such a concession would be inexpedient and contrary to the best

[8] See p. 486.

mitted shall plead at the bar of any court of this state, except in *his* own cause."[9] (emphasis mine)

or, the Wisconsin statute which specified:

"No *person* shall hereafter be admitted or licensed to practice . . . except in the manner hereinafter provided . . . *he* shall be first licensed by order of. . . . "[10] (emphasis mine)

The battle was waged over the masculine pronoun. That is, could the court (in the *Goodell* and *Bradwell* cases, for example) decide that words specifically importing masculine gender should extend to women and thereby admit women to the legal profession? The general rule of interpretation of the statutes was that "every word importing the masculine gender only may extend and be applied to females as well as males."[11] This was precisely the point on which Mrs. Mansfield was admitted to the Iowa bar. However, the judges in both *Goodell* and *Bradwell* maintained that the rule of interpretation applied "unless . . . such construction would be inconsistent with the manifest intention of the legislature."[12] This brings us to another legal argument utilized to bar women from the legal profession.

Surely, the Legislators Never Contemplated That!

In establishing the rules by which admission to the profession should be determined, the court was bound by two limitations, maintained Justice Bradley in the *Bradwell* decision. The first was to promote the proper administration of justice and the second, ". . . that it should not admit any persons, or class of persons, not intended by the legislature to be admitted even though not expressly excluded by statute."[13]

Supporters of this argument maintained that when the legislators first framed the statutes in the eighteenth century, they did not contemplate that

[8] cont'd.
interests of the Law School." Goebel, at 290. Yale Law School similarly has a shameful chapter in the history of women in legal education. Although Yale was technically one of the first law schools to admit a woman, the school later changed its policy. Alice Jordan entered Yale Law School in the fall of 1885 after studying at Michigan University and after being admitted to the Michigan bar. She received a degree from Yale shortly thereafter. However, as of 1890 the law school had reconsidered this decision and the catalogue specified: "It is to be understood that the courses of instruction above described are open to persons of the male sex only, except where both sexes are specifically included." Dean Wayland of the Law School wrote in private correspondence, "the marked paragraph on page 25 is intended to prevent a repetition of the Jordan incident." Robinson, "Women Lawyers in the United States," 2 Green Bag 13 (1890).

[9] Quoted in "Women May be Admitted as Attorney," Annotated Case, *In re* Hall, 21 Am. L. Reg. 728 (1882).

[10] Quoted in *In re* Goodell, 39 Wis. 233 (1875).

[11] *Ibid.*

[12] *Ibid.* at 241.

[13] Bradwell v. The State, 16 Wall. 130 (1872).

women would ever be admitted to the bar. Hence, in its original enactment, the application of the statute to women was not in the minds of the legislators. This interpretation naturally led to the conclusion that the court lacked the statutory authority to admit women to the legal profession. This was the interpretation utilized in both the *Bradwell* and *Goodell* decisions and by Justice Pardee in his dissent in In re Hall.[14]

In holding to this strict interpretation of legislative intent, the courts seemed influenced by an overriding concern with the social consequences of straying from the interpretation. In both the *Goodell* and *Bradwell* decisions (maintaining this lack of legislative intent) one finds the apocalyptic adumbration of the social consequences entailed by permitting women to enter the legal profession—namely, a sweeping revolution of the social order. As Justice Ryan maintained in *Goodell:*

> "If we should follow that authority in ignoring the distinction of sex, we do not perceive why it should not emasculate the constitution itself and include females in the constitutional right of male suffrage and male qualification. Such a rule would be one of judicial revolution, not of judicial construction . . . . We cannot stultify the court by holding that the legislature intended to bring about, *per ambages,* a sweeping revolution of social order, by adopting a very innocent rule of statutory construction."[15]

Similarly, in the *Bradwell* decision, Justice Lawrence when delivering the majority opinion stated the consequence, fearful beyond imagination, that:

> "This step, if taken by us, would mean that in the opinion of this tribunal every civil office in this state may be filled by women: that it is in harmony with the spirit of our Constitution and laws that women should be made governors, judges and sheriffs. This we are not prepared to hold. . . ."[16]

You Have Not, Ergo You Cannot—Common Law Disability

Another common rationale utilized to bar women from the legal profession was the argument that the impediments growing out of women's legal status at the common law prevented them from gaining access to the profession. The fact that women had never been admitted to the bar had established a common law disability. And, supporters of this argument maintained, inasmuch as women were not known as attorneys at common law, this was sufficient reason for the court to refuse to admit them. It was argued, too, that women had other disabilities at common law which would interfere with their practice of the legal profession, such as their not being

[14] Quoted in "Women May Be Admitted as Attorney," supra note 9, at 735.
[15] *In re* Goodell, 39 Wis. 242, 243 (1875).
[16] *In re* Bradwell, 55 Ill 535 (1869).

able to hold office at this time. This presented a problem because an attorney was an officer of the court. However, the most serious common law disability which would interfere with women practicing law, or so women's opponents maintained, concerned married women's inability to contract.

If You're Married, You Can't be a Lawyer

This legal rationale was based on the fact that married women at this time were disqualified from entering into contracts with third persons without their husband's consent. In both the *Bradwell* and *Lockwood* decisions, it was held that because of this disability at common law, married women could not be permitted to gain admission to the bar.[17]

However, in some decisions which admitted women to the bar, it was held that married women's inability to contract was not an insurmountable obstacle. In the *Kilgore* decision in Pennsylvania (admitting Mrs. Kilgore), Justice Thayer held that the essential basis of the relationship between lawyer and client was not in contract.

> "But what difference does it make if she cannot be sued as upon a contract. There are other adequate remedies for neglect of duty, infidelity, or misbehavior in office, which are provided by law and to which she would undoubtedly be amenable. . . . These laws are an ample security for the client in dealing with an attorney, even if she be a married woman."[18]

It can be seen that this objection was not really the primary obstacle in the minds of opposing judges. Upon the filing of Mrs. Bradwell's printed argument, the Illinois Supreme Court held that *no* female was eligible to practice in the state of Illinois—be she married or single.

In addition to legal arguments, opponents of women's entry into the legal profession also utilized social rationale for barring women. One such rationale included the argument that woman's mental and physical nature rendered her unfit for legal practice.

Inferior in Mind and Body

One objection to women entering the legal profession was that women did not possess a "legal mind." Women's minds were thought to be more emotional than rational and logical—the requisite qualities of the legal mind. Moreover it was argued, women simply did not have the natural aptitude to perform the duties required by the profession. Or, as one woman said:

[17] Kanowitz points out that vestiges of this common law disability remain, as in United States v. Yazell, 382 U.S. 341 (1966). Kanowitz, Sex Roles and Society: Cases and Materials 199 (1973).

[18] Quoted in "Women as Advocates," 18 Am. L. Rev. 479 (1884).

> "We are also told that the successful lawyer must have a logical mind, and since the mind of woman is sadly lacking in this respect, her unfitness for the legal profession is apparent."[19]

Not only did women apparently lack the necessary mental qualities for the practice of law, but also they were thought to lack the physical stamina the profession required. The opposing forces maintained that women did not have the physical strength to follow "so arduous a calling as the law."[20] Women, it would seem, were possessed of an exceedingly delicate constitution which could not withstand the long hours of study and the conflicts of the courtroom. As Justice Ryan maintained in *Goodell*:

> "There are many employments in life not unfit for the female character. The profession of law is surely not one of these. The peculiar qualities of womanhood, its gentle graces, its quick sensibility, its tender susceptibility, its purity, its delicacy, its emotional impulses, its subordination of hard reason to sympathetic feeling, are surely not qualifications for forensic strife. Nature has tempered woman as little for the juridical conflicts of the court room as for the physical conflicts of the battle field."[21]

Nowhere are these stereotypes of woman's mental and physical nature as clearly brought into relief as in the whimsical story published in 1886 by Charles C. Moore (author of *Moore on Facts*) about the first woman lawyer who came to Litchfield Connecticut.[22] The presence of these stereotypes in the story is all the more significant because the author seems in favor of (more precisely, enamoured with) the idea of woman lawyers.

As Miss Mary Padelford steps off the Claremont stage, Lawyer Walter Perry remarks, "and if she possesses enough physical strength I wouldn't be surprised if she makes a success." She chooses Claremont (i.e. Litchfield) because it is 1100 feet above sea-level and "her health has never been exceedingly rugged." When Miss Padelford loses her first case in court, she (what else?) bursts into tears in the courtroom. Later, the constant study out of court "was sufficient of itself to tax her constitution to the utmost and long trials in court brought a mental and physical exhaustion her ambitious nature was hardly able to resist." After another courtroom incident she faints and falls from her chair. When the physician arrives, he diagnoses her condition as "brain fever." In a fitting finale, Lawyer Walter Perry and Miss Mary Padelford are married and enter into partnership. One might surmise that thereafter Mrs. Perry's health improved because of the physical and mental assistance of a male law partner.[23]

[19] Cottle, supra note 6, at 371.

[20] *Ibid.*

[21] *In re* Goodell, 39 Wis 245 (1875).

[22] It may be hypothesized, although it is nowhere stated, that the occasion which prompted this story was the successful application of Miss Mary Hall to the Connecticut bar in 1882.

[23] Moore, "The Woman Lawyer," 26 Green Bag 525 (1914). This story first appeared in the Hartford Daily Times, May 17, 1886.

The belief that women's physical disabilities rendered them unfit for law practice even took the form of maintaining that women's "peculiar physiological condition" (menstruation) would inhibit their practice of law. In answer to this objection, one author remarked: "Do the thousands of women who practice medicine, leave their patients to die when they are suffering from catamenial disturbances?"[24] Interestingly, it was not only men who protested that women's physiological condition would interfere with their practice of law. One woman opponent protested:

> "How would a lawyeress be able to consult with her clients, when she was attacked by the nausea of the first few months of pregnancy? And afterward what a figure she would make in court, when, the months of her interesting situation being advanced, her curved lines become crushed with an anterior round line? And if the pains should come upon her in the heat of argument! That would be fine indeed! Would she invite her colleagues to serve her as midwives? And in childbirth, farewell to business! Poor clients! I assure you that I laugh to myself thinking of the ridiculous figure that a woman lawyer would make."[25]

It was suggested on the death of one of the first woman lawyers, Lavinia Goodell, that perhaps the "hard usage and severe mental application incidental to a legal professional career"[26] had contributed to her early demise. In answer to this, supporters of women entering the legal profession maintained:

> "Miss Goodell was forty-one years of age. Henry Armitt Brown, the noted lawyer of Philadelphia, died recently at thirty-two. We would like to suggest the query whether men are able to endure the hard usage. . . ."[27]

Justice Would Suffer

Another argument proffered against women entering the legal profession concerned the fear that the interests of justice would suffer. The female sex, opponents maintained, was reputedly garrulous and wanting in discretion.[28] Consequently, the interests of clients could not be entrusted to women's hands. This latter opinion is clearly expressed in a rather misogynic British law journal article of this period, "Prudes for Proctors":

> "The fact that women are admitted to practise in the United States is sufficient to prevent the matter being passed off as a joke; but it must be remembered that, in the States, the principle that the client must be protected from the solicitor by the Courts, has almost entirely given

[24] Frank, "The Woman Lawyer," 3 Chic. L.T. 411 (1899).
[25] Quoted in Throop, "Woman and the Legal Profession," 30 Alb. L.J. 466 (1884).
[26] Robinson, supra note 8, at 24.
[27] *Ibid.*
[28] Frank, supra note 24, at 401.

> place to the principle that the client can very well look after himself. In England the question has to be considered, whether the interests of clients can safely be entrusted to a woman's hands."[29]

This concern about the interests of justice also took the form that the introduction of women into the field of advocacy would check the fighting instincts of lawyers. Moreover, it was thought that judgment would no longer be impartial if women lawyers were present in the courtroom. This belief was expressed as:

> "There are some lawyers who go so far as to say that given a woman plaintiff and a woman attorney and the defense might just as well lie down if the case be before a jury."[30]

Strains of this belief can be seen in the following anecdote. A woman lawyer asked her client why he came to her for legal assistance. The client, who had been tried and convicted of a crime and awarded a new trial by an appellate court, replied: "Well, ma'am, I reckon I've had justice. What I need now is mercy, and I figger them jurors will feel mightly sorry for me if all I have is a woman to defend me."[31]

Mothers as Lawyers?—Role Conflicts

However, the primary social rationale utilized to bar women from the legal profession centered on woman's traditional role in the family. The professional role of the lawyer was seen to be in direct conflict with the traditional roles of woman as wife and mother. In both the *Bradwell* and *Goodell* decisions, the judges delivered a lengthy discourse on woman's "sphere." The proper sphere for woman, they maintained, citing by way of authority the law of nature and the law of the Creator, was in the home. The decisions are worth quoting at length. As Justice Bradley stated in *Bradwell:*

> ". . . the civil law, as well as nature itself, has always recognized a wide difference in the respective spheres and destinies of man and woman. Man is, or should be, woman's protector and defender. The natural and proper timidity and delicacy which belongs to the female sex evidently unfits it for many of the occupations of civil life. The constitution of the family organization, which is found in the divine ordinance, as well as in the nature of things indicates the domestic sphere as that which properly belongs to the domain and functions of womanhood . . . The paramount destiny and mission of woman are to fulfill the noble and benign offices of wife and mother. This is the law of the Creator. . . ."[32]

[29] "Prudes for Proctors," 14 L.J. 746 (1879).
[30] "A Woman Lawyer's Chances, 21 Case and Comment 380 (1914).
[31] Quoted in Drew, "Women and the Law," 47 W.L.J. 20 (1961).
[32] Bradwell v. The State, 16 Wall. 141 (1872).

Similarly, Justice Ryan in *Goodell* maintained:

> "The law of nature destines and qualifies the female sex for the bearing and nurture of the children of our race and for the custody of the homes of the world and their maintenance in love and honor. And all life-long callings of women, inconsistent with these radical and sacred duties of their sex, as is the profession of the law, are departures from the order of nature: and when voluntary, treason against it. . . ."[33]

Woman's traditional role conflicted with the professional role of lawyer in terms of the divergent sets of priorities of the role sets. The socially approved role for woman as wife and mother had duties associated with it which were expected to be woman's first and primary obligation, superceding any other claim. For the lawyer, obviously, his occupation was intended to be his first priority. Or, as Justice Ryan had asserted in *Goodell*: "The profession enteres largely into the well being of society: and to be honorably filled and safely to society, exacts the devotion of life."[34] For woman, quite clearly, only her husband and children were supposed to exact the devotion of her life.

The requisite personality attributes of the lawyer, moreover, were seen as incompatible with those necessary for the role of wife and mother. The lawyer was supposed to be aggressive—a skilled combatant in the juridical conflicts of the courtroom. Woman was seen as nurturant, gentle, tender. In short, she possessed personality attributes required for the fulfillment of the role of wife and mother. It was readily apparent that the two role configurations have mutually exclusive sets of attributes.

But what of the unmarried woman? If opponents were concerned with married women straying from their duties, should not the unmarried woman, then, be able to practice law? For the single woman who was not engaged in fulfilling the role of "her destiny," the law was still not to be considered as a possible occupation. The court in *Goodell* had this to say:

> "The cruel chances of life sometimes baffle both sexes, and may leave women free from the peculiar duties of their sex. These may need employment. . . . But it is public policy to provide for the sex, not for its superfluous members: and not to tempt women from the proper duties of their sex by opening to them duties peculiar to ours. There are many employments in life not unfit for female character. The profession of law is surely not one of these."[35]

The single woman, thus, was free to enter some other occupation to provide for herself. The legal profession, women's opponents stoutly maintained, should remain forever barred both to her and to her married sisters.

[33] *In re* Goodell, 39 Wis. 245 (1875).
[34] *Ibis.* at 244, 245.
[35]

The next issue which shall be dealt with here concerns the nation's first women lawyers. Recent articles on women and the law tend to celebrate in passing the nation's first woman to graduate from law school, or the first woman to practice in the United States Supreme Court, or the first woman to be admitted to the bar of particular states. However, in their overriding concern with the position of women lawyers today, authors have neglected to take the historical question one step further. Who were the nation's first women lawyers? What can be discovered about them and about their chapter in the history of American legal education? (Data for this section was based on two "who's who" type articles on women lawyers published in 1886 and 1890, in addition to several obituaries of the nation's first women lawyers).[36]

In 1870 approximately four women were attending the nation's law schools (although not all four would be permitted to graduate). The same year witnessed a total student population of 1,611 in thirty-one law schools.[37] (However, the total number of law students was undoubtedly somewhat greater because it was common in this period to pass the bar through private reading and office apprenticeships without ever having attended a law school). By 1890 the number of women lawyers and law students in the United States had grown to approximately 135. In that same time period, the total law student population in the United States had risen to approximately 7,000.

What can be determined about these first women lawyers? After 1870 when law schools slowly began admitting and graduating women (Union College 1870; Michigan 1871; Washington University, St. Louis, 1871; Howard University 1872; Iowa State 1873; National University, Washington, 1873), the majority of these women attended law school in preparation for the bar, occasionally after having studied for a year or two in a law office. Before that time, the handful of women who were admitted to the bar (or more accurately, who sought admission to the bar), such as Mrs. Belle Mansfield, Mrs. Ada Kepley, Mrs. J. Ellen Foster, Miss Alta Hulette and Mrs. Myra Bradwell, gained their instruction either at home (Mrs. Foster said she read Blackstone while rocking her babies)[38] or in law offices. An interesting fact now comes to light: many of the first women to gain entrance to the legal profession were married women for whom the opportunities of law study and later, law practice, were availed to them by their lawyer-husbands. In 1890 approximately one-third of the total number of women law-

[36] Martin, supra note 8, at 76. Robinson, supra note 8. "Mary A. Ahrens," 21 Case and Comment 430 (1914). "Death of Miss Lemma Barkeloo," 2 Chic. L.N. 409 (1870). "Lelia Robinson Sawtelle Dead," 24 Chic. L.N. 421 (1891).

[37] Friedman, A History of American Law 526, 527 (1973).

[38] Robinson, supra note 8, at 21.

yers were married women and more than half this number were married to lawyers.

Many of these lawyer-husbands helped their wives in their struggle to be admitted to the bar. Many of the first women lawyers received instruction in their husband's law offices; and, some lawyer-husbands, such as P.A.L. Smith, worked to get legislation passed which would open the profession to women. As Mr. Smith wrote refuting the argument that admitting women to the profession would interfere with women's domestic affairs:

> "This is all bosh—for in the first place she may not have any domestic affairs to look after; and in the second place, she herself is the best judge as to whether it pays her better or suits her better to look after other business and pay some one to keep an eye on domestic affairs. One or two little domestic affairs are not expected to occupy all of a smart woman's attention, and in the meantime why shouldn't she be allowed to practice law if she wants to. My wife has studied hard, prepared herself for the bar, and is fully competent to stand the legal exam required of men and I see no reason convincing to me why she should not practice. She has studied at my request and anything I can do to secure her admission to the bar will be done."[39]

After admission to the bar many of these women were further facilitated in their entrance to the legal profession by going into practice with their lawyer-husbands. In fact, Robinson reports that in 1890 there were twenty husband-wife law partnerships in the United States.[40]

It is likely, too, that single women were aided by influential male lawyer relatives. Many single women who sought admission to the bar came from families with notable members in the legal profession. One woman's father (the first woman to be admitted to the bar in Utah in 1871) was Attorney General of the Utah Territory. Another woman who graduated from the University of Michigan in 1888 had a father who was a circuit judge in the Hawaiian Islands. And, of Frederika Perry, it was said "she belonged to the Strong family, which has furnished a great deal of the legal talent in the United States."[41] Other women's fathers were famous judges—Bessie Bradwell's father, for one, and Mary McHenry's father who was renowned in both California and Louisiana. Other single women had fathers who were practicing lawyers and often, after these women were admitted to the bar, they entered into partnerships with their family members.

[39] *Ibid.* at 181. (Miss Robinson commented on Mr. Smith's remarks: "Who would not be willing to stand up in a horse car when this new nineteenth century gallantry is given us in exchange for the superficial kind.") It is interesting to note that some lawyers' wives who studied law did so either at the request of their husbandss (Annie Smith, Corinne Douglass), or as in the case of Myra Bradwell [illegible]der to assist their husbands. See DeCrow, Sexist Justice 30 (1974).

[40] Quoted in Frank, supra note 24, at 409, from personal correspondence.

[41] Martin, supra note 8, at 82.

Surprisingly, in such families one finds family combinations of women seeking entrance to the bar—mothers and daughters or sister pairs. Myra Bradwell and her daughter Bessie both sought admission and Kate Pier and her mother graduated together from the University of Wisconsin in 1887. Among the sister pairs are included the Spaulding sisters from the University of Wisconsin and the Cronise sisters who were admitted together to the state courts in Ohio in 1873. The Pier mother and daughter eventually joined Mr. Pier in a partnership and the Cronise sisters also formed a partnership until one of them married and left the profession. It may be surmised that originating from families with such concentrations of legal talent eased the way into the legal profession for many of these women.

Of the women lawyers who entered into active practice, what was the nature of their practice? Many who "actively" entered the profession, it would appear, ended up doing the office work and occupying a back seat to male lawyers. In the case of Mrs. Mary Haddock (in partnership with her husband), she "devoted herself principally to office work and briefing cases," and for Mrs. LeValley "her share of the work has been principally in the office." Tabitha Holton, in partnership with one of several lawyer-brothers, "devoted herself chiefly to office work," and Miss Jessie Wright after her marriage "assisted her husband in some of his work," similar to Mrs. Frank Helmer (Bessie Bradwell) who from time to time "aids her (lawyer) husband in his business."[42]

Staying in the office was not only the fate of women lawyers in partnership with husbands or brothers. It seems this was also the fate of other early women lawyers as well. Of Miss Emma Gillet it was said, "her work has been principally in the office line—the drawing of papers, taking testimony in equity causes and probate business, together with a large amount of notarial and some financial work." Similarly, Mrs. Eliza Chambers gave her attention to such matters as equity, pensions and land claims.

The preponderance of "office work" done by women lawyers may well have been understandable in view of public prejudice. Many women lawyers may have been anxious to escape criticism and censure from the public and from other members of the legal profession and for these reasons chose to remain inconspicuous. Yet surprisingly enough, one finds a handful of these first women lawyers fearlessly engaging in criminal work. Mrs. Addie Billins in partnership with her husband was involved in several criminal cases and Mrs. Martha Strickland was active in criminal prosecutions as the assistant prosecuting attorney in Detroit. Mrs. Laura De Force Gordon had a substantial criminal practice (and represented a client in People v. Sproule, termed in 1900 "the most remarkable trial in California criminal jurisprudence"). Kate Kane wrote that in criminal law she had either prosecuted or defended every crime known to modern times except treason and piracy. And, Mrs.

[42] Robinson, supra note 8, at 10.

Marilla Ricker's interest in the defense of criminals earned her the name of "prisoner's friend."

Later in the history of women in the legal profession, it appears that the profession was quite willing to allow women to take over this specialty, if one can go by the remarks of Clarence Darrow. In an address to a group of women lawyers in Chicago, Darrow stated:

> "And there is another field [after divorce] you can have solely for your own. You won't make a living at it, but it's worth while and you'll have no competition. That is the free defense of criminals."[43]

Where to Practice?

Where did these first women lawyers practice in light of public prejudice? For married women with lawyer-husbands, as we have already seen, many did not have to face this difficult decision because they entered into practice with their husbands (although occasionally they confronted another difficulty as in the states of Massachusetts and New York where married women were not able legally to form partnerships). However, for single women the answer to where to practice was oftentimes more problematic. In some instances these women were advised to open a practice in their home town and presumably thereby diminish public criticism. Often however, if they wished to practice at all, many women had little choice but to move to a state where it was permitted by law. The case of Mary Hall is illustrative of this. Before applying for admission in her home state of Connecticut, she seriously considered going to a state where women were already admitted to the bar "dreading the noise and criticism to which a pioneer in such a matter is always subject."[44] Miss Lemma Barkeloo furnishes another example. After being refused admission to law school in her native state of New York, she left her home and went to Missouri where she was admitted to Washington University. In her obituary was the following story by the Honorable Albert Todd:

> "At the close of the last session of the law school, she called at my office to consult me about opening an office here. She said her parents lived in Brooklyn, New York. I advised her to open her office at home,

[43] Quoted in Drew, supra note 31, at 21. In an interesting cultural comparison it appears that French women lawyers were similarly 'bestowed' this specialty by the legal profession. As Lilly wrote: "The woman lawyer is everywhere in the criminal courts in Paris. . . . The men lawyers voted this field of the law entirely to her, and most enthusiastically does she fill it. With my American commercialism, I could not help speculating as to whether or not the men would have so gallantly accorded this distinctive place in the law courts to the women had there been any money in this particular field." Lilly, "The French Women Lawyers," 21 Case and Comment 431 (1914).

[44] Robinson, supra note 8, at 28.

> where she would have the support of her friends. She said she had though of that. . . ."[45]

In the end, however, Miss Barkeloo decided to stay in the "West," because "the western people were generous and liberal in their sentiments and she would be better sustained here than in the East."[46]

An interesting discovery that emerged from this research is that the West afforded better opportunities for women lawyers than the East. In fact, Robinson goes so far as to say that "It is undoubtedly owing to the Western spirit of liberality that women have ever been recognized at the bar in this country at all."[47] The first women lawyers were found predominantly in four states: Illinois, Iowa, Michigan and Wisconsin. (It is in these states where law schools first admitted women students).

Two husband and wife teams (Alice Jordan Blake and her husband and Sara Kilgore Wertman and her husband) moved as far west as Washington, although it can only be surmised that the diminution of prejudice against women lawyers was a contributory reason for their move. The most noteworthy case of the western mobility of the woman lawyer was Lelia Robinson Sawtelle. After seeking admission to the Massachusetts bar, she left for the Washington Territory where she "established herself in practice with the expectation of remaining permanently."[48] The opportunities there which were unavailable in the East can be seen:

> "There she gained a valuable experience in court work (which she scarcely attempted in Boston) in trying and arguing cases before mixed juries of men and women in a new and progressive territory."[49]

(It is important to note, of course, that the opportunities in the West not only attracted women lawyers, but attracted male lawyers as well. They also flocked to the West as it opened up).[50]

Lest it be thought that all the women who gained entrance to the legal profession in this epoch eventually practiced, suffice it to say that approximately one-fifth of the total number of women lawyers never practiced at all. Some women studied without the intention of practicing. Others married and became entrapped by domestic duties. In some instances, as with Rebecca May and Mary McHenry, women's husbands refused to let them enter active practice after their marriage.

Some women drifted into other fields because, it may be surmised, there they encountered less prejudice. Of these women some went into education. Belle Mansfield (the first woman to be admitted to the bar of any state) took a

[45] "Death of Miss Lemma Barkeloo," supra note 36.

[46] *Ibid.*

[47] Robinson, supra note 8, at 13.

[48] "Miss Lelia Robinson Sawtelle Dead," supra note 36.

[49] *Ibid.*

[50] See Fried ... supra note 37, at 557 for a discussion of the attraction of the frontier for Eastern lawyers.

chair in history at De Pauw University. Catherine Waugh (before becoming the famed suffragist) was a professor of commercial law. Some women entered the literary field. One woman became a legal editor for West Publishing Company in 1886. Another woman became an author of legal texts (Marietta Shay, author of *Students' Guide to Common Law Pleading*). Bessie Bradwell Helmer compiled the last ten volumes of Bradwell's Appellate Court Reports, while her famous mother (Bradwell v. Illinois) became editor of "The Chicago Legal News." Catherine V. Waite became the editor of "The Chicago Legal Times."

It appears that many of these first women lawyers were well-to-do women, as can be deduced both from their mobility and from the concentration of legal talent in their families. Also, many of these women were extremely vocal. In addition to those women who expressed their opinions by virtue of their positions on periodicals, many women lawyers were involved in the social movement of temperance or in politics, as was Belva Lockwood, the first woman to run for President of the United States. (Mrs. Lockwood quite rightfully argued that although women could not vote, there was no reason they could not be voted for!)[51]

Historical Context

The century of struggle for women to gain admission to the legal profession can only be understood by placing it in its historical context—with its roots in the struggle for women's rights in the United States. Only then can the question be answered as to why this struggle of women lawyers took place at this particular time in American history.

At the beginning of the nineteenth century women were not given access to higher education because of their sex. While they were permitted to attend elementary schools since the early days of American history, their admission into secondary schools and universities took much longer. It was considered a waste of money to educate women—not only because women's minds were thought to be inferior to men's, but also because women's function was to bear and raise children and an education was deemed superfluous for this task.

Before 1814, education for women was limited to the "well-to-do"[52] and consisted of such pursuits as embroidery, painting, French, singing and playing the harpsichord. However, one event significantly altered this—the discovery of the first power-driven loom in Waltham Massachusetts which

[51] For a discussion of this presidential race (which Mrs. Lockwood claimed "did more to awaken American women to their political powers than anything that happened in the nineteenth century") see Abernathy, "Belva A. Lockwood: A First Lady," 33 Phi Delta Delta 8 (1954).

[52] Flexner, Century of Struggle: The Women's Rights Movement in the United States 23 (1973).

launched the first large-scale industry in the United States. During the period of industrial development and westward expansion following the Louisiana Purchase, women not only entered the textile mills in vast numbers but also were in increasing demand as teachers for the rapidly growing population. Consequently, "the need to equip them for the new duties being laid upon them was harder to deny."[53]

The battle for broader opportunities and rights for women really revolved around the issue of education, maintains Atkins.[54] Such early American feminists as Mary Wollstonecraft, Hannah Crocker, Emma Williard and Frances Wright all stressed the importance of education for women. The first publicly endowed institution for the education of women opened in 1821 and by the end of the 1830's seminaries and colleges for women were beginning to be established. Oberlin, in 1833, was the first institution of higher education to admit all students regardless of race or sex (although women here took a shortened literary course in accordance with the belief that their minds could not assimilate the same fare as men's and the belief that their education better prepared them for intelligent motherhood).[55] In 1837 with the founding of Mt. Holyoke, the concept finally took hold that women needed an improved education for more than carrying out their housewifely duties. Later developments in the nineteenth century saw the opening of Vassar (1865), Smith and Wellesley (1875) and the Harvard Annex (Radcliffe) in 1879.

The struggle for co-education for women proceeded hand-in-hand with the struggle for such equal rights for women as custodial rights for their children, owning property, the right to work at a job and the right to control their own earnings. The roots of these various struggles (and of the fight for suffrage which often overshadows them) can be found in the anti-slavery movement: it was the slavery issue that provided the spark which ignited the feminist movement. Before the 1840's feminism was an unorganized social movement. However, after that period women began organizing in several major American cities to form anti-slavery societies. As Flexner describes:

> "It was in the abolitionist movement that women first learned to organize, to hold public meetings, to conduct petition campaigns. As abolitionists they first won the right to speak in public and began to evolve a philosophy of their place in society and of their basic rights. For a quarter of a century the two movements, to free the slave and to liberate the woman, nourished and strengthened one another."[56]

Thus, it was the abolitionist movement which first brought women out of

[53] *Ibid.* at 24.

[54] Atkins, The Hidden History of the Female: The Early Feminist Movement in the United States 3 (n.d.).

[55] Flexner, supra note 52, at 30.

[56] *Ibid.* at 41.

the home and encouraged them to speak out for their rights—one of which was co-education. Once women gained ground in co-education in colleges and universities, it undoubtedly seemed the logical next step to continue the fight for co-education in law schools.

Interestingly, the fight for women's rights netted better results in the western United States than in the East. This also explains the reason why many women lawyers migrated westward. The Wyoming Territory was the first to grant full suffrage rights to women in 1869. And, in addition to giving women state control of their property and protecting them from discrimination as teachers, Wyoming also permitted the first women to sit on juries.[57] The westtern state of Utah, then the Utah Territory, followed Wyoming in 1870 by granting women the vote. (However, the Edmunds-Tucker Act illegalizing plural marriage passed by Congress in 1887 also revoked women's suffrage in Utah and Utah women did not regain the vote until 1896). The realities of frontier life and the shortage of labor there resulted in women undertaking considerable responsibilities in daily activities. This gave little credence to the idea that women were inferior and should lead sheltered and protected lives.

Suffragists?

The obvious question which comes to mind is: how many of these first women lawyers were active in the women's rights movement in the late nineteenth century? One might hypothesize that the majority of the first women to gain entrance to the legal profession would have been staunch women rightists. Perhaps, even, many were early suffragists? Yet, an examination of the biographical materials on the first women lawyers and a cross tabulation of several sources on the suffrage movement reveal that only a few of these women evidenced their support of women's rights by being ardent suffragists. The names of women lawyers in this period which have come to light in the suffrage movement include: Mary Ahrens, Emily Buckhout Baker, Phoebe Cousins, Clara Foltz, Belva Lockwood, Catherine Waugh McCulloch and Marilla Ricker.[58]

The number of suffragist lawyers may have been somewhat greater based on the fact that several additional women lawyers are found in the temper-

[57] Flexner, supra note 52, at 161, maintains that the jury issue in Wyoming caused a greater storm than the issue of suffrage. For a discussion of the first women jurors, see Robinson, "Women Jurors," 1 Chic. L.T. 22 (1886).

[58] Data veryifying the role of these women in the suffrage movement may be found for Mary Ahrens in her obituary, supra note 36; for Phoebe Cousins in Raye-Smith, "A Light that Failed," 2 W.L.J. 45 (1914); for Clara Foltz in Johnson, The Bar Association of San Francisco: The First Hundred Years (1973); for Belva Lockwood in Abernathy, supra note 51; for Catherine McCulloch in Kraditor, The Ideas of the Woman Suffrage Movement 229 (1965); and for Marilla Ricker in Flexner, supra note 52, at 165.

ance movement in this era. It is known that many women's rights supporters came to the suffrage movement through temperance.[59] Among the women lawyers whose names are found in the temperance movement were: Mrs. Ada Kepley, Mrs. J. Ellen Foster and Mrs. Ada Bittenbender. However, it can not be stated conclusively whether these particular women were women's rights supporters.

What of the links between the women's rights movement in the United States and the first women lawyers? The apex of American feminism occurred in the period 1890-1920. A survey of several volumes of the *Women Lawyers' Journal* after its inception in 1911 reveals that many women lawyers in this *later* period actively participated in the suffrage movement. In fact, in these later years, the link between the women's rights movement and women lawyers is very clear. In this period, the *Women Lawyers' Journal* carried frequent articles on suffragists, on the formation of suffrage clubs, on the progress of equal suffrage, and on women lawyers who were appointed to positions in suffrage associations. In addition, many members of the Women's Lawyers Club (which published the *Women Lawyers' Journal*) were prominent suffragists. It was not uncommon to find in the *Journal* a comment such as the following:

> "It is expected that the women lawyers of the country will respond to the call for marchers in the suffrage parade in Washington on March 3, the day previous to the inauguration of President Wilson."[60]

However, of the women lawyers in the earlier period of 1870 to 1890, it can more likely be assumed that the majority of these women were not radical feminists. A few of the first women lawyers may have been "quiet" feminists, such as Mrs. Anne Saveny who practiced for the benefit of women, or the Cronise sisters who took several women law students to train in their office. By and large, however, it appears that the overwhelming majority of these first women lawyers were individualists—individualists who were content to earn their law degrees and then to disappear from public life. Rarely do we find these first women lawyers speaking out publicly for women's issues, demanding the vote or greater rights for women or seeking legislation to further woman's cause.[61]

Rather, what appears to be the case is that these first women lawyers benefitted from the concurrent struggle of the women's rights movement for coeducation. As opportunities for higher education for women opened up, so naturally did opportunities in the nation's law schools. These first women

[59] Firestone, The Dialectic of Sex: The Case for Feminist Revolution 488 (1970).

[60] See 2 W.L.J. 59 (1913).

[61] Women such as Myra Bradwell seem to have been the exception rather than the rule among these first women lawyers. Mrs. Bradwell drafted and urged the Illinois state legislature to pass a law establishing married women's rights to their earnings and also won passage of laws guaranteeing to a widow a share in her husband's estate. See DeCrow, supra note 39, at 31.

lawyers were undoubtedly influenced by the feminist struggles of their day and benefited therefrom. However, the vast majority of these women failed to see woman's cause as a legitimate social issue and only viewed it insofar as it helped their cause in terms of gaining access to the legal profession.

Parallels Today

What parallels and similarities can be noted between the first women lawyers in the United States and women lawyers today? First, it appears that a high proportion of women in the legal profession today, similar to the women lawyers of 1870-1890, tend to have lawyers in their family who are influential in their decision to study law. Barnes discovered in a study at the University of Virgina that the reason most often cited by women law students for studying law was that a member of their family was an attorney.[62]

It also appears that a large number of married women lawyers today are married to lawyers, as was also found among the nation's first woman lawyers. Glancy in a study of Harvard women law school graduates reports that of the married women in the sample 63% were married to lawyers.[63] She noted: "the husbands of the women lawyers tended to be more enthusiastic or approving of their lawyer-wives' legal careers than the wives of the men in the sample."[64] The significance of this finding seems to lie in the influence of a lawyer-husband. Although it was not determined in these cases whether the women's interest in law preceded her marriage or whether her marriage to a lawyer fostered her interest in law, the support of lawyer-husbands seemed to be an important motivating factor to these women in their pursuit of law studies and a legal career. This finding of the importance of supportive husbands of professional women has also been reported in other studies—as with women doctors. Lopata has found:

> "Whatever the girl's hopes may be, however, it is her husband, if she marries, who ultimately determines the possibility of continuing in her profession while being a wife and mother."[65]

Bernard has noted from the sociological literature on the professional woman what she terms the "law of husband cooperation." She explains:

> ". . . studies show that integrating a domesic and a professional role depends on the cooperation of one's husband. Without it, all else is impossible. The road is just too rough. And if there is opposition, the game is up. . . "[66]

In the nineteenth century whether the woman lawyer eventually practiced often depended on the support she received from her husband. If support was

[62] Barnes, "Woman and Entrance to the Legal Profession," 23 J. Leg. Ed. 289 (1971).

[63] Glancy, "Women in Law: The Dependable Ones," Harv. L.S. Bull. 23 (1970).

[64] *Ibid.*

[65] Lopata, "Marriage and Medicine," in Theodore, The Professional Woman 54 (1971).

[66] Bernard, The Future of Motherhood 162 (1974).

given, the woman generally went into practice—often into practice with her husband. However, if support was not forthcoming, she was more likely to remain in the home after marriage, confined to domestic duties. It would be interesting if after 100 years the same were true today: whether the married woman lawyer successfully integrates a professional and domestic career may depend on the degree of support she receives from her husband.

Another similarity is that women lawyers today, similar to the first women lawyers, tend to see fewer clients than their male counterparts. While women lawyers practicing in the late 1890's tended to maintain low visibility by remaining in the office doing office work, this phenomenon of low visibility in terms of client relations seems to hold true even of women today. According to both White and Glancy, women lawyers today deal with fewer clients than do male lawyers.[67] In addition, many women lawyers currently maintain low visibility by going into government-related work and by avoiding high visibility specialties such as criminal litigation. It is likely that by seeking low visibility, women lawyers hope to minimize discrimination and client prejudice toward them.

This characteristic of women lawyers is also true of the professional woman generally. It is a phenomenon Epstein has called "being unobtrusive." She has noted that women in the professions try to be unobtrusive and to avoid attention by accepting work which keeps them in invisible positions.

> "This unobtrusiveness is a reflection of women's position within the informal structure of the profession. Women are sensitive to men's desire to be left to their own company . . . By bowing to pressure to make themselves unobtrusive . . . women are accepting common definitions about the inappropriateness of their presence in the field in which they have chosen to work. . . ."[68]

Perhaps one reason for professional women and for women lawyers specifically to seek a low profile may lie in the conflicting behavioral expectations they face today, similar to those found in the nineteenth century. As Armstrong has noted: "A well-dressed, acquainted and endowed woman applicant arouses immediate suspicion although this is just what firms pray for in a man."[69] The qualities most admired in men—confidence, ambition, self-assurance, assertiveness, aggressiveness, competitiveness—are looked upon with disfavor in women because they conflict with the traditional image of the sex. Yet, paradoxically, these qualities historically have been and still are the qualities which are viewed as prerequisites for the successful lawyer.

[67] White, "Women in the Law, 65 Mich. L. Rev. 1093 (1967); Glancy, supra note 63.
[68] Epstein, Woman's Place: Options and Limits in Professional Careers 192 (1970).
[69] Armstrong, "Women in the Law," Harv. L.S. Record, Dec. 6 and 13, 1951, at 2.

It is important to note that women, historically, have not been the only target of discrimination by the legal profession. Similar exclusionary practices existed throughout the history of American legal education against Blacks, Jews and immigrants. Much of the discrimination against the latter two groups occurred in the period 1900-1922[70] when hostility on the part of leading acadmicians and practicing lawyers was directed at night schools because of the ethnic composition of their student body.

It would appear that the period of the multiplication of law schools which occurred during the peak years of immigration from 1905 to 1914, as documented by Auerbach, bore a striking similarity to the period of Jacksonian democracy described by Stevens.[71] Both periods were marked by pressures upon the legal profession from those who demanded a freely swinging door to the profession. During the Jacksonian period, the surge of feeling which exalted the common man held that all male citizens had the inherent right to practice law. Similarly for immigrants after the turn of the twentieth century, access to the legal profession became an index of American democracy. Both periods witnessed vigorous debates over the qualifications for admission to the bar.

In the first two decades of this century, the plea among members of the legal profession for higher standards was actually thinly concealed anti-Semitism and xenophobia. As Auerbach writes:

> "Cries of overcrowding swelled the chorus of complaints about commercialization and declining ethics. The culprits were the 'unlearned, unlettered and utterly untrained young lawyers with no esprit de corps and little regard for the traditions of the profession.' In translation this meant immigrants and Jews. . . ."[72]

Anti-Semitism in the legal profession goes back even further in American legal history. George T. Strong in his diary in 1874 supported the idea of a test for admission to Columbia Law School by writing:

> ". . . either a college diploma, or an examination including Latin. This will keep out the little scrubs (German Jews mostly) whom the School now promotes from the grocery-counters . . . to be 'gentlemen of the Bar.' "[73]

As might be expected in the history of American legal education, we also find considerable discrimination against Black law students and lawyers. Such discrimination is especially pronounced in the South where until a

[70] Auerbach, "Enmity and Amity: Law Teachers and Practitioners 1900-1922," 5 Perspectives in American History 551 (1971).

[71] Stevens, "Two Cheers for 1870: The American Law School," 5 Perspectives in American History 417 (1971).

[72] Auerbach, supra note 70, at 584.

[73] Quoted in Friedman, supra note 37, at 553.

decade ago, Mississippi had three Black lawyers to serve a Black population of 800,000 and seven years ago Alabama had 20 Black lawyers and Georgia had 34.[74] Seven years ago there were only 22 first-year Black students at 17 predominantly white Southern law schools. Many Southern law schools until recently, "have been white law schools where blacks were simply not admitted."[75] Thus, it appears that women, historically, have shared the dubious honor of being targets of discrimination by the legal profession with such other minority groups as Jews, Blacks and immigrants.

Discrimination Today

What of discrimination and the position of women in the legal profession today? This question has received much attention recently.[76] Women are applying to law schools in greater numbers than ever before. Since 1969 the overall number of applicants to law schools has tripled, while in the same period the number of female applicants has increased 14 times.[77]

Women comprised 16% of all students entering law school in 1972.[78] Although this figure constitutes a dramatic rise from previous years, the figure is strikingly low when one realizes that 51% of the population is female. As of 1975, only one law school, Northeastern University, had yet achieved population parity and it is doubtful if many others will swiftly follow this guideline.

The participation of women lawyers in the legal profession has risen slowly since 1910. In that year women constituted 1.0% of the profession. A half century later, in 1960, they constituted only 3.5%.[79] Moreover, the ratio of women lawyers to the total membership of the legal profession has actually *declined* from approximately 1 in 28 in 1950 to 1 in 40 by 1970.[80]

In terms of job placement, a 1972 Association of American Law Schools (AALS) questionnaire revealed that significant discrimination against women lawyers still exists. Forty percent of the respondent schools said that

[74] Making the Legal System Work: How Black Students Become Lawyers in the South," 22 Carnegie Quarterly 3 (1974).

[75] *Ibid.*

[76] Some of the most comprehensive recent articles include: Barnes, "Women and Entrance to the Legal Profession," supra note 62; Bysiewicz, "Women Penetrating the Law," 9 Trial 27 (1973); Ginsburg, "Treatment of Women by the Law: Awakening Consciousness in the Law Schools," 5 Val. U. L. R. 480 (1971); Read and Petersen, Sex Discrimination in Law School Placement," 18 Wayne L. Rev. 639 (1972); White, "Women in the Law," supra note 66.

[77] Bysiewicz, supra note 76, at 27.

[78] *Ibid.*

[79] Epstein, "Encountering the Male Establishment," in Theodore, supra note 65.

[80] Sassower, "Women in the Law: The Second Hundred Years," 57 A.B.A. J. 330 (1971).

they had received complaints of discrimination from female students being interviewed by law firms.[81] In addition, the AALS study revealed that women tend to be underrepresented on the faculties of law schools and tend to cluster at lower levels than their male counterparts.

Sassower reports that women lawyers have been losing ground in terms of holding positions of prestige within the profession: every woman who left the bench in New York State within the past twenty years was replaced by a man. She further notes that most top courts, federal and state, have yet to break through the sex barrier.[82] In addition, she reports that women hold a very small number of positions in the major law firms. Of 2,700 lawyers employed by forty top law firms in six major cities, only 186 were women.

White has revealed that a significant income differential exists between male and female lawyers.[83] He reported that in the first year of practice, a $1,500 income differential is apparent. Gradually however, men increased their income to the point where they were earning nearly *double* their female colleagues.

That discrimination still exists in the legal profession is scarcely a point in need of belaboring here. Women were absent in the first hundred years of legal education in America. In the second hundred years they made slow progress: one hundred years after Ada Kepley became the first woman to graduate from law school, the last male bastion of legal education finally permitted women to enter the first-year class. It can only be hoped that women will occupy a more prominent position in the legal profession in the century to come.

[81] Bysiewicz, supra note 76, at 27.
[82] Sassower, supra note 79, at 330.
[83] White, supra note 76, at 1069.

'Little World of Our Own': The Pennsylvania Hospital Training School for Nurses, 1895–1907

NANCY TOMES

FOR the daughters of the American middle class, the feminization and professionalization of nursing in the late nineteenth century meant a widening of educational and employment opportunities. Nursing promised good wages and steady work for most of those who undertook the calling. For a few, it offered more—a route to prestige and an uncommon measure of administrative power. Nursing gave highly motivated women the opportunity to create, as one nurse called it, 'a little world of our own,' a professional world of women centered in the nursing school. Through the new nursing education, such women generated a professional identity for the trained nurse, symbolized by the cap, pin, and uniform, and celebrated in the rituals of capping, graduation, and alumnae reunions. Historians have traced the development of this professional identity among the national leaders of nursing education, women like Isabel Hampton Robb, Adelaide Nutting, and Lavinia Dock, and have noted its expression in organizations like the National League for Nursing Education, the national and state alumnae associations, and the nurses' registries. But rarely have historians investigated the professionalization of nursing at the institutional level, as it operated in the training school, and affected the average nurse.[1]

1. The phrase 'little world of our own' comes from Mary Knabb, 'Looking backward,' speech, n.d., p. 5, School of Nursing Papers, Pennsylvania Hospital Archives. All manuscript material hereafter cited is in the Pennsylvania Hospital Archives. Standard nursing histories all concentrate on national leaders and organizations. See, for example, Lavinia Dock, *A history of nursing*, 3 vols. (New York, 1912); Richard Shryock, *The history of nursing* (Philadelphia, 1959); and Isabel Stewart and Anne Austin, *A history of nursing* (New York, 1962). There are several excellent descriptive histories of individual training schools; cf. Ethel Johns and Blanche Pfeffercorn, *The Johns Hopkins Hospital School of Nursing, 1889–1949* (Baltimore, 1954); Eleanor Lee, *History of the School of Nursing of the Presbyterian Hospital, 1892–1942* (New York, 1942); Grace F. Schryver, *A history of the Illinois Training School for Nurses, 1880–1929* (Chicago, 1930); and Mary Stephenson, *The first fifty years of the Training School for Nurses of the Hospital of the University of Pennsylvania* (Philadelphia, 1940)—but they too

The Pennsylvania Hospital Training School for Nurses offers the material for such an institutional case history of late nineteenth century nursing. Its records include not only the activities of the nursing leaders but also those of the nursing students. From such contrasting viewpoints, we can arrive at a sense of what nursing education meant to the individuals who experienced it. This perspective is particularly useful since the socialization of nurses differed markedly from that of doctors. Historians and sociologists have used a model of professionalization based so exclusively on medicine that they have neglected the variations and alternatives evident in the development of other professions at this time. The study of nursing adds needed complexity and detail to the history of professionalization in the late nineteenth century.

This study focuses on the Pennsylvania Hospital Training School under the leadership of its superintendent, Lucy Walker. During her tenure (1895–1907), it became one of America's foremost nursing schools. Trained in England, Miss Walker brought a heritage of British nursing methods—the emphasis on rigid discipline, hierarchical authority, efficient organization, and autonomy of nursing service—which she attempted to recreate in an American hospital. Her successes and her failures are equally revealing.

An understanding of Miss Walker's career must begin with an understanding of the evolution of trained nursing in the Pennsylvania Hospital before she was appointed in 1895. In the first twenty years of the school's existence, the trained nurses made gradual gains, gains which Lucy Walker consolidated and then expanded. The process illustrates many of the familiar features of professionalization: elimination of untrained competition, constant upgrading of standards, systemization of work, consolidation of authority, and establishment of autonomy.[2]

Before the establishment of the training school in 1876, nursing care at the Pennsylvania Hospital was performed by untrained attendants drawn from the urban working class. Convalescent patients routinely served as nurses, and some liked the work well enough to stay on after they recovered. Additional nurses were recruited from the city's servant population. A few of these early nurses achieved a certain professionalism in their skillful management of the wards and were well liked and respected by

concentrate primarily on nursing leaders and advances in nursing education. Jo Ann Ashley, *Hospitals, paternalism and the role of the nurse* (New York, 1976), comes closest to dealing with the professionalization of nursing as it affected the average nurse, but her book is an interpretive essay rather than a detailed history using individual training school records.

2. A brief but thoughtful discussion of the professionalization of nursing is Richard Shyrock, 'Nursing emerges as a profession,' *Clio Medica*, 1968, *3*, 131–147. See also Ashley, *Hospitals* (n. 1).

the doctors. Others exhibited less proficiency and reliability, so that the overall quality of nursing care was very uneven. Whatever their abilities, the nurses performed their duties with little supervision. In theory, the steward and matron directed their work, but in practice interfered very little in the day-to-day routine of the nurses. Each ward formed an 'independent kingdom' under its own head nurse.[3]

The hospital administration lumped nurses and servants in the same category, and they performed much the same work. Nurses carted laundry and supplies to the wards, dusted the furniture, and kept the wards in order. Little labor was involved in patient care. Nurses delivered medicine to the patients' beds, but the patients were responsible for taking it themselves. (Frequently they poured it out the windows or simply ignored it.) Nurses took temperatures only in special cases. There was no night nursing; attendants made the rounds every night to see that the patients were quiet and comfortable. The low ratio of nurses to patients further illustrates the limited nature of nursing care; in the early 1870s, eleven nurses, six men and five women, cared for 160 patients.[4]

'Respectable' women of the middle classes had little place in the hospital. 'Lady Visitors' came to talk and pray with the patients but had no role in the regular hospital routine. The chairwoman of the Lady Visitors' Committee chided the president of the Board of Managers for the 'guarded manner in which we have been admitted to the institution, alluding particularly to the restriction to hours of the afternoon.' And perhaps there was good reason for such caution; one hospital matron recalled that, in these years, 'to go into a men's surgical ward after midnight was a risk no woman should encounter.'[5]

Such was nursing care when, in 1876, the Board of Managers decided to establish a training school. Impressed with its 'success in foreign institutions,' they believed that a nursing school might be 'productive of good to the hospital.' They hoped that bringing 'educated women' into the wards would improve the care of the patients, the cleanliness of the wards, and the hospital's general decorum.[6]

3. Arthur Meigs, 'The old nursing and the new,' address given to the graduating class of the Pennsylvania Hospital Training School in 1897, privately printed, p. 4, School of Nursing Papers. The protoprofessionalism of some nurses in the prereform era is discussed by Charles Rosenberg, 'And heal the sick: hospital and patient in nineteenth century America,' *J. soc. Hist.*, 1977, *10*, 434–435.

4. Meigs (n. 3), p. 4.

5. Women's Committee Minutes, 12 June 1867; Roberta West, *History of nursing in Pennsylvania* (Harrisburg, 1939), p. 573.

6. Board of Managers, Annual report to contributors, 1876, p. 10; Board of Managers Minutes, 27 October 1879, xi, 82.

The training school staff and students began work only on the women's wards, where the untrained women nurses had never been very popular with the doctors. For the first eight years of the school's existence, its superintendent Annie Bunting 'interfered but very little with the management of the men's wards.' Not until 1885 did the president of the Board of Managers suggest putting trained women nurses on the men's wards as well. His suggestion shocked some. One doctor said later, 'I well remember my disgust and the feeling of fear that came over me that I should live to see such a state of things.' The board was determined to go through with the plan, however. At first the women's presence in the men's wards created 'great difficulty and friction.' When Miss Sharpless, the first woman nurse on the male surgical ward, helped a very sick man to change his 'outer garments,' 'a cry of horror went up.' According to one old employee, the nurses themselves were 'soon disgusted, and said it was not fit work for women.' But the women nurses stayed on the men's wards. By 1885, a new superintendent, Marion Smith, had eliminated all the male heads of wards. The remaining male nurses were called 'orderlies.' In 1892 the Board of Managers could report to the hospital's contributors, 'where twenty years ago, a woman's presence would have been thought out of place, all care is now committed to her charge.'[7]

Despite the gradual elimination of untrained nurses and the centralization of authority under the Superintendent of Nurses, the training school was far from well established in the early 1890s. A rapid turnover in superintendents had left discipline lax and the quality of nursing care uneven. A hospital committee in 1894 complained that the student nurses did not receive the 'systematic, thorough and accurate instruction which they rightly expect.' Their work was not well organized, and thus all the nurses overworked. The superintendent also had 'failed to win the confidence and command the respect of her pupils,' and the social life in the Nurses' Home lacked 'healthful tone,' the committee concluded.[8]

In 1895, the Board of Managers interviewed Lucy Walker and decided to appoint her superintendent. Their choice proved wise, for the young Englishwoman possessed the 'teaching experience and gift of organization' needed to upgrade the training school. Born in 1860, Miss Walker trained at St. Bartholomew's Hospital, London, in a program founded in the wake

7. Meigs (n. 3), pp. 5, 8; 'A bit of history of the Pennsylvania Hospital School of Nursing,' n.d., School of Nursing Papers; Meigs (n. 3), p. 8.

8. 'Report of managers Garrett, Shinn and Levis,' 28 May 1895, Board of Managers, Special Committee Reports; Sarah McMullin, 'Reminiscences,' 3 February 1941, p. 4, School of Nursing Papers.

of the Nightingale reforms. She came to Philadelphia in 1892 to visit relatives and stayed on to serve as superintendent of the Presbyterian Hospital Training School. After three years at Presbyterian, Miss Walker decided to take up the challenge of reorganizing the Pennsylvania Hospital's school.[9]

During her years in Philadelphia, Lucy Walker played an important role in national organizations for nursing. She was a charter member of the American Society of Superintendents of Training Schools, founded in 1893. In 1899 she helped organize the graduate course in hospital economics for nurses offered at Teachers College, Columbia; she was the first choice of the American Society of Superintendents' Education Committee to teach the course. Although Miss Walker declined the post, citing her responsibilities to the Pennsylvania Hospital Training School as her reason, she did give a series of lectures on hospital organization. In the Philadelphia area, Miss Walker was involved in founding a nurses' registry at the Pennsylvania Hospital, a county association of training school alumnae, and a preliminary course of nursing affiliated with the Drexel Institute.[10]

While the outlines of her professional career are clear, Lucy Walker remains an enigmatic person. She was a fine administrator who inspired respect or resentment rather than affection from her students. The official documents of her superintendency clearly reveal her sternness and self-discipline, but provide few glimpses of her other characteristics. She suffered frequent attacks of ill health. In 1903 she had a nervous breakdown after the death of a favorite student. One nurse wrote of her, 'Miss Walker had many ups and downs, many worries.' She left the nursing profession in 1907 at the age of forty-seven, to take up a 'private life.' Her personal history suggests the severe emotional and physical strains that professional demands might place on a woman.[11]

Whatever her personal agonies might have been, Lucy Walker had a clear idea of administrative goals and set about achieving them from the day she came to the hospital. Her first concern was to consolidate her authority. As a condition for accepting the post, Miss Walker insisted that she act as both matron of the hospital and superintendent of the training

9. Board of Managers Minutes, 28 October 1895, XII, 17; West, *History* (n. 5), pp. 658, 573.

10. West, *History* (n. 5), p. 658; Dock, *History of nursing* (n. 1), III, 132; L. Walker to B. Shoemaker, 5 September 1899, School of Nursing Papers; *Am. J. Nurs.*, 1900, *1*, 36; Nurses' Alumnae Association Minutes, 15 June 1904, II, 142–143; *ibid.*, 6 December 1901, II, 76; L. Walker to Board of Managers, 28 April 1902, School of Nursing Papers.

11. Board of Managers Minutes, 27 August 1903, XII, 247; McMullin (n. 8), pp. 9–10; West, *History* (n. 5), p. 575; Board of Managers Minutes, 29 July 1907, XII, 473. Lucy Walker became the adopted heir and companion of a relative in Pittsburgh, taking the name Donnel. See Nurses' Alumnae Association of the Pennsylvania Hospital Training School, *Alumnae Notes*, January 1908, p. 11.

school. Previously, the two jobs had been separate, and the matron and superintendent had numerous disputes over their areas of authority. Miss Walker wanted to avoid such conflict by assuming control over all aspects of nursing service. Thus the quality of nursing education, patient care, and the hospital environment were all her responsibilities. She supervised the housekeeping staff as well as all nursing personnel. In order to perform her new duties, Miss Walker brought two personal assistants with her to act as assistant matron and assistant superintendent.[12]

Miss Walker's next goal was to increase her control over the head nurses, who supervised patient care, housekeeping, and instruction of student nurses on each ward. She began by establishing a sense of her authority. Instead of making the rounds of the wards, Miss Walker remained in her office and had the head nurses report to her. 'She came on the wards very little,' remembered one head nurse. 'Her assistant made the regular rounds morning and evening and made her report to Miss Walker.' Then Miss Walker gradually replaced the old nurses with women she had trained. She told the hospital's Board of Managers in 1897 that nursing care would be unsettled 'until I can secure the best of my own graduates for this work.' As soon as she had suitable replacements, Miss Walker asked the resignations of the head nurses she considered inefficient or uncooperative, 'for the reason that they could not or would not carry out my methods.' Miss Walker also did not hesitate to ask her own graduates to resign if they refused to obey her. She fired the night superintendent Sarah McMullin 'as she was not in accord with the methods of training, required by the Superintendent.' Three more graduate head nurses were dismissed at the end of their first year, 'as their influence over the pupils was not what was desired by their Superintendent.'[13]

The transition from the old staff to the new did not proceed without tensions. One of Miss Walker's personal assistants aroused resentment because she was 'inclined to criticize and make us feel they [the British nurses] were far superior nurses,' wrote one head nurse. Of course, the American nurses and doctors disagreed, she observed, 'and I know that there were many difficult times for her and for us to overcome.' The same nurse said

12. Board of Managers Minutes, 28 October 1895, XII, 17.

13. McMullin (n. 8), p. 6; Superintendent's Report, July 1896, School of Nursing Papers; *ibid.*, April 1900 and March 1906. It is interesting that Miss Walker, to increase her authority, distanced herself from the bedside aspects of patient care. The split between the nurse's role in administration and patient care has received considerable attention from sociologists as a major source of conflict within the modern nursing profession. See Fred Davis, 'Nurses,' in *The semi-professions and their organization*, ed. Amitai Etzioni (New York, 1969), pp. 54–81.

that once the transition was completed, the staff worked more smoothly. 'As the positions were filled by our own graduates on the wards and operating room, the atmosphere became better, and we had a better understanding of Miss Walker.'[14]

By 1899 Miss Walker had staffed the hospital entirely with Pennsylvania Hospital graduates.[15] The uniformity and obedience she demanded from her nursing staff aided Miss Walker in creating the educational environment she thought necessary for the student nurses. Hierarchy and discipline were the keynotes of her educational philosophy. Having established both in her staff, she now turned to the creation of them in the student body.

The student nurses ranged beneath the nursing staff in their own hierarchy of four classes; senior, intermediate, junior, and probationer. The senior or third year students acted as assistants to the head nurse of the ward. They delegated and supervised the work of the younger nurses. The intermediate or second year nurses received their first experience on the more demanding services such as surgery, clinic, and night duty. The junior or first year nurses performed the basic practical nursing on the wards, such as making beds and feeding and bathing the patients. The probationers occupied the lowest position in the nursing hierarchy; they served six months to a year doing the most menial tasks—caring for the linen and bedpans—before they were 'capped' and accepted as students.[16]

Distinctions among the classes of student nurses were recognized in their living arrangements as well as in their ward duties. They lived on separate floors in the nurses' home and ate their meals seated at separate tables. As they filed into the dining room, one nurse remembered, 'you would note where those of higher rank took their places.' Seniors naturally had the most privileges. For example, they might be invited to join the Nurses' Club or attend the alumnae association's functions.[17]

Every aspect of the student nurses' behavior was regulated by Lucy Walker's rules. All nurses lived on the hospital grounds in the nurses' home. The rules set hours for arising, eating, resting, studying, and retiring. On leaving the home in the morning, each student nurse had to leave her room ready for inspection. The rules specified that 'before leav-

14. McMullin (n. 8), p. 6.

15. Superintendent's Report, October 1900.

16. This outline of the student nurses' duties was put together from the Record of the Training School, 1894–98; Superintendent's Reports; and Helen McClelland, 'Reminiscences,' n.d., School of Nursing Papers.

17. McMullin (n. 8), p. 6; McClelland (n. 16), p. 2; Nurses' Club Minutes; Alumnae Association Minutes (such invitations were frequent).

ing her room, each nurse must remove all bed clothing from the bed, open the window and door, and leave the room to air thoroughly.' Nurses had to attend meals punctually and 'remain at the table for the time allotted.' One of Miss Walker's assistants presided at every meal, 'to see that the nurses get their meals comfortably and that they attend regularly and punctually.' After eating, the students' napkins and napkin rings had to be placed in pigeonholes outside the dining room.[18]

While on duty, student nurses had to wear a 'simply made' uniform of plain blue gingham with a bibbed white apron. The style of cap worn was Lucy Walker's own, the 'Sister Dora' cap used by her school in London. As for the rest of the nurse's clothing, it also had to be 'simply made' if she expected to have it laundered. 'No clothing will be washed that is ruffled, tucked or flounced,' Walker's rules decreed.[19]

On the ward and in the classroom, more rules regulated the student nurses. They had to obey 'strictly and respectfully' the orders of the nurse in charge. They could not give a patient any medicine or treatment without the order of the physician on duty. While on duty, the students had to treat patients with 'the utmost gentleness.' They were forbidden to bring their charges any extra food or fruit. No needlework or novel reading was allowed while a nurse was on the ward. In addition to their ward work, the students attended three hours of lectures a week. Special hours were set aside for study for the weekly quizzes given by Miss Walker and her assistants. If a student's grades fell below 75% she could be suspended.[20]

Even the little free time given the student nurses was regimented. The rules required them 'to go out in the fresh air for at least half an hour daily in fine weather.' Miss Walker had the gatekeeper note the time the students went out and came in, so that those not taking their walk might be reprimanded. On their two free afternoons a week, nurses might go out between 10 A.M. and 7 P.M. if they signed out at the gate. No visitors were allowed without Miss Walker's special permission.[21]

The discipline imposed on every aspect of the student's life seems at once trivial and overbearing, but it was not pointless. Miss Walker meant to teach the student nurses discipline and absolute obedience; the enforcement of a strict set of rules was one way to achieve such discipline. Many

18. 'Rules for nurses,' manuscript in Lucy Walker's handwriting, n.d., School of Nursing Papers; Superintendent's Report, April 1896; McClelland (n. 16), p. 2.

19. 'Rules for nurses'; Margaret Dunlop, 'Speech at capping exercises,' 1936, p. 1, School of Nursing Papers. 'Rules for nurses.'

20. 'Rules for nurses'; Superintendent's Report, April 1901 and April 1896.

21. Superintendent's Report, April 1896; McMullin (n. 8), pp. 6–7; 'Rules for nurses.'

rules also reflected Miss Walker's concern with the students' health, that they get enough sleep, eat regularly, and get exercise in the fresh air. Since almost every student had a serious illness in her first year of training, these precautions seemed necessary indeed.[22]

Not only was Miss Walker responsible for the students' health, she had to guard their moral characters as well. The reputations of sixty young women away from their parents, many in the city for the first time in their lives, had to be guarded carefully. This was especially important since the nursing profession had a poor reputation; the old image of the female nurse as a servant with suspect morals had not entirely disappeared. The greater responsibilities assigned to the trained nurse also increased concern that she be without reproach. Thus the training school leaders felt that they had to weed out 'unsuitable women' to dispel any doubts in the public mind about the morals and abilities of nurses. 'We do not stand in the position of colleges and universities,' wrote Adelaide Nutting in 1898. 'They do not vouch for character, but only for a certain degree of schooling. We stand in a different and peculiar position. We assume a moral responsibility for the character of the nurses we send out.' The Pennsylvania Hospital's managers recognized this fact in describing the training school diploma as 'a certificate of efficiency and character.'[23]

For these reasons, Lucy Walker worked to create an obedient, disciplined body of nurses. But hers was not an isolated, autonomous discipline; another hierarchy existed in the hospital, of which the nurses were a part. They were taught absolute obedience to the doctors as well as their nursing superiors. The doctors' authority seems to have reinforced, rather than conflicted with, that of the nursing staff, however. Although there is ample evidence of conflicts among the nurses, no problems between the nursing staff and the doctors appear in the hospital records. This does not prove that such tensions did not exist, but rather that doctor-nurse conflict was minimized. Lucy Walker undoubtedly cooperated in the effort to minimize it.

In all matters relating to patient care, the physician remained the final authority. The doctors at the Pennsylvania Hospital stated clearly, 'the nurses in the various wards should be under the direction as far as the medical and surgical treatment of the patient is concerned, of the resident phy-

22. Health records for the students were kept in the Record of the Training School, 1894–98, the Nurses' Record no. 1, 1899–1906, and no. 2, 1906–10.

23. Helen Marshall, *Mary Adelaide Nutting* (Baltimore, 1972), p. 90; 'Return and answer of contributors and managers to writ of alternative mandamus issued in the case of Marianne Wood,' December 1900, Marianne Wood file, Board of Managers Papers.

sician.' The ritual of 'rounds' reinforced the division between prescription and treatment as the basis of the doctor-nurse relationship. As the doctors examined the patients each morning, the nurse in charge of the ward followed them around with a special portfolio containing all orders for treatment. After rounds were over, she took the doctors' orders and prepared a treatment board which the other nurses consulted in caring for the patients. The doctors reported any mistakes on the nurses' part in carrying out their orders to the head nurse or Lucy Walker.[24]

The hospital staff during these years consisted of eight residents who lived in the hospital and eight attending or chief physicians, who visited the hospital a few times a week. The number of nurses averaged between sixty and eighty. The permanent nursing staff—the superintendent, her assistants, and the head nurses, all together ten or eleven in number—were undoubtedly well known to the doctors. But the average nursing student had few direct dealings with the doctors. One student remembered that a certain chief physician had the reputation for being able to diagnose a patient's illness from the foot of the bed. 'I did not see him do that,' she said, 'for though a "cat may look at a king," a diet nurse could not often look at the "Big Chief" when he was making his rounds.' The same student said she 'broke all the rules of the training school, by daring to exclaim out loud in the presence of the chief.'[25]

The nurses knew the doctors—even if only by reputation—much better than the doctors knew them. Doctors' abilities, amusing habits, and annoying traits formed the staple of a nurses' folklore. When asked to reminisce, they told such stories at length. It was unusual, on the other hand, for a doctor to know a nurse's name. One nurse said approvingly of the chief surgeon, 'He was beloved by everyone because he had such a gracious manner and was the one "Big Chief" who always remembered a nurse's name, and addressed her by it when he had occasion to speak to her.' Several other residents were praised because 'they were such perfect gentlemen always, and a nurse's word was never questioned by them.' Such remarks suggest that not knowing a nurse's name, questioning her word, and being less than gracious were common behavior on the part of some doctors.[26]

More frequently, however, nurses provided some doctors with the opportunity to indulge their paternal instincts. One resident recalled a repre-

24. 'Residents' reply to Lucy Walker,' 1896, School of Nursing Papers.
25. Knabb (n. 1), p. 3; Mary Knabb, 'Memories of Dr. Thomas G. Morton,' 18 January 1938, McClelland file no. 2, School of Nursing Papers.
26. Knabb (n. 1), Knabb (n. 25), McClelland (n. 16) are good examples of this tendency.

sentative scene between doctor and nurse: 'Dr. Richard Harte's specialty was the kind of shoes the nurses wore. Many times those of us who worked with him have seen some innocent little nurse—probably a probationer—stopped in her tracks and accosted by, "Matilda, why don't you wear sensible shoes?" She was then and there given a lecture on the proper type of footwear.' (Dr. Harte does seem to have known his victim's name, unless he called all nurses 'Matilda,' which is a possibility.) Doctors evidently preferred such paternalism to romantic interests in the nurses. Only one romance involving a student nurse and a resident physician appeared in the disciplinary records during Miss Walker's tenure. She must have sensed some potential danger, however, for nurses were 'strictly forbidden to go to the doctors' rooms for any reason.'[27]

The student nurses had one other form of contact with the medical staff, their class lectures. Members of the staff gave regular courses of lectures to the nurses. This job was little sought after by the doctors, possibly because the student nurses were not always appreciative. The students had to be reprimanded for talking in lecture and copying one another's notes. Lucy Walker lamented that the younger nurses were not always able to 'appreciate the good advice of the experienced members of the medical staff' given in the lectures.[28]

Most contacts between doctor and nurse reinforced the inequality of their relationship. For the most part, doctors were distant and authoritative. They delivered orders and examinations with equal decisiveness. They inspired awe when present, yet were rarely present. The real people with day-to-day power in the student nurses' lives were Lucy Walker and her staff. This may help explain the relative absence of direct conflict between nurses and doctors. The physicians left matters relating to the student nurses to Miss Walker. It was in their best interests to enforce her authority so that the hospital staff would function smoothly. In turn, Miss Walker worked well with the physicians because she put patient care—the hospital's main interest—before the interests of the students.

Yet Lucy Walker's principles and personality were only one determining factor in shaping the training school atmosphere. Having examined her principles, we must now consider the students' influence on the socialization process. They were not passive recipients of Miss Walker's educa-

27. Dr. Charles Mitchell, 'Speech to graduating nurses,' 1935, pp. 4–5, School of Nursing Papers. Caroline Case was reprimanded for sitting in the summerhouse with a resident, see Record of the Training School, p. 166; 'Rules for nurses.'

28. Board of Managers Minutes, 29 July 1889, XI, 429; L. Walker to B. Shoemaker, July 1896, School of Nursing Papers.

tional philosophy but played a significant part in shaping the training school environment; their background and goals defined a major component of their professional experience. Fortunately, we can examine their contribution to the training school environment through the student records kept by Miss Walker. Information on 205 women entering the training school between 1898 and 1909 provides an idea of the type of women going into nursing, and their individual careers as nursing students.[29]

Applicants had to conform to certain basic requirements established by the training school. They had to be between twenty-one and thirty-five years of age, and of 'at least average height and physique.' They needed a 'common school education,' which was defined as the ability to 'read aloud well, to write legibly and accurately, to understand arithmetic as far as fractions and percent, and to take notes at lectures.' This amount of education was 'indispensable,' concluded the application form, but women 'of superior education and refinement take precedence.'[30]

The women accepted by the Pennsylvania Hospital Training School under these guidelines were usually young; 60% were between twenty-one and twenty-four years old, 88% were under thirty. All but two of the students were single. The exceptions were a childless doctor's widow, aged thirty-four, and a twenty-three-year-old who had 'made an unfortunate marriage' and been deserted by her husband.[31] Though the application form did not specify that a woman must be single to be accepted, this must in practice have been a requirement.

Most of the student nurses had grown up in small or medium-sized towns. Only 9% were born in Philadelphia. Strikingly few came from other cities, probably because those cities possessed their own training schools. Of the Pennsylvania students, half were born in towns with populations under 2,500. Another third came from towns between 2,500 and 10,000 in population. The out-of-state students (29%) also came from small towns in New York, New Jersey, Maryland, Virginia, Ohio, and Indiana. Eight percent were natives of Ontario, 5% of the British Isles.

Not surprisingly, considering their predominantly small-town origins, the nursing students were, with the exception of one Roman Catholic, all Protestants. The majority (62%) were Presbyterians, Episcopalians, and Methodists; 8% each were Lutherans and Baptists; the remainder were

29. This information was compiled from the Record of the Training School and the Nurses' Records no. 1 and 2.

30. 'Rules for nurses.'

31. Nurses' Record no. 1, 291; Nurses' Record no. 2, 71.

Quakers, Congregationalists, Moravians, Reformed or United Brethren.

The students had a wide range of educational backgrounds. Forty-nine percent had at least a high school diploma. Another 17½% had completed eighth grade and a few years of high school. Only 16½% had not finished eighth grade. Seventeen percent had been educated entirely in private schools of uncertain academic level. The education of many had been piecemeal. (Requirements for postgraduate work were casual at this time; women entered colleges or normal schools who had failed to complete high school.) They also had pursued a variety of special educational programs, including business schools, art schools, conservatories of music, schools of elocution, and training schools for kindergarten or missionary work.

Half of the student nurses had had no occupation other than 'home life' before entering the training school. Most of these women were under twenty-four (69%). The small number of older women who had never been employed before had all had some family obligation which prevented them from pursuing their own interests at an earlier age. Once that family obligation ended, they applied to the training school. The older women had kept house for widowed fathers and unmarried brothers, or nursed sick relatives until well past the age for marriage; then death or a male relative's marriage set them free. Margaret Derrickson's case is typical. She helped her mother run a private school for many years. When her mother became an invalid, she took over the school. After her mother's death, Margaret entered the training school.[32]

Half of the student nurses had some occupation before entering the training school. As a group, they were slightly older than the never-employed students.[33] Teaching had been their most common occupation (45%). Many of the women had taught for only a short time before leaving the profession, but a few had taught as many as fifteen years before taking up nursing. The new clerical trades opening up for women in the late nineteenth century had provided jobs for 21% of the employed nurses. They had held positions as stenographers, clerks, and bookkeepers. Several

32. For the life histories of the older, never-employed women see Nurses' Record no. 1, 163, 181, 187, 225, 245, 283; Nurses' Record no. 2, 15, 21, 83. Margaret Derrickson's record is in Nurses' Record no. 1, 163.

33. The following table gives comparative ages for employed and unemployed students:

	employed	*never employed*
ages 21–24	56 %	69 %
ages 25–29	33 %	22 %
ages 30–35	11 %	9 %

had worked for newspapers as proofreaders and compositor-typesetters. Two women had been telephone operators. As with teaching, the length of time spent at this work before entering the training school varied greatly. Only 5% of the nurses had made their living by sewing, as dressmakers, milliners, or shirtwaist makers. The only two women in the group who had done factory work were involved in the needle trades. One woman had been an instructor in sewing machine operation, the other a foreman in a hosiery mill.

The nursing profession clearly attracted women with varying backgrounds and motivations. Some did not have to earn a living but were drawn by the idealism of the nursing profession. Theirs was a mission; as one alumna put it, 'Never feel that your profession is necessarily for a livelihood, but reach out and attain your ideals.' A nursing student from an upper class background distinguished between the 'Nurse who comes for the doubly noble reason of making her own living and doing good . . . and those like myself who come with a more sentimental idea.'[34]

For the educated women, nursing was probably a respectable alternative to medical school. The number of women possessing at least a high school degree is striking. Men with similar educational backgrounds would have had no difficulty in entering medical school. As late as 1910, only two medical schools in Pennsylvania required applicants to have a high school diploma. This may reflect poorly on the status of medical education, but gives a good indication of the caliber of women going into nursing school. If they had been male, they might well have become doctors rather than nurses. This suggests that women were choosing nursing as a more fitting career than medicine. Helen McClelland, who entered the training school in 1908, remembered that two graduates of the school told her that the 'nursing profession was of more value for women than medicine unless one was going into the mission fields.'[35]

For others, nursing was a livelihood rather than a profession. For many girls from small towns, nursing probably functioned as domestic service had for an earlier generation. It facilitated a rural to urban migration of women for whom there were fewer and fewer opportunities at home. It offered training in work considered natural for a woman, within a tightly structured, morally reassuring environment. Once the degree was obtained,

34. Nurses' Alumnae Association Minutes, 19 June 1906, I, 198–199; M. Wood to 'Pupil nurses in training at the Pennsylvania Hospital,' August 1900, Marianne Wood file, Board of Managers Papers.

35. Abraham Flexner, *Medical education in the United States and Canada* (1910; reprint ed., Buffalo, N.Y., 1973), pp. 198–199; McClelland (n. 16), p. 1.

work was plentiful and provided a chance for social mobility. The small-town girl nursing in an urban middle class family could pick up their values and mannerisms, and perhaps enable herself to marry a more upwardly mobile man.[36]

The number of women who left another occupation for nursing suggests more concrete reasons for its popularity. In terms of wages, nursing compared favorably to teaching, clerical work, and factory work. In addition to room and board, hospital work paid an average of $35 a month for head nurses, $50 to $100 for nurse administrators. Pay for private duty work varied, but averaged between $15 and $20 a week. Teaching paid only $25 to $30 a week, clerical work, between $11 and $14 a week, and factory work $9 a week. The demand for both hospital and private duty nurses was consistently high during these decades as well.[37]

The educational and employment histories of the nursing students indicate that nursing neither attracted nor accepted urban working class women. The predominance of Protestants from small towns shows that few recent immigrants entered the training school. The absence of women who had done factory work further supports this impression. Instead, the student biographies suggest that women came to nursing from a wide range of backgrounds within the broad category of the 'middle class.' A few were upper middle class women of 'refinement' with exceptionally good educations; others were small-town girls who had failed to finish the eighth grade. Within these extremes, there were many gradations.

The biographies of four members of the class of 1904 illustrate this variety more concretely. Ella Ferguson, born in Philadelphia, age twenty-two, had completed two years of high school and gone to business college. Since then she had worked as a clerk. Her classmate Mary Hale, born in Virginia, age thirty-two, had gone to art school. After six months in Europe, she found a position as a governess and companion. Mary Swank, born in Lancaster, Pennsylvania, age twenty-eight, had been educated in a 'country school' and attended a few years of high school. Until entering the training school, she had lived with a married brother and cared for his invalid wife. Her classmate Ella Tomlinson, from Westtown, Pennsylvania,

36. The similarities between nursing and domestic service are suggested by J. Jean Hecht, *The domestic servant class in 18th century England* (London, 1956), and Theresa McBride, *The domestic revolution* (Chicago, 1976).

37. Statistics on nurses' wages were taken from the Steward's Monthly Accounts, 1890–1915; see also Marshall, *Nutting* (n. 23), p. 94; for other wage information, see United States Department of Labor, Women's Bureau Bulletin no. 225, *Handbook of facts on women workers* (Washington, D.C., 1928).

age twenty-two, graduated from Westtown Boarding School and taught three years in a private Friends' school.[38]

The mixture of motivations and backgrounds among the student nurses posed special problems for Lucy Walker. Teaching, discipline, even living arrangements were made more difficult by the disparity in education and experience. Miss Walker reminded the Board of Managers of this difficulty when she requested an enlargement of the nurses' home. She wrote, 'It is very trying, and in some cases, a severe ordeal, for women of refinement to be obliged to share their rooms, more especially in a Training School as mixed as one of this size must necessarily be.'[39] Miss Walker's strict discipline was undoubtedly aimed at controlling the potentially disruptive social differences among the student nurses. Enforcing a recognized code of discipline made up for the lack of shared, mutually understood standards of behavior. But as in any would-be 'total' institution, there were cracks in the discipline, cracks which the students explored and exploited. Discipline problems did develop, and the type and pattern of infractions most frequently committed reveal important aspects of the training school regimen and the professional standards which shaped it.

The most common discipline problem was, naturally, disobedience. This term applied not only to direct defiance of the 'authorities,' as Miss Walker referred to herself and her staff; it also included any departure from the rules which seemed in the least deliberate. Thus if a student nurse forgot to take a patient's temperature or relabeled a bottle carelessly, she was disobedient; she had strayed from her prescribed duties.

Patterns of open disobedience reveal stresses among the nursing staff. Few students dared to be impertinent to Miss Walker or her assistants, but they were less respectful to the head nurses. Being rude, impertinent, disrespectful, or disobedient to a head nurse was a common misdemeanor. The number of staff members also opened up the possibilities for playing them off against one another. For example, Eleanor Cadbury 'appeal[ed] to the night superintendent against the Head Nurse.' Marianne Wood went to Lucy Walker 'to make complaint of the night superintendent.' Another student, Mary Groff, chose another means for annoying her nursing superior; she 'made trouble by setting the patient against the head nurse of the ward.'[40] The frequency of such incidents makes Miss Walker's

38. These four student histories were taken from Nurses' Record no. 1, 189, 201, 187, 221.

39. Superintendent's Report, April 1899.

40. See, for example, the Record of the Training School, pp. 84, 166; Nurses' Record no. 1, 173, 293; Nurses' Record no. 2, 99. Quotations come from the Record of the Training School, pp. 176, 164, 98.

concern with the quality of her head nurses more understandable. Any conflict of opinion among the head nurses, or with the night superintendent, could easily be used by the students to evade her strict discipline.

Relations between senior and junior nurses also developed special strains. Some senior nurses exploited their younger charges. Miss Walker noted on one nurse's record, 'spends too much time on lists; younger nurses given her work to do.' Other seniors were too rough or showed a 'want of tact' with the younger nurses. The result was irritation between senior and junior nurses. Seniors also used their power to protect the younger nurses. Miss Walker reported to the Board of Managers that 'some of the senior nurses placed in charge, do not realize the responsibilities of their positions, and . . . will not report irregularities to the Head Nurse.' Some seniors, like Elizabeth Arnold, were guilty of 'doing [the junior nurses'] work rather than seeing that it is done.'[41] Neither irritation nor collusion between the senior and junior nurses made for the proper hospital discipline in Lucy Walker's estimation.

The student nurses occasionally banded together in their acts of rebellion. Miss Walker was especially wary of the influence of troublemakers in the school. For example, Marianne Wood concerned her because of her 'troublesome' effect on the other nurses. Miss Walker wrote that she 'stirs up the other nurses, and promised to use her influence to protect them.' A full-scale defiance took place in May 1899. Fourteen students—a quarter of the student body that year—signed a petition to the Board of Managers protesting the dismissal of a fellow student, and asking that she be reinstated. Miss Walker acted quickly to squash that action. She demanded an apology or threatened dismissal for every nurse who signed the petition. She received the apologies, although she felt that several did so only to save themselves from dismissal, and 'did not honestly regret [their] action.'[42]

Senior nurses often became unruly in more subtle ways in the last months of their terms. Since they were leaving soon, they disregarded rules without fear of serious consequence. This behavior distressed Miss Walker because it tended to unsettle all the student nurses. In 1899, she suggested to the managers that such nurses not be given the silver badge awarded to graduates of the school. Miss Walker wrote,

> Some of the nurses when within a short time of completing their term, grow careless in their work or conduct. . . . At the present time, four of those who

41. Nurses' Record no. 2, 49; Superintendent's Report, April 1901; Nurses' Record no. 2, 49.

42. Record of the Training School, p. 164; Nurses' Record no. 1, 3, 5; Record of the Training School, pp. 172, 182.

leave very soon are setting a bad example in the school by their careless work and conduct. No one offence committed is of a very serious nature, nor such as to warrant any severe measure being taken; but all together, their actions are such as to attract the attention of the nurses, and to merit the disapproval of those in authority.[43]

Next to defiance of authority, the student nurses' work habits proved to be the most troublesome disciplinary problem. According to Lucy Walker's standards, many nurses failed to perform their duties with the proper attitude and method. They fell asleep on special duty or acted half-asleep even when awake. They were too slow or too fussy.[44]

The worst infractions of discipline involved mistakes in executing the physicians' orders. Such errors might have disastrous consequences for the patients. They were scalded with hot water bags while unconscious, blistered with burning alcohol and turpentine, and dosed with too much medicine. Patients were given medicine, douches, cuppings, and doses of salts meant for other individuals. Student nurses neglected to take temperatures or give sponge baths to the fevered. One nurse went so far as to record false temperatures to avoid giving a typhoid fever patient a sponge bath. Such actions must have done little to increase the patients' or the doctors' confidence in the student nurses' ability. Miss Walker noted in one case that a 'nervous private patient was very much alarmed' when he discovered that a student had filled up his water pitcher with carbolic acid. Although errors made 'rather through ignorance than actual carelessness' might merit only a reprimand, mistakes due 'to carelessness and disobedience'—for example, by failing to look at a bottle's label before giving medicine—were punished severely, sometimes by dismissal.[45]

The nursing students' relationships with the patients caused recurrent discipline problems. The young women had difficulty in steering the proper line between being too 'familiar' with their charges and being cruel to them. The most common infraction was being too friendly or 'familiar' with patients, especially men. Frequently student nurses had to be removed from the men's wards for not maintaining the proper distance, emotionally or physically, from the patients. Walker described them as too 'free and

43. Superintendent's Report, October 1899.

44. This is a very common complaint. See, for example, Record of the Training School, pp. 98, 140; Nurses' Record no. 2, 5, 29, 79.

45. For a few examples, see Record of the Training School, pp. 78, 84, 122, 124, 126; Nurses' Record no. 1, 173. Quotations come from Record of the Training School, pp. 394, 200; Nurses' Record no. 2, 83, 95; Record of the Training School, pp. 96, 100, 140; Nurses' Record no. 1, 55; Nurses' Record no. 2, 57.

easy' and lacking 'the proper dignity.' One nurse was nearly suspended when she was found 'dancing before the patients in the ward.' Nurses were discouraged from talking too much to any of the patients, male or female, and having favorites among them. The students developed similar problems with orderlies. Emilie Cox, for example, earned Miss Walker's disapproval when she resigned from the school and 'married very shortly after, one of the men employed in the hospital.'[46] Such incidents suggest that since some of the students found enough in common with the male patients and orderlies to flirt with them, the two groups may have been similar in background.

Student nurses were also frequently reprimanded for roughness, rudeness, and neglect of their charges. Ida White, for example, failed to show the proper respect by 'talking loudly with another nurse, on personal affairs, in a room with two dying men.'[47] The dismissals of Eva Taylor and Marianne Wood for striking patients illustrate some of the personal dynamics which might lead to conflict between patient and nurse. Eva Taylor slapped a woman on her ward named Stella White. Stella White, according to the head nurse on duty, became angry at Miss Taylor for refusing to 'wait on her' during the night and making her get her own breakfast tray. Miss Taylor said the patient became 'impudent and rude, talking loud and noisy and in the most disrespectful manner about nurses, hospitals, *etc. etc.*' Miss Taylor lost her control and struck Stella White on the mouth. She said, 'I only wanted to teach her a lesson.'[48]

When Eva Taylor was dismissed, another student, Marianne Wood, wrote a letter to the chairman of the Board of Managers defending Miss Taylor's action. Her letter reveals the kind of anger at patients which prompted student nurses' blows. She wrote:

> I can only say if you had been in her place, I think it is more than likely you would have sympathy with her as I do. The patients on 'G' ward are the very lowest class of women and can frequently only be kept in order by taking extreme measures. . . . If Miss Taylor is to be expelled for this . . . in justice to yourselves and the other nurses you should go thoroughly through the training school and expel numerous other nurses who have done the same thing. . . . They are allowed to hit us and swear at us, and spit at us, not to mention calling

46. Record of the Training School, pp. 96, 100, 140; Nurses' Record no. 1, 55; Nurses' Record no. 2, 57, 81; Record of the Training School, pp. 84, 106; Nurses' Record no. 1, 5, 55.

47. Record of the Training School, p. 60.

48. 'Statement of Mary E. Wittaker, Head Nurse'; and E. Taylor to L. Walker, 10 August 1900, Marianne Wood file, Board of Managers Papers.

us the most *vile* names and it is not to be wondered at if we lose our patience now and then.

Miss Wood mentioned that she herself had struck a patient who refused to lie still in her bed after an operation. The Board of Managers immediately dismissed Miss Wood on the basis of this statement. She brought a lawsuit protesting their action, but was never reinstated.[49]

Such incidents suggest class conflict between middle class nurses and working class patients. Conflict was inevitable when young women with middle class standards of behavior were asked to supervise individuals whose action and language offended them. The nurses did not know how to manage their social inferiors with the correct combination of tact and authority advocated by Lucy Walker—and thus they resorted to force.

Other discipline problems suggest class differences of another sort. Nurses from rural and lower middle class backgrounds could not conform to the ideal of restraint, dignity, and ladylike behavior required by Miss Walker. From the student records, Miss Walker's preference for women of refinement is very clear. Her notion of refinement included a good education, a quiet manner, and a neat appearance. Such qualities were pleasing and attractive to her. Women who lacked refinement were equally unpleasant. She found them 'loud in talk' and 'loud in dress.' Their manners were rough and uncouth; their appearance was untidy and undignified. They tended to be troublesome and, in Miss Walker's estimation, of doubtful trustworthiness.[50]

But the discipline problems point to another type of conflict in the training school—a conflict between levels of professional ability and consciousness. The student nurse's response to discipline—her behavior with the patients, her work habits, her attitude toward authority—all went into the training school's final evaluation of her professional ability as well as her character. In the student records, Miss Walker assessed each individual's suitability for either hospital work or private duty nursing. While social class certainly entered into her professional opinion of a nurse, Miss Walker had another standard which might conflict with her class bias. Women of refinement did not necessarily excel at the training school; they had to have more than their manners to recommend them.[51]

49. M. Wood to Mr. Townsend, 11 August 1900, Board of Managers Papers.

50. See, for example, Record of the Training School, p. 212; Nurses' Record no. 1, 211, 253, 261, 265; Nurses' Record no. 2, 6, 109. Quotations are from Record of Training School, p. 397; Nurses' Record no. 1, 57, 157.

51. See Record of Training School, p. 182; Nurses' Record no. 1, 253.

The real elite of the training school were the nurses deemed fit for 'institutional work.' The training school regimen was designed to produce nurses who were 'trained to train,' to go into training school work themselves.[52] Those who did not meet this high expectation became private nurses. The distinction between hospital nursing and private duty work shaped the training school's definition of a good nurse.

One aim of the training school was to produce a good private duty nurse. She needed to have a good character; she must perform her work reliably, prove herself trustworthy, and behave correctly with men. She had to have an even-tempered, cheerful disposition. She had to know the rudiments of practical nursing, which included bed-making, bathing, and massaging the patient, and preparing the proper sick diet. She had to be physically strong and mentally alert. She should also be refined in manner, but refined manners were not an essential requirement. Miss Walker felt that a good, clean country girl would make a fine private duty nurse for a middle class family. Women who met these basic requirements were given good recommendations for private duty nursing. Miss Walker's typical evaluation for this sort of student ran, 'Very pleasing personality, fair average ability, below average in class work but a good practical worker. Should make an excellent private nurse.'[53]

A different set of standards applied to the woman 'suited for institutional work.' The requirements were far more rigorous, but the reward in terms of prestige much greater. The hallmark of the hospital nurse was her ability to manage others. She must have displayed 'executive ability' and have proved herself a 'good manager' on the wards. Miss Walker characterized such a student as having 'special aptitude for planning work and taking responsibility . . . can do her own work and see that others work, too. If she enters a ward in an upset condition, in a short time all is quiet and peaceful.'[54]

The hospital nurse had to be intelligent in order to manage the theoretical side of her work, but she also had to possess good common sense. Her work habits were very important; hospital work demanded that she be systematic, steady, and attentive to detail. Sentimentality and emotion were traits the hospital nurse could not afford to indulge. She needed to be 'mentally well-balanced.' Hysterical women were useless in hospital

52. Shryock, *History* (n. 1), p. 281.

53. Nurses' Record, no. 2, 35; see also Record of the Training School, p. 182; Nurses' Record no. 2, 29, 53.

54. Nurses' Record no. 1, 145, Lucy Walker used the phrases 'good manager' and 'executive ability' frequently.

emergencies. The hospital nurse could not be too 'easily excited' or 'given to tears.' She had to be able to manage a large number of patients and student nurses without panicking.[55]

Dedication was another requirement. In hospital work, a nurse could not be 'afraid she may do more than her own share of work,' or 'inclined to be anxious about herself.' Her mind had to be on her work; she could not 'think too much of her time off duty.' In personal appearance, the hospital nurse had to be 'refined.' Her dress had to be neat and tidy, never frivolous or 'superficial.' Most of all, she must have no interest in the 'admiration' of men. A woman might be a good manager and an excellent nurse, but not be suited for institutional work, 'as she seeks the admiration of men, first.'[56]

Finally, the good hospital nurse had to have the proper respect for authority. She had to obey orders without being too 'assertive.' She could not be 'inclined to go ahead of herself.' At the same time, she could not be too timid.[57] For the hospital nurse, there was a careful line to be taken between being too respectful of authority and being too self-assertive.

The student nurses who met such difficult requirements became part of a self-conscious elite within the training school. They were highly recommended for hospital work and usually received excellent positions either within the Pennsylvania Hospital or in other hospital training schools.[58] Hospital nurses formed the Nurses' Club, the alumnae association, and the Guild of St. Bartholomew, professional organizations which served a social function as well. They kept in touch with each other through various organizations for nurses at the state and national levels.[59]

For graduates doing hospital work in Philadelphia, the Pennsylvania Hospital Nurses' Alumnae Association served as a focus for their professional and social ties with one another. The alumnae association was open to all graduates of the training school, whether doing private duty or hospital work. The graduates in hospital work dominated the leadership of

55. Record of the Training School, p. 148; Nurses' Record no. 1, 53, 65, 195, 197; Record of the Training School, p. 69; Nurses' Record no. 2, 89; Record of the Training School, p. 118; Nurses' Record no. 1, 9, 133; Nurses' Record no. 2, 51, 55.

56. Record of the Training School, p. 176; Nurses' Record no. 2, 33; Record of the Training School, p. 222; Nurses' Record no. 2, 17; Nurses' Record no. 1, 171, 113, 149, 199.

57. Nurses' Record no. 2, 45; Nurses' Record no. 1, 291; Record of the Training School, p. 56; Nurses' Record, no. 2, 5.

58. See, for example, the entry for Janet McBride in Record of the Training School, p. 69. She became night superintendent of the Pennsylvania Hospital. Anna Groff and Emma Lindberg—Record of the Training School, pp. 62, 130—both became head nurses.

59. Nurses' Club Minutes, pp. 55–57; and Nurses' Alumnae Association Minutes, I, 76–77, and II, 68, 128.

the association, however; they served as its officers and faithfully attended its bimonthly business meetings. The president of the alumnae association for six of its most active years, Charlotte E. Perkins, was the head of the Maternity Hospital's training school in Philadelphia. Other particularly active members were the head nurses and the superintendent's assistants of the Pennsylvania Hospital.[60]

The purpose of the alumnae association as stated in its bylaws was 'the promotion of unity and good feeling among the alumnae, the elevation of professional character, the protection of professional interests, and the establishment of a fund for the benefit of any sick among its members.' To this end, the association participated in the American Nurses Association (the national organization of trained nurses), helped to found nurse registries, supported the *American Journal of Nursing*, and worked for the state registration of nurses. The meetings of the alumnae served as a forum for discussion of various professional issues. Papers were presented on such topics as 'the nurse in her relation and responsibility to the patient,' institutional nursing, and social service work. As might be expected, the interests of the hospital nurses predominated.[61]

Another organization within the hospital, the Guild of St. Bartholomew, promoted both religious and social aims. Under its auspices, a prayer service was held every morning for the hospital nurses. A regular monthly meeting was held 'for the reading and discussion of some article or book religious in nature.' Every three months, a social meeting was held. One participant reported to the *American Journal of Nursing* that these evenings 'are always enjoyable, and often novel in the nature of the entertainment.' Students could join, and alumnae could retain membership after leaving the school.[62]

Pennsylvania Hospital nurses also formed social ties with nurses in other training schools in Philadelphia. With the other alumnae associations of Philadelphia schools, they formed a Nurses' Club which sponsored frequent social gatherings. The alumnae attended teas, dance and card parties, holiday celebrations, and informal social hours at the Nurses' Club. They contributed money to make the clubhouse more attractive and comfortable. Thus the hospital nurses' professional contacts furnished them with a social life as well.[63]

60. Nurses' Alumnae Association Minutes, I, 164–165, and II, 102, 133.

61. *Ibid.*, vol. 2, printed bylaws tipped in between pp. 16 and 17. Sample paper topics taken from pp. 139, 149.

62. *Am. J. Nurs.*, 1900, *1*, 315.

63. Nurses' Alumnae Association Minutes, I, 38, and II, 66, 113.

For those graduates doing hospital work, nursing became a true profession. Their training school experience made them conscious of a special professional identity and shaped their dedication to the upgrading of the public image of nursing. They worked to 'raise the standard and establish an atmosphere that encouraged the public to consider the real trained nurse.'[64] Their circle was not an all-inclusive one, however. The majority of nurses stayed outside their 'little world.' They passed through the training school, endured its discipline, and then went on to make their living as private duty nurses.[65] For them nursing remained a livelihood rather than a profession. They benefited from the professional activities of their fellow nurses, but did not actively work for them.

The history of late nineteenth century nursing, then, must be understood in terms of the *variety* of women going into the work, and the limited meaning of professionalization for the majority of nurses. The training school itself must be viewed as an institution which brought together women of diverse origin and motivation, and integrated them into a working organization. The discipline problems reveal fault lines in its organization—between nurses and their superintendent, nurses and patients, and among the nurses themselves. These same lines of conflict have persisted in varied forms to this day, and for many of the same reasons.

In one respect, however, the end of Lucy Walker's career marked the end of an era in nursing history. Having transmitted a heritage of British methods to American hospitals, she was followed by American nurses who took the lead in adapting those forms to the twentieth century hospital. Miss Walker left behind a legacy of excellence and the example, as one nurse said, of 'a person who had the ability and nursing at heart, and was doing all she could to impress the nursing world and put it on the highest level.'[66]

History Department
University of Pennsylvania

64. Nurses' Alumnae Association Minutes, 15 November 1913, II, 114.

65. In 1914, a count of Pennsylvania Hospital Training School alumnae showed that of the 105 nurses in Philadelphia, almost 60 % were doing private duty work. Since a sizeable number of women probably married and left nursing entirely, the percentage of women doing hospital work would be an even smaller number of the total alumnae. Nurses' Alumnae Association Minutes, 21 January 1914, II, 136.

66. McMullin (n. 8), p. 9.

Research Note

The Male-Female Earnings Differential

A Historical Overview of the Clerical Occupations from the 1880s to the 1970s

ALBERT W. NIEMI, Jr.
University of Georgia

In this article, we analyze the male-female earnings differential in the single most important sector of female employment, clerical and office work, for the period running from the 1880s to the 1970s. Clerical occupations currently provide jobs for one-third of all females engaged in market employment. Our analysis reveals that intraoccupational earnings differences between the sexes rather than differences in occupational structure have been the major factors underlying the male-female earnings gap in the clerical sector. This finding represents a major break with the conclusion reached in many earlier studies where researchers have argued that sex differences in occupational structure account for most of the sex differential in earnings (Cohen, 1971; Fuchs, 1971; Kreps, 1971; Sawhill, 1971). The empirical evidence presented here also suggests that the sex differential in earnings levels in the major clerical occupations has shown no substantial narrowing in recent decades. This result is surprising given the changing social climate of the post-World War II period. In

---

Author's Note: *The author gratefully acknowledges the suggestions of two anonymous referees and Robert Swierenga on two earlier drafts of this article.*

recent decades we have seen a sharp upsurge in activity by feminist groups, pathbreaking civil rights legislation, increasing female labor force participation, increasing female career orientation, changes in sex roles, and other significant social changes. The results in this article suggest that up to now these social changes have not had a significant impact on the male-female earnings gap in the clerical sector.

Before reviewing the calculated earnings differentials between males and females, a word of caution is in order concerning the interpretation of sex differentials in earnings levels. Our analysis will show that within the major clerical occupations male earnings levels consistently have exceeded female earnings levels. This finding does not necessarily mean that females have suffered wage discrimination. Wage discrimination implies that someone is not being rewarded according to his or her effort and ability. In order to test explicitly for the existence of wage discrimination, we would need to compare male and female earnings levels in the same occupation and in the same firm, standardizing for differences in productivity, seniority, education, and other factors that might influence work performance. Unfortunately, the earnings data are not available in sufficient detail to make these kinds of adjustments, and we cannot separate the forces of sex discrimination from productivity, education, and other forces that might promote earnings differences between the sexes. In reviewing the indexes of male-female earnings differentials, we should be sure to keep this in mind.

The earnings data used in this study largely were obtained from U.S. Department of Labor wage surveys (see the Appendix for a chronological list of the sources). In most surveys, earnings data were provided for full-time workers exclusive of bonuses, supplements, and other income and benefits. The elimination of bonuses and other income supplements allows us to make an accurate comparison of actual earnings differentials between the sexes. In most surveys, the wage data represented earnings for a weekly period, but, in several instances, hourly, daily, and monthly earnings figures were reported.[1]

In our analysis of the sex differential in clerical earnings, we use female-weighted (F) and male-weighted (M) indexes. The indexes are defined as follows:

$$F = \frac{\sum_{i=1}^{n} E_f^i L_f^i}{\sum_{i=1}^{n} E_m^i L_f^i} \qquad M = \frac{\sum_{i=1}^{n} E_f^i L_m^i}{\sum_{i=1}^{n} E_m^i L_m^i}$$

where E = earnings, L = the number of workers, i = the n clerical occupations employing both females and males, and the subscripts f and m represent female and male respectively. The F and M indexes measure the sex differential in earnings after assuming a common set of occupations for both sexes. The F index estimates the earnings differential that would have existed between the sexes if males were employed in the same set of occupations as females. The M index, on the other hand, estimates the earnings differential that would have existed between the sexes if females were employed in the same set of occupations as males. The use of both the F and M indexes provides us with two common sets of occupations and serves as a check on the reliability of the estimated sex differential in earnings.

If the entire earnings differential between males and females in the clerical sector were due to differences in occupational structure, the F and M indexes would equal 1. This result would suggest that sex differentials in earnings resulted from differences in occupational structure. As we noted above, this argument has been made in several earlier studies. If there are differences between male and female earnings levels within particular occupations, the indexes will diverge from unity. If male wages exceeded female wages within particular occupations, the indexes would be less than 1. If female wages exceeded male wages within particular occupations, the indexes would be greater than 1. Our results below will show that male wages consistently exceeded female wages within specified occupations. This finding supports our conclusion that intraccupational wage differences rather than differences in occupational structure have been the major factor underscoring the male-female earnings differential in the clerical sector.

The F and M indexes can be used to derive an estimate of the percentage share of the total sex differential in earnings in an industry or sector that was due to intraoccupational wage differences. This calculation is made as illustrated:

$$\frac{1 - F}{1 - (f/m)_w} \quad \text{and} \quad \frac{1 - M}{1 - (f/m)_w}$$

where F = the value of the female weighted index, M = the value of the male weighted index, and $(f/m)_w$ = the ratio of female to male wage rates for the entire clerical sector.

Columns 4 and 4 in Table 1 show calculated F and M indexes running from the 1880s to the 1970s. The state cross-section data for the 1880s and the 1890s show that female bookkeepers earned 55-60% of male earnings, female clerks earned approximately 65% of male earnings, and female stenographers earned 70-75% of male earnings. A study conducted in Massachusetts in 1903 showed substantial evidence of intraoccupational earnings differences. Within the major clerical occupations, female earnings were 67% (F index)/70% (M index) of male earnings. In columns 6 and 7 we estimate the percentage of the male-female earnings differential accounted for by intraoccupational earnings differences. For 1903, we estimate that sex differences in intraoccupational earnings rates were responsible for 77.1% (F index)/92.6% (M index) of the total sex differential in the clerical sector.

Estimates for the United States based on a Conference Board study of clerical wages in the 1920s indicate a narrower intraoccupational earnings differential than earlier state surveys. However,

Table 1 Index of Earnings Differentials Between Male and Female Office Workers

Period	Region	Occupation Group	Indexes: Female Weighted	Indexes: Male Weighted	Percentage of the Male-Female Earnings Differential Accounted for by Intraoccupational Earnings Differences: Female-Weighted	Percentage of the Male-Female Earnings Differential Accounted for by Intraoccupational Earnings Differences: Male-Weighted
(1)	(2)	(3)	(4)	(5)	(6)	(7)
1880s	cross section of states	Bookkeepers	.623	.547	-	-
1880s	cross section of states	Clerks	.674	.628	-	-
1880s	cross section of states	Stenographers	.706	.726	-	-
1890s	cross section of states	Bookkeepers	.573	.542	-	-
1890s	cross section of states	Clerks	.613	.650	-	-
1890s	cross section of states	Stenographers	.756	.739	-	-
1903	Massachusetts	Clerical and Trade	.673	.702	77.1	92.6%
1926	U.S.	Clerical	.828	.773	64.9	85.7
1940	Houston	Clerical	.747	.729	80.8	86.6
1940	Kansas City	Clerical	.780	.724	69.6	87.3
1940	Los Angeles	Clerical	.843	.812	75.5	90.4
1940	Philadelphia	Clerical	.762	.717	73.0	86.8
1940	Richmond	Clerical	.798	.745	65.2	82.3
1948	Chicago	Clerical	.905	.873	72.5	97.0
1948	New York	Clerical	.900	.866	93.5	100.0[a]
1949	Los Angeles	Clerical	.895	.849	56.2	80.8
1951	Chicago	Clerical	.851	.820	86.1	100.0
1951	New York	Clerical	.876	.867	100.0	100.0
1952	Los Angeles	Clerical	.848	.851	84.0	82.3
1960	U.S. Metropolitan Areas	Clerical	.810	.838	100.0	93.1
1965	U.S. Metropolitan Areas	Clerical	.834	.847	100.0	100.0
1970	U.S. Metropolitan Areas	Clerical	.836	.836	100.0	100.0
1976	U.S. Metropolitan Areas	Clerical	.809	.843	100.0	100.0

SOURCE: See Appendix.

a. A percentage of 100.0 represents an intraoccupational earnings differential between the sexes that equals or exceeds the total earnings gap in the sector.

the F and M indexes suggest that there was still approximately a 20% differential in the occupational earnings structure that favored males. The calculations in columns 6 and 7 also suggest the bulk of the sector-wide earnings differential between males and females resulted from the payment of differential wages to males and females engaged in the same occupation.

The estimates in Table 1 suggest that there was a relative rise in female clerical earnings in the late 1940s. The F and M indexes constructed for Houston, Kansas City, Los Angeles, Philadelphia, and Richmond, VA for 1940 show a range in the estimated intraoccupational earnings differential from .717 (M index-Philadelphia) to .843 (F index-Los Angeles). The F and M indexes also suggest that 65-90% of the sector-wide earnings differential was due to intraoccupational earnings differences between the sexes. The F and M indexes for 1948-1949 constructed from earnings data in Chicago, New York, and Los Angeles reveal a much lower sex differential than the 1940 indexes. The F indexes stood at .895, .900, and .905; the M indexes stood at .849, .866, and .873. These estimates suggest that within occupations male earnings were approximately 10-15% higher than female earnings. The indexes calculated for 1948-1949 were the highest estimates for the entire period under review in this article. Despite the relatively high values for the F and M indexes, we should not fail to recognize that intraoccupational earnings differences rather than differences in occupation structure were still the major factors underlying the overall male-female earnings differential in the clerical sector.

The F and M indexes for the early 1950s were lower than those for the late 1940s, but, compared to the overall period of review, they were relatively high. The indexes suggest that male earnings exceeded female earnings within the major clerical occupations. Furthermore, the estimates indicate that 80% or more of the total male-female earnings differential in office work was due to the payment of higher wages to males than females. The estimated F and M indexes for U.S. metropolitan areas for the 1960s and 1970s show a great deal of stability. The F index ranged between

.809 and .836 and the M index remained between .836 and .847. Our results suggest that male earnings exceeded female earnings within particular occupations by an average of 15-20% throughout this period and that the intraoccupational earnings differences were large enough to explain the total earnings gap between male and female office workers.

Our results show that as the clerical occupations became increasingly female dominated, the indexes of male-female intraoccupational earnings differentials narrowed from a 25-45% gap in the late nineteenth and early twentieth century to a 15-20% gap in the 1960s and 1970s.[2] This convergence between male and female earnings within particular clerical occupations was achieved during a period when females were rapidly displacing males in the clerical occupations. As the clerical occupations became increasingly feminized, the average wage rate in the clerical sector fell relative to wages in the economy as a whole. At the turn of the century, clerical wages were generally double nonclerical wages. By the 1920s, clerical wages were approximately 50% greater than nonclerical wages. By the 1950s, clerical wages were roughly equal to non-clerical wages, and, by the 1970s, clerical wages were 20% below nonclerical wages (see U.S. Bureau of the Census, 1953: Table 129; 1964: Table 208; 1973: Tables 227 and 228). Given the sharp relative decline in clerical wages, we should not underestimate the significance of the current 15-20% wage gap between the sexes.

Our analysis suggests that male-female differences in occupational structure within the clerical sector offer little or no explanation for the persistent sex differential in wages. The overall earnings gap between male and female clerical workers has resulted almost exclusively from the payment of differential wages to males and females engaged in similar occupations. This does not necessarily mean that females in the clerical sector have been chronic victims of wage discrimination. In order to measure the degree of wage discrimination, we would need to adjust the intraoccupational wage differentials for sex differences in education, experience, seniority, productivity, and other performance variables that influence wage determination. Unfortunately, the historical wage data do not permit us to separate the influence of performance factors from the forces of discrimination, and, therefore, we cannot explicitly determine how much of the male-female earnings differential is due to sexist wage determination.

Appendix

The following sources of wage data (arranged in chronological order) were used in this study:

U.S. Bureau of the Census, Fifteenth Annual Report of the Commissioner of Labor, 1900.

Massachusetts Bureau of Statistics of Labor. Thirty Third Annual Report. (1903)

National Industrial Conference Board, Clerical Salaries in the United States, 1926.

U.S. Department of Labor, Women's Bureau, Bulletin No. 188-1, Office Work in Houston, 1940.

U.S. Department of Labor, Women's Bureau, Bulletin 188-2, Office Work in Los Angeles, 1940.

U.S. Department of Labor, Women's Bureau, Bulletin No. 188-3, Office Work in Kansas City, 1940.

U.S. Department of Labor, Women's Bureau, Bulletin 188-4, Office Work in Richmond, 1940.

U.S. Department of Labor, Women's Bureau, Bulletin No. 188-5, Office Work in Philadelphia, 1940.

U.S. Department of Labor, Bureau of Labor Statistics, Bulletin No. 943, Salaries of Office Workers in Selected Large Cities, 1948.

U.S. Department of Labor, Bureau of Labor Statistics, Bulletin No. 960, Salaries of Office Workers in Large Cities, 1949.

U.S. Department of Labor, Bureau of Labor Statistics, Bulletin No. 1034, Occupational Wage Survey: Chicago, Ill., April 1951.

Appendix (continued)

U.S. Department of Labor, Bureau of Labor Statistics, Bulletin No. 1037, Occupational Wage Survey: New York, New York, April 1951.

U.S. Department of Labor, Bureau of Labor Statistics, Bulletin No. 1094, Occupational Wage Survey: Los Angeles, Calif., January 1952.

U.S. Department of Labor, Bureau of Labor Statistics, Bulletin No. 1285-84, Wages and Related Benefits: Metropolitan Areas, United States and Regional Summaries, 1960-61.

U.S. Department of Labor, Bureau of Labor Statistics, Bulletin No. 1430-83, Wages and Related Benefits: Part II, Metropolitan Areas, United States and Regional Summaries, 1964-65.

U.S. Department of Labor, Bureau of Labor Statistics, Bulletin No. 1660-92, Area Wage Surveys: Metropolitan Areas, United States and Regional Summaries, 1969-70.

U.S. Department of Labor, Bureau of Labor Statistics, Bulletin No. 1900-82, Area Wage Surveys: Metropolitan Areas, United States and Regional Summaries, 1976.

NOTES

1. A full description of the wage surveys showing the sex composition of the labor force, the type of earnings data (daily, weekly, etc.), and the specific clerical occupations included can be obtained from this author on request.
2. The female share of total clerical employment rose from less than 10% in the 1880s, to 25% at the turn of the century, to 50% by 1930, and to 80% in the late 1970s.

REFERENCES

COHEN, M. S. (1971) "Sex differences in compensation." J. of Human Resources 6 (Fall): 434-447.

FUCHS, V. (1971) "Differences in hourly earnings between men and women." Monthly Labor Rev. 94 (May): 9-15.

KREPS, J. (1971) Sex in the Marketplace. Baltimore: John Hopkins Univ. Press.

Massachusetts Bureau of Statistics of Labor (1903) Thirty-Third Annual Report. Boston: Wright & Potter.

National Industrial Conference Board (1926) Clerical Salaries in the United States, 1926. New York: National Industrial Conference Board.

SAWHILL, I. V. (1973) "The economics of discrimination against women: some new findings." J. of Human Resources 8 (Summer): 383-396.

Albert W. Niemi, Jr. is Director of Research and Acting Dean of the College of Business Administration at the University of Georgia in Athens. He has written several textbooks and many articles on American economic history. He is currently working on a study of profits in nineteenth-century southern manufacturing.

The Labor Market and the American High School Girl 1890–1928

SUSAN B. CARTER AND MARK PRUS

Girls far outnumbered boys in American high schools at the turn of the century. Despite the fact that women on average spent far fewer years than men in the paid labor force, we argue that a high school education was a better investment for girls than for boys. This was because formal education offered the only opportunity for girls to obtain job-related skills, whereas it was but one of many such opportunities for boys.

"Had I been a boy instead of a girl, with my natural love for my studies, mother might have struggled to send me ahead, much as she needed what little I could earn. But a girl didn't need an education. In fact, it might be a mistake to teach her too much. . . ."[1]

LITERARY evidence suggests that girls faced far more barriers in their pursuit of formal education than boys did in turn-of-the-century America. Formal education was seen as irrelevant to girls' future life work. Leslie Woodcock Tentler concludes, for example, that ". . . when a family made sacrifices to insure the future education of a son rather than a daughter, the young girl had little choice but to accept an educational double standard. Schooling beyond the legal minimum was ultimately justified by future occupational achievement, and such achievement for women was apt to be modest and temporary."[2] Moreover, since a woman's primary loyality was to be to the family, time spent away from the home had a high opportunity cost. Again Tentler finds many examples of school-age girls being kept home to do housework and care for children when the mother—or even a relative or neighbor—was ill or unusually busy.[3]

Econometric evidence also leads us to expect lower school attendance rates for girls than for boys in 1900. Studies of rates of return to education consistently have found lower returns for women than for

Journal of Economic History. Vol. XLII. No. 1 (March 1982). ISSN 0022-0507.

The authors are affiliated with the Departments of Economics, Smith College, Northampton, Massachusetts 01063, and the University of Utah, Salt Lake City, Utah 84112, respectively. They are grateful to Mark Aldrich, Michael Carter, Paul David, and Brian Peckham for valuable suggestions on an early draft of this work.

[1] Lillian Wolfe, "How and Why I Chose My First Job," *The Bryn Mawr Daisy* (July 8, 1922), mimeographed (Hilda Smith Papers), no pagination as quoted in Leslie Woodcock Tentler, *Wage Earning Women* (New York, 1979), p. 102.

[2] Tentler, *Wage Earning Women*, p. 103.

[3] Ibid., p. 102.

TABLE 1
PERCENTAGE OF HIGH SCHOOL STUDENTS FEMALE, BY RACE, 1890–1928

Year	*Whites*	*Blacks*	*Year*	*Whites*	*Blacks*
1890	57.9%	57.5%	1910	56.3%	65.9%
1892	60.2	60.8	1912	55.6	65.4
1894	59.9	63.9	1914	55.4	65.7
1896	58.5	63.8	1916	54.5	65.0
1898	57.8	68.1	1918	57.0	67.9
1900	58.2	68.4	1920	55.5	65.6
1902	58.7	68.1	1922	53.5	62.9
1904	58.0	67.4	1924	53.8	62.4
1906	57.6	67.5	1926	51.9	62.5
1908	57.4	66.0	1928	51.6	62.0

Source: U. S. Department of the Interior, Office of Education, *Annual Report of the Commissioner of Education*, various years, 1890–1916, and *Biennial Survey of Education*, biennially, 1918–28.

men.[4] The lower returns come about not because of a relatively lower wage *rate* in jobs available to educated women—the wage-rate differential in jobs requiring a college education as compared with those requiring a high school education is essentially the same for women and men—but because women on average spend less time in the paid labor force than men.[5] Since women's labor force participation rate (one measure of average time devoted to wage labor) in 1900 was less than half its current level, we would expect women's school attendance rates to be much lower than men's. But girls far outnumbered boys in the high schools!

One measure of the differential rates of school attendance is contained in Table 1, which shows by race the percentage of all high school students who were female, for alternate years between 1890 and 1928. These figures show that girls outnumbered boys by over four to three among whites and over three to two among blacks through the second decade of the twentieth century.

In this paper we attempt to explain gender and racial differences in high school attendance rates in terms of differential labor market opportunities. We show that access to good jobs for men was acquired through on-the-job training, while access to the good jobs for women was acquired in schools. Thus, in contrast to Tentler, we argue that schooling was much *more* critical for girls' future life work than for boys'.

In 1890, even more so than today, there were "women's jobs" and "men's jobs," but very few that employed both women and men.[6]

[4] See Cynthia B. Lloyd and Beth T. Niemi, *The Economics of Sex Differentials* (New York, 1979), pp. 109–22.

[5] See Janice Madden, "The Economic Rationale for Sex Differences in Education," *Southern Economic Journal*, 44 (April 1978), 778–97.

[6] Francine Blau and Wallace Hendricks, "Occupational Segregation by Sex: Trends and Prospects," *Journal of Human Resources*, 14 (Spring 1979), 197–210.

Domestic and personal service claimed 41.2 percent of the female labor force in 1890, but only 3.5 percent of the male. Forestry and fishing, extraction of minerals, transportation and communication, and public service employed almost ten percent of the male labor force but less than one half of one percent of the female labor force.[7] The areas of economic opportunity for women and men differed as well. Aside from self-employment, the good jobs for men were to be found in the skilled occupations in large-scale manufacturing. Median weekly earnings in 1900 for heaters in the iron and steel mills were $27.50 and for rollers $35.00. Those at the upper quartile of wage earners in these occupations earned $45.00 and $50.00, respectively.[8] By contrast, male teachers averaged only $11.63 per week.[9]

Wages were high in the skilled blue-collar occupations for several reasons. (1) To the extent that employees financed the training by receiving extremely low wages during the learning period, the wages of skilled workmen had to be kept above those of unskilled workers to continue to attract a new supply of learners. (2) Employers often financed part of the investment in skills and therefore had an interest in retaining workers once they were fully trained. High wages reduced voluntary turnover.[10] (3) Overt and covert actions by skilled workers in the trade restricted the supply of skilled workers below the level that would have been forthcoming in the absence of barriers to entry. The restricted supply of skilled workers, combined with overcrowding in the unskilled jobs, added to the skilled/unskilled wage differential.[11] Skilled workers were able to restrict the number of workers they would admit to their ranks, and they were also able to decide to a large extent just who would receive training. Male relatives received favored status.[12] Blacks, the foreign-born, and women were universally discriminated against.[13]

Thus we find that women's wages in blue-collar occupations were low in large part because women were restricted to the unskilled occupations. In the rope mills, for example, average weekly earnings of female

[7] H. Dewey Anderson and Percy E. Davidson. *Occupational Trends in the United States* (Stanford, 1940), pp. 18–19.

[8] U. S. Department of Commerce, Bureau of the Census. *Twelfth Census of the United States. 1900.* "Employees and Wages" (Washington, D.C., 1904).

[9] U. S. Department of the Interior, Office of Education. *Annual Report of the Commissioner of Education for the Year 1900* (Washington, D.C., 1901).

[10] This motive seems to have been growing in importance around the turn of the century, especially as mechanics' skills became more homogeneous across industries. See Walter E. Weyl and A. M. Sakolski, "Conditions of Entrance to the Principal Trades," U. S. Bureau of Labor. *Bulletin* 67 (Washington, D.C., 1906).

[11] Michael J. Carter, "Behind the Backs of the Producer: The Determinants of Relative Wage Structures," unpublished Ph.D. Dissertation (Stanford University, 1981).

[12] See Massachusetts Commission on Industrial and Technical Education, "What the Value of the Years from Fourteen to Sixteen Might Be for Boys," in its *Report, 1906*, (New York, 1906), pp. 57–69.

[13] See George E. Barnett, *The Printers* (New York, 1909).

employees were $6.50, in the cotton and woolen mills $6.00, in the paper mills $4.50, and in candy factories only $3.50.[14] It was true that a few women worked as skilled cigar packers and as starchers in the collar and cuff industry, and that women at the upper quartile of wage earners in these occupations in 1900 earned $10.99 and $15.99 per week, respectively. But census enumerators were able to find fewer than 200 women in these relatively high-paying blue-collar occupations at the time of the Twelfth Census.[15] Even the most enthusiastic supporter of women's vocational education, Susan M. Kingsbury, was forced to admit that ". . . opportunities at the top are limited" and that women in blue-collar occupations were employed in "unskilled industries which offer little or no opportunity to rise or develop."[16] By contrast, the Bureau of Education found 293,759 female school teachers in 1900 with *average* weekly earnings of $9.73.[17] Although much has been made of the fact that wages of women teachers were low, it is also true that, when compared with other employment opportunities open to women, teaching was a *good job*.[18] Independent women with the means to finance an investment in job-relevant skills were well advised to pursue a teaching career even though a similarly endowed man would not have been.

Wages in teaching and other white-collar occupations were high in part because the occupation required school attendance (at zero wage) beyond the legal school-leaving age at a time when opportunities for paid employment did exist. In order to continue to attract teachers, the teacher's wage had to be kept above the wage in occupations that did not require such schooling. But because training for white-collar occupations took place outside the workplace, skilled workers in those trades never controlled access to training in the same way as skilled blue-collar workers did. Thus, except for short periods of extremely rapid increase in demand for skilled white-collar workers, the skill-related wage differential in white-collar work, when length of training is held constant, was never as large as the skill-related wage differential in blue-collar work. We would expect then that those for whom both blue- and white-collar training opportunities were open—namely, native-born white males—would select blue-collar training, and all the other ambitious, talented people with the money to invest in job-related skills would go to school.

Evidence supporting some of these propositions is presented in the

[14] *Twelfth Census*.

[15] Ibid.

[16] Susan M. Kingsbury and May Allinson, "A Trade School for Girls," U.S. Department of Interior, Office of Education, *Bulletin 1913*, No. 17 (Washington, D.C., 1913), pp. 12, 39.

[17] *Annual Report of the Commissioner of Education. . . 1900*.

[18] Elyce Rotella calculated that women's clerical wages were an average of 1.8 times women's wages in manufacturing jobs in the same city in 1890 and 1.3 times in 1930. See Elyce J. Rotella, *From Home to Office: U. S. Women at Work, 1870–1930* (Ann Arbor, 1981), pp. 158–59.

tables below. The results shown in Table 2 suggest that schooling enhanced wages in white- but not blue-collar occupations. Equation (a) in Table 2 is an estimate of the wage determination process among female textile operatives. LNWAGE is the natural log of the weekly wage in cents; AF and F are dummy variables that assume a value of 1 for those operatives who were Americans born of foreign parentage and foreign born, respectively; LNEDUC is the natural log of years of formal education; LNEXPER is the natural log of years of experience in the plant, measured in tenths of a year; and IQ is a dummy that assumes a value 0 for those who made slow progress through school, 1 for those who progressed at the normal rate, and 2 for those who made rapid progress. The results indicate that while experience, intelligence, and native parentage enhanced wage-earning capacity among factory operatives, education did not! A girl who planned to work in blue-collar occupations, then, should have left school as soon as possible and begun accumulating the work experience that led to higher wages. A different situation, however, prevailed in teaching. The results of an ordinary least-squares regression (in which gender, experience, and education are used to explain differences in wages paid to secondary school teachers in three midwestern states), shown in Equation (b) of Table 2, reveal a coefficient of education that is positive, significant, and twice as large as the coefficient on experience.[19]

Table 3 presents results of a more direct test of our major proposition that differences in employment opportunities across sex/race groups account for differences in high school attendance rates. The dependent variable is the natural log of the likelihood function P/(1-P), where P is the sum of public and private high school enrollments of a sex/race group in a given year divided by the size of the corresponding population aged 15–19. PROF is the proportion of total employment of the group in professional occupations. It is used to test our major hypothesis that high school attendance was undertaken to prepare for work in the professions. PROF measures one dimension of the attractiveness of professional employment, employment availability. The expected sign of its coefficient is positive, since the greater were the employment opportunities in white-collar work the more young adults would be motivated to prepare for those jobs by attending high schools. We also should have included some measure of the financial attractiveness of white- versus blue-collar occupations by sex-race group. We showed earlier that white-collar employment was more remunerative than blue-collar employment for women but not for men. Unfortunately

[19] For corroborative evidence see Mark Aldrich and Randy Albelda, "Determinants of Working Women's Wages During the Progressive Era," *Explorations in Economic History*, 17 (October 1980), p. 326, and Claudia Goldin, "The Historical Evolution of Female Earnings Functions and Occupations," National Bureau of Economic Research *Working Paper No. 529*. (Cambridge, Massachusetts, August 1980), pp. 6, 12.

TABLE 2

WAGE DETERMINATION IN BLUE- AND WHITE-COLLAR OCCUPATIONS

(*a*) *Cotton Mill Operatives*

$$\begin{array}{l} \text{LNWAGE} = \underset{(0.272)}{6.272^{*}} - \underset{(0.055)}{0.133}\ \text{AF}^{*} - \underset{(0.073)}{0.150}\ \text{F}^{*} - \underset{(0.127)}{0.196}\ \text{LNEDUC} + \underset{(0.034)}{0.204}\ \text{LNEXPER}^{*} + \underset{(0.034)}{0.084}\ \text{IQ}^{*} \end{array}$$

$R^2 = 0.281$

(*b*) *Secondary School Teachers*

$$\text{LNWAGE} = \underset{(0.14)}{5.99^{*}} - \underset{(0.06)}{0.16}\ \text{FEMALE}^{*} + \underset{(0.017)}{0.074}\ \text{EDUC}^{*} + \underset{(0.004)}{0.030}\ \text{EXPER}^{*}$$

$R^2 = 0.418$

Standard errors in parentheses. * indicates significance at 5%.

Sources: Data from Anna C. Hedges, *The Wage Worth of Schooling* (New York, 1915), Table XXXVII; and Edward L. Thorndike, "The Teaching Staff of Secondary Schools in the United States: Amount of Education, Length of Experience and Salaries," U. S. Bureau of Education, *Bulletin 1909*, No. 4 (Washington, D. C., 1909).

data inadequacies have prevented us from including a test of the importance of these considerations in determining the school attendance decision. LFPR is the labor force participation rate of the group. It is proxy for the average percentage of one's lifetime spent in the paid labor force, and its expected sign is positive since the longer the time one expects to spend in the paid labor force the greater is the expected return to training *ceteris paribus*. INCOME, measured by GNP per capita, is a proxy for the ability to finance job-related training. Since lending institutions are unwilling to finance job-related training, even if it is expected to yield a high rate of return, the ability to take advantage of training opportunities is limited by one's own income or the income of one's parents. Thus the expected sign of the coefficient is positive. INCOME also may capture some of the consumption motives for high school attendance.[20] The consumption motive would also lead us to expect a positive coefficient for INCOME. BMALE, WFEMALE and BFEMALE, dummy variables representing black males, white females, and black females, respectively, were entered to test the hypothesis that differences in high school attendance rates among groups can be explained in terms of differences in labor market structures facing each group. We expect coefficients equal to 0 for each of these dummies. Other demand-side variables undoubtedly relevant are the opportunity costs of schooling and the quality of training available. These variables had to be omitted because of data inadequacies. We assumed that the supply of education to each group was perfectly elastic and we therefore included no supply-side variables.

Table 3 shows the results of a generalized least-squares regression on data transformed according to the Cochrane-Orcutt method after an initial run on untransformed data produced highly autocorrelated error terms. Equation (a) presents results of a test of the full model discussed above. While the entire equation is highly significant [F (6,120) = 12.69], only two variables are significant. PROF is significant and positive, supporting our major hypothesis that differences in high school attendance rates might be explained in terms of differences in employment opportunities in professional occupations. The significance of the negative coefficient on the dummy for black males suggests, however, that restricted employment opportunities in the professions are insufficient to explain the low school-attendance rates of this group. Discrimination in access to schooling or exceptionally low wages in professional work need to be explored. On the other hand, we cannot reject the hypothesis that employment opportunities alone explain the high school attendance patterns of women.

We suspected that the reason for the high significance of the equation

[20] See F. P. Austin, "What High School Graduates Do," *Journal of Education* (March 28, 1907), p. 355.

TABLE 3
SCHOOL ATTENDANCE RATES BY EMPLOYMENT OPPORTUNITIES, 1890–1928

(*a*) *Economic and Demographic Variables*

$$LN(P/(1-P)) = \underset{(11.20)}{-16.66} - \underset{(0.95)}{3.22}\ BMALE^{*} + \underset{(10.49)}{7.75}\ WFEMALE + \underset{(6.79)}{5.58}\ BFEMALE + \underset{(0.017)}{0.030}\ PROF^{*} + \underset{(0.012)}{0.015}\ LFPR - \underset{(0.04)}{0.01}\ INCOME$$

$R^2 = 0.388$, D.W. = 2.51

(*b*) *Economic Variables Only*

$$LN(P/(1-P)) = \underset{(0.59)}{-6.64^{*}} + \underset{(0.005)}{0.031}\ PROF^{*} + \underset{(0.0005)}{0.003}LFPR^{*} + \underset{(0.03)}{0.07}\ INCOME^{*}$$

$R^2 = 0.30$, D.W. = 2.42

Standard errors in parentheses. * indicates significance at 5%.

Sources: Public and private high school enrollment figures by race and sex from *Annual Report of the Commissioner of Education* and *Biennial Survey of Education*. Population by age, race and sex from *Historical Statistics of the* United States, series A-121, 122 and 123. Occupational distribution of the labor force by sex and race from Dale Heistand, *Economic Growth and Employment Opportunities for Minorities* (New York, 1964). Labor force participation rates by sex and race from Clarence Long, *The Labor Force Under Changing Income and Employment* (Princeton, 1958). Per capita income from *Historical Statistics of the United States*, series F-4. We assumed average income for blacks was one half of the real GNP per capita in a given year.

as a whole combined with high standard errors for many of the estimates is multicollinearity among the dependent variables. In particular, casual examination of the raw data suggests a high degree of correlation between our dummies and our economic variables. To gain some appreciation of the power of the economic variables alone to explain the pooled cross-section and time-series high school attendance ratios, we reran Equation (a) without the dummy variables. The results are shown in Equation (b) of Table 3. The equation as a whole is highly significant (F (3,123) = 17.18). All the economic variables are highly significant and display the expected signs. Together the independent variables explain nearly as much of the total variation in school attendance ratios as did the first form of the equation which included dummy variables. We interpret these results as supportive to our contention that differences in labor market opportunities were the most important determinants of differences in high school attendance rates around the turn of the century.

Woman's Place is at the Typewriter: The Feminization of the Clerical Labor Force

Margery Davies

A large proportion of the recent historical research about women in the labor force has focused on industrial workers, using their specific factory experiences as a model for viewing the class as a whole. On the other hand, relatively little attention has been given to clerical workers. This is surprising: in 1968 for example, over 40 percent of women in the U.S. labor force were employed as clerical and sales workers, while only 16.5 percent were employed in the industrial workforce. (1) This essay is a contribution to a discussion aimed first at clarifying the role of a "secretarial proletariat", and secondly at broadening the definition of the working class to include other than those in industrial production. In particular, there are millions of low-level clerical workers, most of them women, who form an important segment of the working class.

The essay is historical in scope and focuses on the feminization of the clerical labor force. Women now form the majority of the clerical workforce, but this was not always the case. How did women enter and come to dominate clerical work? How did the ideology with respect to women office workers change? What are the connections between a sexual segmentation of the clerical labor force and hierarchical relations in the office? The first step in answering these questions is to look at the "19th-century office". (2)

THE NINETEENTH-CENTURY OFFICE (3)

> Mr. Vhole's office, in disposition retiring and in situation retired, is squeezed up in a corner, and blinks at a dead wall. Three feet of knotty floored dark passage bring the client to Mr. Vhole's jet black door, in an angle profoundly dark on the brightest midsummer morning, and encumbered by a black bulk-head of cellerage staircase, against which belated civilians generally strike their brows. Mr. Vhole's chambers are on so small a scale, that one clerk can open the door without getting off his stool, while the other who elbows him at the same desk has equal facilities for poking the fire. A smell as of unwholesome sheep, blending with the smell of must and dust, is referable to the nightly (and often daily) consumption of mutton fat in candles, and to the fretting of parchment forms and skins in greasy drawers. The atmosphere is otherwise stale and close. (4)

Two of the basic characteristics of 19th-century offices, in the United States as well as Dickensian England, are that they were small and staffed almost exclusively by men. Census data for 1870, for example, show that out of 76,639 office workers in the United States, women numbered only 1869; men were 97.5 percent of the clerical labor force. (5) With the exception of a few banks, insurance companies and governmental branches, most offices in the United States prior to the Civil War usually contained about two or three clerks. This is not surprising, since most capitalist firms were also relatively small until the last decades of the 19th century. For example, in "Bartleby," (6) Herman Melville described a Wall Street lawyer's office of the 1850's which consisted of the lawyer, three copyists and an errand boy.

The small size of offices at this time meant that the relationship between employer and employee tended to be a very personalized one. The clerks worked under the direct supervision, and often the direct eyesight, of their employers. Although the tasks of a clerk were generally well-defined — the job of the copyists in "Bartleby" was to transcribe legal documents — they were also often asked to do numerous other tasks by their employers. It was clearly the employer who set the limits of the clerk's job — there was no question here of the clerk being ruled by the inexorable pace of a machine.

The personal benevolence of an employer could go a long way toward making the hierarchical relations within an office more tolerable. An employer who spoke nicely to his clerks, let them leave early if they were feeling sick, or gave them a Christmas goose helped to create working conditions against which the clerks were not likely to rebel. By treating his clerks with kindness or politeness, a paternalistic employer was also likely to be able to get them to work harder for him.

This personalization of the work relationship between the clerk and his employer in the 19th-century office lies at the root of the phenomenon of employees being "devoted to the firm". A clerk who spent forty or fifty years of his life working for the same small office of an insurance company did not necessarily work so long and so hard out of a belief in the importance of promoting that particular company's kind of insurance. The source of the devotion of this hypothetical employee was much more likely the network of personal relations he had built up in the office over the years. It was probably more important to the employee to "produce" a good working relationship with his boss, with whom he was in constant contact, than to produce, for example, improvements in the insurance company's filing system. Needless to say that that good working relationship no doubt depended in part on the employee producing improvements in the filing system. But whether the employee cared more about the selling of insurance or his personal relationship with his employer, the end result tended to be the same: the clerk became a "devoted employee of the firm" who was not likely to rebel or go out on strike.

Not all clerks in the 19th-century office spent all their working days in clerical positions. A clerkship also served as an apprenticeship for a young man who was "learning the business" before he moved on to a managerial position. These young men were often nephews, sons, or grandsons of the firm's managers and owners — the "family business" trained its sons by having them work as clerks for a period of time. Most clerks, however, ended up with gold watches instead of managerial posts in return for their years of devoted service.

Thus the clerks in an office at any particular time came from different class backgrounds and were likely to have very different occupational futures. (Sons of entrepreneurs

A lunchroom in the Metropolitan Life Insurance Company, New York.

and professionals would work as clerks for only a short period of time before going on to managerial jobs. Men from the working classes, sons of artisans or low-level clerks, would probably work as clerks for the rest of their lives; few would be promoted to managerial positions.)

POLITICAL-ECONOMIC CHANGES

In the last few decades of the 19th century, American corporations underwent a period of rapid growth and consolidation. These changes, which marked the rise of modern industrial capitalism, had been signalled by developments in banks, insurance companies and public utilities; they had spread to manufacturing enterprises by the turn of the century. (7) As business operations became more complex, there was a large increase in correspondence, record-keeping, and office work in general. This expansion of record-keeping and the proliferation of communications both within and between firms created a demand for an expanded clerical labor force. In 1880 there were 504,454 office workers who constituted 3 percent of the labor force; by 1890 there were 750,150 office workers. (8) The number of office workers has been increasing ever since. (See Table #2) In order to fill the need for clerical workers, employers turned to the large pool of educated female labor.

As early as the 1820's, women had been receiving public high school educations: Worcester, Massachusetts opened a public high school for girls in 1824; Boston and New York City did so in 1826. (9) In 1880, 13,029 women graduated from high school in the United States, as compared to only 10,605 men. The figures for 1900 show an even greater disparity: 56,808 female high school graduates and 38,075 male. (10)

Until the end of the 19th century, schools were the main place of employment for these educated women. The feminization of elementary and secondary teaching had taken place with the introduction of compulsory public education and consequent increase in teaching jobs. In 1840 men were 60 percent of all teachers and in 1860 they made up only 14 percent. (11) Women were hired in education because they were a cheap replacement for the dwindling supply of male teachers. "As Charles William Eliot observed some years after the feminization of primary school teaching was largely completed: 'It is true that sentimental reasons are often given for the almost exclusive employment of women in the common schools; but the effective reason is economy . . . If women had not been cheaper than men, they would not have replaced nine tenths of the men in American public schools.' " (12)

But teaching was about the only job that drew on the pool of educated female labor in substantial numbers. The "professions" — law, medicine, business, college teaching — both excluded women and did not employ large numbers of people. The 1890 census, for instance, counted only 200 women lawyers. (13) Social work was still the preserve of moral reformers like Jane Addams; the growth of social work as an occupation with government funding did not come until the 20th century. Nursing was beginning to employ some women by the end of the 19th century: in 1900 there were 108,691 nurses and midwives, although only 11,000 of them had become graduate nurses and achieved professional status. (14)

In the last decades of the 19th century, the situation was, then, the following. There were more women than men graduating from high school every year. These women constituted a pool of educated female labor which was being drawn upon only by elementary and secondary schools. Consequently, there were literally thousands of women with training that qualified them for jobs that demanded literacy, but who could not find such jobs. Excluded from most of the professions, these women were readily available for the clerical jobs that started to proliferate at the end of the 19th century. The expansion and consolidation of enterprises in the 1880's and 1890's created a large demand for clerical labor; the large pool of educated female labor constituted the supply.

WOMEN ENTER THE OFFICE

Prior to the Civil War there were no women employed in substantial numbers in any offices, although there were a few women scattered here and there who worked as bookkeepers or as copyists in lawyers' offices. (15) During the Civil War, however, the reduction of the male labor force due to the draft moved General Francis Elias Spinner, the U.S. Treasurer, to introduce female clerical workers into government offices. At first women were given the job of trimming paper money in the Treasury Department, but, they gradually moved into other areas of clerical work. The experiment proved successful and was continued after the end of the war. Commenting upon this innovation in 1869, Spinner declared "upon his word" that it had been a complete success: "Some of the females (are) doing more and better work for $900 per annum than many male clerks who were paid double that amount." (16) At the time, men clerks were being paid from $1200 to $1800 per year. (17)

Although women started to work in government offices during the Civil War, it was not until the 1880's that women began to pour into the clerical work force. In 1880, the proportion of women in the clerical labor force was 4 percent; in 1890 it had jumped to 21 percent. By 1920, women made up half of the clerical workers: 50 percent of all low-level office workers (including stenographers, typists, secretaries, shipping and receiving clerks, office machine operators, and clerical and kindred workers not elsewhere classified) were women. In 1960, 72 percent of them were. (See Table #2) This tremendous increase in the number of women office workers has changed the composition of the female labor force. While in 1870 less than 0.05 percent of the women in the labor force were office workers, by 1890 1.1 percent of them were. In 1960, 29.1 percent of all women in the labor force were office workers.

When women were hired to work in government offices in Washington during the Civil War, a precedent was established. This precedent facilitated the entrance of women in large numbers into the clerical labor force at the end of the 19th century. Women had gotten a foot in the office door in the Civil War, and the prejudices against women working in offices had already started to deteriorate by 1880. A second factor which eased women's entrance into the office was the invention of the typewriter. By the 1890's the typewriter had gained widespread acceptance as a practical office machine. (18)

Various American inventors had been working on "writing machines" since the 1830's. They had generally been thought of as crackpots by capitalists and the general public alike, and had seldom if every been able to get anyone to underwrite their attempts to develop a manufacturable machine.

By the early 1870's, an inventor named Christopher Latham Sholes had managed to produce a fairly workable machine. The Remington family, which had manufactured guns, sewing machines and farm machinery, bought the rights to start making typewriters. But they did not sell very well. People bought them out of curiosity for their own private use, but businesses were not yet willing to commit themselves. When asked to write a testimonial for the machine he bought in 1875, Mark Twain replied:

> Gentlemen: Please do not use my name in any way. Please do not even divulge the fact that I own a machine. I have entirely stopped using the Typewriter, for the reason that I never could write a letter with it to anybody without receiving a request by return mail that I would not only describe the machine but state what progress I had made in the use of it, etc., etc. I don't like to write letters, and so I don't want people to know that I own this curiosity breeding little joker.
>
> Yours truly,
>
> Saml L. Clemens (19)

People were curious about the typewriter, but it was not until the last two decades of the 19th century that businesses began to buy the machines in large quantities.

It seems fairly clear that it was not until businesses began to expand very rapidly that employers saw the usefulness of a mechanical writing machine. Changes in the structure of capitalist enterprises brought about changes in technology: no one was interested in making the typewriter a workable or manufacturable machine until the utility of having such a machine became clear. But the typewriter no doubt also gave rise to changes in office procedure. Writing was faster on a typewriter. The increase in correspondence and record-keeping was caused in part by the existence of the machine. For example, Robert Lincoln O'Brien made the following comment in the Atlantic Monthly in 1904:

> The invention of the typewriter has given a tremendous impetus to the dictating habit. (. . .) This means not only greater diffuseness, inevitable with any lessening of the tax on words which the labor of writing imposes, but it also brings forward the point of view of the one who speaks. (20)

The typewriter also facilitated the entrance of women into the clerical labor force. Typing was "sex-neutral" because it was a new occupation. Since typing had not been identified as a masculine job, women who were employed as typists did not encounter the criticism that they were taking over "men's work": In fact, it did not take long for typing to become "women's work": in 1890, 63.8 percent of the 33,418 clerical workers classified as stenographers and typists were women; by 1900, that proportion had risen to 76.7 percent. The feminization of low-level clerical work proceeded extremely rapidly.

It is important to determine why women wanted to become office workers. Most women at the end of the 19th century probably worked out of economic necessity. This holds true for the unmarried single woman of middle-income origins who worked until she married and was supported by her husband as well as for the immigrant working-class woman, single or married, who worked to keep her family from starving.

Clerical work attracted women because it paid better than did most other jobs that women could get. In northeastern American cities at the end of the 19th century clerical wages were relatively high: domestic servants were paid $2 to $5 a week; factory operatives, $1.50 to $8 a week; department store salesgirls, $1.50 to $8 a week; whereas typists and stenographers could get $6 to $15 a

TABLE #1

Stenographers and typists, for the United States and by sex: 1870–1930

	Total	Male	Female	% Female
1870	154	147	7	4.5%
1880	5,000	3,000	2,000	40.0%
1890	33,400	12,100	21,300	63.8%
1900	112,600	26,200	86,400	76.7%
1910	326,700	53,400	263,300	80.6%
1920	615,100	50,400	564,700	91.8%
1930	811,200	36,100	775,100	95.6%

Source: Alba M. Edwards, Comparative Occupational Statistics for the United States, 1870-1940. Published as part of Volume IV of the Report on Population of the 16th Census of the United States. Washington, D.C., 1943. Tables 9 and 10. Figures for 1880 and on are to the nearest hundred.

week. (21) Also, clerical work enjoyed a relatively high status. A woman from a middle-income home with a high school education was much more likely to look for clerical work than for work as a house servant or as a factory girl making paper boxes, pickles or shoes. And, as the passage below excerpted from The Long Day shows, a clerical position was coveted by working-class women who usually could find work only in sweatshops, factories or department stores.

The Long Day, the autobiography of Dorothy Richardson, is a good example of the way in which some 19th-century working women regarded clerical work. Richardson came from western Pennsylvania to New York City as a young woman — she is very vague about her background, but the hints she drops lead to the conclusion that she came from a middle-income family that had fallen into bad financial straits. For several months she went from job to job, making paper boxes, shaking out newly-washed laundry, etc. Her account of those days is told in a tone of dismay about the long hours and poor working conditions and a tone of contemptuous pity for the loose morality of the other "working girls". Richardson finally went to secretarial school and got a position as a secretary, clearly a step up in the occupational structure as far as she was concerned:

> I had often thought I would like to learn shorthand and typewriting. (...) I went to night school five nights out of every week for exactly sixty weeks, running consecutively save for a fortnight's interim at the Christmas holidays, when we worked nights at the store. (...)
>
> When I had thoroughly learned the principles of my trade and had attained a speed of some hundred and odd words a minute, the hardest task was yet before me. This task was not in finding a position, but in filling that position satisfactorily. My first position at ten dollars a week I held only one day. I failed to read my notes. This was more because of fright and self-consciousness, however, than of inefficiency. My next paid me only six dollars a week, but it was an excellent training school, and in it I learned self-confidence, perfect accuracy, and rapidity. Although this position paid me two dollars less than what I had been earning brewing tea and coffee and handing it over the counter, and notwithstanding the fact that I knew of places where I could go and earn ten dollars a week, I chose to remain where I was. There was method in my madness, however, let me say. I had a considerate and conscientious employer, and although I had a great deal of work, and although it had to be done most punctiliously, he never allowed me to work a moment overtime. He opened his office at nine in the morning, and I was not expected before quarter after; he closed at four sharp. This gave me an opportunity for further improving myself with a view to eventually taking not a ten-dollar, but a twenty-dollar position. I went back to night-school and took a three months' "speed course," and at the same time continued to add to my general edu-

> cation and stock of knowledge by a systematic reading of popular books of science and economics. I became tremendously interested in myself as an economic factor, and I became tremendously interested in other working girls from a similar point of view. (22)

However, despite the fact that women were pouring into offices at the end of the 19th century, they still met with disapproval. An engraving of 1875 shows a shocked male government official opening the door on an office that has been "taken over by the ladies". (23) The women are preening themselves before a mirror, fixing each other's hair, reading Harper's Bazaar, spilling ink on the floor — in short, doing everything but working. The engraving makes women working in an office seem ludicrous: women are seen as frivolous creatures incapable of doing an honest day's work.

The artist of 1875 shows the horrors that would follow if women were permitted to engage in office work.

Outright contempt was not the only negative reaction to the entrance of women into the office. Bliven cites the following passage from The Typewriter Girl, a novel by Olive Pratt Rayner whose heroine is an American typist fallen on hard financial times in London:

> Three clerks (male), in seedy black coats, the eldest with hair the color of a fox's, went on chaffing one another for two minutes after I closed the door, with ostentatious unconsciousness of my insignificant presence....The youngest, after a while, wheeled around on his high stool and broke out with the chivalry of his class and age, "Well, what's your business?"
>
> My voice trembled a little, but I mustered up courage and spoke. "I have called about your advertisement...."
>
> He eyed me up and down. I am slender, and, I will venture to say, if not pretty, at least interesting looking.
>
> "How many words a minute?" he asked after a long pause.
>
> I stretched the truth as far as its elasticity would permit. "Ninety-seven," I answered....
>
> The eldest clerk, with the foxy head, wheeled around, and took his turn to stare. He had hairy hands and large goggle-eyes....I detected an undercurrent of double meaning....I felt disagreeably like Esther in the presence of Ahasuerus — a fat and oily Ahasuerus of fifty....He perused me up and down with his small pig's eyes, as if he were buying a horse, scrutinizing my face, my figure, my hands, my feet. I felt like a Circassian in an Arab slavemarket.... (24)

The overtones of sexuality in the passage from The Typewriter Girl are hard to miss. The implication here seems to be that a decent girl is risking her morality if she tries to invade the male preserve of the office. Whether or not such sensationalism was backed up by many instances of seduction or corruption, the message seems clear: the office was a dangerous place for a woman of virtue.

Even in 1900, some people counselled women to leave the office and return to their homes, where they rightfully belonged. The editor of the Ladies' Home Journal, Edward

Bok. gave just such advice in the pages of his magazine in 1900:

> A business house cannot prosper unless each position has in it the most competent incumbent which it is possible to obtain for that particular position. And, although the statement may seem a hard one, and will unquestionably be controverted, it nevertheless is a plain, simple fact that women have shown themselves naturally incompetent to fill a great many of the business positions which they have sought to occupy. (...) The fact is that not one woman in a hundred can stand the physical strain of the keen pace which competition has forced upon every line of business today. (...) This magazine has recently made a careful and thorough investigation and inquiry of the hospitals and sanitariums for women, and the results verify and substantiate the most general statement that can be made of the alarming tendency among business girls and women to nervous collapse. No such number of patients has ever been received by these institutions during any previous period of their existence as in the last year or two. (...)
>
> I have recently been interested in ascertaining the definite reasons why employers have felt that the positions in their establishments were not most effectively filled by women. (...) In times of pressure women clerks were found to be either necessarily absent or they invariably gave out. The lack of executive ability was given as the main reason in positions of trust, and the friction caused by the objection of women subordinates to receive orders from one of their own sex. Pending or impending matrimonial engagements were also a very pronounced cause. The proprieties also came in for their share, the merchant not feeling that he could ask his female secretary or clerk to remain after business hours. The trader felt that he could not send a woman off on a mission which required hasty packing and preparations for travel

> at an hour's notice. Then, too, women do not care to travel alone. The newspaper editor felt that he could not give his female reporter indiscriminate assignments or send her out alone at all hours of the night. (...) Illness in the family, which would not necessitate a man's absence at the office, keeping the woman at home, was another reason. (...) And as I carefully went over the reasons each pointed to simply one thing: the unnatural position of women in business. It was not mental incompetence. But God had made her a woman and never intended her for the rougher life planned out for man, and each step she took proved this uncontrovertible fact to her. It was not man that stood in her path; it was herself. (25)

THE SHIFT IN IDEOLOGY

However, sixteen years after Bok used the pages of the Ladies Home Journal to admonish women to return home, another writer in the same magazine not only took for granted the fact that women worked in offices, but also found that certain "feminine" qualities were particularly suited to clerical work. "The stenographer plus" was described:

> I should describe the equipment of the ideal stenographer as follows: Twenty percent represents technical ability — that is, the ability to write and read shorthand and to typewrite rapidly and accurately; thirty percent equals general information — that is, education other than that in shorthand and typewriting; and the last and most important fifty percent I should ascribe to personality. (...)
>
> There are two kinds of personality — concrete and abstract: the one you can see, the other you can feel. The concrete side is that which the stenographer sees when she looks in the mirror. The stenographer who wins must look good — not in the sense that she must be beautiful, for dividends

> are never declared on pink cheeks and classic features; but she should make the very most of her personal equipment. (...)
>
> That other kind of personality — the abstract kind — is the more important element in the stenographer's equipment, for it involves her temperament. Thousands of stenographers stay in mediocre positions because they lack the ability to adapt their conduct to those fixed principles of harmony and optimism which must prevail in all big undertakings.
>
> A large employer of stenographic help said to me once:
>
> "I expect from my stenographer the same service that I get from the sun, with this exception: the sun often goes on a strike and it is necessary for me to use artificial light, but I pay my stenographer to work six days out of every seven, and I expect her all the while to radiate my office with sunshine and sympathetic interest in the things I am trying to do."
>
> It is the spirit in which the stenographer lives and works as well as the volume of her work that makes her profitable. She must be adaptable, agreeable, courteous. Perhaps no single word so underwrites her success as "courtesy"; this is the keyword in all of our new gospels of salesmanship and efficiency. Our great enterprises are showing us to what extent courtesy can be capitalized. (26)

Fortune magazine, in a series of unsigned articles on "Women in Business", carried the argument a step further and equated secretaries with wives:

> The whole point of the whole problem, in other words, is that women occupy the office because the male employer wants them there. Why he wants them there is another question which cannot be answered merely by saying that once there they take to the work very nicely. It is doubtless true that women take to the work nicely. Their conscious

or subconscious intention some day to marry, and their conscious or subconscious willingness to be directed by men, render them amenable and obedient and relieve them of the ambition which makes it difficult for men to put their devotion into secretarial work. But that fact only partially explains the male employer's preference. It indicates that women and by virtue of some of their most womanly traits are capable of making the office a more pleasant, peaceful, and homelike place. But it does not indicate why the employer desires that kind of office rather than an office full of ambitious and pushing young men intent upon hammering their typewriters into presidential desks. To get at that problem pure speculation is the only tool.

One might well speculate somewhat as follows: the effect of the industrial revolution was the de-domestication of women. In the working classes the substitute for domestic servitude was factory servitude. In the well-to-do classes, to which the office employer's wife belongs, the substitute for domestic responsibility was no responsibility — or no responsibility to speak of. Consequently, in the well-to-do classes, women were presented first with idleness, then with discontent with idleness, and finally with that odd mixture of rebellion and independence which changed the face of American society in the years that followed the War. In the process the upper-class home, as the upper-class home was known to the Victorians, disappeared. The male was no longer master in his own dining room and dreadful in his own den nor did a small herd of wives, daughters, and sisters hear his voice and tremble. He was, on the contrary, the more or less equal mate of a more or less unpredictable woman. And he resented it.

He resented the loss of his position. He regretted the old docility, the old obedience, the old devotion to his personal interests. And finding himself unable to re-create the late, lost paradise in his home he set about re-creating it in his office.

> What he wanted in the office was not the office mistress described at least fifty-two times a year by American short-story writers. His very pretty and very clever and very expensive wife was already mistress enough and to spare. What he wanted in the office was something as much like the vanished wife of his father's generation as could be arranged — someone to balance his checkbook, buy his railroad tickets, check his baggage, get him seats in the fourth row, take his daughter to the dentist, listen to his side of the story, give him a courageous look when things were blackest, and generally know all, understand all. (...)
>
> Whether or not any such speculative explanation of the male desire for a female office is sound there can be no doubt that the desire exists and that it is the male employer who is chiefly responsible for the female secretary. (27)

In 1900, the Ladies' Home Journal warned women that they could not stand the physical strain of working in a fast-paced business office, that business girls and women were apt to suffer a nervous collapse. But by 1916 the Journal was comparing the faithful female secretary to some heavenly body who "radiated the office with sunshine and sympathetic interest". It had not taken very long for the ideology to shift and for people to accept the presence of women in offices. Bok had argued in 1900 that women, by virtue of their "nature", were unsuited to the office. But only a few years later, the Journal came close to arguing that the "natural" temperament of women made them good stenographers. And by 1935, Fortune had concocted a full-fledged historical justification for the assertion that "woman's place was at the typewriter".

Women, so the argument went, are by nature adaptable, courteous, and sympathetic — in a word, passive. This natural passivity makes them ideally suited to the job of carrying out an endless number of routine tasks without a complaint. Furthermore, their docility makes it unlikely that they will aspire to rise very far above their station.

Thus their male boss is spared the unpleasant possibility that his secretary will one day be competing with him for his job.

The image of the secretary as the competent mother-wife who sees to her employer's every need and desire was a description which most fitted a personal secretary. Here certain "feminine" characteristics ascribed to the job of personal secretary — sympathy, adaptability, courtesy — made women seem the natural candidates for the job. Not all clerical workers were personal secretaries. For the large proportion of clerical workers who were stenographers, typists, file clerks and the like, another ideological strain developed, emphasizing the supposed greater dexterity of women. These workers were seldom assigned to one particular boss, but instead constituted a pool from which any executive could draw as he wished. In the case of these low-level clerical workers, personal characteristics such as sympathy and courtesy seemed less important. Dexterity — the ability to do work quickly and accurately — was much more important. Not long after the typewriter began to be used as a matter of course in business offices, people started to argue that women, endowed with dextrous fingers, were the most fitting operators of these machines.

Elizabeth Baker states that "women seemed to be especially suited as typists and switchboard operators because they were tolerant of routine, careful, and manually dextrous." (28)

WOMAN'S PLACE IN THE OFFICE HIERARCHY

Whether it was for the warmth of their personalities or the dexterity of their fingers, women came to be seen as "natural" office workers. Why did this ideology develop?

The ideology is obviously connected to the feminization of the clerical labor force. If women were employed in large numbers in offices, then it was not surprising that an ideology justifying their presence there developed. Women were originally employed in offices because they were cheaper than the available male labor force. As corporations expanded at the end of the 19th century, they were forced to draw on the pool of educated females to meet their rapidly increasing demand for clerical workers. But the expansion of capitalist firms did not entail a simple proliferation of small, "19th-century" offices. Instead, it meant a greatly-expanded office structure, with large numbers of people working in a single office. The situation was no longer that of the 19th-century office, where some of the clerks were in effect apprenticing managers. The expanded office structure, on the contrary, brought with it a rapid growth of low-level, dead-end jobs.

It was primarily women who filled those low-level jobs. By 1920, for instance, women made up over 90 percent of the typists and stenographers in the United States. (See Table #1) Women — whose "natural" docility and dexterity made them the ideal workers for these jobs on the bottom of the office hierarchy. By harping upon the docility of the female character, writers like Spillman in the Ladies' Home Journal provided a convenient rationalization for the fact that most low-level clerical workers in dead-end jobs were women.

It is important to point out that differentiating office workers by sex is not the same as dividing them into groups distinguished, say, by eye color. The sexual division of labor in the office — where men hold the majority of managerial positions and women fill the majority of low-level, clerical jobs — is a division which is strengthened by the positions which men and women hold outside the office.

When the ideology of passive female labor first manifested itself in the early 20th century, the United States was, by and large, a patriarchal society. Patriarchal relations between men and women, in which men made decisions and women followed them, were carried over into the office. These patriarchal social relations meshed very conveniently with office bureaucracies, where the means by which the workers were told what to do was often an extremely personalized one. For although the number of clerical workers was large, they were often divided into small enough groups so that five or six typists, stenographers or file clerks would be directly accountable to one supervisor. And if that supervisor was a man (as was generally the case in the early 20th century) and those clerical workers were women, it is easy to see how patriarchal patterns of male-female relations would reinforce the office hierarchy.

The segmentation of the office work force by sex thus promoted a situation where a docile mass of clerical workers would follow without rebellion the directives of a relatively small group of managers. The ideology that women, by virtue of their "feminine docility", were naturally suited to fill the low-level clerical jobs, can be seen as an important buttress of the stability of the hierarchical office structure.

TABLE #2

Feminization of the Clerical Labor Force

		Bookkeepers Accountants and Cashiers	Messengers Errand and Office Boys and Girls (a)
	total	39,164(1)	7,820(3)
1870	female	893(2)	46
	% female	2%	.6%
	total	75,688(6)	12,447
1880	female	4,295(6)	228
	% female	6%	2%
	total	160,968	45,706
1890	female	28,050	1,658
	% female	17%	4%
	total	257,400	63,700
1900(b)	female	74,900	3,800
	% female	29%	6%
	total	491,600	95,100
1910(b)	female	189,000	6,400
	% female	38%	7%
	total	742,000	99,500
1920(b)	female	362,700	8,100
	% female	49%	8%
	total	940,000	79,500
1930(b)	female	487,500	5,100
	% female	52%	6%
	total	931,300	60,700
1940(b)	female	475,700	3,000
	% female	51%	5%
	total	---------	59,000
1950(b)	female	---------	10,600
	% female	---------	18%
	total	---------	63,200
1960(b)	female	---------	11,200
	% female	---------	18%

SOURCES:

For 1870-1940: Janet M. Hooks, Women's Occupations through Seven Decades, U.S. Department of Labor, Women's Bureau, Bulletin #218, Washington, D.C., 1947. Table IIA: Occupations of Women Workers, 1870-1940; Table IIB: Occupations of All Workers, 1870-1940.

CONTINUATION OF TABLE #2

Feminization of the Clerical Labor Force

Stenographers Typists and Secretaries	Shipping and Receiving Clerks	Clerical and Kindred Workers (nec) (c)	Office Machine Operators
		29,655(4)	
		930(5)	
		3%	
		64,151(7)	
		2,315(7)	
		4%	
		219,173(7)	
		45,553(7)	
		21%	
		357,100	
		104,400	
		29%	
		1,034,200	
		386,800	
		37%	
		2,092,000	
		1,038,400	
		50%	
2,754,000			36,200
1,450,900			32,100
53%			89%
1,174,900	229,700	1,973,600	64,200
1,096,400	9,100	702,500	55,100
93%	4%	36%	86%
1,629,300	297,400	2,354,200	146,200
1,538,000	20,700	1,252,900	120,300
94%	7%	53%	82%
2,312,800	294,600	3,016,400	318,100
2,232,600	25,000	1,788,700	236,400
96%	8%	59%	74%

For 1950-1960: Bureau of the Census, Census of Population, United States Summary, Washington, D.C., 1960. Table 201: Detailed Occupation of the Experienced Civilian Labor Force, By Sex, for the United States: 1960 and 1950.

Footnotes for Table #2

(a) "Messengers, errand, and office boys and girls" includes "telegraph messengers" through 1900.

(b) Figures rounded off to the nearest hundred.

(c) N. E. C.: "not elsewhere classified".

(1) Census figures estimated, and 374 added because of undercount in 13 Southern states.

(2) Census figures estimated, and 2 added because of undercount in 13 Southern states.

(3) 70 added because of undercount in 13 Southern states.

(4) Partly estimated, and 494 added because of undercount in 13 Southern states. Figures do not include "Abstractors, notaries, and justices of peace," classified in 1940 in the group "Clerical Workers (n.e.c.)".

(5) Partly estimated, and 6 added because of undercount in 13 Southern states. Figures do not include "Abstractors, notaries, and justices of peace," classified in 1940 in the group "Clerical Workers (n.e.c.)".

(6) Estimated.

(7) 1890 and 1900 data partly estimated, and 1880 data entirely estimated. Figures do not include "Abstractors, notaries, and justices of peace", classified in 1940 in the group "Clerical Workers (n.e.c.)".

Footnotes

1. U.S. Department of Labor, Women's Bureau, 1969 Handbook of Women Workers (Women's Bureau Bulletin #294; Washington: Government Printing Office, 1969), p. 90.

2. Concrete information about female office workers is not easy to find. In a comprehensive bibliographical Guide to Business History, Henrietta Larson points out that "it is significant that the works dealing with the subject (office management) are concerned largely with "systems" and machines — the office worker has been left in neglected obscurity." (Larson; 1948; pp. 771-772)

There are a few analytical studies of office workers, the most notable of which are David Lockwood's The Black-coated Worker and C. Wright Mills' White Collar: the American Middle Classes. Grace D. Coyle focuses on women in offices and the kind of work they do in "Women in the Clerical Occupations" in The Annals of the American Academy of Political and Social Science, vol. 143 (May, 1929); Fortune published a series of articles on "Women in Business" in 1935; the Women's Bureau of the U.S. Department of Labor has issued a number of bulletins on office workers. In addition, there is quite a long list of books addressed to women which tell them how to be better secretaries: the main point of these manuals seems to be that women should be certain to please their (male) bosses and that they should be neat and accurate about any number of office tasks. And dotted throughout the prominent women's magazines are articles about the "business woman".

Finally, there are some fictional works which provide a certain amount of insight into office work. "Bartleby" (1856) by Herman Melville is set in a Wall Street lawyer's office of the 1850's and describes the men who work there as copyists; Alice Adams (1921) by Booth Tarkington is about the daughter of a white-collar employee who is forced to give up her hopes of joining the upper-class social clique in town, accept her own middle-class status, and finally climb the "begrimed stairway" of the local business college in preparation for becoming a "working girl".

But all in all there is very little information about the

history of female clerical workers. However, there are bits and pieces of evidence upon which this essay is based.

3. For the purposes of this discussion the term "19th-century office" will be used to describe those office structures which existed prior to the widespread monopolization and bureaucratization of capitalist corporations, a process which was well underway in the United States by the end of the 19th century. "The modern office" will be used to describe the structures which developed after that bureaucratization. The description of the 19th-century office which follows is based primarily on David Lockwood's The Black-coated Worker and on C. Wright Mills' White Collar: the American Middle Classes.

4. Dickens, Charles, Bleak House (Boston: Houghton Mifflin, 1853), p. 415.

5. Hooks, Janet M., Women's Occupations Through Seven Decades (Women's Bureau Bulletin #218; Washington: Government Printing Office, 1947), Tables IIA and IIB.

6. Melville, Herman, "Bartleby" in The Piazza Tales (first published 1856; Garden City: Doubleday, 1961).

7. See Alfred Chandler, Strategy and Structure, Cambridge, Mass: M.I.T. Press, 1962. Also see Stephen Hymer, "The Multinational Corporation and the Law of Uneven Development" in Jagdish Bhagwati (ed.), Economics and the World Order, MacMillan Company, 1972.

8. Bureau of the Census, Department of Commerce and Labor. Special Report of the 12th Census: Occupations at the 12th Census. Washington, D.C., 1904. Data is for "number of persons engaged in specified occupations". "Office workers" includes bookkeepers and accountants; clerks and copyists; and stenographers and typewriters (typists).

9. Baker, Elizabeth Faulkner, Technology and Women's Work (New York: Columbia University Press, 1964), p. 57.

Baker argues that girls were given high school educations because the number of women teachers was increasing: "Men were being attracted by business opportunities and skilled trades, and the phenomenal growth of public schools created an alarming shortage of teachers. (...) But relief from the scarcity of male teachers of course required that girls as well as boys be taught." (p. 57) However, the fact that so many girls got high school educations in the 19th century still seems rather surprising; unfortunately, recent analysts of the rise of mass education in the United States do not remark upon it. (See Michael Katz, The Irony of Early School Reform, Cambridge, Mass.: 1968; or Samuel Bowles, "Unequal Education and the Reproduction of the Social Division of Labor" in the Review of Radical Political Economics, Winter, 1971.) For more information about the history of women's education, see also Thomas Woody, A History of Women's Education in the United States, New York: 1929.

10. Data for high school graduates from Federal Security Agency, Office of Education; Biennial Survey of Education. Cited in the Statistical Abstract of the United States (1952), p. 121. One possible explanation for the fact that more women than men were graduating from high school at the end of the 19th century is the following: In the case of working-class men and women, the boys left school to work. The money they could earn was badly needed by their families. But if girls entered the factory labor force, their wages would be considerably lower than those of their brothers. This fact, coupled with attitudes that men were the more important breadwinners and that women's place was in the home, may have resulted in working-class girls staying in school longer than their brothers. At any rate, it is clear that figures on high school graduates must be broken down by class, and probably also by ethnic group, before the disparity between male and female high school graduates can be adequately explained.

11. Katz, Michael, The Irony of Early School Reform (Cambridge: Harvard University Press, 1968), p. 58.

12. Ibid., p. 58.

13. Smuts, Robert W., Women and Work in America (New York: Columbia University Press, 1959).

14. Baker, Technology and Women's Work, pp. 62-63.

15. Sumner, Helen L., History of Women in Industry in the United States (61st Congress, 2nd Session, U.S. Senate Document #645; Bureau of Labor, 1911), p. 239.

16. "Women in Business: I", Fortune, XII (July 1935), p. 53.

17. Ibid., p. 53.

18. The following account of the development of the typewriter is based on Bruce Bliven, Jr., The Wonderful Writing Machine, New York: 1954.

19. Ibid., p. 62.

20. Ibid., p. 134.

21. Smuts, Women and Work, p. 90. It is very difficult to find statistics about clerical wages at the end of the 19th century broken down by sex; Bliven and Smuts do not cite sources for their wage statistics.

22. Richardson, Dorothy, The Long Day (1905; reprinted in William O'Neill, Women at Work, Chicago: Quadrangle Books, 1972), pp. 269-72.

23. The engraving is reproduced in Bliven, p. 73.

24. Bliven, Wonderful Writing Machine, pp. 75-76. Bliven gives no date for The Typewriter Girl, but the context of his argument leads to the conclusion that the novel was a late 19th century potboiler.

25. Bok, Edward, "The Return of the Business Woman" in the Ladies' Home Journal (March 1960), p. 16. I am indebted to Elaine Wethington of the University of Michigan at Ann Arbor, and her unpublished manuscript, "The Women's Magazines and the 'Business Woman', 1890-1919" for this reference. Wethington points out that Bok did not shrink from also pointing out that office work was the "best paid and most respectable employment for young women"; he was quite happy to have his magazine reflect opposing opinions in order not to alienate any of its one million subscribers. Wethington's paper is extremely useful as a source for articles about office workers in the prominent American women's magazines.

26. Spillman, Harry C., "The Stenographer Plus" in the Ladies' Home Journal (February 1916), p. 33.

27. "Women in Business: II" Fortune, XII (August 1935), p. 55. It is interesting to speculate why it was in 1935 that Fortune published its defense of women in the office. It is possible that during the Depression there was some criticism of the employment of women as clerical workers when unemployment rates for men, the traditional breadwinners, were so high.

28. Baker, Technology and Women's Work, p. 74.

FEMALE SOLIDARITY AND PROFESSIONAL SUCCESS: THE DILEMMA OF WOMEN DOCTORS IN LATE NINETEENTH-CENTURY AMERICA

Virginia G. Drachman

In 1886, Edna Dow Cheney, the president of the all-woman's New England Hospital for Women and Children, proudly announced that women's struggle to become doctors was over. "We have no longer to plead woman's right to study medicine," she asserted, "no occasion to ask opportunity for her to practice it."[1] Less than ten years after Cheney made her public declaration of women's progress, Dr. Bertha Van Hoosen, the resident physician at the hospital, wrote to the board of physicians in exasperation, "the interns are unhappy . . . they feel they are losing ground."[2] Together these conflicting statements reflect a paradox of progress which confronted women doctors in the last quarter of the nineteenth century. On the one hand, they made significant inroads into the medical profession. On the other hand, the progress they made created new problems which often divided women doctors against each other.

Historians have focused on the first part of this story — women's struggle to enter the medical profession. This interpretation might best be understood as the struggle/victory model: male doctors sought to bar women from medicine; in response, female solidarity overcame male opposition, and women entered the medical profession.[3] The vehicles of entry were the medical institutions founded and run by women for women. From this struggle/victory point of view, historians have understood the all-women's medical institutions as the product of female solidarity in the face of male opposition. One historian has aptly described the New England Hospital, for example, as a "feminist showplace."[4] Indeed, it *was* a triumph to build an all-women's hospital: the New England Hospital and other all-women's medical institutions stood before the public as symbols of the success of feminism.

But, there is a second, more complex chapter to this story which the struggle/victory interpretation masks. As women made inroads into the mainstream of medicine, they struggled more frequently among themselves and acted less and less like a cohesive group with shared values. Many began to question the value of female solidarity. To be sure, some still saw it as crucial to women doctors' professional survival. Yet, others saw female solidarity as an obstacle to their professional progress. This essay focuses on this second chapter in the history of women doctors. It demonstrates that by the late nineteenth century, women doctors no longer faced only a struggle to break the sexual barriers to the medical profession. Rather, the struggle to become a physician was simply their first battle in the more enduring struggle to *be* one.

The arena for this struggle was often the all-women's medical institutions. Within the walls of their hospitals, colleges, and medical societies women doctors attempted to reconcile their commitment to female solidarity with their desire for professional success. The New England Hospital provides an excellent place to examine nineteenth-century women doctors as they faced this challenge. While the history of the New England Hospital is important, the more significant story concerns the women doctors who went there to practice medicine and forge their professional lives. It is their story that makes institutions like the New England Hospital important sources for the social history of women and medicine.

Founded in Boston in 1862, the New England Hospital was unique among nineteenth-century hospitals because its founders were women, its physicians were women, and its patients were women and children. Dr. Marie Zakrzewska, the hospital's founder and central figure until her death in 1902, opened the doors to the New England Hospital with three goals: to provide sick women with medical care from physicians of their own sex, to provide women doctors with clincial training, and to train nurses. To Zakrzewska the central purpose of the hospital was to provide women doctors with equal professional opportunities with male physicians by offering them clinical training. "The most striking feature in its character," Zakrzewska explained of the hospital, "is that it is designed to give to educated women physicians an equal chance of proving their capacity as hospital attendants with their medical brethren, and to admit only female students to its wards, as all other hospitals close their doors to women as medical students."[5] To be sure, clinical training was not readily accessible to the young male doctor-to-be. Since the typical medical school offered lectures exclusively, the would-be doctor seeking practical experience had either to apprentice himself to a physician or work in a hospital.[6] Yet, for the women doctor seeking clinical experience, the situation was even more difficult: hospitals in New York, Philadelphia, and Boston were closed to women. Zakrzewska sought to duplicate for women at the New England Hospital the clinical advantages and professional opportunities available to men elsewhere. Only in this way, she felt, would women doctors be able to participate as equals with the best of male physicians.

Ironically, embedded within this commitment to professional equality for women and men in medicine were the seeds of new problems and challenges which confronted Zakrzewska in the last quarter of the nineteenth century. In fact, the closer she saw women doctors come to attaining her goal of professional equality with men, the more she saw her hospital — which had contributed so significantly to women doctors' professional success — lose ground. In her later years, Zakrzewska watched as women doctors increasingly rejected the New England Hospital for other routes to professional success.

When the New England Hospital opened its doors, however, women had few professional alternatives. Only the New England Hospital and the all-women's New York Infirmary provided women doctors with clinical experience and professional opportunities. Faced with few options, a significant number of women who came to the hospital as interns stayed on after their training. During the hospital's first decade, Zakrzewska steadily built up a staff of physicians primarily from interns within the hospital. By 1875, she had eight women doctors working with her, all of whom dedicated their professional lives to the New England Hospital. By 1900, five of the original physicians still worked with Zakrzewska at the hospital. The other three worked there until they became sick or died. With Zakrzewska, these women were the leaders of the hospital. Having come up the ranks within the hospital in its early years, they comprised a distinct group who understood the role of the New England Hospital as Zakrzewska did. As the hospital's board of physicians, this relatively unchanging group of women doctors ran the New England Hospital day in and day out, setting the direction and pace of growth at the hospital throughout the last quarter of the century.

Yet, running the hospital grew steadily more difficult. As the century progressed, the board of physicians frequently encountered dissatisfaction and conflict as they confronted women doctors with different professional experiences, expectations, and options than their own. Over the next few decades, clinical opportunities for women expanded as women opened other hospitals as well as dispensaries in cities around the country. Together with the more than a dozen women's medical colleges which opened in the second half of the century, the New England Hospital became part of a network of women's institutions born out of a need for female solidarity and a desire to provide women with professional opportunities in medicine. Furthermore, the New England Hospital played a significant role in expanding this network. Several women who trained there went on to open other women's medical institutions: Mary Thompson founded the Chicago Hospital for Women and Children and later the Woman's Medical College in Chicago, while Anita Tyng and Mary DeHart opened dispensaries for women in Rhode Island and New Jersey respectively. Zakrzewska was proud of the contributions her graduates made to expanding this chain of women's medical institutions. "This shows," she boasted publically in her annual report in 1875, "that the seed sown here has fallen on fertile ground."[7]

In the last decade of the nineteenth century, women doctors also began to make inroads into the mainstream of medicine. The formerly all-male institutions began to open their doors to women, thereby providing them with access to equal professional training with men, the goal for which Zakrzewska had originally strived when she opened the New England Hospital in 1862. This breakdown of professional barriers was wide-ranging, encompassing medical schools, medical societies, and hospitals. In 1870, for example, the University of Michigan Medical School became co-educational. By 1893, women could attend Tufts University Medical School or Boston University Medical School in Boston. And in the same year, when John Hopkins Medical School opened to men and women on an equal basis, women finally gained access to medical training at one of the country's top-level universities. When Cornell followed in 1899, it appeared that women had finally climbed the last rung of the medical school ladder.

While women doctors gained educational advantages, they also found professional colleagueship with male physicians in the formally male medical societies. By 1882, seventeen state societies had a total of 115 female members.[8] And in 1884, the women of Boston took a large step forward when the Massachusetts Medical society voted to accept women as members. Finally in 1915, the American Medical Association opened its membershp to female physicians, thereby giving them their ultimate symbol of professional acceptance.

Complementing women's increasing educational and professional opportunities were the expanding clinical opportunities for women at previously all-male hospitals. By the middle of the 1880's, women trained at major hospitals such as Bellevue in New York, Blockley in Philadelphia, Cook County in Chicago, and Boston City in Boston. At the same time, career options for women doctors expanded. Hospitals increasingly placed women on their staffs. By 1890, eight hospitals in New York City alone employed fourteen women doctors in their dispensaries. And by 1890, a new area of work opened for women doctors when several states including New York, Ohio, Pennsylvania, and Massachusetts passed legislation requiring the employment of a woman doctor in every state insane asylum where women were confined.[9] Even private practice proved an increasingly viable option for many women doctors. It took most women doctors only two years to become self-sufficient in their practices, and the average annual income for women doctors by 1881 was $3000.[10]

Zakrzewska applauded the progress women doctors had made. On the occasion of the New England Hospital's twenty-fifth anniversary, she announced with pride that "the woman physician is now called for, respected, and welcome in almost every large town."[11] Yet, while Zakrzewska publically applauded this professional progress, in the privacy of the New England Hospital, she confronted new challenges and problems brought on by the very professional advances she wanted for women doctors.[12]

Between 1863 and 1875, while Zakrzewska built up her nucleus of women doctors for the hospital, relative harmony existed between her and the interns she annually trained. Yet, by the end of 1875, the interns began to demonstrate signs of discontent which continued throughout the winter of 1876. After several months of mounting tension, Zakrzewska called the interns together to hear their grievances. Their strongest complaint was that doctors addressed them as "Misses" rather than with the title of "Doctor."[13] In response, Zakrzewska explained that since the hospital did not require interns to have a medical degree, the doctors had always used the title of "Miss" or "Mrs." to minimize differences between interns, some of whom had graduated from medical schools and some of whom had not.[14] Ultimately, the doctors and interns agreed to a compromise. The doctors would continue to address the interns as "Miss" in the hospital but would address them as "Doctor" in the dispensary, the outpatient department of the hospital where the interns had more direct patient contact.

This initial conflict between interns and physicians was resolved relatively simply. Yet, it takes on larger significance because it illuminated two problems which continued to confront Zakrzewska and her board of physicians over the years — namely, the widening gap between the New England Hospital and the medical opportunities for women outside its walls, and the growing conflict between older and younger women doctors over the needs of women in medicine.

From Zakrzewska's point of view, the hospital offered women valuable clinical training which was unavailable to them elsewhere. But, to the interns the opportunity for clinical training at the New England Hospital was not enough. They came to the hospital with expectations of a quality of experience which transcended their appreciation for the opportunity itself. Their heightened expectations were shaped largely by the fact that by 1875 women doctors no longer faced the same professional obstacles that confronted their predecessors a decade before, leading many women doctors to believe that the prejudice aginst them was fast disappearing. One ex-intern, for example, wrote to Zakrzewska in 1875, "I think whatever prejudice originally existed against women physicians is fast passing away."[15]

The interns who complained to Zakrzewska in 1876 were part of this younger group of medical women whose professional journey was relatively smooth when measured against the rocky path Dr. Zakrzewska and her contemporaries had been forced to blaze. Consequently, they had different expectations and goals from their older colleagues. The meeting in 1876 with the interns illuminated these differences. The interns' request to be referred to as "Drs." rather than as "Misses" revealed their desire for a distinctly professional identity. Zakrzewska, on the other hand, did not seek the same professional identification. "I would prefer never to be called 'Dr.' but rather 'Miss' or 'Madam,' she explained. "For me," she continued, as well as for many of her contemporaries, "it is far more agreeable to be considered first a woman, and secondarily a doctor."[16] Her preferences for highlighting her gender stood in marked contrast to the interns' preference for emphasizing their professional status. Their differences on this specific issue symbolized a larger difference between them — namely their different evaluations of the importance of female solidarity in their professional lives. Of course, these major differences could not be resolved by a simple compromise over the use of titles. Rather, the tension between the older and younger doctors at the hospital persisted long after that particular group of interns left, and continued to produce conflict throughout the century.

In 1863, for example, the interns refused to cooperate with changes in work assignments brought on by an unusually heavy patient load. Having come to the New England Hospital for a year, expecting to spend three months in the hospital's medical, maternity, and surgical wards, respectively, and three months in its dispensary, they were unwilling to make any adjustments in this pattern of rotation. The situation was indeed untenable, for relations between physicians and interns were so strained that they threatened the orderly management of the hospital.

It is perhaps no accident that the interns' insistence on a particular training experience occurred during the decade of expanding clinical opportunities for women. For Zakrzewska, the opening of previously all-male hospitals to women created a dilemma. On the one hand, she saw it as a major step forward for women doctors, bringing them closer to her original goal of equal opportunity for male and female physicians. On the other hand, she recognized that the increasing clinical options for women at larger, more prestigious hospitals could deter women from choosing the New England Hospital.

This dilemma shaped her response to the interns in 1883. She told them that the hospital offered benefits which transcended the professional opportunities available to them at the previously all-male hospitals and medical schools. "Comparisons are often made between the opportunities offered to medical women now, and twenty-five years ago, but the value of seeing women doing skillful medical work, cannot be over-estimated in its inspiring effect . . ."[17] From this point of view, Zakrzewska found intolerable the priorities of her interns which placed each individual's professional interests over the needs of the hospital community as a whole. She explained: "all interns ought to work with us in harmony, not for us personally, but for the *cause* of women practitioners in medicine, for whom we older ones broke the path."[18] Yet, the interns were unwilling to give their loyalty unquestioningly. Instead of coming to the New England Hospital with an eagerness to serve the hospital, as Zakrzewska expected, the interns in 1883 brought to the hospital the expectation that the hospital should serve them.

In the last decade of the century, conflict and discontent continued to polarize Zakrzewska and the board of physicians against the younger women at the New England Hospital. In 1893, for example, the older doctors confronted another group of dissatisfied interns. This time, however, the complaints demanded serious attention as well as accommodation by the older doctors. In a letter to the board of physicians, the interns made a series of complaints that amounted to a strong indictment of the New England Hospital. "After having spent three or four years in medical schools of the highest standing, we enter your hospital ready and anxious to do our best. But, we are allowed to *do* absolutely nothing."[19] The interns also expressed discontent with the attitude of the medical staff toward them. "We have no professional standing," they complained, echoing the feelings of the interns in 1876. "We are considered as mere children who come here to be taught."[20] Overall, their complaints stood as a sweeping critique of the training program at the New England Hospital. "Do you think it pays us to spend a year of our time with you and gain so small an amount of practical knowledge?" they charged. "We are not satisfied with what we are getting here!"[21]

To Zakrzewska and the members of the board, an expression of such feelings would have been unthinkable during their years of training. But the situation had changed markedly since their initial struggle to become doctors. The inroads women had made into the medical profession since the 1870's escalated by the mid-1880's. It was in 1886, for example, that the Boston City Hospital agreed to accept women interns. Two years earlier, the medical women of Boston won a major battle when the Massachusetts Medical Society voted to accept women as members. Dr. Emma Call, a physician since 1875, became the Society's first female member.

While Call and two other long-time doctors at the New England Hospital took the exam for admission, the three oldest physicians at the hospital did not seek membership. Zakrzewska, who had unsuccessfully sought admission in 1859 and again in 1864, refused to take the exam and called the Society's offer in her twenty-seventh year of practice "condescending." Ironically, her decision foreshadowed the future, for it revealed her choice to allow an important symbol of women doctors' achievements and professionalism to pass her by.

In her response to the interns' letter of complaint, Zakrzewska once again harkened back to the past. Referring to the board of physicians, she remarked, "all the ladies present have served as interns in this hospital, and all had their grievances, and all had to endure annoyances . . . but just this training," she continued, "which was borne with dignity and silence, has made them superior women, while everyone of the revolting sisterhood have either remained on the lowest step of success or fallen out of the profession entirely."[22] Calling for the unconditional loyalty of all medical women who passed through the New England Hospital, she urged the younger doctors to follow the lead of the older doctors who understood the value of female solidarity. "You are only helpers in one of the greatest historical reforms, which is still in its infancy, and needs a good deal of self-sacrifice yet to arrive at naturally," she told them. "You ought to be willing to assist in such forms and ways as the experienced workers in this cause think safest and wisest to follow."[23]

To Zakrzewska, the interns had taken the New England Hospital for granted. Yet, to the interns, who faced both opportunities for professional training elsewhere as well as pressure to keep up with rising professional standards, the hospital and its older doctors had failed them on both accounts. Both groups of physicians had a legitimate point of view. The New England Hospital no longer afforded women doctors the best training opportunities. In fact, the hospital lacked the financial base ever to catch up with the major hospitals that were now accepting women. For this, Zakrzewska and the older physicians were not totally responsible. The rapidly rising medical standards were difficult for many doctors and medical institutions to maintain. Yet, the older doctors at the New England Hospital did have some responsibility for the problems there. Even as they provided the hospital with continuity and stability, their failure to adjust to the changing medical scene beyond the hospital's walls starved the New England Hospital of fresh ideas. Furthermore, Zakrzewska's stubborn pride in her hospital made it difficult for her to hear or respond objectively to criticism.

Yet, Zakrzewska did recognize that the contents of the interns' complaints deserved serious attention. She had already received similar criticisms from people higher up the hospital hierarchy. Dr. Bertha Van Hoosen, the resident physician in 1891, had made the same criticisms in her statement of resignation. Van Hoosen was a highly respected member of the hospital staff who went on to become an eminent surgeon, professor of obstretics at Loyola University, and first president of the American Medical Women's Association. Her capabilities and skill were evident to the doctors at the New England Hospital, and her criticisms received serious attention.

Van Hoosen explained that the position of resident physician was "too arduous" and "too disagreeable" for her to continue at the hospital. With despair and frustration she confessed, "I have never felt at the end of any day that I had finished my work in a satisfactory manner." Yet, her problems were small when she compared them to those of the interns whose positions she considered "unendurable." The resident physician, she explained, stood in the way of any practical experience, responsibility, or respect the interns might enjoy.[24]

Van Hoosen proposed a reorganization of hospital staff which included abolishing the position of resident physician. Whereas a similar proposal by the interns had been ignored, within two months of receiving Van Hoosen's letter, the board of physicians drew up a plan for hospital reform which followed the model she proposed.[25] The speed with which such revisions were accepted by the older physicians once Van Hoosen proposed them suggests that by the end of the century the hospital may have needed an influential outsider like her. It needed someone with the objectivity Zakrzewska and the board lacked, who could see that the New England Hospital was becoming out of date. Van Hoosen was more in touch with the growing medical opportunities and pressures for women outside and understood their implications for the New England Hospital. Only a major reorganization of the hospital would help it to maintain its reputation as a valuable training hospital.

But the reforms of 1892 were too little too late. Interns continued to express dissatisfaction in the years immediately following the adoption of Van Hoosen's plan. Lack of clinical experience still prevailed along with an atmosphere of stagnation which made the New England Hospital an increasingly unappealing place for women doctors to train. The tension which had been growing between older and younger physicians since the mid-seventies had by the nineties set the stage for a crisis of faith in the hospital. As the board of physicians and younger doctors continued to lock horns, the older doctors watched as the younger ones turned with increasing frequency away from the hospital to seek their opportunities elsewhere.

The experience of one intern — Alice Hamilton — illustrates this trend. Hamilton was accepted as an intern in 1893. On paper, she seemed to be an extremely attractive candidate. She had a glowing recommendation from her professor of chemistry at the University of Michigan Medical School who described her as "a student of superior scholarship and a person of strong intellectual power."[26] With such a positive report, the board of physicians must have felt confident in accepting Hamilton. Similarly, she was delighted to be accepted. "I feel deliciously animated that I shall go to Boston this fall," she wrote her cousin Agnes.[27] Unfortunately, neither Hamilton's expectations of the hospital nor the physicians' expectations of Hamilton were realized. Before her tenure as intern was up, Hamilton requested dismissal from the hospital, and the board readily let her go.

Hamilton encountered the same disappointment and frustration the previous interns endured — inadequate opportunity for clinical training and lack of professional respect. "It is a very strange novelty to me to be in a place where I actually have not enough to do to keep me busy," she complained three weeks after she began work.[28] Less than four weeks later, the situation became intolerable for her. "I feel that I am simply losing a year when I need practical work," she wrote in exasperation. Yet, Hamilton reserved her most scathing comments for the board of physicians. "They are so bland and patronizing and so convinced that there is no hospital like the New England and no advantages like ours. They are narrow women," she continued, "who escape discovering their own inferiority merely by avoiding their superiors."[29] In the spring, Hamilton asked the board of physicians to release her from her contract, and the board, which usually granted such requests only in cases of illness, voted to accept her withdrawal in "the best interests of the hospital."[30]

Hamilton's actions were part of a trend in the 1890's of growing dissatisfaction with and decreasing loyalty to the New England Hospital. This rejection of the hospital took a variety of forms. For example, more and more young women turned down offers of internships at the hospital. Between 1891 and 1895, of the twenty-seven applicants accepted, seven turned down the offer. Of the four who gave reasons, one took a position at a hospital where she could receive more obstetrical training than the New England Hospital offered, one chose to do "special work" in cystoscopy at Johns Hopkins, one had unspecified "fixed plans," while a fourth received another hospital position.

Once an applicant was on the waiting list, it was even less likely that she would choose to come to the New England Hospital. Of the eight women waitlisted between 1891 and 1895, four rejected eventual offers, while three withdrew their applications. In the interim, all seven made other satisfactory arrangements ranging from finding positions in other hospitals to beginning private practice. Clearly, by the 1890's the New England Hospital was feeling the impact of increased clinical alternatives for young women doctors.

This does not mean that the hospital lacked women seeking to train there. Rather, as the number of women doctors increased throughout the country, so did the number of women seeking internships at the hospital. Whereas sixty-three women applied between 1891 and 1895, ninety-six applied between 1900 and 1904. In addition, women were willing to travel further to come to the hospital. Between 1891 and 1895 more than three-quarters of the applicants were from the northeast. Between 1900 and 1904, more than one-half were from other parts of the country.[31] Furthermore, individual applicants continued to express a strong desire to come to the New England Hospital. One Mary Findlater, upon graduating from the Woman's Medical College of Pennsylvania, wrote in her application in 1905, "Ever since I started the study of medicine, I have looked forward to my senior year, hoping for an appointment in Boston [at the] New England Hospital, of which I had so often heard."[32] Another candiate expressed her interest somewhat more poetically: "Should you favor my application," she wrote, "I promise I will endeavor to do the work entrusted to me on the principle contained in this little poem which I heard:

> If I were a cobbler, I'd make it my pride,
> the very best cobbler to be.
> If I were a tinker, no other beside
> should mend an old kettle like me.[33]

Nevertheless, despite these signs to the contrary, there was mounting evidence that the hospital was falling to disfavor with growing numbers of women doctors. In 1895, Dr. Mary Hobart, who had been at the hospital for nine years, confronted this dilemma. "It is well known," she stated bluntly at a physicians' meeting, "that the staff of the New England Hospital already has the reputation of being narrow and to repulse bright women who might otherwise be valuable co-workers." Advising the older doctors to be more open to the needs of the young women doctors, she warned, "we must get them and keep them about us. In a few years," she continued, "it will be harder to get women clinicians than now."[34]

Particularly problematic was the fact that the disenchantment with the New England Hospital was no longer limited to interns. Women at all stages of their medical careers displayed their dissatisfaction. One way in which they expressed their discontent was by resigning their positions at the hospital. Between 1862 and 1879, when Zakrzewska built up the New England Hospital, only six of the fifteen doctors who served on her staff left. But in the "conflict years" between 1880 and 1899, twenty-five of the forty-three staff physicians left. The reasons women gave for leaving were also cause for alarm. In the hospital's early years, death, illness, or retirement were the reasons women doctors left the hospital. In the last decade of the century, however, only nine of twenty-five women who gave explanations for leaving, left for these same reasons. The remaining sixteen resigned because of dissatisfaction with the hospital's facilities, unwillingness to commit so much time to the hospital, opportunities for more lucrative work elsewhere or a desire to devote more time to private practice.

The irony is inescapable. The closer women came to attaining professional equality with male doctors — the goals for which Zakrzewska founded the New England Hospital — the less they chose the New England Hospital as a route to professional success. This trend revealed a growing difference between the professional route older women doctors had followed in the 1860's and 1870's and the one younger women doctors began to follow in the last decades of the century. Isolated from male medical institutions, the first generation of women doctors relied on the all-women's medical institutions like the New England Hospital. When the male medical institutions began to open to women, a younger generation of women doctors began to turn away from the all-women's institutions in preference for integration into the medical mainstream. To many aspiring women doctors at the end of the century, female solidarity had lost its professional appeal.

Of course, there was not always a sharp division between older women doctors who saw female solidarity as a major priority and younger women doctors who were willing to sacrifice it for their own professional success. There were younger women doctors who continued to share a commitment to women doctors as a group. Gertrude Felker, an intern in 1901, for example, was described as "the kind of girl that will in turn prove helpful to all women."[35] And there were some who stood in both camps. Van Hoosen, for example, went on in later years to found the all woman's American Medical Woman's Association.

Nevertheless, by the last decades of the nineteenth century, there was a clear and growing rejection of the all-woman's New England Hospital by younger women doctors. Zakrzewska watched this trend with a mixture of alarm and despair. To be sure, she took the rejection of the hospital personally. But her often inflexible responses to the interns' complaints over the years also revealed her strong convictions about what was best for women doctors. She firmly believed that female solidarity was the only way women would succeed in the medical profession. Even after women attained equal access with men to the best medical institutions, she still maintained that they had to ban together if they were to survive. To Zakrzewska, the younger women doctors' rejection of the New England Hospital and the female solidarity upon which it was built represented but the first step in the decline of women in medicine.

While Zakrzewska never gave up these convictions, toward the end of her life, she came to understand that the younger women doctors would never fully understand the professional struggles she and her contemporaries had endured. "It is really impossible," she wrote, "to depict the struggles of a pioneer, conditions have so altered, public opinion so changed, that the present generation cannot possible comprehend the life of fifty years ago."[36]

But, in the years following Zakrzewska's death in 1902, young doctors at the hospital realized they had little understanding of their predecessors. In 1910, the interns recognized that they knew so little about the hospital's early years that they requested a recounting of its history.[37] Their lack of understanding of the older doctors' struggles helps explain young women doctors' discontent and impatience with the New England Hospital, Zakrzewska, and the older doctors. At the same time, their complaints reflected conditions which transcended this generational gap. Rather, from the young doctors' point of view, the rapid advances in medicine beyond the hospital's walls created new professional standards which the New England Hospital did not meet.

In the final analysis, the inroads nineteenth-century women made into the medical profession created new problems. Female solidarity was initially the best route to professional success for women doctors. But by the end of the century, women doctors had to make difficult decisions about the importance of female solidarity to their professional careers.

But they were not alone, for this dilemma confronted other women toward the end of the century as well. Club women and suffragists, for example, faced similar conflicts in their respective organizations. The general trend in the women's movement was to tread more carefully, and to concentrate more narrowly on reform or professionalism.[38] Thus, younger women doctors chose their individual professional needs over the female solidarity the pioneer women had carefully cultivated. While they believed this was necessary if they were to keep up with male doctors, hindsight suggests that their priorities were somewhat shortsighted. Indeed, the percentage of women doctors declined in the first half of the twentieth century.[39] Ironically, Zakrzewska, who was unable to keep up with the new professional standards the younger doctors aspired to, anticipated this trend. In 1883, she had warned the interns: "the cause of women practitioners is by no means to be yet regarded as a permanently established reform, even though many women may be successful in their vocation."[40] Her words were, indeed, prophetic, and carried an important message to all nineteenth-century women doctors.

Tufts University Virginia G. Drachman

FOOTNOTES

*Research for this paper was aided by a fellowship from the Rockefeller Foundation and a grant from Tufts University, and was conducted while the author was a fellow at the Bunting Institute. An earlier version of this paper was presented at the Conference on Women in the Health Professions, Boston College, November 15, 1980. For their help in the various stages of writing this paper, the author would like to thank Steven Fuhrman, Douglas Jones, Ann Lane, Regina Morantz, and the members of the Boston area Medical History Group.

1. New England Hospital for Women and Children Annual Report (Boston, 1886), p. 6.

2. Bertha Van Hoosen, Letter of Resignation, September, 1891, in New England Hospital Collection, Smith College, Northampton.

3. In 1950, Richard Shryock first suggested the importance of feminism to nineteenth-century women doctors, arguing that the nineteenth-century women's movement was

crucial to women's successful entrance into medicine. Richard Harrison Shryock, "Women in American Medicine," *Journal of the American Medical Women's Association* 5 (September 1950), reprinted in Richard Harrison Shryock, *Medicine in America: Historical Essays* (Baltimore, 1966), 177-199. John B. Blake examined several of the women who became doctors in the years before the Civil War in "Women and Medicine in Ante-Bellum America," *Bulletin of the History of Medicine* 39 (1965), 99-123. Little else appeared on the topic until Mary Roth Walsh's *"Doctors Wanted: No Women Need Apply": Sexual Barrier in the Medical Profession 1835-1975* (New Haven, 1977). Walsh's book represents the first full-length study of women's entrance into American medicine. Other historians have examined women doctors primarily as professionals and not exclusively within the political sphere. See Regina Markell Morantz and Sue Zschoch, "Professionalism, Feminism, and Gender Roles: A Comparative Study of Nineteenth Century Medical Therapeutics," *The Journal of American History* 67 (1980), 569-588; Regina Markell Morantz, "The 'Connecting Link': The Case for the Woman Doctor in 19th-Century America," in Judith Walzer Leavitt and Ronald L. Numbers, eds., *Sickness and Health in America: Readings in the History of Medicine and Public Health* (Madison, 1978), pp. 117-128; and Regina Markell Morantz, "The Lady and her Physician," in Mary Hartman and Lois W. Banner, eds., *Clio's Consciousness Raised: New Perspectives on the History of Women* (New York, 1974), pp. 38-53. See also Virginia G. Drachman, "Gynecological Instruments and Surgical Decisions at a Hospital in Late Nineteenth-Century America," *Journal of American Culture* 3(1980), 660-672.

4. Walsh, *"Doctors Wanted: No Women Need Apply"*, chapter three.

5. New England Hospital Annual Report, 1865, p. 12.

6. For a discussion of nineteenth-century medical education see William G. Rothstein, *American Physicians in the 19th-Century: From Sects to Science* (Baltimore, 1972), and Robert P. Hudson, "Abraham Flexner in Perspective: American Medical Education, 1865-1910," in Leavitt and Numbers, pp. 105-116.

7. New England Hospital Annual Report, 1875, p. 16.

8. Mary Putnam Jacobi, "Women in Medicine," in Annie Nathan Meyer, ed., *Woman's Work in America* (New York, 1891).

9. *Ibid.*, p. 191.

10. *Ibid.*, p. 200.

11. New England Hospital Annual Report, 1887, p. 44.

12. The first signs of problems were isolated events brought on by conflicts among the doctors in the hospital. One should not dismiss these conflicts lightly as the expression of normal tension between interns and doctors. Rather, later these specific conflicts began to fit together to reveal a more general pattern of dissatisfaction at the hospital. When taken together, they reveal that larger issues were involved.

13. Marie Zakrzewska, Address to Students, April 1, 1876 in New England Hospital Collection, Smith College, Northampton.

14. *Ibid.*

15. New England Hospital Annual Report, 1887, p. 17.

16. Zakrzewska, Address to Students, April 1, 1876.

17. Marie Zakrzewska, Address to Students, March 30, 1883 in New England Hospital Collection, Smith College, Northampton.

18. *Ibid.*

19. Interns' complaints, October 1891, New England Hospital Collection, Smith College, Northampton.

20. *Ibid.*

21. *Ibid.*

22. Marie Zakrzewska, Response to Interns, October 30, 1891 in New England Hospital Collection, Smith College, Northampton.

23. *Ibid.*

24. Bertha Van Hoosen, Letter of Resignation, November 1891 in New England Hospital Collection, Smith College, Northampton.

25. Revision of Hospital Management, October 2, 1891 in New England Hospital Collection, Smith College, Northampton.

26. Letter of recommendation from Albert V. Prescott to Dr. Sarah Palmer, April 13, 1893 in New England Hospital Collection, Smith College, Northampton.

27. Alice Hamilton to Agnes Hamilton, August 13, 1893 in Schlesinger Library, Radcliffe College, Cambridge, Ma.

28. Alice Hamilton to Agnes Hamilton, October 2, 1893 in Schlesinger Library, Radcliffe College, Cambridge, Ma.

29. Alice Hamilton to Agnes Hamilton, October 26, 1893 in Schlesinger Library, Radcliffe College, Cambridge, Ma.

30. Minutes of Board of Physicians Meetings, Volume III, May 4, 1896.

31. All information on interns calculated from applications for internships at the New England Hospital, New England Hospital Collection, Smith College, Northampton.

32. Mary Findlater application for internship to New England Hospital, New England Hospital Collection, Smith College, Northampton.

33. EliZaketh McMaster application for internship to New England Hospital, New England Hospital Collection, Smith College, Northampton.

34. Mary Hobart to Board of Physicians, November 1, 1895 in New England Hospital Collection. See also: Francis Kyle to Zakrzewska, April 15, 1890 for alarmed response of a professor at University of Michigan Medical College to practices at New England Hospital; letter from Delia Rice to Zakrzewska, January 6, 1894 expressing concern about applying to the hospital as an intern because of negative rumors about the hospital, both in New England Hospital Collection, Smith College, Northampton.

35. Harriet Lathrop to Emily Pope, May 31, 1900 in New England Hospital Collection, Smith College, Northampton.

36. Marie Zakrzewska to Pauline Pope, October 28, 1901 in New England Hospital Collection, Smith College, Northampton.

37. Interns' request, December 20, 1910 in New England Hospital Collection, Smith College, Northampton.

38. See Karen J. Blair, "The Club Woman as Feminist: The Woman's Culture Club Movement in the United States, 1868-1914," unpublished Ph.D. Dissertation, SUNY Buffalo, 1975. Also Mary Jo Buhle, "The Nineteenth-Century Woman's Movement: Perspectives on Woman's Labor in Industrializing America," presented at the Bunting Institute, February 1979.

39. See Walsh, *"Doctors Wanted: No Women Need Apply,"* particularly chapter six.

40. Marie Zakrzewska to students, March 30, 1883 in New England Hospital Collection, Smith College, Northampton.

THE TENDER TECHNICIANS: THE FEMINIZATION OF PUBLIC LIBRARIANSHIP, 1876-1905

DEE GARRISON

"The law of nature destines and qualifies the female sex for the bearing and nurture of the children of our race and for the custody of the homes of the world," stated the Wisconsin Supreme Court in 1875 when ruling that women could not be admitted to their bar. The judges conceded that the "cruel chances of life" might leave some women free of the sacred female duties. "These may need employment, and should be welcome to any not derogatory to their sex and its proprieties."[1] Most Americans of the time would have agreed with the Court that only financial need justified a woman's going to work and that only limited jobs should be opened to her. But in the decades before and after 1900 Americans became the unobservant participants in a social revolution, as profound changes took place in the attitudes toward women and their work. The American public libraries played an important role in the revolution, for the feminization of librarianship proceeded rapidly. In 1852 the first woman clerk was hired at the Boston Public Library;[2] by 1878 fully two thirds of the library workers there were female.[3] In 1910 78½ percent of library workers in the United States were women; only teaching surpassed librarianship as the most feminized "profession."[4]

Educated women, while meeting resistance in other more established professions, flooded into library work during the last quarter of the nineteenth century for a variety of reasons. Librarianship was a new and fast-growing field in need of low-paid but educated recruits. With a plentiful number of library jobs available, male librarians offered no opposition to the proliferation of women library workers, partly because women agreed that library work

Professor Garrison is a member of the history department of Livingston College, Rutgers University.

matched presumed feminine limitations. Librarianship was quickly adjusted to fit the narrowly circumscribed sphere of women's activities, for it appeared similar to the work of the home, functioned as cultural activity, required no great skill or physical strength and brought little contact with the rougher portions of society. For all these reasons, Melvil Dewey could predict, when writing at the turn of the century of the ideal librarian, that "most of the men who achieve this greatness will be women."[5] The feminization of librarianship, however, had unexpected long-range results. The prevalence of women would profoundly affect the process of professionalization and the type of service the library would provide. The nature of library work itself, one of the few sources of economic opportunity open to educated women in the late nineteenth century, would serve to perpetuate the low status of women in American society. Above all, female dominance of librarianship did much to shape the inferior and precarious status of the public library as an important cultural resource and to cause it to evolve into a marginal kind of public amusement service.[6]

The rapid growth of libraries in size, number and complexity between 1876 and 1905 was an important cause of the feminization of librarianship. The monumental 1876 "Report on Public Libraries" listed 3,682 libraries containing a little over twelve million volumes.[7] Total yearly additions of library books in the nation passed the one million mark in 1876.[8] A conservative estimate raised the total to forty million volumes held in 8,000 libraries in 1900.[9] Because a heavy demand for trained librarians coincided with other national developments, particularly the advance of women's education and the increase of women workers, many women found employment in library service. Very probably, women would have flocked into any new field into which their entry was not opposed. Because male librarians heartily welcomed women into library service, the eventual feminization of the library staff was assured.

The low cost of hiring women was perhaps the most important reason that male library leaders welcomed women assistants. The public library, supported by taxes and voluntary donations, was by necessity obliged to practice thrifty housekeeping. Trustees and taxpayers expected that the major portion of the yearly income would be invested in books. Because women were notoriously low-paid, the annual cost of library administration could be appreciably lowered by the introduction of women workers. Frederick Perkins, in an 1876 article entitled "How to Make Town Libraries Successful," recommended that "women should be employed as librarians and assistants as far as possible." Perkins was no crusader for women's equality; he only pointed out that the hiring of women, along with the use of "mechanical appliances...better arrangements of book rooms and other sufficient contrivances of that American ingenuity," would lessen the excessive cost of library administration.[10] Justin Winsor, speaking at the 1877 conference of British and American librarians in London, emphasized the importance of women workers in American libraries.

> In American libraries we set a high value on women's work. They soften our atmosphere, they lighten our labor, they are equal to our work, and for the money they cost—if we must gauge such labor by such rules—they are infinitely better than equivalent salaries will produce of the other sex....We can command our pick of the educated young women whom our Colleges for Women are launching forth upon our country—women with a fair knowledge of Latin and Greek, a good knowledge of French and German, a deducible knowledge of Spanish and Italian, and who do not stagger at the acquisition of even Russian, if the requirements of the catalogue service make that demand. It is to these Colleges for Women, like Vassar and Wellesley, that the American library-system looks confidently for the future.[11]

The limited opportunities open to educated women for paid employment served to bring larger numbers of competent women than competent men into low-paid library jobs during this period. Of the eight leading women librarians of the time, four had some college and the rest at least a high school education.[12] In view of the constant references made in library literature to the necessity of finding workers with an educated knowledge of books, a high intelligence and preferably a familiarity with a few languages, it is safe to assume that most women entering library service at this time were either self- or formally-educated to at least the extent expected of an urban schoolteacher.[13] The same economic factors were at work in librarianship and teaching, for educated women, with few other job opportunities flocked into both fields, with a depressing effect on wages. Library work required similar qualifications to teaching and was little worse in pay. In librarianship women could exercise their presumed special feminine talents and could, besides, remain isolated, in a way teachers could not, from the rough workaday world.[14]

The feminine movement into new occupations like nursing and teaching or clerical and industrial employment began in the middle of the nineteenth century when both the right to individuality and the myth of women's sphere held extremely important places in American popular thought. Two such conflicting ideas could not exist together unless individualism was reserved for man alone. Thus man took the world and all its activities as his "sphere," while confining women to domesticity and the guardianship of culture. Women were just as guilty of inconsistency. The gradual expansion of women's claim to the right of individual choice was on the whole unaccompanied by any feminine calls for radical social change. Instead, as each new job became filled by women, charming theories were developed by both sexes to explain why the feminine mind and nature were innately suited to the new occupation. Thus it was decided that teaching was much like mothering; women, it was said, were uniquely able to guide children into piety, purity and knowledge. Women were cleared to work as writers, musicians and artists because of their inherent sensitivity, elevated moralism and love of beauty. Women doctors and nurses were intuitively kind, sympathetic and delicate of touch. The woman social worker expressed inborn feminine qualities of love, charity and idealism. Factory, business and clerical work fit the feminine nature, for women were naturally industrious, sober and nimble-fingered, as well as better able than men to endure the boredom of detailed or repetitive tasks. These various expansions of the work of women served to modify the concept of woman's proper sphere but the process was gradual and involved no radical threat to traditional social ideals.[15] Yet each expansion led to others, with a snowballing effect, so that within a hundred years the limits of woman's claim to individual freedom of choice had undergone considerable and drastic change.

This redefinition of woman's sphere, always in accord with the characteristics presumed to be innately feminine, also came to encompass librarianship as one of the proper fields open to women. The course to library work had already been cleared for women because libraries held books and books denoted Culture with a capital "C". By the late nineteenth century, woman's sphere decidedly included the guardianship and enjoyment of culture. It was believed that through their refining and spiritualizing influence women could exalt all human society. It would be almost impossible to overemphasize the Victorian conviction that men were physically tamed and morally elevated by the sway of the gentle female. Moreover, by the 1870s American popular literature was consciously designed to please feminine readers. Therefore the advent of women to library work required little stretching of the popular ideal regarding the female, for "books...should be treated by reverent hands... should be given out as a priest dispenses the sacrament, and the next step to this ideal ministry is to have them issued by women."[16]

> The librarian...is becoming...the guardian of the thought-life of the people....The library, in its influence, is whatever the librarian makes it; it seems destined to become an all-pervading force...moulding [sic] public opinion, educating to all of the higher possibilities of human thought and action; to become a means for enriching, beautifying, and making fruitful the barren places in human life....Librarians have an important part to play in the history of civilization and in the conservation of the race.[17]

Women in librarianship were merely making more visible the female position as the guardian of cultural ideals.

Just as the concept of "culture" had been generally accorded to the care of women, so the functions of providing education and of overseeing charity to the poor had been deemed suitable fields for female concern. The provision of education and moral uplift to the masses was a prominent mission of the early library; thus, women library workers, with their presumed inborn talents and temperaments, seemed uniquely suited to the new field of librarianship. The popular library brought the librarian "in hourly contact with her constituency of readers, advising, helping and elevating their lives and exerting a far-reaching influence for good not to be exceeded in any profession open to women...."[18] The great mass of men in all fields worked to secure prestige or a higher income but the librarian worked "with as distinct a consecration as a minister or missionary....The selfish considerations of reputation or personal comfort, or emolument are all secondary."[19] For Melvil Dewey, library work offered more opportunity to the altruistic than did the work of the clergyman or teacher. The library would reach those who never entered a church or who did not go to school.

> Is it not true that the ideal librarian fills a pulpit where there is service every day

> during all the waking hours, with a large proportion of the community frequently in the congregation?...[The library is] a school in which the classes graduate only at death?[20]

Dewey encouraged educated women who might ordinarily have become teachers to consider a library career. Physically the library was less exacting than the school. The librarian avoided the "nervous strain and the wear and tear of the classroom" and escaped the bad air of crowded rooms. Dewey could think of no other profession "that is so free from annoying surroundings or that has so much in the character of the work and of the people which is grateful to a refined and educated woman."[21] The genteel nature of library work would compensate, he believed, for the regretable fact that women librarians normally received half the pay of men librarians and often received even less than urban teachers did.

As women became dominant in library work, library literature began to reflect the concept that the ideal library would offer the warmth and hospitality of the home to its patrons. To nineteenth-century man, of course, woman's sphere was, above all, the home, for which she was originally intended and which she was so exactly fitted to adorn and bless. Not surprisingly, it was anticipated that the feminine influence of the librarian would soften the library atmosphere. Like a visitor to a home, the reader must be welcomed; he must be given kind and individual attention; he must be treated with tact and gentle manners. Not the cold impersonality of the business world should pervade but rather the warmth of the well-ordered home, presided over by a gracious and helpful librarian. Counsel like the following is pervasive in the library literature of the 1870s and 1880s:

> Something may be said of the desirableness of making the library wear a pleasant and inviting look. The reading-room offers perhaps the best opportunity for this. A reading-room lately seen has a bright carpet on the floor, low tables, and a few rocking-chairs scattered about; a cheerful, open fire on dull days, attractive pictures on the walls, and one can imagine a lady librarian filling the windows with plants. Such a room is a welcome in itself, and bids one come again.[22]

It was this ideal of the librarian as the accommodating and heartily receptive hostess which Miss Theresa West had in mind when she said that "the personal equation of the librarian may easily become the exponent of the power of the library."[23] On the surface the likening of the library to the home was but one of several devices which library leaders used to entice the reluctant patrón and to make the library into a more "popular" institution. Operating more subtly, underground, were the effects of the prevalence of women in library work. Just as the school had been likened to the home, in order to make more acceptable the dominance of women teachers, so did the library readjust to reflect the widening of woman's sphere. The position of librarian required a certain "gracious hospitality" and here "women as a class far surpass men." Women would not feel humiliated by serving, by playing in the library the part they played in the home: "Here it is said her 'broad sympathies, her quick wits, her intuitions and her delight in self-sacrifice' give her an undoubted advantage."[24]

Women workers were also preferred, it was generally conceded, for the tedious job of cataloging. Again, it was the unique nature of woman which qualified her for this work because of her "greater conscientiousness, patience and accuracy in details."[25] Because women had greater ability than men to bear pain with fortitude, women had stored great reserves of patience and thus could perform the most monotonous tasks without boredom. All the routine, repetitive work of the library was quite generally agreed to fall within the scope of women's special talents.[26]

It is evident that the role of domesticity imposed upon women also worked to create the emphasis which was early given to library service for children.[27] By 1900 the children's library had "passed its first stage—all enthusiasm and effervescence—"[28] and had moved into its current position as a major department of the public library. From the beginning, the supervision of children's reading was given over to the woman librarian.

> The work for children in our libraries, like many other of our best things, is woman's work. To them it owes its inception, its progress and present measure of success, and its future is in their hands.[29]

Here in the children's sections was woman's undisputed domain. And here the librarians waxed eloquent over the attributes and accomplishments of the reigning queen. Work with children is "the most important, and in its results, the most satisfactory of all library work," reported Minerva Sanders. "As our personal influence is exerted, in just such a proportion will our communities be uplifted."[30] Another librarian commented that woman, alone, has "that kind of sympathetic second-sight that shall enable her to read what is often obscure in the mind of the child."[31] Edwin M. Fairchild summed up the prevailing attitude toward woman's natural role in library work—not as a bluestocking, but as a traditionally defined female with intrinsic traits.

The chief source of enthusiasm for the children's library is the librarian....[She] needs to be...a woman grown, herself the realization of the educational ideal, which by the way is not the smart, but the intelligent, great souled woman....[32]

Originally conceived and theoretically maintained as an educational institution, the children's department was, in fact, even by the turn of the century, becoming mainly a provider of recreational reading for pre-adolescents.[33] Misgivings over the nature of library service to children were rarely expressed, however. Most often, sentimentality over-ruled any attempt at a realistic assessment of the work being accomplished in the children's department. The romantic air of enthusiastic tenderness so prominent in any discussion of children in the library is in sharp contrast to the more normal tendency of librarians to indulge in searching self-criticism in every other phase of library work. This incongruity becomes more understandable when it is remembered that the children's section of the library was created and shaped by women librarians. Here, as in no other area, library women were free to express, unchallenged, their self-image. Because their activities did not exceed the Victorian stereotype of the female, their endeavors remained substantially unquestioned and unexamined by male library leaders.

Despite the respect paid them, however, women soon learned that they were seldom paid the same as men who were doing the same work; and that even though women easily dominated the library field in numbers, male librarians headed the largest and most prestigious libraries. In the library literature of this period there is hardly a hint that the hundreds of women librarians across the country were seriously disturbed at the inequality which was freely admitted to be their lot.[34] Rather, one finds feminine pride repeatedly expressed over the prevalence of women in the library, at the increased participation of women in the national association and of America's flattering contrast with England where women were meeting resistance in library work. A situation which really amounted to the exploitation of women in the American library was publicly touted as a liberal concession to women in America and was contrasted with women's supposedly less favorable position in the Old World to indicate the superiority of American freedoms and the liberal attitudes of the male leaders of the American library movement.[35]

The twelve women present at the 1876 American Library Association meeting set the submissive tone which few women librarians were to challenge. They were "the best of listeners, and occasionally would modestly take advantage of gallant voices, like Mr. Smith's, to ask a question or offer a suggestion."[36] The next year Miss Caroline Hewins had the distinction of being the first woman to speak up at the national convention; she asked if the dog tax were used to support a library outside Massachusetts. Perhaps this small temerity earned her the reputation of fearless spokesman for it was Miss Hewins who presented in 1891 the first general discussion of the "woman question" in the *Library Journal.*

Library work was difficult for women, Miss Hewins said. For a salary varying from three to nine hundred dollars annually, a library assistant must write steadily six or seven hours a day, know half a dozen languages, be absolutely accurate in copying, "understand the relation of all arts and sciences to each other and must have...a minute acquaintance with geography, history, art and literature." A successful woman librarian would work eight to ten hours a day and "those who are paid the highest salaries give up all their evenings." Miss Hewins added that "librarians and library attendants sometimes break down from overwork." With unconscious humor, the intrepid Miss Hewins had a remedy for impending exhaustion—"plenty of sleep and nourishing food, with a walk of two or three miles every day."[37] Presumably this stroll was to be taken in the hours of early dawn or late evening.

The year after Miss Hewin's article appeared there was an abortive attempt to establish a Woman's Section in the national organization. The sole meeting of women in 1892 was a tame affair, with only the barest expression of stifled rage at women's low wages and subordinate position. An official statement secured from 25 of the nation's most prominent libraries revealed that "women rarely receive the same pay for the same work as men."[38] But no matter. "The palm of honor and of opportunity waits for her who shall join a genius for organization...to the power of a broad, rich, catholic and sympathetic womanhood." In "the long run" the woman librarian "will win appreciation."[39]

The Woman's Section of the American Library Association did not meet again, although the 1892 session appointed a committee to report at the next conference in Chicago. There was no formal explanation of the failure of this committee to report but it may be that a protest movement, sparked by Miss Telsie Kelso of the Los Angeles Public Library, would explain the demise of the Woman's Section. Miss Kelso stoutly disapproved of any deference paid to women as a group.[40]

> In the...14th American Library Association Conference I note that there is a movement toward establishing a woman's section....For years woman has worked, talked, and accepted all sorts of compromises to prove her fitness to hold the position of librarian, and to demonstrate that sex should have no weight where ability is equal. In all these years the accomplishment is seen in the table of wages paid women librarians in comparison with those paid men....For women to now come forward with the argument that a woman librarian has a point of view and such limitation that they must be discussed apart from the open court of library affairs is a serious mistake....The use of the name of the association should not be permitted in such a direction....[41]

Such a truculent defense of women's equality, however, was not in accord with the expressed attitude of most women librarians. They accepted with little protest the traditional view of women as inherently limited in the working world. Certainly women library leaders had no utopian plans for woman's sexual and social emancipation. Of course they wanted to do things not customary for women in the past, such as managing a library with pay equal to men's, but this they considered as no more than a slight modification of the traditional ideal, and certainly not as a basic change in the male-structured view of women. As late as 1896 the influential Mary Ahern, editor of ***Public Libraries***, warbled that "no woman can hope to reach any standing...in the library profession...who does not bring to it that love which suffereth long and is kind, is not puffed up, does not behave itself unseemly, vaunteth not itself, thinketh no evil...." Every woman owes it to herself to live up to the ideals expected of womanhood; "no woman striving ever so hard to play the part of a man has ever succeeded in doing more than to give just cause for a blush to the rest of her kind." Every woman in library work should seek not "to detract from the reputation so hardly earned of being faithful conscientious workers."[42]

In 1904 one hundred representative libraries were asked by the American Library Association to comment on the limitations of women library workers.[43] Economic reasons were most often cited to explain women's low pay scale; women who did not demand as much salary as men were in abundant supply. Women were generally acknowledged to be hampered by their "delicate physique" and "inability to endure continued mental strain." Mary Cutler (now Mrs. Fairchild), an important woman library leader, commented that she could not see how women's physical disability could ever be eliminated. Whether women would ever hold high positions in the library "may remain perhaps an open question." While having decided advantage wherever "the human element predominates," Mrs. Fairchild went on, women too frequently lacked the will to discharge executive power and most trustees "assume that a woman would not have business capacity." Reviewing all the facts she concluded that "on account of natural sex limitations, and also actual weakness in the work of many women as well as because of conservatism and prejudice, many gates are at present closed to women."[44]

Recognition of women's limited potential was probably justified when applied to women library workers in general. The average woman accepted the current ideal which taught that her success in life would be judged by her marriage and not by her work. With this concept central in her mind, she was being wholly practical if she spent much of her time in conforming to the popular ideal of "femininity" rather than in thinking about business achievement. Women librarians who had given up hope for marriage were also less apt to strain for advancement since they realized that society would discourage them from a display of "male" aggressiveness. Of course, some talented and energetic women librarians did realize their ambitions to a considerable degree, primarily because these ambitions were exceedingly modest and did not threaten the prevailing notion of woman's place.

Perhaps the most striking point to be made about women's adaptation to library work is the extent to which they supported the traditional feminine concern for altruism and high-mindedness. They invoked the Victorian definition of proper female endeavors at the same time as they were widening it. Librarianship, when defined as self-denying and spiritual, offered women the opportunity not to change their status but to affirm it, not to fulfill their self but their self-image. When women's advance became justified in terms of the good they could do, rather than of their human right to equality, it became conditional in nature.

Even if some librarians did not subscribe to the concept of woman's sphere, with all its connotations, they had to appear to do so in order not to offend the many who did. Not to surrender to the Victorian mystique was to run the terrible risk of being judged deviants in their society, of being judged abnormal because of a challenge to well-established norms. Perhaps, too, both men and women librarians wished to avoid any real discussion of the injustice which library women suffered because of the eagerness of all library leaders to establish librarianship as a profession. To publicize the prevalence of women in the library or to increase their influence could only harm the drive toward professionalization. A woman-dominated profession was obviously a contradiction in terms.

Librarians have been absorbed to a marked degree, from 1876 to the present, with the question of professionalization. Melvil Dewey and other early library leaders made repeated claims to professional status.[45] Not until the Williamson report of 1923 was there open and general admission among librarians that significant elements common to professional work were lacking in librarianship.[46] In the effort to win professional standing, librarians have concentrated upon improvements in their system of library schools. The education of librarians, it has been commonly lamented, includes too much detail and attention to method, only producing good craftsmen and technicians. True professional education, on the other hand, should present a systematic body of theory and a scientifically-based abstract knowledge upon which the profession rests.

Throughout the debate among librarians as to how best to receive recognition as professionals, the dominant influence of women on librarianship has been strangely shunted, buried under a multitude of words concerning recruitment, accreditation, curriculums and other factors thought to be inhibiting professionalization. There has been no systematic consideration given to the way in which feminization has shaped, in a most significant way, the development of library education and the entire range of activities associated with the field of library work. Carl White, who has written the best study of library education as it developed before 1923, gives thoughtful and scholarly attention to the social and educational setting in which library education began and relates it brilliantly to the traditions which remain today from that early inheritance.[47]

Yet White curiously refrains from considering the effect of the prevalence of women workers upon the shaping of those traditions. Only sociologist Peter Rossi, in a symposium of 1961, has tackled the existence of feminization head-on and applied it to library development. Rossi commented upon the puzzling absence of any real consideration being given to the influence of women upon library history.

> I kept expecting...some comment on *the major reason* [italics mine] why librarians find it difficult to achieve a substantial spot in the array of professions. Any occupation in which there is a high proportion of women suffers a special disability.... Women depress the status of an occupation because theirs is a depressed status in the society as a whole, and those occupations in which women are found in large numbers are not seen as seriously competing with other professions for personnel and resources. It is for this reason that professions such as education, social work, and librarianship develop within themselves a division of labor and accompanying status along sex lines.[48]

Rossi added that the status of librarianship could be raised by a radical division of labor such as that accomplished in medicine where nursing was done by females and doctoring by males. This sharp differentiation between male and female librarians, however, runs counter to the central development of library history. Once formed, the solutions—both planned and accidental—found workable by nineteenth-century librarians closed the possibility of starting over with a clean slate. For this reason it is important that librarians assess the basic meaning of feminization and give precise attention to their early history, for the dominance of women is surely the prevailing factor in library education, the image of librarianship and the professionalization of the field. Women's role in the library was established in the last 25 years of the nineteenth century. An examination of the principal factors in this period of library history should include an emphasis upon the underrated effect of women students in library schools and its relationship to the constant search of librarians for professional standing.

The process of professionalization has received increasing attention by sociologists and historians in recent years.[49] Although it is generally agreed that professions have certain characteristics differentiating them from other occupations, there is no agreement on the precise nature of those characteristics. The conceptual model for this study will be devised so as to examine the professionalization of librarianship under three headings: service orientation, knowledge base and degree of autonomy. These components of professionalization will be examined, first as they apply to nineteenth-century librarianship in general and then as they relate to the feminization of the field.

The service orientation of librarianship exhibits most of the qualities expected in the ethical code of a profession. The professional, in contrast to the non-professional, is primarily concerned with his client's needs or with the needs of society, rather than with his own material interests. A profession also has direct relevance to basic social values on which there is widespread consensus. In law and medicine, for example, the services provided by the professional are justice and health. In librarianship the basic social value served is education. Early library leaders were firm in their commitment of the library to educational purposes; they definitely relegated the recreational function of the library to a secondary place. William Poole's comment typifies this view.

> Our public libraries and our public schools are supported by the same constituencies, by the same methods of taxation, and for the same purpose; and that purpose is the education of the people....If public libraries shall, in my day, cease to be educational institutions, and serve only to amuse the people and help them to while away an idle hour, I shall favor their abolition.[50]

The librarian also showed a professional acceptance of the ideal of sacrificial service to the community. Librarianship was deemed to be second only to the ministry in its aims and standards.[51] Additionally, librarians had the sense of community which is common to professionals. They felt an affinity with other librarians in a way which the plumber, for example, does not feel for all other plumbers. Librarians, like the ministers with whom they liked to compare themselves, sensed an identity as a group, sharing a common destiny, values and norms.

The service and collectivity orientation of librarianship, then, conform to certain important characteristics of a profession. The characteristics used in the definition of the term "profession" are variables, forming a continuum along which an occupation's rise to professionalism can be measured. Although librarianship certainly showed a number of professional traits, significant elements of a truly professional code of service were missing. Specifically lacking in the librarian's professional service code are a sense of commitment, a drive to lead rather than to serve and a clear-cut conception of professional rights and responsibilities. The feminization of library work is a major cause of these deficiencies.

The concentration of women served to lower a professional work-commitment within librarianship. The culture defined woman's responsibility to the home as her primary one and this definition was all-pervasive before 1900. It was perfectly understandable, for example, that Theresa West would in 1896 leave her job as the leading woman librarian heading an important library when she married Henry Elmendorf. Indeed, it would have been shocking if she had chosen otherwise. Nineteenth-century complaints of high employee turnover and of low commitment to excellence among library workers are directly related to the place which women accepted in society. For the library assistant of the nineteenth century to become highly work-committed would require from her an atypical value orientation.[52] The majority of librarians were no doubt eager to marry and to leave library work. Of the eight women leaders selected for this study, five were unmarried and one was a widow. Of the two who married, late in life, both continued to work in the library field, although not as head librarians. All eight of these women were highly educated by the standards of their time. In each case, professional success, high status, extensive training and spinsterhood served to increase their vocational commitment. Despite the positive work commitments demonstrated by these women leaders, it remains generally true that within the field of librarianship, from 1876 to the present, the dominance of women significantly lessened a trend toward professional, life-long commitment to the field of library service.[53]

In established professions the practitioner assumes the responsibility for deciding what is best for his client. Whether or not the client agrees with him is theoretically not a factor in the professional's decision. Thus in the medical field, the doctor does not give the patient whatever treatment he requests, but instead prescribes the treatment which, for professional reasons, the doctor thinks is correct. In contrast to this professional attitude, librarians tended to "serve" the reader, rather than to help him. They felt a strong obligation to meet the needs of the public and were self-consciously sensitive to requests and complaints of the client.[54] This is partly a result of the tax-supported nature of the library and of its early efforts to attract a large public following. But this passive, inoffensive and non-assertive "service" provided by the librarian is also a natural acting-out of the docile behavioral role which females assumed in the culture.[55]

Theoretically the nineteenth-century library could have developed a less demand-oriented code of service. John Dana, Melvil Dewey, William Fletcher and William Poole often urged the librarian to lead his community, to educate the reader and the public. These men strongly felt that the librarian's role was to teach the standards that the public *should* want, not merely to provide access to what the public *did* want. Dewey argued that it was unwise "to give sharp tools or powerful weapons to the masses without some assurance of how they are to be used."[56] The public library, said William Fletcher,

> ...has too often been regarded somewhat as a public club, a purely democratic association of the people for mutual mental improvement or recreation....The public library is an educational and moral power to be wielded with a full sense of its mighty possibilities and the corresponding danger of their perversion.[57]

The assumption of a definitive intellectual leadership, however, did not come to characterize the public librarian. Modern librarians have laid the blame for their general passivity and inferior status upon various factors: the lack of a scientifically-based abstract body of knowledge; the public's lack of differentiation between the "professional" librarian and the library clerk and the inherently weak position of the librarian as implementor rather than creator of intellectual and cultural advance. Rarely given its due as a determinant is the overwhelming presence of women in librarianship. The negative traits for which librarians indict themselves—excessive cautiousness, avoidance of controversy, timidity, a weak orientation toward autonomy, little business sence, tractability, over compliance, service to the point of self-sacrifice and willingness to submit to subordination by trustees and public—are predominantly "feminine" traits.[58] Dana and others who sought to give librarianship a position of community leadership and intellectual authority were vastly outnumbered by the thousands of women who were shaping library development across the country. There is no evidence to indicate that these women opposed society's views of woman's nature and function. The traditional ideals of feminine behavior held by women librarians and the reading public had a profound impact upon the development of the public librarian's non-assertive, non-professional code of service.

The second component of library professionalization—the body of knowledge—does not contain as many professional attributes as does the service ideal of librarians. Professional knowledge is generally defined as that knowledge which (1) is organized in abstract principles, (2) is continually revised or created by the professionals, (3) places strong emphasis upon the ability to manipulate ideas and symbols rather than physical objects and (4) requires a long enough term of specialized training so that the society views the professional as possessing skills which are beyond the reach of the untrained layman. William Goode has commented,

> Librarians themselves have found it extremely difficult to define their professional role and the knowledge on which it rests. To use a phrase like 'specialization in generalism' is insufficient....The repeated calls which librarians have made for a 'philosophy of librarianship' essentially expresses the need to define what *is* the intellectual problem of the occupation.[59]

In short, the librarian does not know who he is. Is he a library mechanic, having to do with such clerical, technical work as cataloguing, shelf arrangement and signing-in-and-out management? Or is he an expert guide, with considerable training in knowledge retrieval and organization?

One point, at least, seems clear. Despite the expressed desire of librarians to become admired professionals whose expertise would make available the world of knowledge, the system of library education which developed in the nineteenth century was a form of schooling, in origin and by design, which merely produced good craftsmen, trained to perform jobs which were chiefly mechanical in nature. This relatively low level of training, which made a small intellectual demand on the student, did not evolve entirely because of the feminine majority in library schools. The rate of expansion in both size and numbers of libraries was the first influence. The demand for a rapid production of library workers encouraged library schools to grind out graduates after only a brief course of instruction in the fundamental skills of library economy. The older system of in-service training could not produce enough self-made librarians to satisfy the manpower needs of the country. Carl White has outlined the second great influence on library education—the nineteenth-century development of technical education to fill the vacuum created by the breakdown of the classical curriculum and the medieval system of apprenticeship.[60] Library leaders were aware that a concentrated practical training has been demonstrated in other fields to produce the same results as learning by doing, but in less time and more systematically. Thus, detailed instruction in technical routines became the solid core of library training. Library education was in no sense designed to cultivate intellectual leadership, to produce trained high-level administrators or to develop an abstract knowledge base for library science.

The predominance of women in library schools, on library-school faculties and in library work functioned as an unmentioned but inflexible framework into which "professional" education would have to be fitted. An emphasis upon the influence of women is not meant to downgrade the other elements which shaped library education or to deemphasize the other inherent weaknesses in the librarian's claim to professional status, nor is it meant to impose chauvinistic attitudes upon male library leaders. Nineteenth-century librarians, however, were men and women of their time, governed by traditional views of woman's role in society. They were faced with an unorthodox problem—how to devise "professional" training for young women. Their answer was caught between the upper and the nether millstones. The upper millstone was their hope that librarians would become indispensable educational leaders, with professional scope and value. The nether millstone was the reality of the library school student—a woman who most likely lacked scholarly ambitions or preparation, had no life-long vocational commitment and whose attitudes toward feminine sex roles led her to accept, and expect, administrative controls, low autonomy and subordination to clerical, routine tasks.[61]

No study of why library training developed as it did would be complete without a consideration of how it was influenced by the thought of Melvil Dewey. Dewey so molded library education that the whole period before 1923 is called the "Dewey period." Librarians, too, have their folk heroes; Dewey's whirlwind passage through library history is the source of much of librarianship's most colorful annals. The narrators who have given accounts of intimate contact with Dewey share a common characteristic—they are breathless, either with admiration or with rage.

Tall, powerfully built, astonishingly handsome, Melvil Dewey was priggishly devoted to the truth as he saw it. He had no use for the trivial frolics of life; wasted time was to him a moral issue. He even developed in his wife the habit of writing precise compilations of how each minute of the day had been spent. He was, above all, pragmatic, looking only for what was workable, then and there, to produce the desired results. Dewey has been called a "man-child," for his idealism, enthusiasm and impatience with any obstacle. Childish too was his simplistic assessment of the world and his mission in it. There is something maddeningly pretentious about a man who can decide, at 17, "to inaugurate a higher eduction for the masses,"[62] and who can write, at age 76, in the same shallow prose,

> As I look back over the long years, I can recall no one I ever intentionally wronged, or of whom I should, now, ask forgiveness....I have tried to do right, and so, if my race is run, I can go down into the last river serene, clear-eyed and unafraid.[63]

Yet burning zeal can carry one very far. Dewey's contributions to library development are unequaled by any one man and his personal courage and unflinching faith in his mission will long be admired. It was Dewey who initiated library school education and aggressively promoted his standards of technical training in library mechanics.

A predominant characteristic of Dewey's, and important for its relationship to library education development, is his inordinate fondness for women. His men friends were few; his women friends appear to have been numerous. All through his life he preferred the company of women to men. He worked with them, played with them and repeatedly got into trouble over them.

The trouble began as early as 1883 when Dewey hired six young women graduates of Wellesley to assist him in the organization of the Columbia University Library. At that time Columbia College was closed to women. Four years later Dewey again scandalized the campus by his insistence that women students be admitted to the first library school ever established. When the Trustees refused to allow Dewey classroom space because of the presence of women in the school, he furnished an unused storeroom on the campus and opened on schedule in defiance of the Trustees' orders. Shakily supported by President Frederick A. P. Barnard, the library school survived until 1889 when Dewey submitted his resignation to the Trustees shortly before his impending dismissal. During the time at Columbia, Dewey was sharply criticized for his open recruitment of women students and for his startling application form which included in it a request for height, weight, color of eyes, color of hair and a photograph.[64] Little tempered by time, Dewey's congenial intimacy with women set wagging in 1905 the "tongue of slander in sex matters," which even his eulogistic biographer concedes to have sent "stories sweeping like storms among the library leaders of the nation."[65] Dewey apparently had been guilty of some vaguely defined, but unorthodox, familiarities. The scandal prompted his wife to write scorching letters to the tale-bearers.

> Women who have keen intuitions know by instinct that they can trust Mr. Dewey implicitly. He has so many proofs of this and is so sure of his own self-control, that unconsciously his manner has grown more and more unconventional and familiar....It is most unwise for any man to pass the bounds of convention, and he has been frequently warned of the danger. Knowing that I was absolutely free from jealousy and understood him perfectly, he has doubtless gone farther than with a wife who felt it necessary to watch her husband....A wife who has lived more than a quarter of a century with her husband is surely the best judge as to whether he is pure minded....[66]

Dewey's compatibility with women gave him insight which was unusual among men of his time. This remarkable statement was delivered before the Association of Collegiate Alumnae in 1886:

> Would a father say to his son, 'My boy, your mother and I are lonely without you; you must stay at home, go out to afternoon teas with us, and keep us company in the big, empty house. I have enough for us all, so there is no need of your bothering your head about supporting yourself.' Would he expect his son to be happy under such circumstances? Why, then, his daughter?[67]

Dewey had sincere respect for the intellect of women and successfully contended that Mary Salome Cutler should be chairman of the library exhibit committee for the World's Columbian Exposition of 1893 because she was the most highly qualified candidate. He has often been praised because his defense of women's capabilities led him at times to suffer real personal sacrifice, as at Columbia. Any admiration for his support of women's rights, however, must be tempered by a recognition that Dewey had an unusually strong personal desire for feminine company and an equally strong indifference to the presence of men. Indeed, his role as champion of women is a complex and intriguing one, for beneath it lies a grating note of paternalism. He did not call on women to assert themselves but instead set himself up as their valiant spokesman.

Dewey, with a progressive (as well as erotic) affinity for women, was obviously deflected by his sexist attitudes from his progressive design for a strong, highly intellectual new profession. The library school curriculum which Dewey devised at Columbia and later continued at the New York State Library School ruled out any "attempt to give general culture or to make up deficiencies of earlier education." Dewey, in a characteristically pragmatic decision, would reconcile the library needs of the country with the status of women in society by concentrating upon schooling which would teach the technical skills necessary to perform work on the lower rungs of the library ladder. The American Library Association's committee on the proposed library school at Columbia remarked that those who came to the school would probably wish to become administrators. Dewey quickly corrected them; the committee was told that "the plans all contemplate special facilities and inducements for cataloguers and assistants who do not expect or desire the first place."[68]

By 1905 library education had crystallized around Dewey's core of practical instruction of routine detail to a predominantly female force. Yet even though librarians had established library education as a system of non-professional training for library mechanics, they continued to wonder at the "appalling misconception" in the public mind of their "professional" qualifications and to bemoan the fact that the public had made them "the poorest paid professionals in the world."[69] In that year the American Library Association found an answer of sorts to the dilemma—the great librarians, it was agreed, were born, not made.

> Pooles and Winsors are not and never will be wholly produced by library schools.... Such eminent examples are born librarians. The born librarian will not need a school to teach him principles of classification...he will evolve systems of classifications and cataloging, and methods of administration without ever going near a school....But there will never be many of him, and there will be thousands of library employees.[70]

It was for the low-level employee "that our schools are at present intended."[71] In the discussion that followed a consensus was reached by important library spokesmen like E. C. Richardson, Frederick M. Crunden, S. S. Green, Melvil Dewey and Herbert Putnam.[72] It was agreed that librarians of genius had no need of formal training. Unconsciously the national association had focused upon a central library truth. While females from the library schools became clerks and assistants and heads of small libraries, the most honored and well-paid librarians were men. The "best" librarians of the time were indeed not made, but born—born male.

The prevalence of women librarians also served to strengthen a non-professional bureaucratic system of control and low autonomy base for the library worker. In librarianship, as in teaching and social work, the dominance of women made more likely the development of an authoritative administrative structure with a stress on rules and generally established principles to control the activities of employees. In these feminized fields the highest success was secured through promotion to the administrative levels of the organization. This is in contrast to the pattern within established professions. In university teaching, for example, the productive practitioner is usually more honored within his profession than is the high level administrator of the university. Within librarianship and other feminized occupations, compliance to sex roles caused women to assume low levels of autonomy. Because sexist attitudes still prevail in the society, this basic situation has undergone little change since the nineteenth century.[73]

The changing image of librarianship graphically illustrates the many alterations which feminization brought to library work in the late nineteenth century. To call the public image of librarianship a stereotype does not make it an entirely erroneous concept for the popular image of librarians is a by-product of deeper social realities. In the 1870s the popular concept of the librarian was that of a pre-occupied man in black—a collector and preserver who was never so happy as when all the volumes were safely on the shelf. He was thought to be ineffectual, grim and "bookish." Library literature of this period reflects the attempt of librarians to replace the image of the "old" librarian with a picture of the "new" librarian.

> The mechanical librarian is no more a finality than the acquisitive and conservative librarian. He is succeeded by...a type who is not content with removing the obstacles to circulation that his predecessors have built up, but tries actually to foster it; who leans more to the missionary and pastoral side of librarianship; who relies more on personal intercourse; who goes in for reference lists and annotated and interesting bulletins; who does not so much try to make it easy for an interested public to help itself among the books as to create an interested public.[74]

The popular image had shifted by 1905 to portray the librarian as a woman. The public's mental image of the librarian was consistently deprecatory. Meek, mousy and colorless had been added to the original "old" male librarian's traits of eccentricity, frustration, grouchiness and introversion. The public librarian came to be stereotyped as an inhibited, single middle-aged woman.[75] Librarian Harold Lancour quipped that he had heard so much about this lady that he was "growing rather fond of the old girl."[76] Howard Mumford Jones, musing on the caricature of the librarian, suggested that the image was "partly the product of limited budgets, and in part the product of genteel tradition....This is not to say that all librarians are maiden ladies, but enough of them are to rank librarians with school teachers, Y. W. C. A. secretaries and social workers as persons less likely to go to night clubs than are receptionists or department-store buyers."[77] Unlike the librarians who had shaped public library standards, Jones understood well the chief reason why professionalization continued to elude library workers: the training of librarians should include more about the insides of books and "less technical lore about what to do with the book as an object in space."

The feminization of public librarianship did much to shape and stunt the development of an important American cultural institution. The socially designated sexual roles which women elected to act out had a major influence upon the development of the library's "homey" atmosphere and its staff of "helpful" non-assertive hostesses. Increasingly librarians are seeking to change the traditional role of the public librarian. The hope is to establish librarianship on a scientifically-oriented, abstract-knowledge base and to train the librarian as the indispensable expert in knowledge retrieval. The communication explosion has decidedly created a need for such a person; as the printed material grows to an unmanageable mass certainly someone, if not the public librarian, will move in to perform this vital function. However, until the librarian deals with the implications of feminization—with its varied inhibitory effects on intellectual excellence and leadership— progress toward professionalization will be limited. So long as sexist attitudes essentially govern the society, the basic situation which supported the service ideal and knowledge base of the nineteenth-century librarian seems unlikely to change.

FOOTNOTES

1. Cited in Robert W. Smuts, *Women and Work in America* (New York: Columbia University Press, 1959), 110.

2. [Charles Evans] (ed.), *The Athenaeum Centenary* (Boston: The Boston Athenaeum, 1907), 42. William Poole is generally credited with the hiring of the first woman librarian at the Boston Athenaeum in 1857. Poole's predecessor had barred women from the staff on the grounds that part of the library should be closed to impressionable female minds.

3. "The English Conference: Official Report of Proceedings," *Library Journal*, II (January-February, 1878), 280. The *Library Journal*, organ of the American Library Association, is hereafter cited as *LJ*.

4. Joseph Adna Hill, *Women in Gainful Occupations, 1870-1920*, Census Monograph, No. 9 (Washington: Government Printing Office, 1929), 42. Librarianship has been termed a "profession" by the U. S. Census and is used in that sense here. Hill cites 43 women library workers in 1870, 3,122 in 1900 and 8,621 in 1910. See Sharon B. Wells, "The Feminization of the American Library Profession, 1876-1923" (unpublished Master's thesis, Library School, University of Chicago, 1967) for statistics on the number of women employed in all American libraries, including public libraries, and the number of women enrolled in library schools. Miss Wells counts 191 men and 18 women managing collections of over ten thousand volumes in 1875.

5. Melvil Dewey, "The Ideal Librarian," *LJ*, XIX (January, 1899), 14.

6. This analysis of the feminization of public librarianship rests upon a larger study of the socio-economic backgrounds and social and literary ideals of 36 library leaders in the period from 1876 to 1900. The selected librarians represent the profession's most influential spokesmen and are primarily the heads of urban libraries in the east, although important western library leaders are also included in the group.

7. U. S. Bureau of Education, *Public Libraries in the United States of America: Their History, Condition and Management*, Special Report, Part I (Washington: Government Printing Office, 1876), iii. Hereafter cited as "1876 Report."

8. Carl M. White, *The Origins of the American Library School* (New York: The Scarecrow Press, Inc., 1961), 14.

9. R. R. Bowker, "Libraries and the Century in America: Retrospect and Prospect," *LJ*, XXVI (January, 1901), 5.

10. "1876 Report," 430. It is interesting to note that Perkins, who deserted his family to go West and to become the surly librarian at the San Francisco Public Library, left behind his young daughter, Charlotte Perkins Stetson Gilman, who later became a noted spokesman for women's rights.

11. "The English Conference...," *loc. cit.*

12. The eight women among the selected 36 library leaders are: Mary Bean, Eliza G. Browning, Mary Cutler, Theresa Elmendorf, Caroline Hewins, Hannah James, Mary Plummer and Minerva Sanders.

13. Because librarians, at least until about 1885, were so vocal in their contempt for the low intellectual abilities of teachers in general, I deduce that most women librarians were better educated or of higher social standing than were most women teachers.

14. Mabel Newcomer, *A Century of Higher Education for American Women* (New York: Harper and Brothers, 1959) offers a good overview of the employment opportunities open to educated women in the late nineteenth century. The economic causes which she cites of the predominance of women teachers can also be applied to the feminization of librarianship. In 1870 three fifths of all teachers were women. Also see, Robert E. Riegel, *American Women: A Story of Social Change* (Cranbury, New Jersey: Associated University Presses, Inc., 1970), 132-200.

15. Aileen S. Kraditor (ed.), *Up from the Pedestal* (Chicago: Quadrangle Books, 1968) and William L. O'Neill, *Everyone Was Brave* (Chicago: Quadrangle Books, 1969).

16. Richard le Gallienne, quoted in M. S. R. James, "Women Librarians," *LJ*, XVIII (May, 1893), 148.

17. Linda A. Eastman, "Aims and Personal Attitude in Library Work," *LJ*, XXII (October, 1897), 80.

18. "Library Employment vs. the Library Profession," *Library Notes*, I (June, 1886), 50.

19. *Ibid.*, 51.

20. Melvil Dewey, "Libraries as Related to the Educational Work of the State," *Library Notes*, III (June, 1888), 346.

21. Melvil Dewey, "The Attractions and Opportunities of Librarianship," *Library Notes*, I (June, 1886), 52. See also, Melvil Dewey, Address before the Association of Collegiate Alumnae, March 13, 1886, *Librarianship as a Profession for College-Bred Women* (Boston: Library Bureau, 1886).

22. Lilian Denio, "How to Make the Most of a Small Library," *Library Notes*, III (March, 1889), 470.

23. Theresa H. West, "The Usefulness of Libraries in Small Towns," *LJ*, VIII (September-October, 1883), 229.

24. Mary Salome Cutler Fairchild, "Women in American Libraries," *LJ*, XXIX (December, 1904), 162.

25. *Ibid.*

26. Celia A. Hayward, "Woman as Cataloger," *Public Libraries*, III (April, 1898), 121-23; "Female Library Assistants," *LJ*, XIV (April, 1889), 128-29; John Dana, "Women in Library Work," *Independent*, LXXI (August 3, 1911), 244.

27. Robert Weibe, *The Search for Order: 1877-1920* (New York: Hill and Wang, 1967), 122-23, discusses how sexual roles were expressed in this period by women social workers, lawyers and doctors in their service to children.

28. *LJ*, XXV (August, 1900), 123.

29. *Ibid.*

30. Minerva Sanders, "Report on Reading for the Young," *LJ*, XV (December, 1890), 59.

31. Annie Carroll Moore, "Special Training for Children's Librarians," *LJ*, XXIII (August, 1898), 80.

32. E. M. Fairchild, "Methods of Children's Library Work as Determined by the Needs of the Children," *LJ*, XXII (October, 1897), 26.

33. Sophy H. Powell, *The Children's Library: A Dynamic Factor in Education* (New York: H. W. Wilson Co., 1917), 1-7, 191-96, 255-71, is a careful study of the limited educational function of the children's section of the library. For a history of the development of library service to children see Harriet G. Long, *Public Library Service to Children: Foundation and Development* (Metuchen, New Jersey: The Scarecrow Press, Inc., 1969) and Effie L. Power, *Work With Children in Public Libraries* (Chicago: American Library Association, 1943).

34. For examples of women's mild tone see, Mary S. Cutler, "What a Woman Librarian Earns," *LJ*, XVII (August, 1892), 90; Mary E. Ahern, "The Business Side of a Woman's Career as a Librarian," *LJ*, XXIV (July, 1899), 62; Martha B. Earle, "Women Librarians," *Independent*, XLIX (February 18, 1897), 30.

35. "Woman's Meeting," *LJ*, XVII (August, 1892), 89-94.

36. "Proceedings," *LJ*, I (November 30, 1876), 90.

37. Caroline M. Hewins, "Library Work for Women," *LJ*, XVI (September, 1891), 273-74.

38. Cutler, 90.

39. *Ibid.*, 91.

40. "Library Association of Central California," *LJ*, XXII (June, 1897), 308. Miss Kelso later became a successful businesswoman in the field of publishing and remained an outspoken feminist.

41. Tessa L. Kelso, "Woman's Section of the A.L.A.," *LJ*, XVII (November, 1892), 444.

42. Ahern, 60-62.

43. Fairchild, 153-62.

44. *Ibid.*, 162.

45. Melvil Dewey, "The Profession," *LJ*, I (September, 1876), 5-6; Ernest C. Richardson, "Being a Librarian," *LJ*, XV (July, 1890), 201-02.

46. The first library school opened in 1887 at Columbia College. As a result of Williamson's critical survey of library schools in 1923, the curriculum standards in library education were revised and a national system of accreditation was established. Charles C. Williamson, *Training for Library Service: A Report Prepared for the Carnegie Corporation of New York* (Boston: The Merrymount Press, 1923); Sarah K. Vann, *The Williamson Reports: A Study* (Metuchen, New Jersey: The Scarecrow Press, Inc., 1971); C. Edward Carroll, *The Profes-*

sionalization of Education for Librarianship (Metuchen, New Jersey: The Scarecrow Press, Inc., 1970). For discussions of library professionalization see: Phillip H. Ennis (ed.), *Seven Questions About the Profession of Librarianship* (Chicago: University of Chicago Press, 1961); Pierce Butler, "Librarianship as a Profession," *Library Quarterly*, XXI (October, 1951), 235-47; Robert D. Leigh, *The Public Library in the United States* (New York: Columbia University Press, 1969); Robert B. Downs (ed.), *The Status of American College and University Librarians* (ACRL Monograph, No. 22 [Chicago: American Library Association, 1958]); William J. Goode, "The Theoretical Limits of Professionalization," *The Semi-Professions and their Organization: Teachers, Nurses, Social Workers*, ed. Amitai Etzioni (New York: The Free Press, 1969), 266-313.

47. White, *passim*.

48. Ennis, 83.

49. A. M. Carr-Saunders, *The Professions* (Oxford: Clarendon, 1933); T. A. Caplow, *The Sociology of Work* (Minneapolis: University of Minnesota, 1954); Ernest Greenwood, "The Attributes of a Profession," *Social Work*, II (June, 1957), 139-40; Howard M. Vollmer and Donald Mills (eds.), *Professionalization* (Englewood Cliffs, New Jersey: Prentice-Hall, 1966); Ronald M. Pavalko, *Sociology of Occupations and Professions* (Itasca, Illinois: F. E. Peacock Publishers, Inc., 1971); Raymond M. Merritt, *Engineering in American Society* (Lexington, Kentucky: University Press of Kentucky, 1969); Daniel H. Calhoun, *Professional Lives in America* (Cambridge, Massachusetts: Harvard University Press, 1965); Kenneth S. Lynn (ed.), *The Professions in America* (Boston: Houghton Mifflin Company, 1965).

50. William F. Poole, "Buffalo Conference Proceedings," *LJ*, VIII (September-October, 1883), 281. See also, William H. Brett, "The Present Problem," *LJ*, XVIX (December, 1894), 5-9; S. S. Green, *Libraries and Schools* (New York: F. Leypoldt, 1883), 56-74; Max Cohen, "The Librarian as an Educator and Not a Cheap-John," *LJ*, XIII (November, 1888), 366-67; Melvil Dewey, "Public Libraries as Public Educators," *LJ*, XI (June, 1886), 165.

51. Charles Knowles Bolton, "The Librarian's Duty as a Citizen," *LJ*, XXI (May, 1896), 219-22; S. S. Green, "Personal Relations Between Librarians and Readers," *LJ*, I (November 30, 1876), 74-81.

52. Smuts, 36.

53. For a thorough documentation of characteristic behavior of women workers see Richard L. and Ida Harper Simpson, "Women and Bureaucracy in the Semi-Professions," in Etzioni, 196-265. The nineteenth-century woman would demonstrate even more strongly the traits which the Simpsons outline.

54. Ennis, 7, 9; Marjorie Fiske, *Book Selection and Censorship* (Los Angeles: University of California Press, 1959), 100-12.

55. Sociologist Talcott Parsons has also noted the "tendency for women to gravitate into 'supportive' types of occupational role, where functions of 'helpfulness' to the incumbent of more assertive and ultimately, in the social function sense, more responsible roles, is a major keynote." Parsons points to sex composition as "both a symptom and a partial determinant" of the pattern of "the 'quietness,' the rather passive character of the attributes of librar-

ians as a group, wishing as it were to be unobtrusively 'helpful' but avoiding assertiveness." Talcott Parsons, "Implications of the Study," *The Climate of Book Selection*, ed. J. Periam Danton (Berkeley: University of California, 1959), 94-95.

56. U. S. Bureau of Education, *Report of Commissioner of Education, 1887-1888* (Washington: Government Printing Office), 1033.

57. William Fletcher, *Public Libraries in America* (Boston: Roberts Brothers, 1894), 32-33.

58. My interviews with a leading university librarian and with several public librarians indicate a recent twentieth-century trend toward male homosexuals in library work. Their presence may be connected to the role-playing assumed by librarians in general. That is, to the extent that the homosexual male takes on the characteristics of femininity, he proves quite adaptable to playing a female service role. It may be, too, that male homosexuals, having been driven from most of the high status professions by prejudice, find women less hostile to their presence and thus feel more comfortable in a feminized working environment. On this point, note the formation of the Task Force on Gay Liberation during the 1970 American Library Association annual meeting.

59. William E. Goode "The Librarian: From Occupation to Profession?" Ennis, 13.

60. White, 32-33.

61. Normal schools were faced with similar problems during this period. A predominantly bureaucratic control is evident in school-teaching and librarianship. See Simpson and Simpson, 196-221.

62. Fremont Rider, *Melvil Dewey* (Chicago: American Library Association, 1944), 8.

63. Grosvenor Dawe, *Melvil Dewey: Seer, Inspirer, Doer* (Albany, New York: J. B. Lyon Company, 1923), 76.

64. Ray Trautman, *A History of the School of Library Service: Columbia University* (New York: Columbia University Press, 1954), 3-23.

65. Dawe, 70.

66. Letter from Annie Godfrey Dewey, June 15, 1906, cited in Dawe, 70.

67. Dawe, 91-92.

68. "Report of the Committee on the Proposed School of Library Economy," *LJ*, X (September-October, 1885), 293.

69. Lutie E. Stearns, "The Question of Library Training," *LJ*, XXX (September, 1905), 68, 70.

70. "Fifth Session," *LJ*, XXX (September, 1905), 167-68.

71. *Ibid.*

72. *Ibid.*, 164-76.

73. Simpson and Simpson, 260-65. For current feminist protest see, Anita R. Schiller, "The Widening Sex Gap," *LJ*, LXXXXIV (March 15, 1969), 1098-100; Janet Freedman, "The Liberated Librarian," *LJ*, LXXXXV (May 1, 1970), 1709-711; Anita R. Schiller, "The Disadvantaged Majority: Women Employed in Libraries," *American Libraries*, IV (April, 1970), 345-49.

74. "Editorial," *LJ*, XVII (September, 1892), 371. For discussions of the old and new librarian see, "The New Librarians," *LJ*, XV (November, 1890), 338; R. R. Bowker, "The Work of the Nineteenth Century Librarian for the Librarian of the Twentieth," *LJ*, VIII (September-October, 1883), 247-50.

75. William H. Form, "Popular Images of Librarians," *LJ*, LXXI (June 15, 1946), 851-55; Robert Leigh and Kathryn W. Sewny, "The Popular Image of the Library and of Librarians," *LJ*, LXXXV (June 1, 1960), 2089-091.

76. Ennis, 74.

77. Howard Mumford Jones, "Reflections in a Library," *Saturday Review*, XXXXIII (April 9, 1960), 34.

WOMEN IN THE PROFESSIONS: A RESEARCH AGENDA FOR AMERICAN HISTORIANS

Joan Jacobs Brumberg and Nancy Tomes

The development of the modern professions has been at the center of historical analysis over the last two decades. Inspired no doubt by the interdisciplinary gospel of the "new social history," historians have enthusiastically rediscovered the relationship between occupational groups and the social order, first marked out by Emile Durkheim in 1902.[1] As a result, the study of the professions is no longer exclusively a sociological domain. Hardly a history of education, health, religion, or reform does not include professionalization as a central focus. More importantly, the professions act as a linchpin in much larger historical arguments. In his sweeping analysis of American society from the colonial to the Progressive periods, David Rothman presents psychiatrists, educators, lawyers, and social workers as the chief architects of the institutional welfare state. Burton Bledstein posits the existence of a "culture of professionalism" that shaped the educational system, and through that system, the whole ethos of the American middle class. Robert Wiebe locates the professional at the core of the "new middle class" responsible for integrating the "island communities" of the late nineteenth century into a cohesive national society. Last, but not least, Christopher Lasch indicts a vast army of professional "help-providers" for the rise of the "therapeutic state" and the consequent decline of American family life.[2]

While these influential interpretations sparked invaluable historical debate, they fail to incorporate a crucial element in the modern evolution of the professions: the entry of middle class women into the professional milieu. Although gender is obviously an important factor in structuring occupational hierarchies, it has not been considered in any substantive way in the historical analysis of the professionalization process. The primary actors in the standard works are inevitably male. The working definition of "profession," in sociology as well as history, excludes fields dominated by women because they seem to lack the qualities of autonomy and expertise central to professional power.[3] Even in those historical works that have examined a predominantly female profession, such as social work or education, the issue of gender is overlooked.[4] Thus, it appears that the existing scholarship pro-

0048-7511/82/0102-0275 $01.00

ceeds on two assumptions: that the "culture of professionalism" shaped men, not women, and that women's professional activities represent an anomaly, a deviation from the larger pattern of professional participation in American life.

The current renaissance in history writing on women and work has also neglected the study of gender and professionalization, devoting its major intellectual energies and its emotional heart to the history of anonymous American working class women. The reasons for this semi-exclusion of professional women are complex but essential to understanding the "state of the art." First, the failure to tackle head-on historical issues in female professionalization may well reflect the ambivalence of women historians about the meaning and consequences of professionalism in their own personal lives. In fact, the contemporary feminist push for professional opportunities has all the characteristics of a love-hate relationship. Women rightly demand equal access to and treatment in professional life, yet when professional success arrives often question both the social relations and the values implied by their new status.

Second, the conceptual power of the work of E. P. Thompson, the *Annales*, and the "new social history" has prompted a generation of historians, both male and female, to rewrite history from "the bottom up." In the effort to correct the total neglect of working class women by traditional American historiography, interest in professional women—who were largely in the middle and upper classes—has been less intense. Professional women who were first in a field, such as Elizabeth Blackwell or Jeanette Rankin, generally had their names in the history books already since "women worthies" have been a long established part of a reverential antiquarian tradition. In the effort not to perpetuate a Whiggish women's history, historians gave working class women center stage.[5]

This ordering of research priorities in the direction of the working class has to do as well with the personal politics of many women historians. Without doubt, Marxist or Socialist Feminism is an influential and provocative analytical tool for women in a profession whose social organization, as well as its essential products (i.e., history writing and teaching), remain male dominated. Given this perspective, it makes perfectly good sense to focus on the laboring classes where both individual and family lives demonstrate the full disruptive force of industrial capital development. Unfortunately, because the nineteenth-century woman professional existed somewhere between the exploited female industrial laborer and the nonproductive bourgeoise lady, she has been relegated to the periphery of research and writing in the field of women's history. Consequently, the sorely needed concentration on working class women, for all that it offers, fueled an unnatural dichotomy that elevated class over gender, obscuring the ways in which the history of all working women, be they professional, clerical, or manual laborers, may be marked by enormous continuities.

Those scholars who do work in the history of female professionalization have been heretofore methodologically conservative, writing the history of discrete occupational specialities without creating works of synthesis.[6] These separate histories of individual professions do, however, constitute a crucial first step. Dee Garrison's pioneering work on librarians, *Apostles of Culture* (1979), and Mary Roth Walsh's *"Doctors Wanted: No Women Need Apply": Sexual Barriers in the Medical Profession, 1835–1975* (1979) began the process of charting the development of important professional career patterns for women. By the early twentieth century, the designation "lady librarian" was sheer redundancy while "lady doctor" was not, despite the existence of a substantial feminist medical community in Boston in the nineteenth century. In the case of medicine, male practitioners openly acted to deny women entrance to their profession and its training schools; in the case of librarians, men sought more lucrative opportunities elsewhere at the very moment that libraries, as agents of culture, expanded. Women doctors were tied to the feminist movement, supporting suffrage and utilizing female support groups in both their personal and professional lives; women librarians, in contrast, generally opposed the suffrage and eschewed organized feminist activities.[7] Both books, despite radically different scenarios of professional development, speak to the power of cultural conceptions in defining and shaping what is considered appropriate women's work.

In the field of nursing history there exists a vast amount of literature (written predominantly by nurses) and a lingering tendency to write "mega-history": nursing from prehistory to modern times. But a new generation of historians—Susan Armeny, Janet James, Darlene Hine, Barbara Melosh, Jane Mottus, Susan Reverby, and Nancy Tomes—is now at work on more carefully defined studies that place nursing in its social context, i.e., in its relationship to hospitals and welfare services, the medical profession, urban development, and existing educational and work opportunities for women.[8] Midwifery, once a totally female employment, has been the subject of great interest since the 1960s when an emerging feminist critique of the medical establishment led many pregnant women to consider alternatives to hospital births. Work by Jane Donegan, Judy Barrett Littoff, Frances Kobrin, and Richard and Dorothy Wertz, drawn largely from the medical controversy over midwifery both in England and the United States, explains why this female employment was subsumed, as Donegan clearly demonstrates, by male-dominated obstetrics and gynecology as early as 1850.[9]

Surprisingly, we have as yet no substantive historical analysis of women as teachers, from their improvisational role in the Colonial Dame school to militant teacher unionism.[10] Despite the popularity of Kathryn Kish Sklar's classic biography of Catherine Beecher and the demographic work of Richard Bernard and Maris Vinovskis (both of which point in different ways to the centrality of teaching in the lives of American women), a good collective biography of the American "school marm" has yet to be done.[11] And, there are additional observable gaps: neither social work, authorship, law, nor the academic profession has been scrutinized by historians with an eye to the complex interactions of gender, work, and career.[12]

On the basis of what we do know, some important conceptual distinctions can be made and an agenda suggested for future research and writing. First, as we chart the social history of women in different professional employments, it becomes immediately apparent that a comparative approach helps to clarify the issues. As Garrison and Walsh have demonstrated, women's struggle to enter the "classic" male dominated professions (e.g., medicine, law, engineering, the academy, the clergy) is markedly different than the process by which large numbers of women entered the feminized service professions (e.g., teaching, nursing, social work, librarianship). The point here is simply this: the complex web of social, cultural, economic, and life-cycle factors affecting women's work will be impossible to disentangle so long as we maintain a historical myopia that focuses on one class or a single occupational group.

Second, a comparative approach to the history of women in the professions must be coupled with a conceptual orientation, born of the current renaissance in historical writing about women; that is, what we have learned in the last decade about the experience of women must guide our future investigations of the subject. Rather than to simply structure research and writing around disheartening stories of how national professional associations denied women access to specialized training and advancement, historians of American women might pursue an entirely different course. Some suggestions follow here.

Women, Work and the Family

In setting an agenda for research in the history of female professionalization we draw first upon the considerable body of scholarship that has been done on women and work in the nineteenth century. Joan Scott and Louise Tilly, Virginia Yans-McLaughlin, Thomas Dublin, and Tamara Hareven have all demonstrated that the entrance of working class women into the industrial labor force involved the complex interaction of economic, structural, and cultural forces. Economist Elyce Rotella's study of the expansion of female clerical employment (1870–1930) indicates that opportunities responded to long term supply factors (such as a decline in the family economy and rising levels of education) as well as short term demands related to technological advances.[13] To what extent can this same model help to interpret the entry of middle class women into professional fields? How might this model be enlarged or refined to accommodate class distinctions at different points in time?

In antebellum America, the polarized image of the "lady" and the "mill girl" has obscured the extent to which middle class women, like their working class counterparts, pursued work outside the home in the service of familial interest. The powerful idea of a leisured female class, busily perpetuating a "cult of domesticity," has diverted our attention from the very real economic necessity that moved many women who were neither urban, immigrants, nor laboring poor into the work force.[14] In the early nineteenth century, rural New England farm families sent their daughters into teaching as well as millwork in service of a family economic strategy not unlike that suggested by Scott and Tilly. In the late nineteenth century, nursing schools continued to draw most of their students from among the native-born in small towns and rural areas.[15] Parents seem to have regarded training as a teacher or nurse, like dairying or beekeeping in an earlier day, as a good investment for a daughter's future, inasmuch as it provided skills for marriage, allowed for the possibility of accumulating a meager dowry, and protected against a destitute widowhood. The disruption of the "family economy" by the loss of a male breadwinner set many a middle class widow or daughter to writing for a living (as Ann Douglas suggested) or seeking employment in the expanding federal bureaucracy (as demonstrated by Cindy Aron).[16] While many middle class girls were not raised explicitly to face the prospect of supporting themselves, few could have been unaware that for some women of their background work became an imperative. Cycles of economic boom and bust, a skewed sex ratio, death, and desertion ensured a goodly number of households without male wage-earners. Consequently, the lack of preparation given girls for just such eventualities was consistently used to rationalize the nineteenth-century campaign for women's education which brought about a spectacular rise in female literacy and attainments, changing the nature of the labor supply.[17]

While the need to support one's self or one's family first sent the middle class woman outside the home, the economic imperative did not long remain the sole rationale for women's work. Using Scott and Tilly's line of argument, we hypothesize that once outside the home environment, some girls and women kept working for their own reasons. In other words, a familial orientation toward work gave way to a more autonomous impulse to develop or fulfill one's own interests and aspirations. For example, once teaching began to be considered an acceptable way of life for an unmarried woman, individuals like Catherine Beecher, who had their own visions to pursue, used the profession as a means to achieve independence from family constraints. So, too, throughout the nineteenth and well into the twentieth century, countless numbers of women, activated by their commitment to evangelical principles, realized their personal "missions" in the form of paid careers in the service of the church, education, and "Social Housekeeping."[18] With teaching to fall back upon, the more ambitious could eventually venture into other fields as well. Only after several years in the classroom did Elizabeth Blackwell decide to study medicine at the Geneva (New York) Medical College; Emily Chubbuck Judson developed the pseudonym "Fanny Forester" and began writing and selling fiction precisely because she was fed up with teaching in rural district schools in upstate New York.[19] It is possible that the peripatetic movement that characterized male careers in the nineteenth century has something of a female equivalent, despite the fact that women's options were so much narrower.

Among women, however, commitment to work outside the home occurred in varying degrees. As we have already suggested, nineteenth-century women continued to go into fields like teaching, nursing, and librarianship both for the sake of family interests and for personal fulfillment. Some women wanted to work only a few years before marriage; others planned to stay in the field permanently, but looked upon their work simply as a means of earning a living; a few conceived of their enterprise as a higher "calling" and as a lifelong commitment to providing skilled services. Within the field of nursing history, recent scholarship suggests that these varying orientations to work created significant internal professional strains.[20] We expect similar problems will materialize in future historical studies of the dynamics of women at work as teachers and as social workers.

The problems inherent in combining a career with traditional married life in the nineteenth century only exacerbated these tensions. The biographies of well-known feminists such as Angelina Grimke and Charlotte Perkins Gilman deftly illustrate how the choice between family and career caused searing personal conflict.[21] Many women felt that they had to make an unnatural choice between the two. According to Roberta Frankfort, among the first generation of American women's college graduates over 50 percent never married. Among Wellesley College faculty in the period 1880–1920 there were no married women.[22]

Collective biography of the first generation of women graduates at Wellesley has been used by both Joyce Antler and Patricia Palmieri to test Jane Addam's charge that when women graduates returned home from college, eager to apply their knowledge and skills to the larger social realm, their parents refused to sanction the legitimacy of this "social claim" and reasserted familial authority. Both Antler and Palmieri admit the power of the "family claim" but also demonstrate that in many cases the family acted in support of professional life. Palmieri proposes that certain daughters were actually selected by their achievement oriented families for professional careers; "dutiful daughters," in the form of sisters, acted as domestic support systems making professionalism a reality for the "designated daughter." Antler's research points to the importance of nontraditional family arrangements in the lives of professional women, particularly mother-daughter support systems and female friendships of longstanding.[23] Some women, like Wellesley's Vida Scudder or Bryn Mawr's M. Carey Thomas, made the single state a conscious choice. Strong female networks—in the form of national organizations and informal associations of friends and alumnae—provided the emotional and physical intimacy these women needed for personal satisfaction and professional success. In many cases, a rejection of heterosexuality and a commitment to career were interrelated. Biographical accounts of Jeanette Marks, Mary Wooley, M. Carey Thomas, and Mary Garrett suggest that early twentieth-century professional women who earned their own way were more free than their dependent sisters to pursue longstanding lesbian relationships.[24]

Clearly, the whole question of professional women's lifestyles requires considerably more attention. It may well be, for example, that the small number of women who entered male-dominated fields like medicine and law actually married in larger numbers than we might expect. For example, in her biographical survey of women doctors, Regina Morantz has found that between 1860 and 1900, 30 to 40 percent of women doctors were married, a rate four times that of other professionals. For the decades from 1900 to 1960 the figure sometimes went as high as 50 percent. The scant data available on nineteenth-century women lawyers suggest that women who married attorneys often used their husbands as a means of access to professional life, circumventing legal encumbrances to female practice at the bar. And, among women considered in Jean Gordon's study of women artists before 1850, 17 percent belonged to families in which there were artist relatives: husbands, fathers, and brothers. Given Carl Degler's claim that women and the family are intrinsically "at odds," the point seems worth emphasizing: family can act as either inhibitor or stimulus to a woman's professional life.[25]

Less clear is the issue of social mobility for the professional woman and her family. The historical record suggests a number of different scenarios, varying across class, ethnic, and regional lines. For middle class women, as distinct from their male counterparts, careers were usually prompted by the downward mobility of families. Yet this trend does not rule out the possibility of hungry female careerists, that is, female "Horatio Algers," who consciously charter their own route out of family and factory, ethnic neighborhood or ghetto, by going to normal schools, library training institutes, or nursing and medical schools. We suspect that at certain points and locations in time, native-born daughters of certain ethnic groups became teachers or nurses in disproportionately large numbers. For example, studies need to be done of the influx of Jewish women into the New York City public school system and black women into post World War II nursing. In these studies we might ask how their salaries were utilized: To build a nest egg for marriage? To support parents? To help pay for the professional educations of their siblings?

Finally, in examining the interrelationship between professionalism and social mobility, experience prompts us to consider those women who in the midst of professional training of one kind or another truncated their own careers in order to marry, raise children, and act as "helpmates" to aspiring professional husbands. Helpmates, particularly those with relevant skills, are oftentimes a central ingredient in the success of male careers and, hence, social mobility. If we take the prefatory statements of gratitude in academic books as any indication, the educated wives of American university scholars have been particularly obliging. University archives, which oftentimes hold the papers of faculty wives, ought to be culled with an eye to this helping relationship. Support services provided by clerical wives might be considered in a similar light.[26]

The Dimensions of Occupational Segregation

However varied the impulses that sent middle class women out to work in the nineteenth century, most of them ended up performing the same kinds of services. Whereas middle class men might choose from a wide range of employment, their female counterparts remained segregated in only a few fields. The development of the predominantly female professions paralleled the expansion of education and welfare institutions. By the 1840s, the spread of the public school system had brought middle class women into teaching just as the antebellum "print revolution" facilitated their careers as authors. In the late nineteenth century, the proliferation of urban welfare services, hospitals, and public libraries led to the entry of women into social work, nursing, and librarianship. In all these areas the need for a cheap, abundant labor force harmonized with prevailing notions of "innate" female abilities.

What are the consequences of an occupational field becoming disproportionately female, as teaching, nursing, librarianship, and social work soon did? Borrowing from sociology, historians venture some ready answers, including lower wages and a decline in status. Although there is little reason to believe that this is not the case, these two measures of the effects of a female majority need to be tested in each field at different points in time, and in varying locales.

Significantly, some of the best-known literature takes a negative view of the feminization process. In other words, aside from its depressive effect on salaries and status, feminization has negative consequences for skills and services because it allegedly alters and debases the nature of the work. Ann Douglas's *The Feminization of American Culture* (1977) and Redding S. Sugg's *Motherteacher: The Feminization of American Education* (1978) are both cases in point. Douglas links the vapidity and sentimentality of Victorian culture to the hegemony of women; Sugg asserts that the substitution of female for male teachers subverted academic authority and led to a "pedagogy of love" which fostered anti-intellectualism in American schools. To a lesser extent, the pejorative effects of feminization are also suggested by Dee Garrison in her book on libraries, and by David Tyack and Myra Strober in their commentaries on American schools. Garrison posits that the feminized concept of the library's purpose diluted its role as cultural agent and information center; Tyack and Strober see a positive association between the feminization of teaching and the growth of school bureaucracy.[27]

In the history of health care, however, a different set of assumptions has prevailed. Several feminist historians have claimed that women fostered a noninterventionist, holistic, prevention-oriented approach toward health. Accounts of childbirth, for example, suggest that the transfer of authority from the female midwife to the medical man brought with it greater emotional trauma, needless use of instruments and surgical techniques, and higher maternal and infant mortality rates.[28]

Two recent articles on women in health-related fields suggest the need for a healthy skepticism with respect to claims about "female therapeutics." In a study of hospital case records, Regina Morantz and Sue Zschoche found no significant differences in the way men and women physicians treated their patients in childbirth; for example women used forceps and drugs no less than men. Morantz and Zschoche did find that female physicians expressed more concern for the moral and emotional welfare of their charges, but this difference in attitude did not translate into gender-specific medical practice. Similarly, Susan Reverby's article on nursing and the organization of hospital work suggests the caution needed in promoting the "nurturant" qualities of the women's professions. While nurses as individuals may have contributed to the better care of patients, the nursing profession's ethos greatly facilitated the depersonalization of institutional medical care.[29]

Undoubtedly, feminization occurred because there was a "fit" between economic need and cultural conceptions of gender roles. Where no such fit existed, professional opportunities for women remained bleak: the male preserves of engineering, law, and the ministry, for example, made no place for female aspirants in the nineteenth century. Between 1850 and 1890, women made some gains in medicine, primarily because a small specialized market for their services developed among women clients while the profession itself was too weak to resist their encroachments effectively. The idea that innate feminine modesty and virtue necessitated treatment by women doctors stimulated the growth of a small but significant female presence within medicine, especially in obstetrics, gynecology, and psychiatry.[30] Studies of the transition from a male-dominated missionary movement to a post-Civil War women's crusade reveal that nineteenth-century Protestant evangelicals legitimated female missionary careers because women could penetrate that physical space, purdah, where heathen women were secluded. In the same vein, Franz Boaz allegedly encouraged women students, such as Ruth Benedict, to become anthropologists because they might gain access to cultural rites denied to male scholars in the field.[31] Conversely, we might argue that the abysmal legal status of nineteenth century women—their inability to sue, collect debts, and establish credit—prevented the formation of a similar market for woman's law.

Although the entry of middle class women into the professional workplace appeared quite revolutionary at the time, the patterns of occupational segregation and distribution that developed reflected and sustained male authority.[32] The feminized service or "semiprofessions" remained low in autonomy, prestige, and financial reward. The highest positions of power within the women's fields, i.e., the school superintendent, head librarian, and the agency director, were usually occupied by men. In nursing, where a female-headed hierarchy did develop, women still operated under the formal and informal guidance of doctors and hospital administrators; in contrast, in the development of home economics as a professional field, women retained control of the educational institutions until the premier generation of careerists retired and was replaced by male social scientists, generally in the 1960s. Recent studies have begun to move beyond the simplistic oppressor/victim models of earlier work on women in the professions, and focus on the complex strategies women used to pursue their interests in the face of consistent opposition. Still, we need a much fuller understanding of how occupational hierarchies developed and persisted through periods of profound professional and social change.

Professional Women and Women's Culture

A central problem in women's history is the articulation of the links between work and culture. Carroll Smith-Rosenberg, Nancy Cott, Ann

Douglas, Mary P. Ryan, and others posit a causal relationship between the nineteenth-century sphere of women, with its sex-specific language, customs, and institutions, and female participation in larger public spheres. Consequently, the current feminist debate over the development and demise of the nineteenth-century "female world" has significant implications for the history of women in the professions.[33]

The notion of women's culture implies an important new perspective on the relationship between professionalism and female volunteer activity. Within the nineteenth-century woman's sphere, unpaid work outside the home became a route to self-respect and power oftentimes involving a lifetime commitment to a single organization or cause. As volunteers, women participated in a broad range of activities: religious schools and missions, military nursing, social work, and institutional management. Patterns of female persistence in volunteer groups suggest that we consider seriously the notion of a volunteer "career" which embodies some important professional qualities. The history of American philanthropy is largely the story of networks of women volunteers who were the mainstay of urban reform and charity as early as 1850.[34] Yet, the story of how "friendly visiting" by female charitable societies was transformed into social casework remains virtually untold. Biographies of major female figures in the evolution of social welfare services, such as Mary Richmond, Belle LaFollette, Julia Lathrop, Jessie Hodder, and Katharine Bement Davis, remain to be written.[35]

Moreover, in the guise of the volunteer or amateur, women apparently ventured into less traditional female settings. Sally Kohlstedt's work on women in science traces the gradual evolution of their participation through three stages: first, women's contributions from the periphery of scientific endeavor, as lone women correspondents observing and categorizing natural phenomena, and as the female relatives of male scientists, collaborating on scientific works without any public recognition; second, women's role as popularizers of scientific information through teaching, writing, and organizing clubs; and finally, the establishment of small enclaves of women scientists in academia, especially in women's colleges. According to Kohlstedt's schema, the activities of the amateur and popularizer gradually helped to legitimate an institutional role for the woman scientist, albeit a small one.[36]

A similar relationship between professional and volunteer plagues our own discipline, in which the traditional sexual division of labor is symbolized in the distinctions drawn between academic and local historians. Professional historians are generally men in colleges and universities who get paid for teaching, research, and writing; local historians are disproportionately unsalaried women who act as keepers of community records and provide guidance for those interested in the community's past. Many such women have post-secondary school educations and have combined careers as school teachers and librarians with childrearing, all the while pursuing their local historical and genealogical interests with great passion. In part, the dichotomy between the academic and local history worlds reflects changes in the maturing profession which, in the 1880s and 1890s, moved away from local to regional and national studies. Male historians assumed teaching posts in colleges and universities; women historians taught public school and were active, on a volunteer basis, in building local historical societies and their collections. This gender schema is captured in New York State, where as a result of a 1919 law that mandated the formal appointment of a historian in every municipality, there is still an active network of close to 1600 such volunteer historians. In 1981, close to 80 percent of these local historians were women, generally over the age of fifty-five.[37]

The existence of a distinct female culture also helps us to understand the expansion and contraction of professional opportunities for women. As Jessie Bernard noted in 1966, the level of women's participation in nontraditional fields has not increased steadily over time.[38] On the contrary, there were more women doctors and college professors between 1900 and 1920 than at any other time in American history, suggesting the importance of further study of various cohorts and their historical experiences.[39] Until very recently, both the absolute number and the proportion of women in male-dominated fields had been declining. The precise timing of this downturn remains subject to debate; most scholars assume that it began in the 1920s, but more recent calculations point to the 1950s as the critical decade.[40] Estelle Freedman has linked the decline in women's professional presence, as well as political visibility, to the abandonment of the separatist structures which characterized nineteenth-century women's culture. In the 1920s, Freedman argues, "Women gave up many of the strengths of the female sphere without gaining equally from the man's world they entered."[41]

In another sense, the ethos of professionalism probably hastened the demise of female culture by widening the distance between career and non-career women. As small groups of elite women made gains in the work world, they inevitably imbibed the "culture of professionalism" and its hostility to both the amateur and the volunteer. Perhaps professional women felt that they had to subvert the long tradition of female voluntarism in order to make their own positions secure. Nancy Tomes makes this argument in an analysis of the World War I debate over the relative virtues of using Red Cross volunteers or student nurses in military hospitals. This conflict suggests that professionalism became an ideology that aligned the nursing leadership with doctors, rather than with women volunteers of familiar social backgrounds.[42]

Finally, the consideration of the link between women's work and women's culture raises this difficult but important question: to what extent does the traditional professional distaste for "popularization," whether in science, history, or literature, constitute a rejection of female aspiration? Given that the canon in most fields has been dominated and defined by men, women have oftentimes been relegated to the realm of what we euphemistically call "popular culture." In American literature, Nathaniel Hawthorne's often-quoted remarks about the "damned lot of scribbling women" symbolically set the stage for the subsequent devaluation of women's writing and women's art.

The recent work we have surveyed here raises some larger methodological and interpretive questions concerning the "rise of professionalism" in nineteenth- and twentieth-century America. In terms of methodology, our review of the literature suggests two critical points. First, the history of women's participation in the professions underscores the inadequacy of traditional approaches to the professionalization process. The "retarded" entry of women into the nontraditional fields and the anomalous position of the so-called "semiprofessions" simply cannot be explained in terms of the professional attributes women have individually or collectively failed to acquire. Rather the structuring of women's participation in the professional workforce must be seen as a complex process in which gender distinctions are an organizing principle. Second, a comparative perspective is essential in analyzing this complex process. Only by charting the development of women's fields in relation to one another, as well as to the male-dominated fields, can we begin to comprehend the interconnections between sex roles and the occupational structure. Women's professional opportunities did not develop within a vacuum, but as part of a larger occupational hierarchy shaped by interprofessional competition and accommodation. To understand the expansion and contraction of women's professional options, then, historians and sociologists must begin to place the development of individual fields within this broader framework.[43] Some initial insights garnered from the comparative approach employed in this essay follow.

What women have traditionally taken as their province have been the "dirtiest" areas of professional service, i.e., those involving the most human contact with all its attendant complexities. By and large, women have staked their professional claims in areas abandoned or unwanted by men. Over the course of the nineteenth century, they assumed primary care of the most unrewarding and disorderly of clienteles: the young, the poor, the immigrant, the intemperate, the sick. Women found their "golden opportunities," so to speak, in the massive social dislocation caused by immigration, poverty, economic uncertainty, and labor exploitation—social problems that necessitated the creation of a vast army of social workers, public health nurses, and public school teachers. The diversion of this human "capital" into welfare services no doubt greatly reduced the threat of social chaos at the turn of the century. Thus the rise of the female "helping professions" becomes an essential ingredient in understanding the Progressive era's "triumph of conservatism."[44]

As women have been relegated to the unattractive peripheries of professional work, prestige within the professions has increasingly come to depend upon precisely those qualities least associated with the ideal "feminine." High status professions do not maintain close contact with their clients; philosophical abstraction and distance from human complications characterize their elite cadres. Thus among doctors, the physician engaged in "pure" research has greater prestige in his colleagues' eyes than the family practitioner; in legal circles, the corporate attorney has more status than the divorce lawyer. As Andrew Abbott has posited in a recent article on professional status, a process of "regression" or retreat from "front line" contact with all but the most rewarding and mannerly of clients has characterized professional behavior over the course of the twentieth century.[45]

We might conclude, then, that the development of subordinate female professions greatly accelerated this process. Only by recruiting a vast workforce of helpers, regarded as intellectually inferior but altruistically superior, could the male-dominated professions pursue their course of abstraction and isolation. The rise of professional nursing obviously freed doctors to pursue the "pure" objectives of laboratory medicine. Just as nurses now assist doctors, elementary and secondary school teachers (not to mention part-time lecturers) underwrite the university professor, and social workers facilitate the administration of judicial and bureaucratic decrees. From this perspective, the patterns of women's participation appear not as an anomalous aspect of the modern professions, but rather as an integral part of their development. Ultimately, this juxtaposition of male and female professions has become an essential facet of the modern structuring of higher learning, technological advance, and social order.

Professor Brumberg, who has a joint appointment in the Department of Human Development and Family Studies and the Women's Studies Program, Cornell University, is the author of "Zenanas and Girlless Villages: The Ethnology of American Evangelical Women, 1870–1910," Journal of American History *(June 1982). She is currently at work on a book about the changing experience of female adolescence, 1850–1980.*

Professor Tomes, Department of History, State University of New York at Stony Brook, is the author of The Persuasive Institution: Thomas Story Kirkbride and the Art of Asylum-Keeping, 1840–1883 *(forthcoming, 1983).*

The authors are indebted to Faye Dudden for her perceptive reading of an earlier version of this paper and to Andrew Abbott for sharing his work-in-progress on interprofessional relations.

1. Emile Durkheim, *The Division of Labor in Society* (Glencoe: The Free Press, 1947).

2. David Rothman, *The Discovery of the Asylum* (Boston: Little Brown, 1971) and *Convenience* (Boston: Little Brown, 1980); Burton Bledstein, *The Culture of Professionalism: The Middle Class and the Development of Higher Education in America* (New York: Norton, 1976); Robert Wiebe, *The Search for Order, 1877–1920* (New York: Hill and Wang, 1967); Christopher Lasch, *Haven in a Heartless World* (New York: Basic Books, 1977). Other important work on the professions includes Daniel Calhoun, *Professional Lives in America, Structure and Aspiration, 1750–1850* (Cambridge: Harvard University Press, 1965); William R. Johnson, "Education and Professional Life Styles: Law and Medicine in the 19th Century," *History of Education Quarterly* 14 (Summer 1974): 185–207; Joseph F. Kett, *The Formation of the American Medical Profession: The Role of Institutions, 1780–1860* (New Haven: Yale University Press, 1968); W. J. Reader, *Professional Men: The Rise of the Professional Classes in Nineteenth-Century England* (London: Weidenfeld and Nicolson, 1966); Charles Rosenberg, *No Other Gods: On Science and Social Thought* (Baltimore: Johns Hopkins University Press, 1976) and *The Trial of Assassin Guiteau: Psychiatry and Law in the Gilded Age* (Chicago: University of Chicago Press, 1968); William G. Rothstein, *American Physicians in the Nineteenth Century: From Sects to Science* (Baltimore: Johns Hopkins University Press, 1971).

3. Robert MacIver (1922), Talcott Parsons (1939), and others laid the groundwork of the structural-functional approach which stood, until quite recently, as the classic description of the professions. In the past decade, a new breed of sociologists has replaced the notion of immutable professional criteria fostered by the structural-functionalists with a more dynamic analysis which places the process of professionalization within specific historical contexts. Not surprisingly, this approach calls for more sociohistorical studies of the development of individual professions. For examples of the older approach to the professions, see Robert MacIver, "The Social Significance of Professional Ethics," *The Annals of the American Academy of Political and Social Science* (May 1922): 5–11; Talcott Parsons, "The Professions and Social Structure," *Social Forces* 17 (May 1939): 457–67; Ernest Greenwood, "Attributes and Social Structure," *Social Work* 2, 3 (July 1957): 44–55. Among those using the new "dynamic" models of professional development are Elliot Freidson, *The Profession of Medicine* (New York: Harper and Row, 1970); Terence Johnson, *Professions and Power* (London: MacMillan, 1972); Margali Sarfatti Larson, *The Rise of Professionalism* (Berkeley: University of California Press, 1977). Despite the recent ferment in the sociological study of the professions, however, none of the new sociological work has developed a schema including the female-dominated fields. The standard reference remains Amitai Etzioni, ed., *The Semi-Professions and Their Organization: Teachers, Nurses, Social Workers* (New York: The Free Press, 1969).

4. Roy Lubove, *The Professional Altruist: The Emergence of Social Work as a Career, 1880–1930* (Cambridge: Harvard University Press, 1965); Paul Mattingly, *The Classless Profession: American Schoolmen in the 19th Century* (New York: New York University Press, 1975).

5. On the history of working class women, see Alice Kessler-Harris, *Women Have Always Worked: An Historical Overview* (Old Westbury: Feminist Press, 1981); "Where Are the Organized Women Workers?" *Feminist Studies* (Fall 1975): 92–110; Susan Kennedy, *If All We Did Was to Weep At Home: A History of White Working Class Women in America* (Bloomington: Indiana University Press, 1979); David Katzman, *Seven Days a Week: Women and Domestic Service in Industrializing America* (New York: Oxford University Press, 1978); Faye

Dudden, "From Help to Service: American Servants, 1800–1880" (Ph.D. diss., University of Rochester, 1981); Carol Groneman, "Working Class Immigrant Women in Mid-Nineteenth Century New York," *Journal of Urban History* 4 (May 1978): 255–74, and "She Earns As a Child, She Pays as a Man: Women Workers in Mid-19th Century New York City," in *Class, Sex, and the Woman Worker*, eds. Milton Cantor and Bruce Laurie (Westport, Conn.: The Greenwood Press, 1977), pp. 83–100; Susan Kleinberg, "Technology and Women's Work: The Lives of Working Class Women in Pittsburgh, 1870–1900," *Labor History* 17 (Winter 1976): 58–72; Barbara Wertheimer, *We Were There: The Story of Working Women in America* (New York: Pantheon, 1977); Daniel J. Walkowitz, "Working Class Women in the Gilded Age: Factory, Community, and Family Life Among Cohoes, New York Cotton Factory Workers, *Journal of Social History* 5 (Summer 1972): 464–90; Rosalyn Baxandall, Linda Gordon, and Susan Reverby, eds., *America's Working Women* (New York: Vintage, 1976). For an example of the "women worthy" approach, see Madeleine Stern, *We The Women: Career Firsts in 19th Century America* (New York: B. Franklin, 1974).

6. Barbara Harris in *Beyond Her Sphere: Women and the Professions in American History* (Westport, Conn.: The Greenwood Press, 1978) provided a preliminary, but now outdated, synthesis. Harris, a Tudor-Stuart specialist, delivered these essays as public lectures at Pace University in 1976.

7. Dee Garrison, *Apostles of Culture: The Public Librarian and American Society, 1876–1920* (New York: The Free Press, 1979); Mary Roth Walsh, *"Doctors Wanted: No Women Need Apply": Sexual Barriers in the Medical Profession, 1835–1975* (New Haven: Yale University Press, 1979). In the history of women and medicine, Regina Morantz's work is also noteworthy (her published articles on women physicians appear in later footnotes). She is presently working on a book entitled *Natural Guardians of the Race: Women Physicians and American Medicine 1840–1980*. She has also edited with Cynthia Pomerleau and Carol Fenichel a collection of oral histories with women physicians, *In Her Own Words* (Westport, Conn.: The Greenwood Press, forthcoming).

8. Susan Armeny, "Resolute Enthusiasts: The Effort to Professionalize Nursing, 1893–1923" (dissertation in progress, History Department, University of Missouri); Janet James, "Isabel Hampton and the Professionalization of Nursing in the 1890s," in *The Therapeutic Revolution*, eds. Charles Rosenberg and Morris Vogel (Philadelphia: University of Pennsylvania Press, 1980), pp. 201–44; Darlene Hine, "A History of Black Women in the Nursing Profession, 1890–1950" (book in progress); Barbara Melosh, *The Physician's Hand: Nurses and Nursing in the Twentieth Century* (Philadelphia: Temple University Press, 1982); Jane E. Mottus, *New York Nightingales: The Emergence of the Nursing Profession at Bellevue and New York Hospital, 1850–1920* (Ann Arbor: University Microfilms International, 1981); Susan Reverby, "Apprenticeship to Duty: The Rationalization of American Nursing, 1860–1945" (dissertation in progress, American Studies, Boston University); Nancy Tomes, "Little World of Our Own: The Pennsylvania Hospital Training School for Nurses, 1895–1907," *Journal of the History of Medicine and Allied Sciences* 33 (October 1978): 507–30. For an old but still useful article on American nursing, see Richard Shryock, "Nursing Emerges as a Profession: The American Experience," reprinted in *Sickness and Health in America*, eds., Judith Leavitt and Ronald Numbers (Madison: University of Wisconsin Press, 1978), pp. 203–16. For an excellent piece on the moral premises of early nursing thought, see Charles Rosenberg, "Florence Nightingale on Contagion: The Hospital as Moral Universe," in *Healing and History*, ed., C. Rosenberg (New York: Science History Publications, 1979), pp. 116–36.

9. Jane Donegan, *Women and Men Midwives: Medicine, Morality and Misogyny in Early America* (Westport, Conn.: The Greenwood Press, 1978); Judy Barrett Litoff, *American Midwives, 1860 to the Present* (Westport, Conn.: The Greenwood Press, 1978); Frances Kobrin, "The American Midwife Controversy: A Crisis of Professionalization," *Bulletin of the History of Medicine* 40 (July-August 1966): 350–63; Richard W. Wertz and Dorothy C. Wertz, *Lying In: A History of Childbirth in America* (New York: The Free Press, 1977).

10. Interest in women in the teaching profession shaped a recent session at the Social Science History Association meeting. See these articles from the SSHA program, Nashville, Tennessee,

October 1981: Myra Strober and Audri Lanford, "The Percentage of Women in Public School Teaching"; Elyce Rotella and Robert Margox, "Sex Differences in the Careers of Public School Teachers: The Case of Houston, Texas 1892–1923"; Susan B. Carter, "Discrimination and Market Forces as Determinants of Women's Academic Employment Patterns: Some Cross Sectional and Time Series Results."

11. Kathryn Kish Sklar, *Catherine Beecher: A Study in American Domesticity* (New Haven: Yale University Press, 1975); Maris Vinovskis and Richard Bernard, "The Female School Teacher in Antebellum Massachusetts," *Journal of Social History* 10 (March 1977): 332–45, and "Beyond Catherine Beecher: Female Education in the Antebellum Period," *SIGNS* (Summer 1978): 856–69; Keith Melder, "Woman's High Calling: Teaching Profession in America, 1830–60," *American Studies* 13 (Fall 1972): 19–30; Redding Sugg, *Motherteacher: The Feminization of American Education* (Charlottesville: University Press of Virginia, 1978); Robert E. Doherty, "Tempest on the Hudson: The Struggle for 'Equal Pay for Equal Work' in the New York City Public Schools, 1907–11," *History of Education Quarterly* 19, 4 (Winter 1979): 413–34. For articles that discuss gender issues in the larger context of educational history, see Geraldine J. Clifford, "Home and School in Nineteenth Century America: Some Personal History Reports from the United States," *History of Education Quarterly* 18, 1 (Spring 1978): 3–34; Barbara J. Finkelstein, "Pedagogy as Intrusion: Teaching Values in Popular Primary Schools in Nineteenth Century America," *History of Childhood Quarterly* 2 (Winter 1975): 349–78, "In Fear of Childhood: Relationships Between Parents and Teachers in Popular Primary Schools in the Nineteenth Century," *History of Childhood Quarterly* 3 (Winter 1976): 321–35), and "The Moral Dimensions of Pedagogy: Teaching Behavior in Popular Primary Schools in Nineteenth Century America," *American Studies* 15 (Fall 1974): 79–89. The *History of Education Quarterly* 19, 1 (Spring 1979) devotes a whole issue to the theme "Women's Influence on Education." Nancy Hoffman, ed., *Woman's "True" Profession: Voices from the History of Teaching* (Old Westbury, N.Y.: Feminist Press, 1981) is a useful collection of primary source material. See also Barbara Finkelstein, "Schooling and Schoolteachers: Selected Bibliography of Autobiographies in the Nineteenth Century," *History of Education Quarterly* 14 (Summer 1974): 253–300; and, although dated, Frances Donovan, *The School Marm* (New York: Arno Reprint Co., 1969. Reprint of 1938 ed.).

12. On the historical development of social work, see Lubove, *The Professional Altruist;* John Rousmaniere, "Cultural Hybrid in the Slums: The College Woman and the Settlement House, 1889–1894," *American Quarterly* 22 (Spring 1970): 45–66; Alan Davis, *American Heroine: The Life and Legend of Jane Addams* (New York: Oxford University Press, 1973), and *Spearheads for Reform* (New York: Oxford University Press, 1967); Marvin E. Gittleman, "Philanthropy as Social Control in the late 19th Century: Some Hypotheses and Data on the Rise of Social Work," *SOCIETAS* 5 (Winter 1975): 49–60; Jill Conway, "Women Reformers and American Culture, 1870–1930," *Journal of Social History* 5, 2 (Winter 1971–72): 164–77. On women and the evolution of the profession of authorship, see Ann Douglas, *The Feminization of American Culture* (New York: Knopf, 1977); Nina Baym, *Woman's Fiction: A Guide to Novels By and About Women in America, 1820–1870* (Ithaca: Cornell University Press, 1978); Ann Douglas Wood, "'The Scribbling Women,' and 'Fanny Fern': Why Women Wrote," *American Quarterly* 23, 1 (Spring 1971): 3–24; Elaine Showalter, "Women Writers and the Double Standard," in *Women in Sexist Society*, eds., Vivian Gornick and Barbara K. Moran (New York: Basic Books, 1971), pp. 452–79. On the history of women in law, see D. Kelly Weisberg, "Barred from the Bar: Women and Legal Education in the United States, 1870–1890," *Journal of Legal Education* 38 (1977): 485–507; Frank Stricker, "Cookbooks and Law Books: The Hidden History of Career Women in 20th Century America," *Journal of Social History* 10 (Fall 1976): 1–19. Cynthia Fuchs Epstein's *Women in Law* (New York: Basic Books, 1981) discusses some of the consequences of increasing female participation in the legal profession. For references on women and science, see Helen Owens, *Early Scientific Work of Women and Women in Mathematics* (State College, Pa.: Pennsylvania State University, 1940); Mary Louisa Willard, *Pioneer Women in Chemistry* (State College, Pa.: Pennsylvania State University, 1940); Helen Wright, *Sweepers of the Sky: The Life of Maria Mitchell* (New York:

Macmillan, 1949); Anne Sayre, *Rosalind Franklin and D.N.A.* (New York: W. W. Norton, 1975); Agnes O'Connell and Nancy Russo, eds., "Eminent Women in Psychology: Models of Achievement," special issue of *Psychology of Women Quarterly* 5, 1 (Fall 1980). Expected in Fall, 1982, from The Johns Hopkins University Press is Margaret Rossiter's *Struggles and Strategies: Women Scientists in America, to 1940*. For women in the arts, see Claire Richter Sherman and Adele M. Holcomb, eds., *Women as Interpreters of the Visual Arts, 1820–1979* (Westport, Conn.: The Greenwood Press, 1981). This collection deals with women as art critics, art historians, archaelogists and museum professionals. See also Claire Sherman, "Pioneers in American Museums: Dorothy Miner," *Museum News* 59 (March/April 1981): 36–41, 54, 57. A recent biography dealing with an important figure in American aesthetic criticism is Joan Shelley Rubin, *Constance Rourke and American Culture* (Chapel Hill: University of North Carolina Press, 1980). On the issue of women's careers in American religious movements, see Rosemary Radford Reuther and Eleanor McLaughlin, *Women of Spirit* (New York: Simon & Shuster, 1979) and R. Laurence Moore's splendid chapter on spiritualism, "The Medium and Her Message: A Case of Female Professionalism," in his book *In Search of White Crows: Spiritualism, Parapsychology, and American Culture* (New York: Oxford University Press, 1977), pp. 102–129. A collective biography of women clergy could be developed from the original edition of *Notable American Women*.

13. Joan W. Scott and Louise A. Tilly, *Women, Work and Family* (New York: Holt, Rhinehart, and Winston, 1978); Virginia Yans-McLaughlin, *Family and Community: Italian Immigrants in Buffalo, 1880–1930* (Ithaca: Cornell University Press, 1977); Thomas Dublin, *Women at Work: The Transformation of Work and Community in Lowell, Massachusetts, 1826–60* (New York: Columbia University Press, 1979); Tamara Hareven, "The Family as Process: The Historical Study of the Family Cycle," *Journal of Social History* (JSH) 7 (Spring 1974): 322–29; "Cycles, Courses and Cohorts: Reflections on Theoretical and Methodological Approaches to the Historical Study of Family Development," *JSH* 12 (Fall 1978): 97–109, "The Dynamics of Kin in an Industrial Community," *American Journal of Sociology* 84 (1978 Supplement): 151–82; Elyce Rotella, *From Home to Office: U.S. Women at Work, 1870–1930* (Ann Arbor: University Microfilms International, 1981).

14. Gerda Lerner, "The Lady and the Mill Girl: Changes in the Status of Women in the Age of Jackson," *American Studies Journal* 10 (Spring 1969): 5–14; Barbara Welter, "The Cult of True Womanhood," *American Quarterly* 18 (Summer 1966): 151–74.

15. See, for example, James, "Isabel Hampton"; Mottus, *New York Nightingales*, especially chapter 5; Reverby, "Apprenticeship to Duty," especially chapter 5; and Tomes, "Little World of Our Own," pp. 518–22.

16. Wood, "The Scribbling Women"; Cindy S. Aron, "To Barter their Souls for Gold: Female Clerks in Federal Government Offices, 1862–1890," *JAH* 67, 4 (March 1981): 833–53.

17. For a useful overview on the argument for women's education, see Eleanor Flexner, *Century of Struggle* (New York: Atheneum, 1973), especially chapters 2 and 8. The literature on women's education has grown too vast to cite here. In addition to the articles cited in notes 22 and 23, a student might find useful these newer works: Charlotte Conable, *Women at Cornell: The Myth of Equal Education* (Ithaca: Cornell University Press, 1977); Patricia A. Graham, "Expansion and Exclusion: A History of Women in American Higher Education," *SIGNS* 3, 4 (Summer 1978): 759–73. Of course, the new educational institutions for women came to play an important role in deflecting female aspiration into a narrow range of occupations. As numerous studies have shown, coed and female colleges, with few exceptions, developed curricula designed to fit girls for "woman's work." See, for example, Roberta Wein, "Women's Colleges and Domesticity, 1875–1918," *History of Education Quarterly* 14 (Spring 1974): 31–47.

18. Sklar, *Catherine Beecher*; Joan Jacobs Brumberg, *Mission for Life: The Story of the Family of Adoniram Judson* (New York: The Free Press, 1980). Mary P. Ryan in *Womanhood in America* (New York: Franklin Watts, 1979) uses the term "Social Housekeeping" to designate women engaged in reform careers.

19. Elizabeth Blackwell, *Pioneering Work in Opening the Medical Profession to Women*,

with an introduction by Mary Roth Walsh (New York: Schocken, 1977); Brumberg, *Mission*, pp. 120–22.

20. See, for example, Susan Armeny, "Resistance to Professionalization by American Trained Nurses, 1890–1905" (Berkshire Women's History Conference, 1978); Reverby, "Apprenticeship to Duty," especially chapter 6; Tomes, "Little World of Our Own," pp. 526–28.

21. Gerda Lerner, *The Grimke Sisters from South Carolina* (New York: Houghton Mifflin, 1967); Mary A. Hill, *Charlotte Perkins Gilman: The Making of a Radical Feminist, 1860–1896* (Philadelphia: Temple University Press, 1980).

22. Roberta Frankfort, *Collegiate Women: Domesticity and Career in Turn of the Century America* (New York: New York University Press, 1977); Patricia A. Palmieri, "Patterns of Achievement of Single Academic Women at Wellesley College, 1880–1920," *Frontiers* 5, 1 (Spring 1980): 63–67.

23. Palmieri, *Frontiers*, pp. 64–65; Joyce Antler, "After College What? New Graduates and the Family Claim," *American Quarterly* 32, 4 (Fall 1980): 409–33. See also Sarah Gordon, "Smith College Students: The First Ten Classes, 1879–1888," *History of Education Quarterly* 15 (1975): 147–67; Cynthia Horsbaugh Requardt, "Alternative Professions For Goucher College Graduates, 1892–1910," *Maryland Historical Magazine* 74, 3 (Fall 1979): 274–81; David Allmendinger, Jr., "Mount Holyoke Students Encounter the Need for Life-Planning, 1837–1850," *History of Education Quarterly* 19 (1979): 27–47.

24. Anna Mary Wells, *Miss Marks and Miss Wooley* (Boston: Houghton Mifflin, 1978); Laurence R. Veysey, "M. Carey Thomas," *Notable American Women*, 3 vols., eds., Edward and Janet James (Cambridge: Harvard University Press, 1971), vol. 3, pp. 446–50. For other works on the social context of lesbianism, see Smith-Rosenberg, "The Female World," and Nancy Sahli, "Smashing: Women's Relationships Before the Fall," *Chrysalis* 8 (1979): 17–27. For a study of the historical trends in the never-married population of the United States, see Edward Kain, "The Never Married in the United States, 1890–1980" (Ph.D. dissertation, University of North Carolina, Chapel Hill, 1980).

25. Regina Morantz, Personal Communication, February 1982. Morantz has examined women physicians' marital status using both the records of the Women's Medical College of Pennsylvania and the United States Census. The only profession in which the marriage rate for women came close to that of medicine was the law. See also Weisberg, "Barred from the Bar," pp. 485–507; Jean Gordon, "Early American Women Artists and the Social Context in Which they Worked," *American Quarterly* 30, 1 (Spring 1978): 54–69; Carl Degler, *At Odds: Women and the Family in America from the Revolution to the Present* (New York: Oxford University Press, 1980).

26. See Leonard I. Sweet, "Women in the Ministry: The Minister's Wife in American Religion" (Thesis, Colgate-Rochester Divinity School, 1977). Marilyn Hoder-Salmon, "Collecting Scholar's Wives," *Feminist Studies* 4, 3 (1978): 107–14, does a textual analysis of male scholars' acknowledgments to their spouses. The decisive role of male mentors in women's professional careers needs historical attention. Clearly this was an important phenomenon in the "hard sciences," e.g., Edward C. Pickering at the Harvard College Observatory recruited many women into astronomy in the late nineteenth century. The papers of male scholars could be examined for the light they shed on this and other issues of female professionalization but the evidence is scattered and, generally, fragmentary. For example, the papers of both Carl Becker (at Cornell University) and J. Franklin Jameson (at the Library of Congress) include some passing references to the problems of young female academic historians. A better approach might be to develop collective biography of early women in a particular field, drawn from the faculties of the women's colleges and universities. In history, the following women are of interest. Lucy Salmon, Emily Hickman, Marie Becker, Betty Bohanon, Julia Spruill, Alice Morse Earle, and Elizabeth Dexter. We are indebted to Michael Kammen for his suggestions in this area. In the social sciences, Willystine Goodsell, Elsie Clews Parsons, Ruth Reed, Ruth Benedict and Margaret Meade are some obvious suggestions.

27. Douglas, *Feminization of American Culture*; Sugg, *Motherteacher*; Garrison, *Apostles*;

David Tyack, *The One Best System* and Myra Strober and David Tyack, "Why Do Women Teach and Men Manage? A Report on Research on Schools," *SIGNS* 5, 3 (Spring 1980): 494-503; Beatrice Kachuck, "Comment on Strober and Tyack's 'Why Do Women Teach and Men Manage?'" *SIGNS* 6, 3 (Spring 1981): 542-44. A forthcoming review essay by Joan Jacobs Brumberg suggests how the feminization of schoolteaching was linked to competition among the Protestant denominations. See Brumberg, "The Feminization of Schoolteaching: 'Romantic Sexism' and American Protestant Denominationalism," *History of Education Quarterly* (forthcoming, 1982).

28. Barbara Ehrenreich and Deidre English, *Complaints and Disorders* (Old Westbury, N.Y.: Feminist Press, 1973) and Barbara Ehrenreich, *Witches, Midwives and Nurses: A History of Women Healers* (Old Westbury: Feminist Press, 1973) represent the most extreme statement of this view. Nancy Schrom Dye presents a more scholarly, balanced interpretation in her review essay, "History of Childbirth in America," *SIGNS* 6, 1 (Autumn 1980): 97-108. See also in the same issue Judith W. Leavitt, "Birthing and Anaesthesia: The Debate Over Twilight Sleep," pp. 147-64.

29. Regina Morantz and Sue Zschoche, "Professionalism, Feminism, and Gender Roles: A Comparative Study of 19th Century Therapeutics," *Journal of American History* 67, 3 (Dec. 1980): 568-88; Susan Reverby, "The Search for the Hospital Yardstick: Nursing and the Rationalization of Hospital Work," in *Health Care in America*, eds., S. Reverby and David Rosner (Philadelphia: Temple University Press, 1979), pp. 206-25. See also Regina Morantz, "Feminism, Professionalism and Germs: A Study of the Thought of Mary Putnam Jacobi and Elizabeth Blackwell," *American Quarterly* (forthcoming) for an interesting discussion of gender and professional identity.

30. Walsh, *Doctors Wanted*; Regina Morantz, "The 'Connecting Link': The Case for the Woman Doctor in 19th Century America," in *Sickness and Health in America*, eds., Judith Leavitt and Ronald Numbers (Madison: University of Wisconsin Press, 1978), pp. 117-28; Constance M. McGovern, "Doctors or Ladies? Women Physicians in Psychiatric Institutions, 1872-1900," *Bulletin of the History of Medicine* 55, 1 (Spring 1981): 88-107.

31. Barbara Welter, "She Hath Done What She Could: Protestant Women's Missionary Careers in Nineteenth-Century America," *American Quarterly* 30, 5 (Winter 1978): 624-38; Joan Jacobs Brumberg, "Zenanas and Girlless Villages: The Ethnology of American Evangelical Women, 1870-1910," *Journal of American History* (June 1982). For more on women anthropologists, see Nancy Oestreich-lurie, "Women in Early American Anthopology," in *Pioneers of American Anthropology*, June Helm [MacNeish], ed. (Seattle: University of Washington Press, 1966), pp. 29-82.

32. The literature on occupational segregation has grown rapidly in the last decade. Two useful overviews, albeit very different in format, are Cynthia F. Eptstein, *Woman's Place: Options and Limits in Professional Careers* (Berkeley: University of California Press, 1970), and Martha Blaxall and Barbara Reagan, eds., *Women and the Workplace: The Implications of Occupational Segregation* (Chicago: University of Chicago Press, 1976). See work on nursing cited in note 8. For the history of home economics, see Margorie East, *Home Economics: Past, Present, and Future* (Boston: Allyn and Bacon, 1980).

33. For the generative works on nineteenth-century women's culture, see Carroll Smith-Rosenberg, "The Female World of Love and Ritual," *SIGNS* 1, 1 (Autumn 1975): 1-29; Nancy Cott, *The Bonds of Womanhood* (New Haven: Yale University Press, 1977); Douglas, *Feminization of American Culture*; Mary P. Ryan, "The Power of Women's Networks: A Case Study of Female Moral Reform in Antebellum America," *Feminist Studies* 5 (Spring 1979): 66-86. See also the recent debate, Ellen DuBois et al., "Politics and Culture in Women's History: A Symposium," *Feminist Studies* 6 (Spring 1980): 26-64.

34. The literature on antebellum female voluntarism is diverse and there is, as yet, no synthesis. For different approaches see Joan Jacobs Brumberg, "Benevolent Beginnings: Volunteer Traditions Among American Women, 1800-1860" and Margaret Steinfels, "Women Volunteers: From 1860 to the Present: An Historical Sketch and Modest Critique" in *Women,*

Volunteering, and Health Policy, Proceedings of the United Hospital Fund of New York City (forthcoming, 1982); Susan Porter Benson, "Business Heads and Sympathizing Hearts: The Women of the Providence Employment Society, 1837-58," *Journal of Social History* 12, 2 (Winter 1978): 302-313; Keith Melder, "Ladies Bountiful: Organized Women's Benevolence in Early 19th Century America," *New York History* (July 1967): 231-54; Mary P. Ryan, "The Power of Women's Network"; Marion Hunt, "Women's Sphere and Pediatrics: St. Louis Children's Hospital, 1879-1919" (Berkshire Conference on Women's History, 1981).

35. The papers of all these women are at the Schleslinger Library or other major university repositories. See Muriel W. Pumphrey, "Mary Richmond and the Rise of Professional Social Work in Baltimore," (Ph.D. diss., Columbia University, New York School of Social Work, 1956).

36. Sally Kohlstedt, "In From the Periphery: American Women in Science, 1830-1880," *SIGNS* 4, 1 (Autumn 1978): 81-96; Margaret W. Rossiter, "Women Scientists in America before 1920," *American Scientist* 62 (May-June 1974): 312-23. Jane Gover posits a similar relationship between women's participation in amateur "camera clubs" and the entry of women into professional photography in her work "The Positive Image: Women and Photography 1880-1930," a dissertation-in-progress at the History Department, State University of New York at Stony Brook. One could also argue that mid-nineteenth-century middle class women's involvement in "self-help" medicine helped to legitimate the rise of women physicians. See, for example, Regina Morantz, "19th Century Health Reform and Women: A Program of Self-Help," in *Medicine Without Doctors*, eds., Guenther B. Risse, Ronald L. Numbers, and Judith W. Leavitt (New York: Science History Publication, 1977), pp. 73-94; and Martha Verbrugge, "The Social Meaning of Personal Health: The Ladies' Physiological Institute of Boston and Vicinity in the 1850s" in *Health Care in America*, pp. 45-66. As a final example it seems very likely that women's volunteer activities in the Civil War contributed to the acceptance of trained nursing in the 1870s. See Ann Douglas, "The War Within a War: Women Nurses in the Union Army," *Civil War History* 18 (Sept. 1972): 197-212.

37. The history of women as local historians and genealogists has not been systematically pursued. Information on New York State provided through Edmund Winslow and Stephan Bielinski, Division of Historical and Anthropological Services, Office of Cultural Education, New York State Department of Education.

38. Jessie Bernard, *Academic Women* (New York: Meridian, 1966).

39. Patricia M. Hammer, *The Decade of Elusive Promise: Professional Women in the United States 1920-1930* (Ann Arbor: University Microfilms International, 1979); Susan B. Carter, "Academic Women Revisited: An Empirical Study of Changing Patterns in Women's Employment as College and University Faculty, 1890-1963," *Journal of Social History* 14, 4 (Summer 1981): 675-700; Stricker, "Cookbooks and Lawbooks"; the latter two articles stress the persistence of women's professional activities into the 1950s. Yet another chronology is suggested by Rudolph C. Blitz, "Women in the Professions 1870-1970," *Monthly Labor Review* 97, 5 (May 1974): 34-39. Using indices that measure change in the sex ratio in a profession as well as changes in occupational structure, Blitz asserts that female professionalism reached a peak in 1930 and thereafter declined. See also Blitz and Chin Hock Ow, "A Cross-Sectional Analysis of Women's Participation in the Professions," *Journal of Political Economy* 81 (Jan/Feb 1973): 131-44.

40. Glen H. Elder's method of cohort analysis would make a useful model for such an undertaking. See Glen H. Elder, Jr., "Age Differentiation and the Life Course," in A. Inkeles, ed., *Annual Review of Sociology* (Palo Alto: Annual Reviews, 1975); Elder and Richard C. Rockwell, "Marital Timing in Women's Life Patterns," *Journal of Family History* 1 (Autumn 1976): 34-53.

41. Estelle Freedman, "Separatism As Strategy: Female Institution Building and American Feminism, 1870-1930," *Feminist Studies* 5, 3 (Fall 1979): 512-29. Recent work on women in medicine strongly confirms Freedman's argument. See Walsh, *Doctors Wanted;* Morantz, "Feminism, Professionalism, and Germs"; Virginia Drachman, "Feminist Showplace or Profes-

sional Priorities at an All-Woman's Hospital, 1862–1910," Berkshire Conference, June 1981, and "From Female Solidarity to Professional Opportunity: The Dilemma of Women Doctors," American Historical Association Meeting, Los Angeles, 1981; Edna Manzer, "Women Doctors' Choices of Specialties: The Vanishing Woman 'Woman's Doctor'" Berkshire Conference, June 1981.

42. Nancy Tomes, "A Collision of Nursing's Two Worlds: Volunteer and Professional Nurses in World War I" (Berkshire Conference on Women's History, June 1981).

43. Gabriel Kolko, *The Triumph of Conservatism* (Chicago: Quadrangle, 1967).

44. Andrew Abbott in an unpublished paper entitled "Inter-professional Relations," presented at a Sociology Department workshop, Rutgers University, makes the same argument for the professions as a whole. His work has been very useful in developing our perspective on the female-dominated professions.

45. Andrew Abbott, "Status and Status Strain in the Professions," *American Journal of Sociology* 86, 4 (1981): 819–35. This insight helps explain the tension between the male professions and female "semi-professions." To use a medical example, if doctors retreat too completely from the hospital ward or family practice, they find that nurses are only too willing to take over some of the doctor's "charismatic functions," i.e., providing basic medical services, relieving pain, and dispensing advice. As a result, nurses gain in public estimation. To quote a recent popular account of nuring (later turned into the television series "Nurse") the lay person begins to believe that "Doctors don't save you, nurses do." In a more serious vein, the nurse-midwife and nurse-practitioner movements represent a real threat to medical hegemony over the "heartland," to use Abbott's term, of professional service and have prompted doctors to reassert control over the "public-pleasing" aspects of medical work and limit nursing's autonomy.

Self-Assertion and Social Commitment: The Significance of Work to the Progressive Era's New Woman

LeeAnne Giannone Kryder

"A happy necessity," "that wonderful battlefield," "a broadening experience,"...these were but some of the happy expressions used by early twentieth-century career women to describe their work. But how does this clear affirmation of work correspond with that troubled concern about the "lost" work ethic so readily detected in the ruminations of their contemporaries? Indeed, as American historians Daniel Rodgers, James Gilbert and Herbert Gutman have noted, a concern for the loss of meaning in work was common among many turn-of-the-century Americans.[1] As work rapidly industrialized and the laborer became a depersonalized element in a vast corporation, middle-class Americans began to question if the American "work ethic" could survive. The increasing number and severity of labor-capital clashes added to their pessimism. But within that troubled middle class, women often expressed an opposite sentiment. They asserted that work was meaningful, and they determined to somehow enter the workforce and make a life-long commitment to work.

Although economic necessity typically explains female as well as male participation in the workforce, these middle-class women seemed to attribute a deeper significance to work. This article examines the work experiences and rhetoric of four Progressive era women who were deeply commited to work: Jane Addams, M. Carey Thomas, Ida Tarbell, and Charlotte Perkins Gilman. This is a preliminary effort to call attention to the significance of work in the lives of middle-class women, and to encourage scholars to consider not only class but gender distinctions in the so-called "American work ethic."[2]

Historian Frank Stricker has noted that turn-of-the century middle-class women mixed a "career impulse" with their feminist desire for political equality.[3] Work, for these women, became part of women's rights, their means of securing personal independence as well as advancing the status of womankind. Family and Progressive era history also provide insight into why women found so much significance in work. Historical studies of the American family indicate a growing individualization of family members; as the family modernized, individual interests rather than interest of the family as a whole took precedence. Recent studies such as that by Joan Scott and Louise Tilly indicate that perhaps this "modernization" of the family took place at different rates for each sex. That is,

> long after their husbands and children had begun to adopt some of the individualistic values associated with industrialization, these women continued the self-sacrificing, self-exploitative work...that was characteristic of the peasant or household economy.[4]

If this is accurate, perhaps the turn-of-the-century commitment to work outside the home can be understood as a delayed expression of new female emancipation and self-assertion. Work-for-wages became symbolic of woman's new sense of individuation. As more and more middle-class women participated in higher education, this experience served to further emphasize the development of women as individuals. The resulting informed, articulate, self-possessed "New Woman" opted for work which would ensure her independence from family and reflect her individual interests and capabilities.[5]

Yet the New Woman's rhetoric of work and her actual participation in work reflected not simply personal emancipation but a strong commitment to people and causes beyond herself. The New Woman surfaced during the Progressive era (c.1890-1917) when middle-class Americans were encouraged to look beyond their immediate personal circumstances and to engage in broader activities to benefit all of society. This reform impulse could understand work as a useful way to shape a new order and a better world. While it seems contradictory to find in work both personal independence and social connection, Addams, Thomas, Tarbell and Gilman seemed to find in it a means to assert their individuality as well as to participate in a larger social order.

Jane Addams was born September 6, 1860 in Cedarville, Illinois, the eighth of nine children.[6] Her mother and the ninth child died when Jane was two; when she was eight, her father remarried a woman whom Jane dutifully obeyed but never loved. Her graduation from Rockford Female Seminary in 1881 coincided with her beloved father's death. Although this loss plunged her into despair, she left for the Women's Medical College of Pennsylvania to pursue her ambition to become a doctor. Disenchantment with medical studies, her step-mother's continued interference in her studies, and ill-health led to Jane's abandonment of medical studies at the end of her first academic year. The next seven years were full of restlessness ("I was absolutely at sea" she later confessed.)[7] During this period her life was consumed by illness, family responsibility and two trips to Europe. Finally, in 1889 Addams and her best friend Ellen Gates Starr solicited help to begin Hull House, a settlement house in Chicago's crowded Nineteenth Ward. This marked the beginning of Addams' life-long career in social work, through which she gained national and international prominence. Her social work broadened to include lecturing, writing and national and international work for such causes as woman suffrage, labor reform and peace. The recipient of hundreds of awards and citations, she shared the 1931 Nobel Peace Prize with Nicholas M. Butler. Addams died May 21, 1935.

For Jane Addams, work signified several things.

It was a necessary revolt and avenue of escape from "the family claim." After college Jane had her career plans initially frustrated by her step-mother and continually thwarted by family demands. Work provided an escape from the "suffocation" and wastefulness of a protected, domestic life of the educated middle-class daughter in the late nineteenth century. Two quotes best express Addams' feelings:

> You do not know what life means when all the difficulties are removed. I am simply smothered and sickened with advantages.
> I have seen young girls suffer and grow visibly lowered in vitality in the first years after they leave school...[the daughter] is besotted with innocent little ambitions and does not understand this apparent waste of herself, the elaborate preparation, if no work is provided for her....[8]

Most frequently, however, Addams spoke of work as a means of connection with "the world" and with "life." No one can mistake the wistfulness and alienation in the following passage:

> The stream of laboring people goes past you as you gaze through the plate-glass window of your hotel. You see hard-working men lifting great burdens; you hear the driving and jostling of huge carts. Your heart sinks with a sudden sense of futility....[9]

World would provide an opportunity to make one's talents useful to society, thus ensuring a place in that society. For example, it was Jane's "business acumen, her well-organized mind, her ability to get along with all kinds of people, her penchant for compromise..." which eventually made Hull House a success.[10]

Addams spoke of her years between college and work as being adrift at sea..."clinging only to the desire to live in a really living world and refusing to be content with a shadowy intellectual or aesthetic reflection of it." She spoke of her eventual commitment to work at Hull House as being "launched into the strong intercourse of human life."

It comes as no surprise that her personal life and her work were inextricably connected. That interconnection of work and self, and the intensity of that commitment to work are best expressed in this poem she wrote to a close friend, Mary Smith, in 1895;

I had forgotten love
And only thought of Hull House then...
That is the way with women folks
When they attempt the things of men;
They grow intense, and love the thing
Which they so tenderly do rear,
And think that nothing lies beyond...[11]

Bryn Mawr, for M. Carey Thomas, was like Hull House for Jane Addams. It too marked the one career commitment which lasted for a lifetime and which led to national and international prominence. M. Carey Thomas was born January 2, 1857, the first of ten children of a Quaker couple, James and Mary Thomas.[12] "Minnie," as she was then called, enjoyed much independence from her earliest days. According to her private journals, she began to question her parents' belief in female inferiority at an early age. She became determined to disprove that inferiority:

Oh it is too unjust, too horrible, that things should be so. Of course I don't believe it. I believe that I have as much sense as any boy I know...and more too. And if I live we'll see who'll be worth the most. It seems to me I'd die if I could do anything to show that a woman is equal to a man.[13]

Minnie resolved to become a doctor but for reasons that had little to do with medicine. A medical career was an alternative to female dependency and domesticity; "I'm making my mind up to be a doctor for when I grow up I can't be dependent on father or mother, and I ain't going to get married... I can't imagine anything worse than living a regular young lady's life..."[14].

Much of M. Carey Thomas' resistence to marriage came from her sense that her father was to blame for burdening her mother with so many children. Expressing a common sentiment among New Women, Thomas identified children as a threat to one's work: "If a woman has children I do not see but she will have to, at least for some time, give up her work, and of all things taking care of children does seem the most utterly unintellectual."[15]

While at Howland Institute, a girl's school at Union Springs, New York, Thomas responded to "the cause of women." She decided to become a scholar rather than a doctor because her head mistress advised her that "the cause" needed women scholars "to advance woman's position in the world." After graduating in 1874 she spent a year at home preparing for college studies. She then enrolled in Cornell, graduated with a BA, and entered Johns Hopkins graduate school. There she encountered continual obstruction of her studies due to sexual discrimination. Thomas and her friend Mamie Gwinn then pursuaded their reluctant fathers to send them to the University of Leipzig in 1879. Because Leipzig refused to grant the Ph. D. to women, the two transferred to the University of Zurich where Carey graduated summa cum laude with her Ph. D. in 1882.

In December of 1883 she gained her first job at the newly-founded Quaker college of Byrn Mawr. She was hired as Dean and professor of English. In 1894 she became president, holding that post until retirement in 1922. M. Carey Thomas' work as scholar and academic administrator held great purpose for her; through it she could remain economically independent from her family and free from marriage. It gave her connections to a group of college women, faculty, administrators and educated Americans who shared her taste for "culture" and passion for academic excellence. It gave her a means to prove to herself and to contemporaries that women were not inferior to men.

Of all four subjects, only Ida Tarbell seemed to have had second thoughts about her career choice; but not about work itself. These regrets, however, came much later in her life. Born November 5, 1857 on a farm in Erie County, Pennsylvania, Ida was the eldest of three surviving children. Her mother had been a schoolteacher before her marriage; her father prospered with the oil business in Titusville, Pennsylvania but suffered financially due to his resistance to the Standard Oil Company. At an early age she was influenced by the woman's rights movement, and became convinced of woman's right to education and to economic independence. Sounding much like the young M. Carey Thomas, she wrote "the older I grew, the more determined I became to be independent."[16]

Planning to be a biology teacher, she went to Allegheny College in Meadville, Pennsylvania, as one of five females in her class. She graduated four years later in 1880. Apparently she saw this as part of "woman's cause," for years later she wrote "to go to a man's college and fit myself for man's work... that was to be my contribution to the cause." At this stage of her life Tarbell, again like Thomas, viewed marriage as an obstacle to work and to freedom; "I would never marry. It would interfere with my plans; it would fetter my freedom.... When I was fourteen I was praying God on my knees to keep me from marriage."[17]

Upon graduation she took her first and only teaching position, at Poland (Ohio) Union Seminary. After two years she quit and returned to Allegheny College to get her Master's degree. In 1883 she began work as an editorial assistant for the *Chautauguan Magazine*. After eight years of this work she left for Paris. There she began researching women and their role in the French Revolution, studying at the Sorbonne and College de France, and writing articles for *Scribners*. In 1892 she met S.S. McClure and began to contribute to his new magazine, *McClure's*. In 1894 she returned to the United States to join his staff. From 1906-1915 she co-edited *American Magazine* with several former writers from *McClure's*. In 1917, after two years as a lecturer on the Chautaugua circuit, she contributed to the war effort by joining Woodrow Wilson's Council of National Defense. In 1919 she joined the *Red Cross*

Magazine staff in Paris, then returned home to her farm in Connecticut. There she continued to write and occasionally teach until her death January 6, 1944.

Perhaps best remembered as a "muckraker" (against her wishes), Tarbell saw herself as a writer and an historian. The words Tarbell uses to describe her first job and in discussing "woman doing a man's job," may indicate the emotional centrality of work for Tarbell:

> If I had been going on my honeymoon I should scarcely have been more expectant or more curious than I was in August when I left my home to take my first position....

> But the woman sternly set to do a man's business, believing it better than the woman's, too often views life as made up of business. She throws her whole nature to the task. Her work is her child.... It is hers, a personal thing to which she clings as if it were a living being....[18]

Work not only provided an emotional focus throughout her life, but served to connect her with other people and to give her a place in the world. In words similar to Jane Addams, she recounted how the girl of today "is not needed. There is no place for her...she is a member of a group that has no responsible place in the community...." She must leave her home and family and she must seek work, "less for the sake of work than for the sake of life."[19] In France, Tarbell discovered that she was accepted because of her work ("I was treated with respect because of my working quality"). That acceptance through work continued upon her return to the United States and throughout her remaining years. Tarbell had found her place in the world through work.

But it seems that later, when "it was too late," Tarbell had regrets about her renunciation of marriage:

> A few women in every country have always and probably always will find work and usefulness and happiness in exceptional tasks. They are sometimes women who are born

with what we call "bachelor's souls"...they are not the women upon whom society depends; they are not the ones who build the nation.[20]

In both her autobiography and in *The Business of Being a Woman* she placed some blame on the women's movement for this, since she (and other girls of her generation) had been exposed to its ideas at too impressionable an age. Marriage and children were presented as obstacles to meaningful work and, when given a choice, Tarbell (and others) had remained single. She never seemed to doubt the value of work, however; her regret seemed to be for the type of work (a "man's work") which seemed to necessitate sacrificing the joys of marriage. Instead, she counseled, women should make homemaking their work. Sounding much like Catherine Beecher sixty years earlier, Tarbell argued that instead of renouncing homemaking as viable work, it should be given "a more scientific treatment...revitalizing its vocabulary, reformulating its problems, giving it dignity it deserves, that of a great profession."[21]

Professionalizing the work of the home was also a goal of Charlotte Perkins Gilman, but with the idea that this would free most women from the home to find their appropriate work elsewhere. Charlotte, identified by suffragist Carrie Chapman Catt as "the most original and challenging mind which the woman movement produced," was born July 3, 1860 in Hartford, Connecticut.[22] Her parents were Mary and Frederick Beecher Perkins, but she was raised by her mother after her scholarly father deserted his wife, son and infant daughter. Her early life was shaped by his desertion because it left the family penniless, her mother emotionally withdrawn, and Charlotte always craving love. She received little formal schooling until she attended the Rhode Island School of Design in her late teens. Like many adolescents, she often worried about the nature of life and her place in the world. At age sixteen she found evolution to be a key explanation:

I figured out that the business of mankind was to carry out the evolution of the human race, according to the laws of

> nature, adding the conscious direction... proper to our kind. The first duty of a human being is to assume right functional relation to society...more briefly, to find your real job and do it.[23]

Charlotte's "real job," as she determined it, was "to help humanity." She longed for a "sphere of her own" from which to work, but because of her mother's wishes she remained at home until her early twenties. At twenty-four she married artist Charles W. Stetson, but with strong doubts that perhaps this personal happiness would thwart her complete devotion to her work. After her marriage Charlotte became depressed and listless, but she and her husband attributed this to her pregnancy. But after her daughter's birth Charlotte's condition worsened so that "I, the ceaselessly industrious, could do no work of any kind."[24] After treatment by nerve specialist S. Weir Mitchell made her condition worse, she left husband and infant for a vacation with friends in California. This brought instant relief. Her return to home and family brought on another breakdown, so Charles and Charlotte reluctantly separated, attributed her nervous condition to the restrictions of domestic life.

With this separation, at the age of twenty-eight, Charlotte then began what she felt was her "serious work:" writing and public speaking on behalf of mankind. She saw her work less as social reform than as philosophy:

> I worked for various reforms, as Socrates went to war when Athens needed his services, but we do not remember him as a soldier. My business was to find out what ailed society, and how most easily and naturally to improve it.[25]

From 1888 until her death in 1935 she continued her work. She wrote numerous books, among them her widely-read *Women and Economics* (published in 1898, it was translated into at least seven languages by 1911) and a magazine titled *The Forerunner*. In 1900 she joyfully married her first cousin George Gilman, this time able to achieve a balance between marriage and work. This time, she recorded in her journal, the personal happiness of marriage would not hurt her. It would not "dull my sensitiveness, check my sympathy, stop my work. It will not, I know; it has not so far and it will not. On the contrary I shall do more work and better...."[26]

Work, according to Charlotte Perkins Gilman, would help individual women and men as well as the entire human race. Through work, woman would regain her rightful connnection to the world, and would become an even closer comrade to man. According to Gilman, at some point in the past, woman had been wrongfully confined to the house while man had left it to wrestle with the world. Because of this restriction, woman had become dependent and crippled. She was in the degrading position of having to rely on her sexual attraction to catch a man who would then sustain her. Work outside the home would free woman of this degradation and help her regain economic independence. It would also restore to her true friendship, which she had lost because in the home she was left alone. Work, finally, would restore men and women to one another. With the separation of workplace and home, a separation between man's world and woman's world developed, resulting in the absence of a "natural" and honest relationship between men and women:

> The economic independence of women will change [this] as naturally and inevitably as her dependence has introduced it.... We shall live in a world of men and women, humanly related, as well as sexually related, working together as they were meant to, for the common good of all.[27]

All four of these Progressive era women seem to affirm the value of "work" in general (only Ida Tarbell, late in life, came to advocate a more specific type of work for women). This generalized affirmation is significant when contrasted to earlier nineteenth-century discussions of women's work, which almost always prescribed a particular job for women. Because these four women viewed work as a "liberation" from previous dependency and restriction, it probably was important to avoid narrow prescriptions as to what now was appropriate. No longer was the American woman to be torn between two spheres, one expansively public and one restrictively private. As Gilman wrote triumphantly, "Home was the World...the World was Home to me!"[28] Also, the general reference to "work" may also indicate its symbolic value, similar to "education" for the newly-freed slave or the recent immigrant. Work was idealized as a passport to "life"—a development of self, a new awareness of others, a participation in a broad range of experiences.

Work served as an important remedy for ennui and alienation. Three of the four women here considered spoke of an interim period of "restlessness;" for Addams and Thomas it followed their college education, when they returned to their families and domestic restrictions. For Gilman, who did not attend college, it followed her marriage and reached its nadir after her child's birth. Could this restlessness be connected with the return to the family sphere and the absence of meaningful work? For each the "cure" was to leave the family and to find her place in the world via work: Addams as a social worker at Hull House; Thomas as a student and administrator at Bryn Mawr; Gilman as a writer/lecturer/philosopher "at large." Only Ida Tarbell seemed to have avoided this restless period, perhaps because she entered the workworld after college and never really stopped working?

For all these women, work seemed to symbolize independence from family. This might explain why they, like other New Women, found it difficult to reconcile the idea of marriage and children with a career. For all the women, female friendships seemed to be a "safe" alternative to marriage. Addams and Thomas each had a supportive group of three to five close female friends who remained friends throughout their adult years. Most, if not all the friends remained single and most held jobs. In addition, Addams, Thomas and Gilman had intimate female friends with whom they lived and traveled for several years at least. While it could not be determined if Tarbell had such intimate friendships outside her immediate family, certainly her mother, sister Sarah and Sarah's two daughters were constantly close to Tarbell throughout her life. Female friendships could provide stability, love and intimacy but would not jeopardize work commitment or personal independence as marriage seemingly would.

But if work enabled the New Woman to escape the restrictions of traditional family life, might not she run the risk of alienation? Christopher Lasch suggested that female restlessness, the sense that life was "out there" beyond home and family, was part of a general intellectual alienation at the turn-of-the century. In that case, women might assert their individuality and leave the family unit but still find themselves adrift because of the turmoil within larger society. But the experience of the four women here considered does not substantiate this theory. For them, work was both an expression of individuality *and* a means of establishing connection with the world. Charlotte Perkins Gilman pointed to this new balance:

> The growth, individualization of democratic life brings inevitable change to our daughters as well as our sons. Girls do not all like to sew, many do not even know how.... As the race becomes more specialized, more differentiated, the simple lines of relation in family life draw with less force, and the more complex lines of relation in social life draw with more force....[29]

Through work a woman left her "merely personal" obligations to take on the larger concerns and obligations of "society." This seems to fit a pattern identified with the Progressive era...the transition from personal and local concerns to social and supra-local concerns. Within the new order, individuals would join associations and it was through these associations that the "public welfare" (no longer "my" interests or "your" interests) would be ensured. An examination of the work ethic as expressed by these women reveals that work, for them, was *not* primarily a means to success or personal recognition. Work served the individual woman only in that it released her from the limitations of family concerns and left her free to make her choice of commitments. Work "re-connected" her to the more expansive concerns of society. For these American women, the work ethic meant usefulness and a place in the world. Perhaps because their actual work was professional and was not affected by the dislocation of mechanization, these American women found work far from alienating. For them, as Jane Addams expressed it, work "launched [them] into the strong intercourse of human life."

Notes

[1]Daniel Rodgers, *The Work Ethic in Industrial America, 1850-1920* (Chicago and London: University of Chicago Press, 1978); James Gilbert, *Work Without Salvation: Amercica's Intellectuals and Industrial Alienation, 1880-1910* (Baltimore: Johns Hopkins University Press, 1977); Herbert Gutman, *Work, Culture and Society in Industrializing America: Essays in American Working-Class and Social History (*New York: Alfred Knopf, 1976).

[2]See Patricia Branca's important discussion of the possibility of a "female work ethic" (not specifically an American work ethic), Patricia Branca," A New Perspective on Women's Work: A Comparative Typology," *Journal of Social History* IX (December 1975), pp. 129-153.

[3]Frank Stricker, "Cookbooks and Law Books: The Hidden History of Career Women in Twentieth Century America," *Journal of Social History* 10 (1976), p. 1.

[4]Joan Scott and Louis Tilly, "Women's Work and the Family in Nineteenth-Century Europe," in *The Family in History*, Charles E. Rosenberg, ed. (Philadelphia: University of Pennsylvania Press, 1975), p. 173; Tamara Hareven, "Modernization and Family History: Perspectives on Social Change," *Signs* 2(Autumn 1976): 196-206.

[5]Roberta Frankfort, *Collegiate Women: Domesticity and Career in Turn-of-the-Century America* (New York: University Press, 1977); Carolyn Forrey, "The New Woman Revisited," *Women's Studies* 2 (1974): 37-56.

[6]For biographical material see Jane Addams, *Twenty Years at Hull-House with Autobiographical Notes* (New York: Macmillan Company, 1910); Anne Firor Scott, "Jane Addams," in *Notable American Women 1607-1961: A Biographical Dictionary* (Cambridge, Massachusetts: Harvard University Press, 1971), p. 16.

[7]Addams, *Twenty Years*, p. 64.

[8]Ibid., p. 73 and Jane Addams, "The Subjective Necessity for Social Settlements," in *Philanthropy and Social Progress* (New York: Thomas Y. Crowell, 1893), p. 12.

[9]Addams, "Subjective Necessity," p. 11.

[10]Allen Davis, *American Heroine: The Life and Legend of Jane Addams* (New York: Oxford University Press, 1973), p. 61.

[11]Quoted in Christopher Lasch, *The New Radicalism in America, 1889-1963: The Intellectual as Social Type* (New York: Alfred Knopf, 1965), p.

[12]For biographical material see Edith Finch, *Carey Thomas of Bryn Mawr* (New York: Harper and Brothers Publishers, 1947); Laurence R. Veysey, "Martha Carey Thomas," *Notable American Women 1607-1950: A Biographical Dictionary* (Cambridge, Massachusetts: Harvard University Press, 1971), p. 446.

[13]Finch, *Carey Thomas*, p. 32.

[14]Ibid., p. 36.

[15]Ibid., p. 79.

[16]Quote from Ida Tarbell, *All in the Day's Work* (New York: The Macmillan Company, 1939), p. 34. For additional biographical material see David M. Chalmers, "Ida M. Tarbell," *Notable American Women 1607-1951: A Biographical Dictionary* (Cambridge, Massachusetts: Harvard University Press, 1971), pp. 428-431.

[17]Mary Tomkins, *Ida M. Tarbell* (New York: Twayne Publishes, 1974), p. 104; Tarbell, *All in the Day's*, p. 36.

[18]Tarbell, *All in the Day's*, p. 49; Ida Tarbell, *The Business of Being a Woman* (New York: Macmillan Company, 1928), pp. 44, 45.

[19]Tarbell, *The Business*, pp. 170, 171

[20]Ibid., p. 241.

[21]Ibid., p. 108.

[22]Quoted in Carl Degler, "Charlotte Perkins Gilman on the Theory and Practice of Feminism," *American Quarterly* 3 (Spring 1956), p. 21. For biographical information see Charlotte Perkins Gilman, *The Living of Charlotte Perkins Gilman: An Autobiography*(New York: Arno Press 1972; rpt. of 1935 ed.); Carl Degler, "Charlotte Anna Perkins Stetson Gilman," *Notable American Women 1607-1951: A Biographical Dictionary* (Cambridge, Massachusetts: Harvard University Press, 1971), pp. 39-42.

[23]Gilman, *The Living*, p. 42.

[24]Quote, Ibid., p. 91; also see pp. 45, 70, and 83.

[25]Ibid., p. 183.

[26]Carol Berkin, "Private Woman, Public Woman: the Contradictions of Charlotte Perkings Gilman," in *Women of America: A History*, ed. by Carol Berkin and Mary Beth Northon (Boston: Houghton Mifflin, 1979), p. 172.

[27]Charlotte Perkins Stetson, *Women and Economics: A Study of the Economic Relation Between Men and Women as a Factor in Social Evolution* (Boston: Small, Maynard and Co., 1898), p. 63.

[28]Berkin, "Private Woman," p. 175.

[29]Stetson, *Women and Economics*, pp. 154-155.

Dr. Kryder has taught women's history at Findlay College and at Bowling Green State University. At present she is a free-lance historian, with a special interest in women and business.

Bei Fragen zur Produktsicherheit wenden Sie sich bitte an:
If you have any questions regarding product safety,
please contact:

Walter de Gruyter GmbH
Genthiner Straße 13
10785 Berlin
productsafety@degruyterbrill.com